To Pa[illegible]

my [illegible]ted Op. 2,

Stephen Studd
August 25th
1999.

SAINT-SAËNS

a Critical Biography

SAINT SÄENS.

SAINT-SAËNS

a Critical Biography

Stephen Studd

cygnus arts

London **Cygnus Arts**
Madison & Teaneck **Fairleigh Dickinson University Press**

Published in the United Kingdom by
Cygnus Arts, a division of Golden Cockerel Press
16 Barter Street
London
WC1A 2AH

Published in the United States of America by
Fairleigh Dickinson University Press
Associated University Presses
440 Forsgate Drive
Cranbury
NJ 08512

First published 1999

ISBN 1 900541 65 3
ISBN 0 8386 3842 2

BRITISH LIBRARY CATALOGUING-IN-PUBLICATION DATA

Studd, Stephen
Saint-Saëns : a critical biography
1.Saint-Saëns, Camille, 1835–1921 2.Composers – France – Biography
I.Title
780.9'2

ISBN 1900541653

LIBRARY OF CONGRESS CATALOGUING-IN-PUBLICATION DATA

Studd, Stephen.
Saint-Saëns : a critical biography / Stephen Studd.
p. cm.
Includes bibliographical references, discography, and index.
ISBN 0-8386-3842-2 (alk. paper)
1. Saint-Saëns, Camille, 1835–1921 2. Composers – France
Biography. I. Title.
ML410.S15S78 1999
780'.92 – dc21
[B] 99–25256
CIP

PRINTED IN THE UNITED KINGDOM BY BIDDLES LIMITED, GUILDFORD

To the memory of
Anne-Maree Sheehan

CONTENTS

ILLUSTRATIONS

PREFACE

IT WAS AS A SIX-YEAR-OLD THAT I FIRST CAME ACROSS SAINT-SAËNS, when, along with many children of my generation, I danced round the school hall in the part of a skeleton animated by Death's fiddle in *Danse Macabre.* Later we were introduced to *The Carnival of the Animals* (under its English title, of course) and, like Ogden Nash, were amused by both the spelling and the pronunciation of the composer's name. Later still, I joined the menagerie as a pianist in a sixth-form performance of the *Carnival.*

It was only with serious concert-going that I began to be aware of Saint-Saëns as someone more than a curiosity, as he was usually dismissed, when the second piano concerto appeared at a Henry Wood promenade concert as representing a rather more considerable canon. Many years later a performance of the 'Organ' symphony in the same concert series finally impelled me to the bookshelves for reading matter on the life and works. What did I find there? Nothing, not a single volume, however slim.

This struck me at first as odd, then as extraordinary and finally as almost nonsensical, for by then entries in reference books had given some indication of the significance of Saint-Saëns and the extent of his contribution to the repertory. The last English biography, James Harding's *Saint-Saëns and his Circle,* had appeared a quarter of a century earlier and, as its title suggests, is as much about the composer's contemporaries as the man himself. This remarkable lack of material was what prompted me to undertake the present work.

Publication of a translation of Stegemann's detailed and highly technical study of the concertos in no way invalidated the project. My intention was to take the reader through the whole spectrum of Saint-Saëns's life, character and music, and as an amateur musician I hope I have been able to give the subject something of the appeal of the interested layman while at the same time meeting the needs of the scholar. I do not pretend that the book is a thoroughly comprehensive account: such a claim would be a bold one in view of the length and productivity of Saint-Saëns's many-faceted life. There are several areas ripe for further exploration, such as the songs and the many unaccompanied choruses which Saint-Saëns wrote with greater frequency towards the end of his career. I see the book rather as opening doors to a new and serious consideration of Saint-Saëns's music, instead of the dismissive finality which has characterised the comments of so many commentators in the past.

The first to be thanked for helping to produce this book, in a chronological sense, is the teacher who put on that record of *Danse Macabre* at Winns Avenue Primary School, Walthamstow, all those years ago. Little did she know what it would lead to. There have been many teachers since who have indirectly and belatedly been influential in the work, too many to acknowledge individually, but I am especially indebted to the late Joseph and Lilian Weingarten, for reading the chapter on Saint-Saëns as pianist and for giving unfailing encouragement. I remember them with much fondness and gratitude. Library staff are, of course, indispensable in a project of this kind and my thanks are due for the help I received from librarians at the Bibliothèque nationale de France in Paris, the British Library and Newspaper Library, the main public library in Edinburgh and at the Central Music Library at Victoria, London, where many a journey was necessary down two floors to the basement and back to retrieve the most obscure items.

I should also like to thank the publishers Editions Durand for permission to consult and to quote from the composer's letters in the Jean-Manuel Mobillion de Scarano Collection, kept in the Bibliothèque Gustav Mahler in Paris, where also the curator was most courteous and helpful. I am grateful as well to Paul Collen, of the Department of Portraits and Performance History at the Royal College of Music in London. Every effort has been made on the part of myself and the publisher to trace all copyright holders – we regret if any have been inadvertently omitted, and will of course ensure that any such omissions are rectified in future editions of this book.

Other individuals I should like to thank are my former newspaper colleague the late Val Weeks, for help in the course of my research; Patrick McGinley for much valuable advice; and my sister Sheila Collier for her support and for undertaking the weighty task of transferring the manuscript into the realms of the new technology.

London, October 1998.

SAINT-SAËNS

a Critical Biography

INTRODUCTION

OF THE VAST AMOUNT OF MUSIC WRITTEN BY SAINT-SAËNS DURING HIS long life, almost continuously from his infancy to his last year, a small number of works have kept their place in the concert hall and record collection with a resilience that has stood up both to time and the critics. The second piano concerto, the third violin concerto and third symphony, the *Danse Macabre*, *Samson et Dalila* and, of course, *Le Carnaval des Animaux* are hardy evergreens familiar to many, if not most, music lovers. The third symphony and *Le Carnaval*, indeed, are among the most recorded works in the catalogue. With the rest of Saint-Saëns's achievement, however, twentieth-century iconoclasm has been rather more successful, ensuring that this controversial and, in some ways, enigmatic composer is kept out of his rightful place in musical evolution – a process that stems as much from the personal animosity which Saint-Saëns aroused during his lifetime as from purely musical considerations. The marked imbalance between the over-familiarity of a few of his works and the under-familiarity of the many has, if anything, compounded the injustice by seriously distorting the general picture of his wide-ranging contribution to music. It is good, therefore, that the movement towards reappraisal is gathering momentum, with the compact disc revolution giving wider access to Saint-Saëns's remarkable output and radio broadcasting more of his compositions more frequently, chipping away at decades of encrusted prejudice.

What has tended to be overlooked for too long is the crucial role that Saint-Saëns played in the development of French music in the period between Berlioz and Debussy, the period in which his creative life reached its peak. Berlioz died in 1869; two years later the National Music Society (Société Nationale de Musique), dubbed "the cradle and sanctuary of French art" by the contemporary writer Romain Rolland, was formed.[1] Saint-Saëns was one of its chief instigators. His work in the field of orchestral and chamber music, a major achievement for a Frenchman of the time, did much to broaden the scope of the national school beyond its fixation with the theatre and light opera, and gave a lead to a new generation of French composers of 'serious' music. By taking the classical models of sonata, symphony and concerto as his starting point and adapting them to his own ends he paved the way for the development of a French symphonic tradition that was largely non-existent before the mid-nineteenth century, just as Tchaikovsky used classical models as a framework for the development both of a personal and of a distinctively Russian symphonic style. Both composers are of a nineteenth-century type – Dvořák is another – who, through their use of Austro-German forms, espouse a national cause while belonging to the wider

European musical culture. It is a position that goes some way to explaining Saint-Saëns's sometimes paradoxical and apparently contradictory views on the German influence on French music and the place of nationalism in composition and performance.

In the opera house he set out to curb the dominance of the Italian style in favour of a form of opera more sympathetic to the French language and more in keeping with French culture as he saw it, and some of his songs – there are more than one hundred of them, all woefully neglected – are gems that are among the glories of French *mélodie*. In this respect he is almost a Gallic Schubert, a prolific songwriter who yet could not translate his vocal skills into full-length dramatic works that could command a regular place on the operatic stage. Of his dozen operas, only *Samson et Dalila* has held a lasting place in the repertory.

As he set out to tread a new path in French music, the young Saint-Saëns drew on several influences that helped shape his musical language. In considering them it should be borne in mind that the oft-repeated claims that he was a mere imitator are a distortion of the formative process which in many, if not most, composers is accepted as perfectly normal and usual. And in the work of his early maturity we can already see a distinctive, individual voice emerging, one which has not been sufficiently appreciated.

Of the influences that helped to articulate that voice, then, that of Schubert is evident in the warm lyricism and open, airy texture that characterise much of his music. From Haydn he derived a strong formal sense coupled with a readiness to experiment with departures from the norm; from Schumann a rhythmic drive and inventiveness (and sometimes obsessiveness); and from Mendelssohn a lightness and delicacy of touch. Of his own acquaintances, Gounod helped to impart a feeling for vivid orchestral colours, while Liszt inspired dash and bravura.

He revered Mozart, inheriting from him a taste for elegance and precision, both in form and content. For one of the most obvious qualities of his works is their conciseness. His concertos are of Mozartian rather than Beethovenian proportions, and even such works as the early Mass and the *Oratorio de Noël* are considerably shorter than some of their more famous namesakes. The major exception is the monumental third, or 'Organ', symphony which, as the composer himself realised, is on a scale way beyond his normal field.

The third symphony is something of a swan song for a dynamically productive period, spanning about twenty years from the mid-1860s, that saw the appearance of most of his more famous and characteristic pieces. It was a period when he hardly ever stopped writing, for here was a man of a phenomenal mental and intellectual energy that was always threatening to overload a small and weak physical frame. The child prodigy became the eternal scholar who, besides being a prolific composer, was also one of the greatest organists of his day, a touring pianist of awesome technique and pearly brilliance, the producer of scholarly, diligently researched editions of other composers' works, a contributor to a variety of newspapers and journals, a writer on literature, philosophy and the sciences – especially astronomy – as well as music, a poet and a playwright, and an inveterate traveller. A member of the Légion d'Honneur and feted by royalty, he had the rare distinction – for a musician – of being alive to see the unveiling of a statue of himself.

Behind the public triumphs were the years of struggling for recognition, the setbacks and the frustrations, a short-lived marriage that ended in disaster and – the biggest emotional blow of all – the death of an adored mother. Yet a cast-iron resolution withstood them all, just as a firm intellectual honesty remained unswayed by the shifts of fashion and taste. Saint-Saëns always expressed his mind on music and other matters forcefully and cogently, regardless of prevailing opinion and the likely reaction, and he made many enemies along the way. He alienated the establishment by his early championing of innovators like Schumann, Wagner and Liszt, and later his strong views on the 'Wagner question' as it had become by the 1880s, stirred around him a furious controversy which never really cleared. In his old age he railed against the twentieth-century radicals and his published views on musical 'progress' are classics of conservative thinking. The often violent extremes of opinion which he aroused in others created a legacy of prejudices and assumptions which has for three-quarters of a century remained largely unchallenged and has militated against a more sober assessment of his music and its place in musical history.

A new century approaches that is likely to re-appraise the nineteenth century after decades of iconoclasm and derision, in the same way as the eighteenth century has been re-evaluated – and revalued – by the present age. It is time, therefore, to look again and in depth at the life and work of one of the nineteenth century's most significant products – doubly significant because he is, in different ways, both typical and atypical of it.

I • CHILD PRODIGY

THE LIFE OF SAINT-SAËNS BEGAN IN THE PARIS OF CHOPIN AND BERLIOZ and ended away from the Paris of Stravinsky and Les Six. His birth followed that of a new music in the *Symphonie fantastique* and of a new European order in the revolutions of 1830, when Chopin, newly arrived in the French capital, watched street battles from his apartment window. His death followed that of the old music in *Le Sacre du Printemps* and of the old Europe in the First World War. And it was a musical as well as a merely mortal life that spanned such a long and eventful period, one with few, if any, equals among composers. Saint-Saëns was writing music in the last year of his life, 1921; he was also a child prodigy, the wonder of the Parisian salons of Orléanist France, whose patrons compared him to Mozart and Mendelssohn.

Yet the boy pianist and composer grew from no family musical nursery of the kind which favoured those illustrious predecessors. He brought innate musical gifts to a household from which music had been entirely absent, its only token a disused piano, untouched by a Leopold or a talented older sister to emulate and accompany. For Saint-Saëns was an only child who was not quite three months old when his father died. Jacques Joseph Victor, a civil servant, was not without influence on the child, however. Writing was his hobby: he collaborated on a comedy, *La Petite Maison*, performed after his death,[1] and was in the habit of breaking into whimsical verse when writing to friends and relatives—a habit his son was to inherit, along with a biting wit and a general sensitivity to and creativity with words. Two songs to Joseph Victor's lyrics were published, and among his poems is an Elegy on the death of his brother, the abbé Camille.[2]

The Saint-Saëns family roots went back to the Normandy village of the same name, a corruption of Saint Sidonius, an Irish monk of the abbey of Jumièges, who founded a monastery nearby in the seventh century (no trace of which remains). As far as is known the much-travelled composer never once set foot in the village whose name he bore.

Born into a farming family at Rouxmesnil-Bouteilles, a small village near the port of Dieppe, Joseph Victor was of that Norman stock noted for its sober industry, quiet confidence and respect for the rules. While some of his ancestors conquered England and sailed round the world, others stayed at home and worked the land, self-willed but prudent, with a regard for order and correct procedure, unruffled either by triumph or disaster. His father, the local mayor, was a farm labourer turned first-generation smallholder at a time when revolutionary pressures were mounting against the old feudal restraints, and his newly-won status was consolidated by the overthrow of the old order in 1789. Of his eight children most stayed in farming, but Camille took holy orders, becoming a priest at Pollet, near Dieppe, Nicholas became a grocer, and Joseph Victor left the countryside for a government office in Dieppe, eventually moving to Paris in 1823 as an audit clerk in the Department of the Interior. In 1834, while living with his brother Nicholas, he met and married Françoise Clémence Collin, a carpenter's daughter from the Champagne district who had been adopted by her childless uncle and aunt (who were, incidentally, cousins).[3] A year later, on 9th October 1835, he abandoned the verse he was composing in a letter to a friend to announce, "in vile prose", the birth (at 6.45 a.m. that day) of a son. The mother suffered great pain for some fourteen hours, but the father wrote that both mother and baby were now "doing well". "My son shows the very best disposition for living", he added.[4] Seven weeks later, at the church of St Sulpice, the baby was christened Charles Camille, after his late uncle the abbé Camille and his mother's aunt Charlotte Masson, who was also his godmother. Five weeks after the christening, at the end of December, Joseph Victor died of consumption at the age of thirty-seven, leaving the baby under the guiding spirits of his mother and great-aunt.

Under the care of the Massons, Clémence showed artistic talent from an early age and became a competent painter of still-life watercolours. Until her marriage at twenty-five, she lived with her adoptive parents at their Rue Mignon bookshop, a business which failed shortly before the couple were due to retire. Salvaging as much as they could, they moved in with the newlyweds at a third-floor flat at 9 Rue du Jardinet, a narrow street in the Latin quarter of Paris, within sight of the dome of the French Institute (Institut de France), a landmark of Saint-Saëns's childhood. The uncle never got over the collapse of his business and in March 1835 he died, according to the composer, "of a broken heart".[5]

Clémence hoped for a family that would shine in the arts. She often spoke to her son about another uncle who was artistically gifted and "was passionately fond of music". Saint-Saëns recounts that this uncle played a drawing room organ which he built himself and, while running his fingers through his niece's long black hair, talked enthusiastically to her about art, music and "beauty in every form" so that "she got it into her head that if ever she had sons the first would be a musician, the second a painter and the third a sculptor".[6] Fate was to allow only the first stage of this triple design, but even this did not look certain at the outset, for the baby's "disposition to live" was beset by alarming symptoms of an inherited tuberculosis. Latent consumption was to remain with him, flaring up at intervals over the years, and throughout his long life the composer of the *Danse Macabre* was never far from death.

Mme Saint-Saëns, fearing that her son might develop the disease which had killed her husband, followed medical advice and sent him into the country, at Corbeil, south of the capital, where he was looked after for two years by a nurse. Here he breathed for the first time the clear country air he was to delight in throughout his life: the precedent was set for the regular escape from the city, on both health and aesthetic grounds, of his later years. It was in childhood visits to his mother's native district of Champagne where, he said, he learned to love the countryside. Up to the age of twelve he spent summer holidays at the house of one of her uncles near Chaumont, enjoying the freshness of open spaces and acquiring a sensitivity to the sounds of nature and the subtle nuances that distinguished them.[7] Yet this effect on his aural senses seems already to have been made at Corbeil, for when he returned home after his two years there he began to show signs of a remarkable musical instinct.

The American critic Harold Schönberg has called Saint-Saëns "probably the most awesome child prodigy in the history of music".[8] Champions of Mozart may disagree. Certainly there is nothing from the infant Saint-Saëns of the minor masterpieces – symphonies, operas and smaller works – of the kind that Mozart had produced before the age of twelve. Saint-Saëns, always careful of his reputation, suppressed most of his earliest compositions and destroyed many of them, including overtures and cantatas, piano pieces and songs. "Oblivion will enshroud these gropings after effect, for they are of no interest to the public", he insisted,[9] so it is not possible to assess accurately the infant prodigy's standing as a composer, although these early pieces certainly impressed his elders. It was chiefly as pianist and scholar that he was to astonish the adult world.

Even so, he beat Mozart for a first known composition by two years, with a piano piece dated 22nd March 1839, when he was three. He could already read and write, and heard in musical terms the everyday sounds of striking clocks and creaking doors. These and the sounds of nature were his musical stimulants, in a home where there was no music as such. There was also the "symphony of the kettle", the gradual crescendo of a kettle coming to boil in front of the fire, featuring a rising oboe note which, the composer wryly recalled, he later recognised in the 'Ride to the Abyss' in Berlioz's *La Damnation de Faust*.[10] Outside the windows, the cries of travelling merchants "rendered him mute with astonishment", the magazine *L'Illustration* later reported, and he ran from room to room almost in a frenzy hearing and comparing every sound.[11] It may be supposed that these and other stories of a precocious childhood were supplied by a proud mother in later years, but Saint-Saëns insists: "I was not told all these details, I remember them perfectly."[12] And we should not be cynical about his claim to remember the minutest particulars of infancy – including being bathed and fed – given the restless intellectual curiosity which characterised him all his life and which betokens an active consciousness from an early age.

Apart from the stimulus of common sounds, his gifts seem to have stemmed entirely from pedigree. His mother, whom he resembled in facial features, notably in the large beak of a nose, had little formal education but a strong artistic imagination and an ability to learn which, her son said, "bordered on the miraculous".[13] Added to these qualities was his father's literary bent, tempered by a Norman love of order and restraint. But the decisive influence came from his godmother, great-aunt Charlotte, who had some practical musical knowledge. Recognising the infant's intelligence after his return from Corbeil, she opened the miniature Zimmermann piano that stood neglected among her furniture and her niece's paintings and sat the two-year-old in front of it.[14] Instead of crashing his hands down on clusters of keys, as children often do on seeing an open piano, little Camille picked out one by one the narrow, closely packed keys, listening intently to each note, allowing the sound to die away before striking another, and comparing the difference.[15] Within a month he had learned from his great-aunt all the notes, as well as posture, fingering and positioning of the hands.

Mme Masson, a small, tough, wiry woman, was the family precedent for infant precocity. Like her niece, she was looked after by a childless aunt and an uncle who was a wealthy lawyer. She was walking at nine months and quickly learned to sing, paint, embroider and play the piano (then still something of a novelty), all of which she taught as a young girl to earn a living when her adopted family was ruined by the Revolution. She was, wrote Saint-Saëns, a woman "of keen intellect and brilliant attainments" who "remembered perfectly the customs of the *ancien régime*, which she enjoyed talking about, as well as the Revolution, the Terror and all the times that followed".[16] She was his personal link back to the eighteenth century. A close relationship with a grandparent or other elderly relative often gives a child a vivid impression of the lives, attitudes and outlook of an older generation that stays with him and matures to an indefinable perception of the reality of a bygone age. Mme Masson's belongings and even her clothes seemed to give off the scent of France before Napoleon, and the composer could breathe it all his life.

Showing little interest in the usual playthings of childhood, the young Saint-Saëns became so wrapped up in the piano that his worried mother occasionally closed it to prevent it becoming an obsession. But the boy "cried like a lost soul" until it was opened again. The instrument seemed to be part of his personality. Lacking the company of children his own age, he spoke and understood its language as if it were a boyhood friend. For he had perfect pitch, as remarkable as Mozart's. He amazed everyone by naming the note at which a glass was struck or a clock chimed, and the notes sounded on the piano as it was being tuned in the next room.[17] Even the inspirational kettle was heard to boil on A. It was this ability that first spread the boy's fame into the world beyond the family apartment – and it was to humble Professor Pierre Zimmermann at the Paris Conservatoire. Zimmermann, son of the piano manufacturer, was sceptical of stories about this amazing gift and put the youngster to the test. It appeared his scepticism was confirmed when the boy's naming of the note sounded was apparently incorrect by a semitone. Saint-Saëns insisted he was right, and was vindicated by a tuning fork. Unknown to the mortified professor, the piano had been tuned a semitone down.[18] The acute musical sensitivity that caused tantrums when the boy was denied access to the piano also caused a scene when he was taken to his first symphony concert, still in his mother's arms. The sound of the violins delighted him, but when the brass and percussion entered fortissimo he screamed for them to be silent, shouting "I can't hear the music", and had to be taken from the hall.[19] But he soon came to appreciate brass and percussion when, a little older, he went to watch the ceremony of the military retreat, one of the pageants of pre-1848 Paris, with its "ingenious combination of trumpets and drums":

I can still recall the shades of night beginning to invade the Luxembourg Garden, the shooting stars (then an unexplained phenomenon) falling across the sky, and the drums and trumpets making a complete tour of the immense vault of heaven and ravishing my youthful senses as the strains alternately approached and died away in the distance.[20]

At home piano lessons made rapid progress. He lost patience with children's pieces, with their simple tunes above tonic-dominant accompaniment, because "the bass doesn't sing", so the two women searched for suitable pieces from the classics. Thus it was that he was introduced to the sonatas of Haydn and Mozart (those of Beethoven were soon to follow) at such an early age,[21] his great-aunt teaching him to follow carefully the composer's markings, without distortion or exaggeration. She did not then foresee the direction in which the talents of her charge would take him. "When he is fifteen, if he can write a dance I shall be satisfied", she said. The dance was to come sooner than expected. The boy began to write very many of them, mainly galops and – which he considered better – waltzes, at first improvised at the piano but later written straight down. He recalled later that these waltzes were beyond the scope of his little fingers, so that a family friend had to play them. And his musical instinct was such that the harmonies of these pieces conformed to the rules even though he had as yet had no formal training in harmony. "They are insignificant, but it is impossible to find a technical error in them", he declared when looking over them in later life. "Such precision was remarkable for a child who had no idea of the science of harmony."[22]

His musical intuition was further expressed and developed in an early facility for improvisation, which was to be especially valuable to the future organist. As young as two, he could sit at the piano and improvise a descriptive piece at will, guided by a vivid and precocious imagination. Regular involvement with the musical life at St Sulpice, the church of his christening and first communion, made him especially sensitive to religious subjects. Asked to improvise a piece describing the taking of the veil, the toddler sat at the keys and after a few moments played an introduction, some dance tunes to suggest the nun's early days, a melancholy passage as she says her last farewells to the world, solemn bells, a hymn, the tears of her parents and finally the calm of the holy life.[23]

The intuitive feel for technique in the child was to lead to an almost total absence of self-criticism in the man, whose works, like Mozart's, had a finished quality as soon as they were written down, and were rarely revised. Instead there was a solid self-assurance that, while it was to see him over considerable obstacles, sometimes led him to overlook lapses of judgement and discernment. Only in adolescence, when many childhood and student pieces were destroyed, and to a lesser degree in early manhood, did Saint-Saëns show any serious doubt as to his ability.

The first wholly independent account of the boy's musical prowess appeared in the Parisian journal *Moniteur Universel*, a report of a drawing-room performance of a Beethoven violin sonata in which the four-year-old accompanied the young Belgian violinist Antoine Bessems (for whom he later wrote a three-movement sonata of his own). It referred to his "surprising musical instinct and aptitude, rare at such an age, for seizing, with perfect accuracy and a refined touch, on everything that is impressive in the melody, rhythm and harmony". He held out the promise that "through his truly exquisite and well-cultivated gifts, the great masters will one day find in him a worthy rival . . . Such a graceful yet delicate sapling needs only to be nurtured" because "too strong a feeding and too premature a brilliance could become detrimental to it".[24]

This warning was heeded by Mme Saint-Saëns and her aunt, who – unlike Leopold Mozart – were to see to it that their child prodigy would be exposed neither too much nor too soon to the limelight. They were only too aware of his delicate health and the consequent dangers of precocity and overwork, from which they constantly sought to protect him. From them he learned that applause did not matter, only artistic integrity. When called to play at gatherings of friends and neighbours, he insisted that he would play Haydn and Mozart only to people capable of understanding and appreciating them, so that "it was necessary to tell me that there was a lady in the audience who was an excellent musician with fastidious tastes".[25]

As well as performing he was also studying and analysing music, graduating from piano works to orchestral scores, including operas, particularly those of the eighteenth-century French composer André Grétry. It was, however, Mozart's *Don Giovanni* that was to be the biggest single inspiration to a career as a composer, as it was to be for Tchaikovsky. The human tragedy of that darkly dramatic work appealed to the Russian's passionate nature; for Saint-Saëns its wonder lay in the simple means used to great effect, "their placing, reciprocal harmony, contrasts and overall balance". This sense of proportion, he came to believe, was "the style, the secret of genius".[26]

He was five when he was introduced to Mozart's opera. The full score, in two volumes bound in red morocco, in French and Italian text, was a gift from an old soldier for whose daughter the boy had written a ballad ("twelve bars long, four of them consisting of a ritornello"), in which he accompanied her on the piano. "I had written it down in pencil and my great-aunt . . . had piously gone over it in ink." The boy studied his score of *Don Giovanni* – a somewhat unusual gift for a five-year-old – every day, "acquainting myself with both the vocal and instrumental parts. . . . Unconsciously, with that wonderful ease of assimilation which is the great characteristic of childhood, I lived in the music."[27]

The handsome score was the first of many gifts from admirers that were to multiply over a lifetime to an Aladdin's cave of musical and artistic treasures. Another was a medallion presented by the painter Ingres in return for an Adagio dedicated to him "in all seriousness". ("Fortunately this masterpiece has been lost", the composer wryly noted in later years.) The medallion bore Mozart's profile and signature, and was inscribed: "To M. Saint-Saëns, charming interpreter of the divine artist." The boy played Mozart when his mother took him to visit Ingres, whom she had met through his pupil Jean-Pierre Granger, a fellow tenant of 9 Rue du Jardinet. Little Camille liked to play with one of the gold paper crowns used by Granger's model for one of the kings in his painting of the Adoration, while Mme Saint-Saëns and Granger's daughter would spend many hours together at the Louvre copying pictures.[28] As well as sharing a love of art Mlle Granger was also a keen singer who wrote many of her own songs, and one of Saint-Saëns's first songs was composed for her when he was six. Called 'Le Soir' it is a setting of verse by the actress-poet Marceline Desbordes-Valmore, in which a girl waits for her lover at the close of the day.

Visits to Ingres's home were undoubtedly a formative influence on Saint-Saëns's artistic outlook. To an extent Ingres represents in art a model for the career of Saint-Saëns in music (he lived, incidentally, to the same age). Something of a loner and a rebel in his youth, he became a staunch defender of classicism against the prevailing trends of his later years, asserting the supremacy of draughtsmanship and clarity of line over expression, using his academic standing to rubbish the ideas of the younger generation, and accused by his enemies of clinging to an outdated tradition that had descended into mediocrity. Famous for his portraits and oriental scenes featuring voluptuous nudes, the sixty-year-old painter was by this time as conservative in his views on art as on music. He retained a passion for music from the days when he played second violin in his youth, but regarded everything written after Mozart as worthless. He was popularly supposed to have been more interested in music than in painting, so that an 'Ingres violin' was a phrase used to mean a hobby that was more important than a profession. Saint-Saëns never heard him play and the only time he ever saw the violin in question was years later in the Ingres museum at Montauban.[29] Nevertheless, conversations about art between Ingres and Mme Saint-Saëns, which surely touched on oriental exoticism and the virtues of classical form, in music as well as art, could not have been lost on the young composer.

Saint-Saëns received a private general education from the age of seven, from specialist teachers outside the local authority system set up by the Orléanist government in the 1830s. His ability, within a month or so, to grasp the intricacies of Latin grammar as well as geometry and the natural and mechanical sciences were as astonishing as his musical gifts. He so quickly outpaced his tutors that plans to learn Greek came to nothing, much to his lifelong regret, but he became an avid reader of the Latin as well as of the French classics. He also regretted not having a sufficient grounding in mathematics, which he thought would give him a more solid base not only for musical theory but also for scientific inquiry.[30] For science, that popular pursuit of nineteenth-century amateurs, was a lifelong passion, expressed early on in observing the growth of seeds in a window box on his apartment balcony, breeding caterpillars, collecting fossilised shells and studying rock formations at Fontainebleau. Of all the sciences, though, astronomy was his greatest love, from the day he was taken to the Paris observatory by the writer and poet Amable Tastu, and saw the mountains of the moon through its telescope. A pair of opera glasses were his first means of regular stargazing, but he was later to acquire his own telescope to pursue what was to be a lifelong 'Ingres violin'.

Formal piano lessons also began at the age of seven, on 13th March 1843. His teacher was Camille Stamaty (the name betrays Greek parentage), who complimented Mme Masson on the training she had already given her great-nephew. Stamaty was of the Clementi school of playing, with its emphasis on strength and independence of the fingers, and evenness of touch. Clementi's method of achieving these ends was to place a coin on the back of the pupil's hand, but Stamaty copied his own teacher Friedrich Kalkbrenner in having a rod fixed along the front of the keyboard on which the forearm rested in such a way that all muscular effort was confined to the hands. Saint-Saëns later dismissed the method as suitable only for the harpsichord and forte-piano, and useless for the modern instrument, deploring the aim of producing a continuous legato "which is both false and monotonous" and "opposed to my natural feelings".[31] He was often to attack the editorial fashion for marking almost everything legato even when it ran counter to the composer's intentions as indicated on original manuscripts. Nevertheless, Stamaty's training undoubtedly developed that power and independence in the fingers and the refinement of sound they produced, so essential for playing Mozart, of whose concertos Saint-Saëns was to become such a noted exponent. Stamaty also had the far-sightedness to encourage an interest in Bach, whose music was to be another important influence on the boy.

Also studying at Stamaty's studio was the American composer and pianist Louis Gottschalk, Saint-Saëns's senior by six years. Having been lauded as a child prodigy in his native New Orleans, he was crestfallen on seeing his younger contemporary's precocity and never forgot the way he used the hand rail on the piano "as though amusing himself with a toy" and, when it was removed, played "with brilliance one of his own compositions".[32]

There were lessons in accompaniment from the cellist Auguste Franchomme, a Conservatoire professor noted for the expressive tone he produced using a special smooth, light bow technique, and the memory of whom surely helped to inspire the richness of Saint-Saëns's later writing for the cello. He went to the church of St Germain l'Auxerrois for organ lessons with Alexandre Boëly, an early champion of Bach among French organists who passed his advocacy on to his young pupil. For composition and harmony, Stamaty recommended Pierre Maleden, described by Saint-Saëns as "an incomparable teacher" who derived from the German theorist Gottfried Weber the idea of considering chords in relation to their pitch and scale as well as in relation to each other. The Conservatoire regarded his ideas and methods as unorthodox and rejected his application for professorship, but Saint-Saëns regarded them as "a wonderful tool with which to reach the depths of music . . . Chords acquire different characteristics according to the place they occupy, and as a result certain things are explained that are otherwise inexplicable." He regarded his introduction to Maleden as the best service Stamaty ever did him. Under his influence he composed overtures, cantatas and songs as well as piano pieces, none of them published. But the boy had his own ideas too and lessons sometimes became stormy affairs. Maleden, normally "a kind and timid soul", would pin his young charge's ear to the desk to get him to accept a point, only to give up in the end: his precocious pupil would have his own way.[33]

His insatiable thirst for knowledge kept the young Saint-Saëns for the most part isolated from other children, apart from those at the church of St Sulpice. There he met one of the first of his lifelong friends, Theodore Biais, who was to become a church ornament maker. Otherwise it was a childhood of music and study rather than friendship and fun, during which he served his apprenticeship as a pianist at those select gatherings of family and friends that were a prominent feature of Parisian musical life in the 1840s. He was joined by another musical prodigy, Francis Planté, destined to become one of the greatest French pianists of the century, at one such gathering, at the home of an in-law of the young organist and composer Charles Gounod, whom Saint-Saëns had met at St Sulpice. Gounod already knew of the boy's musical gifts and may well have been at this soirée, joining in the embraces and congratulations before the evening ended with cakes and chocolate.[34]

At a matinée concert in July 1844 Saint-Saëns first attracted the attention of the influential critic Henri Blanchard with his playing of pieces by Field, Bach and Handel, and a concerto by Mozart. Blanchard praised the "ringing tone of a musician who really feels what he is playing", the "expressiveness without mannerism", a strong rhythmic sense and a "miraculous facility". Only the trills needed perfecting. He noted also an evenness in the tone which he was later to criticise, describing it more adversely as a lack of dynamic contrast.[35] As he did at all these informal, private concerts, Saint-Saëns played the programme from memory, following the pioneering example of Liszt, a practice that was then not only unusual but actually frowned upon.

Mme Saint-Saëns organised two further matinée recitals for her son, in January and February 1846, and bought him a grand piano, on which the ten-year-old, dwarfed rather by the instrument, gave a further recital at home. These events were a preliminary to his first public concert, which took place at the Salle Pleyel on 6th May 1846, with members of the Théâtre-Italien orchestra. His programme comprised Mozart's B flat Concerto K.450, for which he played his own cadenzas, and Beethoven's C minor concerto, either side of solo pieces by Bach, Handel, Hummel and Kalkbrenner, all played from memory. Looking like a junior Chopin, with his frail physique, long curved nose, small, delicate mouth and a complexion hinting at the latent consumption that had haunted his first years, he sat impassively throughout the performance, all movement confined to the small hands that belied the strength of tone they produced. All was achieved without excess, exaggeration or mannerism. The *Gazette Musicale* reported the apparent effortlessness of the performance, and phrases given with "clarity, elegance and even expression in the midst of the powerful effects of a numerous orchestra using all its resources".[36] *L'Illustration* commented that while other children of his age had played works as difficult, "none has equalled him for purity, sagacity and purpose". He was "one of those high intelligences that are epoch-making . . . It is above all in the slow movements that he shows the exquisite feeling with which he is endowed. What grace, what breadth, what perfect understanding of the styles of different composers."[37] Note that these first reviews talk of an expressive quality in the playing, something which in the adult pianist had all but disappeared.

The concert brought the young Saint-Saëns to the attention of a wider musical world. In the United States the *Boston Musical Gazette* reported on 3rd August "a boy in Paris, only ten-and-a-half, who plays the music of Handel, Bach, Mozart, Beethoven and more modern masters without any book before him". But it was not to be the start of the illustrious – and lucrative – concert career that Stamaty hoped for from his star pupil. A planned engagement with the Conservatoire Concerts Society (Société des Concerts du Conservatoire) – there was even a rehearsal – was cancelled at the instigation of François Seghers, the Belgian violinist, who was influential in the orchestra's affairs, and who disliked Stamaty. The society, he declared, was not there to play children's accompaniments. Mme Saint-Saëns was greatly hurt by this rebuff.[38] The lesson she learned was that amid public acclaim treachery lurked, and she passed on to her son her deep mistrust of adulation, which he retained for the rest of his life. In his old age he recalled that his mother "had something of a horror of praises and from the outset put me on my guard against their duplicity".[39] In fact he came to regard his role as a musician, and especially what he felt to be an inborn need to compose, as existing independently of any kind of critical comment. "I am so little sensitive to criticism and even to praise", he told a Berlin journalist at the height of his fame, "not out of an exaggerated sense of my own worth – that would be stupid – but because, producing works to fulfil a function of my nature, as an apple tree produces apples, I have no worries about what may be said on my account."[40]

In the wake of the aborted Concerts Society appearance, Mme Saint-Saëns and her aunt – much to Stamaty's disappointment – decided it was best to steer the boy clear of the potentially exhausting lifestyle of a touring virtuoso. Instead the "graceful sapling" was to go on being nurtured out of the public gaze, partly because of his still delicate health, partly because a further education was seen as the best means of enhancing prospects of advancement and security. The contrast with the infant Mozart could not have been greater.

Like Mozart, though, the infant Saint-Saëns played to royalty. Stamaty, returning from a winter break in Italy, introduced him to Helen, the Duchess of Orléans and daughter-in-law to King Louis-Philippe, and on 24th March 1847 he played to her at the Tuileries Palace. Her young son the Count of Paris was more interested in playing with his toy drum and rocking horse, but the Duchess was delighted by her little guest and afterwards sent a gold watch to the "young artist and future teacher".[41] In addition to this royal audience, a precursor to many that were to follow in later life, Mme Saint-Saëns allowed the occasional public appearance. Stamaty wanted her son billed as his pupil on these occasions, but as the boy was no longer being taught by him this was refused, signalling the end of relations with the teacher. The emphasis was no longer on performance but on learning: the child prodigy was about to become the prodigious student. His mother must have had a strong notion of his future. Warned about allowing him to play such advanced music as the Beethoven sonatas while still so young (he knew them all by heart), she was asked: "What music will he play when he is twenty?" She is said to have replied: "His own".[42]

II • STUDENT

THE PRODIGIOUS CHILDHOOD OF SAINT-SAËNS COINCIDED WITH A WORLD of music that was emerging from a period of momentous development. The romantic movement, in all its various aspects, had, under the impact of Beethoven and the revolutionary ideals of the 1790s, broadened the stylistic and emotional range of music to a degree unprecedented in the history of the art. Composers and performers were asserting themselves as free artists, no longer the salaried servants of kings, clergy and aristocrats, and although church employment and aristocratic patronage inevitably continued to play an important role in supporting musicians, both composers and performers were coming to regard themselves as being responsible ultimately to their art rather than to their paymaster.

Alongside this concept of artistic independence went a greater emphasis on personal expression, on music as a vehicle for the communication of emotions, anxieties, aspirations and ideals, which outweighed considerations of form and balance. 'Liberalism in art', to use Victor Hugo's definition of romanticism, meant that the formal certainties and tonal relationships of symphony, sonata and concerto of what was now seen as the 'classical' period – that is, the latter half of the eighteenth century, the period of Haydn, Mozart and their contemporaries – were increasingly undermined by the uncertainties and imbalances of the human psyche. A fascination with the macabre, the supernatural and the fantastic, together with attempts to ally music more closely with other arts, visual and literary, were among the manifestations of this free-ranging imagination. The *Symphonie fantastique*, which opened the decade in which Saint-Saëns was born, stood like a beacon of the new age, coming just three years after the death of Beethoven. Berlioz, however, represented just one of a widening variety of stylistic developments that was a natural consequence of the greater freedom and individuality of the composer. Contrast the style of Berlioz with, in turn, that of Chopin, Mendelssohn, Schumann, Liszt, all of whom were coming of age at about the time the *Symphonie fantastique* was first heard.

One outcome of the new artistic 'liberalism' was the growth of nationalism in music, varying in character from one part of Europe to another according to political circumstance. Wagner and Verdi were to become focal points in the movements for, respectively, German and Italian nation states. In Paris, Chopin turned Polish national dance forms into high art while dreaming of the homeland he would never see again; and in 1848, as the thirteen-year-old Saint-Saëns prepared to enter the Paris Conservatoire, the Czech nationalist Smetana took to the revolutionary barricades in Austria, as Wagner was to do in Dresden the following year. In Russia, a long established imperial power, it was the lack of a musical tradition that had prompted Glinka to launch a national school. In France, for centuries both a political entity and an artistic force, musical nationalism, with Saint-Saëns at the forefront, set out to challenge both German form and Italian melody, but was to come to a head later on largely as a reaction to political and military disaster.

Another aspect of the romantic movement – a paradoxical one at first sight but in fact wholly consistent with the stylistic expansion of the period – was the growing interest in and re-assessment of music of the more distant past. It was a process that had been going on for a century or more, at least since 1726, when Johann Pepusch set up his Academy of Ancient Music in England, but the new spirit of adventure in music gave it a new impetus. Bach had been attracting a growing number of enthusiasts since Johann Forkel's biography of 1802: Samuel Wesley's Bach concerts in London in 1808–09 and Mendelssohn's revival of the St Matthew Passion in Berlin in 1829 introduced Bach's music to a wider audience. Meanwhile, a growing number of choral societies across Europe spread interest in the pre-classical era, especially in the works of Palestrina, Bach and Handel. In Paris the publisher Alexandre Choron's school of singing gave recitals of Renaissance and baroque choral music in the 1820s, a mantle taken over by the Society of Vocal Classical Music (Société de Musique Vocale et Classique) in the 1840s, attracting an upper class clientele in search of sober alternatives to a rich diet of Italian opera.[1] It was the revivalists' mission to counter the prevailing notion of musical progress, that the music of the past was inferior to that of the present. (Berlioz, for instance, tended to dismiss such music – Gluck excepted – as "superannuated and childish".)[2] The Belgian scholar François-Joseph Fétis, who in 1832 organised a ground-breaking series of concerts at the Paris Conservatoire surveying the history of opera from 1600, declared that "art does not progress, it transforms itself".[3]

In his formative years Saint-Saëns came into direct contact with this revivalist movement, or at least its supporters, from whom he acquired an early enthusiasm for both Bach and Palestrina. Among them was Gounod, who at the time he met the infant prodigy, was also a friend of that other early influence on the boy, Ingres. The painter was director of the Villa Medici in Rome, where he became well acquainted with Gounod during the latter's stay there as winner of the Prix de Rome. Stamaty and Boëly have already been mentioned as fostering an interest in Bach in the young pianist and, as a thirteen-year-old student, Saint-Saëns was to come into contact with yet another Bach exponent, François Benoist. Saint-Saëns entered the Paris Conservatoire in November 1848, in the wake of Louis-Philippe's overthrow and the setting up of the short-lived Second Republic. On the advice of Stamaty, in his last role as shaper of the boy's destiny, he joined Benoist's organ class, while continuing the organ lessons with Boëly at St. Germain l'Auxerrois.

As the Church was a major employer of musicians the organ option seemed a wise career move, wiser than pursuing the more glamorous but more hazardous path of a concert pianist. But student years at the Conservatoire did not have a promising start. Asked to play to Benoist and the assembled class, the newcomer was so nervous and "the sounds I made were so extraordinary that all the pupils roared with laughter". He was admitted as an 'auditor', allowed to sit in on classes but not to take part. At home he studied Bach's *Art of Fugue*. Later the 'auditor' was asked to play again to the class, and this time performed so well that he was immediately accepted as a full student. At the end of the first year he won a second prize, blaming his failure to win a first on his youth, and "the inconvenience of having me leave a class where I needed to stay longer".[4] Nevertheless, he failed to gain a first prize again the following year. He did not blame Benoist, an inspiring teacher who produced "a veritable galaxy of talent" that already included César Franck. Despite a disconcerting habit of doing other work, like editing ballet scores, as a student played to him during a lesson, Benoist still gave the most masterly advice and guidance.[5] One of Saint-Saëns's contemporaries in the class was Auguste Durand, his future publisher.[6]

Benoist had a knowledge of counterpoint that was exceptional for his time and was highly skilled in fugal improvisation. Although Saint-Saëns did not rate him very highly as a performer, he acknowledged that "nothing he said lacked weight or authority". At St. Germain l'Auxerrois, his other teacher Boëly was distinguished as one of the most brilliant, subtle and knowledgable organists of his day, even more skilled in counterpoint than Benoist. He gave his pupil a grounding not only in Bach, but also in the wider repertory of the seventeenth and early eighteenth centuries, a speciality that was in part Boëly's reaction to what he regarded as the flippant tastes of the Parisian public.

Thus Saint-Saëns, in his formative years, came under the direction of two of France's foremost practitioners of the classical organ discipline. Boëly, however, was an important influence on the young composer as well as the future organist, as his organ pieces showed him how the archaic could be blended with the advanced, how adherence to traditional theory and practice could be combined with an adventurous and chromatic treatment of harmony to produce imaginative effects and nobility of line, just as Maleden had shown how regular chords could be used to achieve different moods and colours.

Saint-Saëns was preparing to enter a musical world that was at once stimulating and stifling. Paris had regained the artistic and cultural preeminence it had lost during the Revolution, eclipsing Vienna as the musical capital of Europe and attracting a young generation of musicians from abroad – including Chopin, Liszt, Paganini and Wagner – with its lively atmosphere of artistic debate and innovation of which the revolution of 1830 was the political counterpart. Yet for the native composer, Paris for the most part was an artistic straightjacket which confined him to the stage, turning out comic operas of passing value or grand operas, most of them equally short-lived, in the style of Rossini or Meyerbeer. Orchestral and chamber music, though performed more often in the period after 1830 than is generally supposed,[7] was a small world confined mainly to the works of Germanic – and deceased – masters, and open only to a few dedicated enthusiasts who could afford to be less concerned about earning a living, or, like Berlioz, were prepared to make huge personal sacrifices.

The French composer was inhibited on two fronts, first by the French taste for foreign spice, which for a century had savoured Italian opera, was now being fed by Beethoven's symphonies, and would in turn find relish in Wagner, the Russian ballet and the black American eroticism of Josephine Baker. Second, he was of a culture dominated by the visual and decorative, to which music was subservient in that it existed primarily to provide operatic and balletic spectacle. And even in opera, he was expected to work in a style essentially at odds with native tradition. Italian bel canto had long been regarded as the supreme form of musical expression, with its strong, lengthy melodic line over chords that are mere accompaniment. This style was alien to a French tradition in which melody, of more slender and feminine proportions, and harmony, often of a complex and subtle nature, combine on a more equal expressive basis to form an integrated whole. Italian opera fed an appetite for pomp, pageantry, spectacle and melodrama derived in part from the monumental and heroic style of First Empire art, and provided audiences of newly rich financiers and industrialists with regular doses of ostentatious diversion and escapism. Of the operas of Rossini, who directed the Théâtre Italien in Paris from 1824, *Le Comte Ory* became a model for comic opera as *Guillaume Tell* was for serious opera. "*Guillaume Tell* had its admirers from the start. I heard it spoken of constantly in my youth", recalled Saint-Saëns,[8] who shared from an early age the aspiration of French composers to shake off this Italian stylistic yoke. Had he not, at the age of three, already stated his position when he spurned simple melody-plus-accompaniment pieces because "the bass doesn't sing"?

Composers accommodated themselves to the prevailing Italian style in varying degrees, from whole-hearted adoption towards a more distinctively national idiom, for which comic opera – that is, opera with spoken dialogue – gave the greater scope. Here, Boieldieu and Hérold, inspired by the example of Weber in Germany, pioneered a romanticism characterised by lightness of touch, grace and elegance, a trend continued by Auber, in whose comic operas the orchestra plays a more integral role than in conventional Italian opera. But grand opera remained firmly in the tradition of spectacle and melodrama, and its mantle fell on the shoulders of another non-Frenchman, the Berlin banker's son Meyerbeer who, with his imitators, dominated the grand opera of Paris for the next three decades.

It was another foreign influence that provided the impetus for a renewed interest in purely orchestral music after a long decline. Beethoven's works were widely regarded before 1828 as ugly, barbaric and contrary to the French taste for elegance and refinement. In that year François Habeneck founded the Conservatoire Concerts Society (really a revival of the public 'exercises' by Conservatoire students which were abolished in 1824 for political reasons) specifically to spread the Beethoven gospel in Paris. The concerts were a revelation, starting what Berlioz described as "a fever of enthusiasm". The heroism, defiance and struggle in the symphonies caught the romantic imagination and struck like lightning the highly charged atmosphere of revolution, kindling a wider awareness and appreciation of orchestral works which a growing number of performances aimed to cater for.

But Beethoven came to dominate the movement to the disadvantage of French composers. His works were by far the most frequently performed – "no city in the world devoted itself more completely to the cult of Beethoven than Paris"[9] – with the other Austro-German masters Haydn, Mozart, Mendelssohn and Weber the next most widely played, though even they were some way behind. Paris was not, on the whole, fertile ground for French music of any originality, hence the seemingly superhuman efforts of Berlioz to have his works performed. By the mid-1840s he was thoroughly disillusioned by the state of music in the capital, which, he declared, was "absorbed by material interests, indifferent and inattentive to all that is dear to the poet and artist, devoted to scandal and banter, and laughing sarcastically whenever that strange taste is satisfied".[10] With typical exaggeration, he nevertheless caught the native composer's sense of frustration, of potential falling on stony ground, when he wrote in 1842: "There is scarcely any music in France now . . . and yet what unbounded resources we possess in this Parisian whirlpool, the centre of the restless ambition of all Europe!"[11]

Saint-Saëns was a child prodigy at a time when the revolutionary and revelatory mood of 1830 was giving way to a reassertion of conservative attitudes even among converts to the orchestral cause, who now regarded Beethoven as the last word in that medium. The pioneering spirit of Habeneck was a spent force by 1847 when he retired from the Conservatoire Concerts Society, and other societies that had sprung up in its wake were discontinued. As well as the operatic preferences of most aristocratic and upper middle class audiences there were political restraints on the playing – and hence the composition – of orchestral music. Beethoven was still associated with revolution and the government was suspicious of large musical gatherings around individuals and groups outside the institutions – like the Opéra, Opéra-Comique and Théâtre Italien – that it subsidised and could therefore influence, especially after a political demonstration was unwittingly inspired by a concert organised by Berlioz in 1844.[12]

Of the musical establishments supported by the government only the Conservatoire Concerts Society was a purely orchestral body. But the Conservatoire itself enshrined the supremacy of opera, regarding instrumental music as an inferior branch of the art. Its director Cherubini and his successor Auber, like the majority of its teachers of composition, were chiefly, though by no means exclusively, concerned with vocal music. In this situation, a student had few opportunities to hear orchestral and chamber music. Some outdoor events were free, but salon concerts were exclusively for invited, and usually wealthy, guests, and subscription concerts, like those of the Conservatoire Concerts Society, involved an outlay beyond the pockets of all but the very well-off. For Saint-Saëns, not yet part of the salon set except when performing, the Society offered the main chance of hearing orchestral works but "it was a paradise guarded by an angel with a burning sword, in the form of a porter named Lescot, whose job it was to prevent the profane from defiling the sanctuary". Luckily M. Lescot grew fond of the persistent student and "made his rounds as slowly as possible in order to throw me out only at the last minute". After hiding in the corridor or crouching on the floor of a box listening to concerts, Saint-Saëns took back to his classroom "the odour of Beethoven and Mozart" which in a student was regarded as "a strong taint of heresy".[13] Not that he always approved of the performance of works whose scores he had studied assiduously. Listening to the Sunday concerts as a respectable member of the audience after a wealthy acquaintance allowed him a place in his box, he noticed "grave defects in the Society's much-vaunted execution. . . . No one would stand them now, but then they passed unnoticed." And he was not popular for pointing them out.[14]

Saint-Saëns was growing up in an era when many musicians no longer looked beyond the Alps for inspiration but beyond the Rhine. The success of Beethoven in France confirmed their view that the Italian vocal tradition was decadent and that the Austro-German symphonic tradition was the dynamic force in the ascendant. Chief among French composers working in the classical symphonic forms were Théodore Gouvy, Louise Farrenc, the half-British George Onslow, and Henri Reber, but in so far as their work lay outside the theatre they enjoyed only limited appeal. When Gouvy produced his first symphony in 1847 one critic asked: "When he has the talent to be performed at all the lyric theatres . . . why the deuce does he write symphonies?"[15] So that although Berlioz was not strictly correct when he lamented that Frenchmen wrote nothing but comic operas, he nevertheless pointed to the dilemma of the native composer in the Paris of 1850: whether to accept the mould of musical reality – to compose comic operas, or grand operas in the style of Meyerbeer – or to break new ground and face hardship, ridicule, contempt or, worse, obscurity. Only Berlioz stands out as having had the strength of character to tread a new, unfamiliar path, that of a distinctive symphonic style, but he was reviled, misunderstood or simply ignored by an essentially conservative public, and the effort killed him in the end. For him recognition was to come posthumously, but he still sometimes gives the impression of a man feeling his way in the dark. A son of the temperamental, passionate south, he was finally overcome by disappointments and a morbid self-pity. It was to take a confident Saint-Saëns, with all the phlegmatic determination of his Norse forefathers, with his thorough grounding in form and technique, and from a base of domestic and financial security, to make resolute progress along the symphonic path. And just as he was to take his cue from Germanic forms, so he was to score many of his early triumphs, both as performer and composer, in Germany.

Of the French 'classical' composers, he most admired Henri Reber, and took part as pianist in several of his chamber works. He described Reber as a man of the eighteenth century living in the nineteenth ("his grey hair even looked powdered"), casting a disapproving eye on all around him.[16] His comic operas are a reaction against what he regarded as Italianate bombast in favour of the more restrained style of early eighteenth-century opéra-comique, with orchestration on a more modest scale. His orchestral and chamber works adhere rigidly to classical Austro-German models, and Saint-Saëns, who was to transcribe four of his symphonies for piano duet, regarded him as the first Frenchman to succeed in symphonic form. He was the example Saint-Saëns followed in making his own first symphonic essays, rather than going down the well-trodden road towards opera. Among the many compositions begun and either discarded or suppressed in his first two years as a student were two symphonies, the first written in 1848, the second two years later. This Symphony in A of 1850 clearly shows the Reber stamp. For a modest orchestra, it is Haydnesque in style and scale, but sometimes, in its boyish simplicity, reminiscent of early Schubert (incidentally the only composer of his own time that Reber liked). The outline of the four movements is strictly classical, with a repeat of the exposition in the first and last movements, and a conventional scherzo and trio. There is some rhythmic monotony – something which was to reappear in later works – and the charming if not very original tune of the larghetto receives little in the way of variation or development. Nevertheless it is a creditable effort by a fifteen-year-old, achieving an engaging degree of individuality in the boisterous finale, with its chattering quavers.

Alongside organ studies and composition, Saint-Saëns continued to work at the piano, with occasional public appearances as pianist. One of these was a matinée in aid of the poor on 3rd May 1849, organised by the opera librettist Eugène Scribe. He played Beethoven's C minor variations, sharing the bill with the mezzo-soprano Pauline Viardot, then in her late twenties, who had that year created the role of Fidès in Meyerbeer's *Le Prophète*. Daughter of the Spanish bass and impresario Manuel Garcia, who taught singing at the Conservatoire, she belonged to one of the most influential musical families of Europe, and Saint-Saëns's long friendship with her was to prove not only artistically inspiring but also extremely useful for his personal advancement.

More might have been heard of Saint-Saëns the pianist during this period but for the man who had earlier blocked his engagement with the Conservatoire orchestra. This time Seghers meant well. Perhaps regretting his earlier hostility, perhaps swayed by the fact that the young musician was no longer the protégé of his enemy Stamaty, Seghers asked him to join in a series of chamber concerts he was planning. Saint-Saëns was quite fired by the idea, but did not realise that Seghers, whom he described as a violinist of masterly execution, admirable tone and first-rate musical intelligence, "Herculean in appearance and tenacious in purpose", went to pieces before an audience. He spoke enthusiastically about the concerts to Seghers's mother-in-law as she sat at her embroidery, and was somewhat surprised when she looked up and replied: "Don't count on it too much. He'll never give them." Preparations were made and about thirty people invited to a trial performance. It was a disaster, and the project was abandoned. Before even this modest-size audience, Saint-Saëns recalled, "all the depth of tone had gone from his violin as well as the skill from his fingers".[17]

Saint-Saëns finally gained the first prize for organ on 28th July 1851, and with such superior marks that neither a second prize nor even an honourable mention was awarded to anyone else. The prize was a copy of a course in fugue and counterpoint by the Conservatoire's former director Cherubini, but said to have been largely ghost-written by Fromental Halévy, whose composition class Saint-Saëns entered in October.

Halévy's *La Juive* was the only one of his thirty-two operas, all largely in the Meyerbeer mould, to achieve any lasting success. Its spectacle and sensationalism – the heroine is thrown into a cauldron of boiling water – made it an immediate hit on its first appearance in the year Saint-Saëns was born, but its popularity did not outlive its composer and in his lifetime gave him a reputation which his easy-going personality was ill-equipped to build upon. Halévy, whose class Gounod had attended in the 1830s, was much sought after as a teacher because of this reputation, but it is doubtful whether he had any important influence on Saint-Saëns for he was often absent from his class, instead writing lucrative pot-boilers for the stage, attending to the singers and other favour-seekers whom his good nature made it impossible for him to dismiss and keeping up with his administrative work as permanent secretary of the Academy of Fine Arts at the Institute. He gave his students little direction, saying it was not his job to interfere with their 'inclinations' and confining himself to correcting the compositions they brought to him of their own volition. In his absence his students would discuss each other's work and the ideas they had gleaned from textbooks.

Saint-Saëns's work included orchestration, and vocal and instrumental pieces, most of which would never see the light of day. "And rightly," he insisted, "for my work was very uneven."[18] One of these student works was an uncompleted oratorio, *The Israelites on the Mount of Horeb*, a subject which held his interest throughout his long career but which he did not finally turn into an oratorio until his last years, in *The Promised Land* of 1913. From the beginning he sought perfection in the translation of ideas and sounds to manuscript, so that many a piece was begun and abandoned because "it doesn't go".[19] Throughout his life he was to draw a veil over the preliminary working out of his compositions so that he gave the impression of being able to turn out a polished product apparently without preparation. And those completed works which he felt were not of sufficient merit, or might damage his reputation, he withheld from publication. The A major Symphony of 1850, for instance, was not published until 1974.

When he was not composing he was reading scores in the Conservatoire library. "There, as a matter of fact, I completed my education. The amount of music, ancient and modern, I devoured is beyond belief."[20] His study of Bach was so advanced as to enable him, while still in his teens, to be among the first contributors to the first complete edition of Bach's works, a huge project begun in Germany in 1850 that was to take half a century to achieve – his name appears on the fourth volume, published in 1854. He was to go on 'devouring' music and in that sense at least he never ceased to be a student. He was familiar with the works of other masters, to the minutest details, to an extent far greater probably than any other composer before or since and he was immensely proud of his knowledge. According to Gabriel Fauré, as reported by Marguérite Long, "he sought to understand everything that he might love everything".[21] Yet his extraordinary powers of absorption have been seen as a source of weakness rather than strength, in that his own development of an original, personal style might otherwise have been greater than it was. In later years, while he enjoyed discussing, and displaying his thorough grasp of, other men's music, he cheerfully accepted charges of eclecticism. "I am an eclectic. This is perhaps a great defect, but it is impossible for me to correct it: one cannot alter one's nature."[22] To Saint-Saëns, eclecticism meant intellectual honesty and freedom of thought, taste and criticism (which was later to bring him into conflict with the Wagnerians). He was naturally disposed to praise and emulate the strengths of other composers, and to point out their weaknesses, without fear or prejudice or thought for the consequences of his expressed opinions. Gounod said of him that he could "write at will a work in the style of Rossini, of Verdi, of Schumann or Wagner," and that "he possesses his art like no one else; he knows the masters by heart".[23] Gounod adds, however, that this thorough knowledge of the masters was "the surest safeguard, perhaps, against him imitating any of them".[24] In any survey of his life the scholar can sometimes seem greater than the musician, but too much emphasis has been laid on this aspect of his art, leaving his distinctive, individual style greatly underestimated. His own voice is not silenced by scholarship but acquires from it an aura of authority and wisdom, breathed from the past, that gives it its own peculiar quality. Romain Rolland came close to defining this quality when he wrote that Saint-Saëns's resemblance to the old masters was spiritual rather than actual. "One seems to be travelling in a country that one knows and loves; and yet . . . one does not find any direct resemblance to the works of other composers, for . . . it is his spirit that is akin to theirs . . . His compositions are like fragments of another world."[25]

In combining his knowledge of music with the evolution of a style of his own, Saint-Saëns was again taking a lead from Reber, who, he recalled, openly advocated imitating the 'ancients' – "for they are the best" – yet had the "power and the depth of genius" writing "some particularly individual music when he thought he was imitating Haydn and Mozart". Reber was also a musical mentor to Ingres, that other classical influence on the young student who, like Reber, "affected the most profound contempt for all modern music and would not even listen to it". Saint-Saëns saw that some of Reber's compositions, "in their perfection of line, their regard for detail, their purity and their moderation are reminiscent of Ingres's drawings which express so much in such a simple way". And just as Reber was both imitative and individual, so Ingres, "although he tried to imitate Raphael, could only be himself".[26]

Reber and Ingres were members of a musical revivalist group, headed by the tenor François Delsarte, Bizet's uncle, a small but dedicated band of serious musicians, artists and wealthy amateurs who looked for true beauty in the 'ancients' and rejected what they regarded as the frivolous, comic opera tastes of their contemporaries, imagining a pristine purity in a distant past from which subsequent ages were a falling away. Dismissing such "false notions"[27] – and indulging what was to be a lifelong taste for comic opera, often queuing hours for a ticket[28] – Saint-Saëns was nevertheless inspired by Delsarte to further his own study of pre-classical music. He attended, as did Gounod before him, a series of lectures on declamation and gesture given by Delsarte, who, in his late thirties, had already acquired a reputation as an eccentric, both from his ill-fitting clothes and his antiquarian tastes. He claimed that his voice had been ruined by the Conservatoire's training, but Saint-Saëns thought it more likely that his own method did the damage. He could still croak out a Gluck aria, with Saint-Saëns at the piano. The young student thought him a "disastrous and deadly teacher of singing": what interested him were Delsarte's ideas on dramatic expression, speech and movement, which involved elements of psychology and physiology, with a touch of mysticism, in character interpretation, and which showed "why the accent should be on such a word and not on another, to bring out the sense".[29]

They undoubtedly helped to tune his fine ear for the music of words, and his fastidious sense of metre and the correct placing of words in vocal settings.

Delsarte deepened the young man's appreciation of opera from the period before Mozart's maturity, at a time when, for instance, Gluck was so much neglected that, as Saint-Saëns ruefully recalled, first editions of his scores could be picked up for a few francs in second-hand bookshops. Delsarte was typical of the revivalists: although his scholarship was dubious his dedication was undeniable, and Saint-Saëns saw in him a "visionary" who "played an important role in the evolution of French music in the nineteenth century". Thanks to him "the lamp of our old French school was kept dimly burning until the day when inherent justice permitted it to be revived".[30] From Delsarte he gained a wider perspective on the continuity of musical history, and took over the mantle of musical revival by including in his recitals and concerts works from the seventeenth and early eighteenth centuries, as well as by editing Bach, Gluck and the old French masters like Rameau.

His interest in and sympathy with former times was reflected in the fond memories he retained of the old Conservatoire building in the Rue Bergère. By 1851 conditions had become so cramped that the sound emanating from the classrooms – "the wailing of sopranos and tenors, the rattle of pianos, the blasts of trumpets and trombones, the arpeggios of clarinets" – seemed to sit on top of each other in what he described, in a side-swipe at the musical contemporaries of his latter years, as a kind of "ultra-polyphony which some of our composers have tried to attain, without success". But what appealed to him most about the building, soon to be vacated for more spacious accommodation, was its "antiquity, its utter absence of any modern note, its atmosphere of other days" which – like great-aunt Charlotte's clothes and furniture – were a tangible link with a bygone age.[31]

"Everything in my youth seemed calculated to keep me far removed from romanticism."[32] Thus Saint-Saëns, in later years, acknowledged the influence of tradition in shaping his musical outlook in the romantic era. As a teenager he was thoroughly immersed in the great masters from Bach to Beethoven, while, encouraged by Boëly and Delsarte, he extended his knowledge and appreciation further back into the musical past. Yet at the same time he remained very much alive to contemporary developments, and his formative years as a composer were to see him using classicism as a point of departure for new ideas and means of expression, much as an organ piece by Boëly can take flight into adventurous harmonies, while remaining strictly traditional in conception.

His first taste of romanticism was literary, a fact that led to the composition of songs which, though little known, are among the finest fruits of his early years. By the late 1840s he was familiar with Lamartine, and set several of his poems, though with indifferent results. It was the gift of a volume of Victor Hugo that was to have the most inspirational and lasting impact. He became an ardent admirer of Hugo, eagerly awaiting each new work up to the writer's death in 1885. He was to set many of his verses, which he always read in musical terms "as my temperament is essentially musical in everything".[33] The first known setting is 'Guitare' from 1851, and with 'Rêverie', despite its imperfections of form and prosody, Saint-Saëns reaches an early mastery of the solo song, both in style and atmosphere. He saw no contradiction in his admiration for the classics (literary as well as musical) and for one of the literary giants of romanticism. "I never could see why it was unfaithfulness to Hugo not to despise Racine. I have seen the most fiery romantics . . . revert to Racine in their later years and repair the links in a golden chain that should never have been broken."[34] For the young Saint-Saëns this golden chain in music was to stretch from the earliest times to Berlioz, Schumann, Wagner and Liszt, and it carries the golden key to the understanding and appreciation of his own music. It is wrong to regard him as the first neo-classical composer, for that implies a divide between the present and the past which for Saint-Saëns did not exist.

A singer, Mme Forgues, gave him much valuable advice on writing for the voice, and in gratitude he dedicated to her his early song 'La feuille du peuplier', a setting of a poem by another woman he had cause to thank, Mme Tastu, the writer who had introduced him to the delights of astronomy. In his songs, as in other forms, he set out to break from the Italian style, in which accompaniment is subsidiary to melody, towards a more integrated approach in which the accompaniment plays an equal part in conveying the poetic idea; and as in symphonic music, he took a lead from Austro-German models, in this case those of Schubert and Schumann, with their warm lyricism and their expressive use of accompaniment. His setting of Hugo's poem about a medieval military tournament, 'Les pas d'armes du roi Jean', written when he was seventeen, is a small masterpiece comparable to those of Schubert at the same age, an evocative blend of bravado and tenderness. In his writing he brings to German lyricism a French feel for the picturesque – and the whimsical, as in 'La cigale et la fourmi', to La Fontaine's fable.[35] He was to go on writing songs all his life (except for a fourteen-year gap in mid-career), yet his contribution to the repertory of French song has been generally unrecognised.

Despite his great industry as a student Saint-Saëns was no dry academic. Although of frail constitution and sickly complexion, he had an outgoing personality, playful, even exuberant, loving tricks and games, and with a ready, quick wit. These characteristics were given full rein in the company of his fellow students, as if to make up for his cloistered childhood. Among his contemporaries in Halévy's class who were to prove lifelong friends were Edward Silas, who became a concert pianist, and the future composer of comic operas Charles Lecocq, who shared Saint-Saëns's enthusiasm for Gluck and Rameau.

It is probable (there is nothing to confirm it) that he had also by this time met Bizet, who had entered the Conservatoire the same year, though three years his junior. Although a contemporary at the Conservatoire, Bizet was never with Saint-Saëns in the same class – he studied piano and did not join Benoist's class until 1852, nor Halévy's until the year after – but his uncle Delsarte frequently used the elder student as his accompanist, and it is almost certain that the two would have come into contact through this family connection.

Saint-Saëns also accompanied Pauline Viardot at her Thursday evening soirées in the Rue de Douai, which attracted some of the most eminent musicians of the day, and where he was to make many useful contacts. He was deeply impressed by everything about her: her personality, which transcended her plain looks and led the Russian writer Turgenev to become her lover; her fluency in foreign languages, chiefly Italian, English and German; her wide literary knowledge and her considerable powers as both pianist and composer, about which she was quite self-effacing. Her voice he remembered as "tremendously powerful, prodigious in its range" but "a little harsh, like the taste of a bitter orange": it was a voice made for tragedy and epic, perfect for the part of Delilah which Saint-Saëns was to write for her. She had, he recalled, "an astonishing facility for assimilating all styles of music", which, of course, matched his own, and she shared with him an enthusiasm for Bach. She also gave him valuable insights into the playing style of Chopin, who had often accompanied her at George Sand's house at Nohant. Through her descriptions of Chopin's playing, especially in its rubato melody over a strictly controlled bass, he came to see in it another link between classical precision and romantic eloquence which avoided the extremes of both, "as far removed from any show of bad taste as it was from cold correctness".[36]

His musical outlook was further developed by his collaboration with Gounod. There was a strong bond of sympathy between the two, despite the age difference of almost twenty years. Gounod was born in the same district as Saint-Saëns, had also lost his father early in life and had displayed miracles of perfect pitch in infancy. Deeply impressed by the student's musical skills, he asked him to help with the scoring of his incidental music for Ponsard's tragedy *Ulysse*. Saint-Saëns relates that Gounod "had some trouble playing his scores. At his request I went nearly every day to spend a short time with him and between us we played – well and badly, but more often well – fragments of the work blossoming on freshly written pages". Gounod would expound his ideas and aims, especially for orchestration, declaring that "sonority is yet unexplored . . . His great preoccupation was to discover beautiful colour on the palette of the orchestra; and far from adopting established methods from the masters, he sought directly, in the study of timbre, in new combinations, the tones needed for his paint brush." For the nymphs' chorus in *Ulysse*, for instance, he achieved a special aquatic effect with a glass-plated harmonica and a muted triangle. The music as a whole attempts to evoke the ancient world through the use of pseudo-antique rhythms and key sequences, a piece of period reconstruction which Saint-Saëns was later to emulate in his own stage works. Having played such an enthusiastic role in the creation of the score, and "wanting passionately for the music of my great friend the success it deserved", he shared its composer's great disappointment when *Ulysse* failed on its première at the Comédie-Française on 18th June 1852, despite a fine performance. The audience, Saint-Saëns noted, was "for the most part purely literary and only a little concerned about the musical art". By the last act there were howls of derision, and he had "the melancholy sight of my friend, whom I had managed to restrain up to then, laughing heartily".[37]

Working with Gounod, whom he had come to regard as something of a father figure, undoubtedly influenced his own attempts at orchestral tone colour as well as period evocation. "He discussed things with me as with an equal: it is thus that I became, if not his pupil, at least his disciple, and that I completed my formative period in his shadow, or rather in his brightness."[38] Gounod had dabbled in painting, and he saw the orchestra as a canvas on which to paint the most subtle and evocative sounds. He knew, said Saint-Saëns, that "it was not necessary to put all his colours on the canvas, and he restored sobriety to the theatre orchestra, the mother of accurate coloration and delicate nuances".[39] This restraint and delicacy marked a new break from the aggressively vocal Italian style towards a distinctively French approach in which the imaginative use of harmony plays as important a part as melody. Gounod had rediscovered, said Ravel, "the secret of a harmonic sensuousness lost since the French harpsichordists of the seventeenth and eighteenth centuries".[40] Saint-Saëns also shared with Gounod an admiration for French opera of the eighteenth century, especially Gluck, and a desire to recover what they saw as the expressive clarity and directness of the old school in the face of the prevailing Italian style.

An event which had a profound effect on the young Saint-Saëns came in 1852, when he called at Seghers's house to find Liszt teaching piano to one of Seghers's daughters. The great Hungarian was a frequent guest there and had given piano lessons to Mme Seghers, herself a competent pianist. Saint-Saëns was awestruck, for Liszt was already "part of the world of legend". He recalled:

You would not believe with what glamour, what magical prestige this name Liszt appeared to young musicians in the first years of the imperial era, strange to us French, pointed and whistling like the blade of a sword that whisks through the air, crossed by its Slav 'z' as by a streak of lightning . . . I already considered him to be a genius. Imagine my astonishment then, when I found that he far exceeded even this expectation.[41]

That astonishment at Liszt's formidable personality and pianism left a permanent mark on the young student. Many years later he recalled that "he seemed like an apostle, when he played 'St Francis of Paule Walking on the Waters', and you could believe you saw it, really saw the foam of the raging waves flying round about his pale, impassive face, with its eagle look and sharp profile."[42] Of all his illustrious contemporaries it was Liszt whom he was most to admire and revere.

He declared his aspirations to be a composer by entering for the Prix de Rome. He was still only sixteen when, in June 1852, he and five other hopefuls were each locked away in solitary confinement, according to custom, to write a cantata to a given text. The subject was *Le Retour de Virginie* by the minor poet Auguste Barbier, written as a sequel to Bernardin de Saint-Pierre's love story *Paul et Virginie*. The winner was a twenty-five-year-old, Léonce Cohen, who thereafter sank into obscurity. The judges perhaps considered that Saint-Saëns was too young to benefit from the prize, which financed two years of study in Italy, one in Germany and two in Paris, but when he again competed unsuccessfully twelve years later, the rumour was that Auber, the Conservatoire director, had adversely influenced the judges on both occasions because he bore him some grudge (perhaps because of some typically outspoken comment, or remembering his heretical pursuit of orchestral above operatic success). Saint-Saëns refused to believe this and years later told the pianist Georges Mathias that the idea of Auber being in some way ill-disposed towards him "is exactly contrary to the truth . . . he always showed me the greatest interest and sympathy".[43]

The failure of the first Prix de Rome attempt, far from discouraging the young composer, spurred him on to enter, on 15th October, a competition held by the Society of St Cecilia, founded two years before by Seghers to promote new and otherwise unfamiliar works by such contemporaries as Schumann and Wagner. The authorship of entries was not revealed to the selectors – who, as well as Seghers, also included Halévy, Reber and Gounod – until after a decision was made. The prize was awarded unanimously to Saint-Saëns's *Ode à Sainte Cécile*.

But even this success was soured by the *Ode*'s reception when Seghers conducted it at the Casino Paganini on 26th December. It showed the composer still bound by his devotion to the classics, without a voice of his own, the *Gazette Musicale* lamenting a lack of what it called "high inspirational flashes of genius" and the spirit to show "a young man's desire to create a personality for himself."[44] Seghers was to conduct it again two years later but it was never published and the manuscript, like so many of Saint-Saëns's student works, has not survived. Three pieces for harmonium, written in 1852 and published six years later, became his Opus 1.

III • ORGANIST

THE YEARS OF ORGAN STUDY BROUGHT SAINT-SAËNS THE HOPED-FOR dividend in an appointment as organist at the Church of St Séverin, beginning a twenty-four-year period of regular income and material comforts at the outset of his working life. Not for him the debts and hardships of many an aspiring composer; instead, the encouragement and loving attention of his mother and her aunt, who saw to his every need and were proud and delighted that their wonder child had become the family breadwinner while at the same time making the most of his carefully nurtured gifts. But his work as an organist was no mere job, held simply to finance his aims as a composer: he brought to it the same thoroughness, dedication and artistic purpose with which he approached most other branches of music. From his twin bases of home and organ loft he was certainly able to work at composition without financial worries, but he was also to become one of the greatest organists of his generation.

After a few months at St Séverin he took over as organist at the sixteenth-century church of St Merry, half an hour's walk from his home: in his spare time, encouraged by Seghers, he worked on a symphony in E flat, which, on completion, he sent in manuscript – anonymously, like the *Ode* – to the Society of St Cecilia. Fearing prejudice against a symphony by a Frenchman – and one not only still living but even still in his teens – Seghers led the selectors to suppose that it was the work of a mature German. That the pretence worked says as much about Saint-Saëns's early mastery of symphonic form and his identification with German style as it does about the attitudes of the selection committee. The symphony – still unattributed – was awarded the honour of a performance at a concert conducted by Seghers on 18th December 1853. At a rehearsal attended by Gounod and Berlioz, as well as Saint-Saëns and his mother, the eighteen-year-old overheard the two older composers discussing the work enthusiastically. They were astonished to discover the identity of its author. Gounod wrote to his young friend next day of the joy he felt at hearing the symphony. "You are far in advance of your years", he told him, adding that with the symphony he had "contracted the obligation of becoming a great master". Saint-Saëns greatly valued this encouragement, and kept the letter for the rest of his life.[1] As for Gounod, his admiration may well have been what prompted him to produce two symphonies of his own two years later.

The warm reception given to the E flat symphony, published as No. 1, is understandable. Despite occasional faults of immaturity, it is a delightful work full of the ardour and exuberance of youth, touched by the freshness and delicacy of a spring breeze but also by a certain lofty nobility. It shows its composer emerging from the somewhat dry formality of the A major symphony with early indications of an identity of his own: here is symphonic matter of greater vitality, tonal and rhythmic variety and orchestral colour, qualities in part fostered by the collaboration with Gounod the previous year. The scoring is for a much larger orchestra than that of the earlier symphony: the finale involves four harps, cymbals and extra brass, including two saxhorns. Such extravagance shows a readiness to follow Berlioz in orchestral adventurousness, and the use of the saxhorn, invented by Adolphe Sax just eight years before, also shows an early interest in new instruments for creating new orchestral sound combinations. (Saint-Saëns was later to experiment with the saxophone and the rival sarrusophone.)

Blanchard, who did not share in the general welcome for the new symphony, was especially critical of the opening allegro, which he described as vague and characterless. It is significant, in view of Saint-Saëns's leanings towards the German symphonic style, away from Italian bel canto, that Blanchard thought the first movement lacking in thematic ideas "which the young composers of our day neglect very much".[2] The criticism misses the point: the melodic interest is subservient to the symphonic design and atmosphere of the movement, which, opening with a short slow introduction, combines a grandeur of conception with a lightness of touch. There are some purely functional moments, such as in the transition between first and second subjects, but these are far outnumbered by passages of real inspiration, especially in the development.

Melody is more in evidence in the jaunty march-scherzo, whose main theme has a Schubertian felicity and a familiarity that gives the first-time listener the odd feeling of having heard it before. An adagio of wistful delicacy, in which the harp is prominent, creates a mood of gentle nostalgia, looking back fondly to a past, real or imagined. It leads straight into the blazingly triumphalist finale, the first of a type that was to characterise many of Saint-Saëns's later works. Based on a single theme, its towering grandeur and full-volumed intensity also point to the occupation of the composer, for the organ, as well as the ideas of Gounod, was opening his ears to the as yet untapped resources of the orchestra. The organ, as he well appreciated, was an orchestra in itself, and one literally at his fingertips. The organist, he said, had "manifold resources . . . obedient to his slightest wish", the keyboards, stops and pedals placing a broad spectrum of sound, nuance and inflection at his command,[3] and it is perhaps no coincidence that the two foremost orchestral writers in France to emerge in the second half of the nineteenth century, Saint-Saëns and Franck, were both distinguished organists. Berlioz certainly appreciated this dual nature of Saint-Saëns's musical mastery. Having hailed the composer of the E flat symphony, he called on him to play the organ at the first performance of his Te Deum in April 1855, after Henry Smart cancelled from London. (His first choice was Liszt.)[4] Because of the short notice Saint-Saëns could not oblige, but his pianistic gifts were of use to Berlioz – no pianist himself – in preparing the piano reduction of the dramatic monologue *Lélio*.

As a pianist he was able to supplement his salary at St Merry by accepting concert engagements all over the country, a once-discouraged occupation that added to an already busy life, giving his mother and her aunt fresh grounds for concern about his health. Often, and especially in winter, he was stricken by fever, coughing and shortage of breath, brought on by the slightest dampness in the air and aggravated by undue physical and mental strain. His concert performances, and the attendant socialising which he could not resist, caused the two women no end of anxiety: he is known, on more than one occasion, to have arranged for a friend to take his place in bed so that his mother, seeing the bed occupied, could retire in the comforting belief that her son was safely tucked in for the night.[5] As for great-aunt Charlotte, the industrious youth repaid her for the tuition and guidance she had given him by dedicating to her his piano quintet in A minor.

For his first major chamber work Saint-Saëns clearly took his cue from Mendelssohn, who had died prematurely only eight years before. It has many of Mendelssohn's lyrical and rhythmic qualities, from the cloistered, hymn-like serenity of the slow movement to the agitated presto with its whirling chromatic runs and diminished chords and intervals, but the Mendelssohnian lightness is countered by the thickness of some of the piano writing. The dramatic series of chords that opens the work is combined with a bold, assertive figure to form a composite first subject, to which the lilting second subject is in pleasant contrast. The final allegro begins with a conventional fugue giving way to a noble, march-like theme: these alternate and combine in a variety of configurations to often exhilarating effect, and the return of the first movement's second subject at two climactic points shows Saint-Saëns's early interest in cyclical form, something which he was to explore in many different ways in later compositions in pursuit of the rounded, self-contained, fully integrated work of art.

His contribution to instrumental music at the outset of his career has created the impression that he was not interested in opera and was therefore untypical of the France of the period. In fact he considered and even began several operatic projects in the early 1850s, prompted by both Halévy and Auber, and from another quarter, by Pauline Viardot, who, in view of the young man's admiration for her, is likely to have had the most decisive influence on him. Among the plans for serious opera were *Macbeth* – he set the sleep-walking scene to an Italian text – and Scott's *Kenilworth*. He wrote an overture and several airs for an opéra-comique on a Persian theme, an early indication of interest in oriental subjects that was to shape an important part of his later output. And in 1854 the librettist Jules Barbier suggested another opéra-comique, the overture to which has survived and was first played in London nearly sixty years later.

But all these tentative beginnings left Saint-Saëns dissatisfied, and he turned back to vocal forms in which he felt more sure of himself. Songs of the period include 'Plainte', set to another of Mme Tastu's poems, a masterly creation of emotional effect with simple means, and more settings of his beloved Victor Hugo, including 'La Cloche', evocative of the darkly Gothic atmosphere of the poem, with its mingling of iron-clad solemnity and human love, a song that should be heard by all who think that Saint-Saëns lacks passion. It is dedicated to Pauline Viardot.

On a larger vocal canvas is the Mass of 1856, the most substantial of a number of religious works, many unpublished, written for the St Merry choir. Church music was another branch of the art that had been undergoing profound stylistic changes brought about by the romantic movement. Opposed to what had come to be regarded as eighteenth-century formality and pomposity was a greater emphasis on mysticism and devotion, in an age when Catholicism was undergoing something of a spiritual revival, as well as reasserting itself politically in the wake of Napoleon's downfall. Its manifestations included the restoration of the Jesuits as a world order, the fostering of a new Marian cult and, across the Channel, the Oxford Movement and neo-Gothic architecture.

One of the features of the new approach to church music was a greater use of plainsong, as a way of recapturing the imagined simplicity and piety of earlier centuries. Among its leading advocates was the Abbé Guéranger at Solesmes, who aimed to restore the 'authenticity' of chant by omitting harmonised accompaniments and replacing regular metre with more flexible speech rhythms.[6] The movement for church music reform was thus clearly associated with that of the musical revivalists with their fondness for the pure sounds of Palestrina and his contemporaries.

The danger for the reformists was to be led astray by this association towards dry, fossilised, academic 'restorations' instead of the new, living intensity and immediacy they sought. Saint-Saëns understood this: he was quick, for instance, to criticise a performance of a Palestrina Mass by the Society of Vocal Classical Music as "lifeless".[7] Just as with instrumental music he saw the blend of formal balance and harmonic adventurousness as a creative force, so with church music he shared the view of Liszt, that it should seek to combine ancient austerity with the living force of modern harmonies and have the power to inspire the worshipper to divine contemplation and imaginings of paradise.

So it is not surprising that his Mass Op. 4 was warmly, even extravagantly praised by Liszt, who, in a letter to the composer some thirteen years later, called it "capital, grand, beautiful, admirable, extraordinary". This was a piece of gushing adulation typical of Liszt, but even so the Mass is a worthy achievement for a twenty-year-old. Saint-Saëns creates an archaic effect by drawing on his knowledge of sixteenth-century harmony and polyphony, recreating it in his own fashion, and going back even further in time, to plainsong, in the delightful 'O

Salutaris' for women's voices. There is little of the concert-style Mass that had developed since the time of Haydn: the style is lighter, more ethereal, and more in keeping with current notions of devotional music, which preferred hushed humility and restraint. There is nothing of the Italian opera house here. None of the four soloists has any substantial passage to sing, save where a solo introduces the full chorus. All are integrated into the structure, notably in the Credo where the vocal quartet alternates with the choir. Yet while the assimilation of old styles and the sparing use of soloists lend an appropriate sobriety to the work, Saint-Saëns, following the example of Boëly, often adds chromatic interest to the harmonies, as in the organ accompaniment to the Christe eleison. In the Quoniam he reaches the heights of that grandeur admired by Liszt, who likened the Mass to "a magnificent Gothic cathedral" and begged to be allowed to keep the manuscript "for I must possess this extraordinary work".[8]

The Mass was first sung at St Merry on 21st April 1857 and dedicated to the Abbé Gabriel, curate at the church, who rewarded its composer by taking him to Rome. This was a visit that was to be more than just a brief alternative to a Prix de Rome tenure, for it was to have a lasting impact on Saint-Saëns. Seeing at first hand the ruins of the ancient city stimulated what was to be a lifelong interest in classical archaeology and the Latin writers. And hearing the choir of the Sistine Chapel sing Palestrina not only gave him fresh insight into sixteenth-century polyphony but also helped to determine his approach to both performance and composition, with the idea of 'pure music' seeming to confirm what he had been taught since childhood, that musical beauty existed dispassionately, without, as he put it, "nuance or expressive intent". The memory of this Vatican performance was to assume greater significance in his later years, when he was advancing with greater forthrightness the idea of form as the essence of music, and when he recalled also hearing as a young man choirs in Germany who sang "without any emotion or expression of any sort".[9] This was entirely consistent with his criticism of some performances of older music as dull and lifeless: the aim should be to convey the living spirit of the music that existed independently of any expressive input by the performer.

It would be a mistake to think that the Symphony in F, called *Urbs Roma*, was inspired by the visit to Rome – it was written the year before, in under eight weeks during June and July 1856, for a competition held by the St Cecilia Society of Bordeaux. It won first prize and Saint-Saëns was awarded honorary membership of the society. As he had not been to Rome when he wrote it, the title, especially in its Latin form, must be seen rather as referring to an imagined view of the Rome of literature, legend and history: the generally grand festive manner of the music certainly suggests some sort of tribute to the Eternal City. Or it may simply be a rueful comment on failure to win the Prix de Rome. Saint-Saëns does not tell us: he was unhappy about the work and after conducting it in Paris on 15th February 1857 with the newly formed orchestra of the Society of Young Conservatoire Artists (Société des Jeunes Artistes du Conservatoire) – his first public appearance as a conductor – he withheld it from publication and it was never performed again in his lifetime. Yet it is a work of some interest. A slow introduction built on a fanfare figure announced by the horns gives way to an allegro whose $\frac{6}{4}$ time creates a strong forward drive and a bright, sunny mood before the fanfare returns to launch the coda. A vigorous A minor movement generates a climax of tremendous energy, with a quieter central section based on a flighty descending/ascending figure on the flutes in thirds which become caught up in the concluding outburst of exhilaration. The slow movement provides a retreat from the bustle with a ponderous, rather shapeless theme on the cellos, which is contrasted with a lighter central section, and the finale is a set of variations – one in $\frac{5}{4}$ time – using a smaller orchestra than that of the E flat symphony's finale but building to a brilliant climax in keeping with the overall mood of energetic optimism.

Urbs Roma, like the earlier A major symphony, was not finally published until 1974. Both have been recorded, and both certainly deserve to be heard. Indeed, there is a case – especially in view of another, still unpublished, symphony, the one in D written in 1859 – for renumbering Saint-Saëns's symphonies, in the same way that Dvořák's fifth became his ninth after publication of his four early symphonies in the 1960s.

A major career advance followed Saint-Saëns's visit to Rome in 1857, when he was appointed organist at the church of the Madeleine, that imposing neo-classical building in the heart of Paris, commissioned by Napoleon I as a temple to military glory but not completed until 1842. The Abbé Deguerry, the Madeleine's curate and confessor to the Empress Eugénie, had for some time been an admirer of Saint-Saëns's musicianship and had already lined him up to succeed Louis Lefébure-Wély. At twenty-two, the new organist commanded a comfortable salary of 3,000 francs a year and the considerable prestige of presiding over the music of one of the capital's greatest churches. The instrument at his command was one of the first major works of the great organ builder Aristide Cavaillé-Coll, the pioneer of a number of technical advances to improve tonal combinations and brilliance. Saint-Saëns had already met him, for he had lately installed another of his creations at St Merry, a three-manual instrument for which the composer retained a strong affection. In the years to come, Saint-Saëns was to join other eminent organists in inaugurating many of Cavaillé-Coll's instruments, in France and overseas.

The Madeleine's new organist took up his post in the high gallery over the door on 7th December. During his nineteen years at the church he acquired such a formidable reputation that Liszt, after hearing him play a transcription of his 'St Francis Preaching to the Birds', hailed him as the greatest organist in the world. Writing to his friend Olga von Meyendorff in 1877, he declared that as an organist "Saint-Saëns is not merely in the first rank but incomparable, as is Sebastian Bach as a master of counterpoint". The recipient of this letter, Liszt notes, did not care much for the instrument, "but were you to hear Saint-Saëns play an organ worthy of his extraordinary virtuosity I am convinced that you would be moved and amazed. No orchestra is capable of creating a similar impression; it is the individual in communion with music rising from earth to heaven".[10] Saint-Saëns's improvisations, usually on a plainchant used in the day's service, were his particular glory. Already as a child an imaginative improviser at the piano, he believed strongly that this ability was the mark of the organist who really knew his art, for the instrument provided him with "an extraordinary means of expressing himself", its touch stimulating the imagination so that "the unforeseen rises from the depths of the unconscious . . . as an enchanted island comes from the sea".[11] Organ improvisation was also to be a major source of composition in other media: he was later to reveal that parts of the second piano concerto, the andante of the first cello sonata and the finale of the third symphony all had their origins in exploratory sessions at the organ.[12]

The church organist's job, he declared, was to produce music that would "harmonise with the service and aid meditation and prayer", so that even a mediocre improvisation whose harmonies suited the occasion was better than a fugue by Bach or Mendelssohn that did not, "on the principle that nothing in art is good unless it is in its proper place". He was to attack what he saw as the 'German tendency' to regard the 'precise' pieces of Bach and Mendelssohn as superior to improvised ones. This, he believed, was "the negation of eloquence". The organ "furnishes a harmonious noise rather than precise music". Works of the old masters "are very fine, but they belong to concerts and are entirely out of place in church services". The true worth of the organist was not the works he left behind him, written down for posterity, but the music inspired by the moment. Saint-Saëns's predecessor at the Madeleine, Lefébure-Wély, was "a wonderful improviser" but "he left only a few unimportant compositions for the organ". The same can be said of Saint-Saëns. His faith in the power of the organ to set the mood of a service was shared by at least one member of the congregation, who asked him to play funeral music at her wedding because she wanted to cry during the ceremony "and as she had no natural instinct to do so, counted on the organ to bring tears to her eyes".[13]

Soon after Saint-Saëns started work at the Madeleine his household moved to an apartment on the top floor of 168 Rue du Faubourg St Honoré, nearer the church. The new home had more room than the apartment where he was born, and so was better able to accommodate the family's musical gatherings that had now become a weekly event. Every Monday evening Mme Saint-Saëns was hostess to an increasing number of guests attracted by her son's growing fame. The new address also had the advantage of having a courtyard open to the sky, allowing the young organist greater ease to indulge his passion for astronomy. These were the days before electricity, when the night sky could be observed clearly even from a great city like Paris, before the advent of the astronomer's curse of 'light pollution'. He bought a small telescope, made to his own requirements, for 500 francs which he earned from the Six Duos he had written for piano and a new type of harmonium (they were dedicated to Lefébure-Wély). One of his first delights through the lens of his new toy was a clear view of Donati's comet. Watching the stars remained a lifelong enthusiasm, for they seemed to make a strong appeal to his aesthetic sensibility, in a way a physical counterpart to the tonal colorations and luminosity he sought in music, ranging, as he put it, "through the most varied hues – yellows, reds, greens – looking like brilliantly illuminated strings of precious stones". Guests were expected to share these delights, being ushered into the telescope room to put their eye to the glass, and in later years Saint-Saëns was to become a fervent advocate of the popularisation of astronomy as a hobby, declaring the stars to be "breathtaking splendours which everyone should see".[14]

Everything at home was organised for his comfort and convenience by the two women, but he was far from being a home bird, preferring to strut and chatter among the convivial company of clubs and soirées. Short in stature, he was like a bird, in looks, movement and speech. His large, long nose, crossed by a pince-nez, was like a huge beak curving down between lively, penetrating eyes over a small mouth which was covered for a time by a downy moustache. He shaved off the moustache – "as a result my nose looks twice as long!"[15] – but it was soon replaced by the first growth of full beard. He walked with quick, purposeful steps, and talked just as rapidly, on all kinds of subjects, in a loud, high-pitched chirp which could be heard from across the street, and with a lisp that was to be a lifelong characteristic, too consistent to be affected. It was as if bodily movement and speech were trying to keep pace with a hyperactive mind: he dashed off letters also at high speed, some including an occasional doodle or decoration of whimsical nature, often in the form of a flower or insect, and many of his compositions were written down extraordinarily quickly. For Saint-Saëns time was always at a premium.

His high voice made him a popular performer as the female lead in operatic parodies, complete with costumes, which he arranged with friends to enliven his Monday soirées and the informal Sunday gatherings at the home of Pauline Viardot which, unlike her more formal Thursday evenings, were reserved for her closest acquaintances. From 1859, when Marie Miolan-Carvalho created the role of Marguerite in Gounod's *Faust*, a favourite party piece was a re-enactment of the Garden Scene with the bearded Saint-Saëns, in bonnet and false hair plaits, doing a hilarious impersonation of the diva, his falsetto mimicking her to the finest detail, including her habit of singing slightly sharp. At other times he would dance an impromptu ballet, suitably attired.

There was a ready audience for his wit also at the Trop Serrés, a dining club so called because members were so tightly packed round the table that they virtually sat in each other's laps. They were regularly entertained by Saint-Saëns's improvised verses and songs, by a wittily pompous march written specially for them and thundered out on the piano, and by Chico Marx-like pianistic contortions such as the eleven-note trick – eleven notes played at once or in quick succession using all the fingers of both hands and his enormous nose as the eleventh "finger".[16] His ceaseless chatter on matters artistic, scientific, political and philosophical made him many friends, who found him a lively, stimulating companion, but it must also have seemed at times exasperating and tiresome, and was not without the occasional withering reply and flash of sarcasm (more politely described as "caustic wit") that were likely to make as many enemies. He could be especially rude to women: a female guest at one of his Monday evenings who dared to suggest that he perhaps spent too much time and money on astronomical pursuits was told: "You spend as much on fancy clothes".[17]

Among his allies were composers whose works he honoured with his great powers of technique and performance. Berlioz, of course, was one – as well as the piano score of *Lélio*, Saint-Saëns also produced piano reductions of the Easter Hymn from *La Damnation de Faust* and, in collaboration with Mme Viardot, of *Les Troyens*. The Russian composer-pianist Anton Rubinstein became another close friend when, in 1858, he was astounded to hear Saint-Saëns play at sight on the piano the full score of his 'Ocean' Symphony. Rubinstein, at twenty-nine, was already one of the giants of Russian music, and the young French composer was quite in awe of this intense looking man with the long flowing hair when, the year before, he saw him play his C major concerto during his first visit to Paris. "From the first notes I was felled, harnessed to the chariot of the conqueror! More concerts followed and I did not miss one." He was offered an introduction, but "the idea of seeing him close up, of speaking one word to him, positively terrified me". During Rubinstein's second visit to Paris a year later, he plucked up the courage to meet him, and when he played the 'Ocean' Symphony on the piano "the ice was quickly broken between us".[18]

Saint-Saëns's first years at the Madeleine saw the composition of his first published concertos. The first piano concerto and the first two violin concertos were all written in the two years from 1857, showing that the restless versatility and lively industry of the composer were in no way curtailed by the demanding duties of the organist. Rather, the two worlds of organ and orchestra, as has been suggested, seemed to complement, stimulate and inspire each other.

The Piano Concerto in D of 1858 is France's first major work in this form, eclipsing the already largely forgotten four piano concertos of Rigel and the two esoteric and rarely heard chamber concertos of Alkan. It is the first French concerto to gain international standing, its three-movement form owing much to German models and its material showing the influences of Schumann, Mendelssohn and Liszt. The piano writing, which has a certain thickness of texture already encountered in the quintet, is also strongly Lisztian in its grand gestures and dazzling virtuosity. But there are also many distinctive features, like the slow introduction – unusual for a concerto – with its horn calls in echo effect that are transformed into the first subject proper, and the ghostly tremolando that ushers in the piano's cadenza-like entry, like the last shiver of night before the dawn – an effect that was to be used again more famously in the *Danse Macabre*. The cascading runs on the piano were to become a favourite device in future works, and the second theme, a curious leaping tune of rhythmic repetitiveness, is characteristic of its composer in the way it promises strong dramatic development but is instead steered back into home key cadences before it asks any soul-searching questions. This stylistic backing away from confrontations, and retreat into harmonic safe havens, was to recur in many later works, sometimes musically satisfying, sometimes not, as much a means of maintaining formal equilibrium as an indication of personal distaste for any hint of emotional turmoil.

The slow movement provides another instance of rhythmic repetition: there always seem to be too many repetitions of the triplet figure high on the piano in the cadenza-like passage. Nevertheless, we are ultimately rewarded with the final resolution as this figure floats with a gently beautiful pathos down the minor scale to its rest. The movement as a whole is a reflective dialogue between soloist and orchestra that gives an impression of improvised fantasy but is in fact in the regular form of ABC repeated. The finale, despite its obvious debt to Mendelssohn, is full of Saint-Saëns's own brand of youthful verve and humour. A briefly thoughtful subsidiary theme is at first interrupted by mocking laughter on the woodwind but is gradually transformed into a virile paean and the concerto ends with a triumphant restatement of its opening material. There is much to savour in this now largely forgotten work, inspired, said its composer, by the forest at Fontainebleau, where he enjoyed picnics with friends.[19] It certainly suggests, as well as the boisterousness of youth, the spirit of youthful company and contentment in surroundings of sylvan charm. Although in D, it seems to want to climb on to the sunnier plateau of E flat.

With the violin concerto Saint-Saëns was following in a much stronger French tradition, of which the works of Rodé and the Belgian-born Vieuxtemps are notable examples. After acquiring some knowledge of the technicalities of the instrument from the violinist George Bridgetower – a one-time acquaintance of Beethoven – he wrote the Concerto in C in 1858, published over twenty years later as No. 2. It is remarkable how this work has been so persistently ignored, not only by performers and concert managers but also by critics and historians. Its tunefulness and warm, good-natured humour give it an appeal that would serve as an attractive alternative to the familiar fare trotted out with unfailing regularity by violinists on the concert platform. Its interest to the music historian lies in its blend of classical and romantic elements and in the striking formal and stylistic contrast to the A major concerto which was to follow almost immediately. Its lyrical warmth places it firmly in the tradition of the Liège school, which set out to recreate on the violin the cantabile style of Italian opera. There are the usual three movements, the second leading into the finale without a break, but the violin's announcement of the opening material before it is heard on the orchestra is unusual, as is the disregard for sonata form in favour of a looser, freer structure. Yet, as in the classical concerto, there is a cadenza introduced in starkly conventional form by a second inversion on the orchestra. The first movement material includes a fine, noble melody for the soloist, and there is a notable chord sequence in the central portion in which traditional harmonies are used in imaginative juxtaposition.

Saint-Saëns's powers of orchestral colouring are most evident in the slow movement, such as in the solo oboe descant, but mostly in the announcement of the plaintive main theme on the violin accompanied by the harp, a combination that anticipates Rimsky-Korsakov's *Scheherazade* by thirty years. The rondo finale, with its jauntily amiable main subject, suffers from a lack of contrast, but the work as a whole is a pleasing apprentice effort. The facility and flexibility with which Saint-Saëns invests his later writing for the violin are already in evidence, but the development of these qualities in the second concerto, published as No. 1, is nonetheless astonishing because it follows so closely on the previous work.

The fifteen-year-old Spanish virtuoso Pablo Sarasate was the inspiration behind this development, and indeed the instigator of the concerto itself. This flamboyant youth, whom Saint-Saëns described as "fresh looking as the spring and already a celebrity, though a dawning moustache had only just begun to appear", called at the composer's home "to ask me, in the most casual way imaginable, to write a concerto for him".[20] The result was a violin concerto which, according to the writer Emile Baumann, Saint-Saëns preferred both to its predecessor and to the much more famous third concerto, and which gave him the greatest pleasure in writing.[21] It caused him some annoyance, therefore, when it came to be referred to as a 'concert piece' because of its short duration – little over ten minutes.[22] It represents a radical modification of classical forms on the lines of the Liszt piano concertos (both of which, incidentally, Liszt had been revising at this time), in its condensing of the traditional three movements into a single, cyclical whole. Schumann's D minor Symphony may also have been in his mind (he could play all four symphonies in piano reduction from memory).

But a more likely model is the single-movement fifth Violin Concerto of Vieuxtemps, which appeared in 1858, the very year when Saint-Saëns received his commission from Sarasate. The form is that of a sonata movement in which a central slow section with new material replaces the development. Oddly, the principal subjects of the opening allegro are recapitulated, after the lyrical andante, in reverse order, creating a kaleidoscopic effect.

While the formal contrast with the earlier concerto is striking, the greater integration of form is matched by a greater integration between soloist and orchestra. In the C major concerto the two remain largely distinct from and independent of each other, with passages dominated by the violinist alternating with ritornello-style orchestral sections. In the A major concerto there is much more of a partnership, the soloist blending with the orchestra in a more unified sound. Saint-Saëns again demonstrates his grasp of the lyrical and virtuosic possibilities of the instrument, but is here more in tune with Sarasate's personal style, of tonal purity and transparency, with a lightness that marks a break from the rich sonority of the Liège school.

The A major concerto marked the start of a friendship between composer and violinist that was to last up to Sarasate's death in 1908. Saint-Saëns acknowledged much valuable advice from him about writing for the instrument, and the friendship led directly to the composition of the Introduction and Rondo Capriccioso and the later concerto in B minor. It also stimulated in the composer a love of Spain and Spanish musical idioms which was to produce many other works of a Spanish flavour, both vocal and instrumental. The two men, although nearly ten years apart in age, had much in common. Sarasate was as hopeless in dealing with the practicalities of everyday life as Saint-Saëns (with his mother and great-aunt running the household) was careless of them. Both were lively conversationalists as Saint-Saëns was later to describe:

Those who attended my Monday musical soirées have not forgotten the brilliant effect produced by my distinguished friend. This was so much the case that for several years after no violinists could be persuaded to perform at my home, so terrified were they of the idea of inviting comparison. Nor did he shine by his talent alone, but also by his brilliant intellect and the inexhaustible animation of his conversation, which was always interesting and suggestive.[23]

In between the two violin concertos the church musician reasserted himself in the *Oratorio de Noël*, written in just twelve days and completed just over a week before Christmas Day 1858, when it was sung at the Madeleine. It harks back to the eighteenth century, both to the baroque and rococo periods, but builds bridges to its own time in many ways, such as the use of the harp with small orchestra and organ, and in the shifting, chromatic harmonies in the 'Quare Fremuerunt' and the beautiful Trio. The two arias are in a freer form than that of the eighteenth-century version, and the Pastoral prelude, while clearly an idea borrowed from *Messiah* or Bach's *Christmas Oratorio*, in turn undoubtedly influenced Liszt in his prelude to *Christus*. There is a special delicacy about the orchestration, and another distinctive feature is the reappearance of the opening material towards the end – in this case the Pastoral becomes the basis of the Quintet and Alleluia chorus – to give a sense of cohesion. There is also an example of the composer's reluctance to develop the emotional possibilities of a theme: the opening phrase of the Gloria throws out a challenge only to be tamely answered by a half-close in the home key. This inhibition, though, here seems in keeping with the overall mood, one of simple piety, in line with the period's aims in church music, and innocent joy lit by the decorative serenity of a nineteenth-century stained glass window.

Another important work of this extraordinarily productive period is the Symphony No. 2 in A minor, in which Saint-Saëns takes another step along the road to symphonic mastery, developing his material with ingenuity and flair, and again using elements of formal compression and thematic recollection to mould the four movements into a concise unity. In the opening allegro, which is unusual in having a fugue as a first subject (a feature that "scandalised many listeners", Saint-Saëns recalled),[24] the development and recapitulation are much condensed, and the adagio is more like a short interlude than a complete movement, a brief glimpse of an imagined past, of great-aunt Charlotte as a little girl among the perfumed elegance of an eighteenth-century drawing room, intuitively perceived across two generations. An important theme of the scherzo is recalled and developed amid the whirling triplets of the tarantella-like rondo finale, followed by hints of the first movement's fugue and a brief reminder of the wistful mood of the adagio, before the symphony is brought to a dizzy end in a spirited coda.

The symphony was first performed on 20th February 1859, not in Paris but in Leipzig, a city that was also to hear the first performance of the piano concerto. Paris first heard it on 25th March 1860, conducted by Jules Pasdeloup, but it was not published until eighteen years later. After composing it, Saint-Saëns seems to have lost faith in the symphony as a form: the D major work of 1859 remained unpublished, and he did not return to the symphony as such until a quarter of a century later, after his international reputation had been established, in the meantime developing his symphonic style instead in the concertos and the chamber works.

The stony ground on which the early symphonies had fallen was indicative of a lack of interest in French orchestral music in the France of the Second Empire. It was the age of Offenbach operettas and Labiche farces, the diversion and delight of the aristocracy and newly rich industrialists and financiers who were investing in the empire's economic and commercial expansion, with its railway building, its industrial exhibitions and Haussmann's grand designs for Paris as an elegant imperial capital. Saint-Saëns could enjoy the froth of Offenbach and the humour of Labiche as much as the next man, but he also lamented the limited scope for serious young composers. He illustrated the attitude of the time by quoting a newspaper article of 1864, which asserted that would-be composers should positively be discouraged and made instead to listen to "accredited talent". "What use", it asked, "is it to encourage them and their efforts when the public obstinately refuses to pay any attention to them?"[25] It is true that beneath the veneer of frivolity and ostentation that overlay 'La vie Parisienne' flowed an undercurrent of interest in serious music, but its devotees were popularly regarded as poseurs listening to music they did not understand. The artist was alienated in such a world, and if the Second Empire was an age of the socially pretentious it was also an age of the Bohemian.

Serious music was certainly being played: the demise of many musical societies in the political uncertainty of the late 1840s was followed in the more stable and confident 1850s by new groups, such as Pasdeloup's Society of Young Conservatoire Artists, which took over from the disbanded Society of St Cecilia in presenting contemporary works. Blanchard wrote of a thriving concert season and a growing interest in chamber music.[26] But, as in the last years of Louis-Philippe's reign, there was still official suspicion of groups outside government control, and it was not easy to form organisations giving opportunities for new music without authorisation. Most of the music that was performed was still Austro-German, and there is evidence that the impetus towards new music inspired by the empire's promised security was a spent force by the end of the decade, when complaints could be heard about a lack of variety and new works in programmes.[27] Pasdeloup helped to promote Schumann and, even more controversially, Wagner, but came to the conclusion that the public simply did not like new music. Beethoven was still the most frequently played, while French composers remained on the sidelines. "The name of a composer at once French and living on a programme had the effect of putting everyone to flight,"[28] Saint-Saëns ruefully recalled of a time when Pasdeloup would tell his compatriots: "Write masterpieces like Beethoven's and I'll play them." Anything else was likely to provoke a witheringly dismissive remark, as when Saint-Saëns began to play him his *Oratorio de Noël*: "after eight bars he stood up, crying contemptuously 'but this is Bach!' and refused to hear any more".[29]

It may of course be that Saint-Saëns was exaggerating the frustrations of the period in order to enhance the role he was later to play in overcoming them, and to be fair to Pasdeloup, he did include the occasional French work in his concerts, like Saint-Saëns's *Urbs Roma* and A minor symphonies and the two symphonies of Gounod. But it is certain that native composers were losing what little ground they had once gained in the Parisian concert halls. Berlioz, increasingly infirm and embittered, was fading from the scene, and of Saint-Saëns's orchestral works only the A major Violin Concerto is known to have received more than five performances before 1870.[30] It was no use looking to the Conservatoire Concerts Society, where conservatism reigned supreme. Even Beethoven could be too much for its director, Narcisse Girard, who, after looking over Saint-Saëns's E flat Symphony, told him that symphonies should not include trombones. The composer humbly begged to remind him that Beethoven used trombones in his fifth and sixth symphonies. "Yes," Girard replied, "but it would perhaps have been better if he had not."[31] The Paris Opéra, undergoing a grand rebuilding in one of the most splendid and ambitious of Napoleon III's plans for the capital, was also becoming more rigidly conservative than ever, as Berlioz and Bizet were discovering. There were few new works at the Opéra-Comique either, and only the Théâtre Lyrique under Léon Carvalho offered any real outlet for composers: Gounod, Berlioz and Bizet all enjoyed premières there. One area of promise was chamber music, where Adolphe Blanc was achieving some success, but on the whole it was a limited outlook for French composers. Berlioz was characteristically pessimistic, declaring in 1855 that "apart from Saint-Saëns, a fine musician nineteen years old, and Gounod . . . I can see nothing but ephemeral insects hovering over this stinking morass we call Paris".[32]

It was not in Saint-Saëns's nature to be discouraged by these circumstances, whatever the views of the newspaper columnist. He could have lived well enough as an organist and pianist, but he had to write music: it was in his bones. As he said later, he produced music "as naturally as an apple tree produces apples", regardless of obstacles or criticism.[33] Composition sprang from the impulse to improvise, present in him from infancy. His post at the Madeleine required him to supply pieces for services almost every day, usually short canticles in French or Latin; but he could not help composing music of all kinds, in the same way that he could not help talking. Indeed, the two often went on at the same time, for he had Mozart's ability to carry on a conversation while scoring a new work. It was an irresistible force that was to break the mould of French music.

For some of his critics, this facility proves his work to be facile, an equation no one would dream of applying to Mozart. Even more perversely, it has been argued that, because he grew up in an age noted for its shallow frivolity and questionable taste, his music is therefore shallow and tasteless. Certainly there is an element of the boulevardier, of the *bon viveur*, in Saint-Saëns's work and personality: but there is also the serious musician at odds with the times he lived in, whose outlook was shaped to a large degree by the seriousness and solemnity of the organ loft. From here, he looked down, metaphorically as well as physically, on the ostentatious vulgarity of an industrial upper class that liked to display the trappings of its new-found wealth in church as well as in the opera house. According to the Baedeker guide of 1907, midday mass was popular with fashionable 'society' and "the departure from these services at the principal churches is one of the sights of Paris, at the Madeleine in particular";[34] and there is no reason to suppose that it was very much different fifty years before. Saint-Saëns, with his strong views on the appropriateness of church music to religious devotion, was often at odds with a clergy anxious to keep its congregation happy with music more akin to that which they were used to hearing in the theatre. The movement for the reform of church music was still a missionary movement that had yet to convert the vast majority of churchmen, many of whom had little or no musical education let alone discernment: it was not until early in the next century that a minimum standard of musical knowledge was laid down for Catholic clergy. Saint-Saëns's old teacher Boëly had fallen foul of his employers at St. Germain l'Auxerrois because of what they regarded as his austerity and obscurity, and he was forced to resign in 1851. Saint-Saëns soon acquired the same reputation. "The public was led to believe that I played nothing but fugues", he recalled, so that "one young woman about to be married begged me to play no fugues at her wedding." But he stood his ground, telling the priests he would play music appropriate to the opéra-comique only when he heard the language of the opéra-comique preached from the pulpit, and not before. Anything 'serious' was liable to be met with incomprehension: once, when he played Liszt's 'St Francis Preaching to the Birds' at a wedding, a puzzled priest asked why he should be tuning the organ during the service.[35]

The young composer's social life took a new turn when the Viardots introduced him to Rossini, then a replete sixty-five-year-old living in splendid retirement at his home on the corner of the Chaussée d'Antin. He recalled:

All Paris sought the honour of being admitted to his magnificent, high-windowed apartment. As the demi-god never went out in the evening, his friends were always sure of finding him at home. At one time or another all sorts of social sets rubbed elbows at his great soirées. The most brilliant singers and the most famous virtuosi appeared there. The master was surrounded by sycophants, but they did not influence him . . .

The newcomer was received with Rossini's "usual, rather meaningless cordiality", but after a month the great man invited him to visit during the morning. Then he found Rossini far more relaxed, "intensely interested in and open-minded to ideas". One evening the Tarantella for flute and clarinet which Saint-Saëns had composed in 1857 was played before the assembled guests, who were allowed to believe it was the work of their illustrious host. When it was over Rossini received the customary extravagant praises, and only then pointed his mortified admirers towards the real author, holding him firmly by the hand so he could not escape. Saint-Saëns became a regular pianist at the Saturday evenings, deputising for Rossini (who, he said, played the piano "to perfection"), and thus met and accompanied some of the most famous singers of the day.[36] He no doubt relished too the lighter side of the proceedings, the skits and music hall items that were an extension of the Rossini wit. Meyerbeer and Auber were frequent guests, as were Gounod and Liszt.

Saint-Saëns made another notable acquaintance in 1859. Wagner, who had come to Paris to promote his operas there, wrote to him in October asking him to call at the villa he was renting in the Rue d'Aumale. Wagner had heard about his exceptional musical gifts from the conductor Hans von Bülow, who had attended Saint-Saëns's Monday soirées. At a time when Schumann's symphonies were hardly known in France, von Bülow had been

most astonished to hear him reproduce them on the piano with such a degree of ease and accuracy that I was dumbfounded . . . In talking to him I found that nothing was unknown to him, and what made him appear still greater to me was the sincerity of his enthusiasm and his complete modesty.[37]

Wagner wanted to confirm all this for himself, and was not disappointed: his guest sat at the piano and played at sight from the recently completed full score of *Tristan und Isolde.* On a subsequent visit, Wagner showed Saint-Saëns the bacchanalia he had just written for the planned Paris production of *Tannhäuser* (the ink was still wet, the visitor recalled)[38] and in his memoirs wrote that

with an unparalleled sureness and rapidity of glance with regard even to the most complicated orchestral score, this young man combined a not less remarkable memory. He was not only able to play my scores, including Tristan, *by heart but could also reproduce their several parts, leading or minor themes, and with such precision that one might easily have thought that he had the music before his eyes.*

On a later occasion, von Bülow and Wagner were talking together when Saint-Saëns, bored because he could not yet follow German, picked up the still uncompleted manuscript of *Siegfried* in full score and played it through on the piano, reproducing the essence of the work at sight. "No man living could have performed that feat after Saint-Saëns," von Bülow declared. "He is the greatest musical mind of our time."[39] Wagner called him "that excellent musician" and was delighted to hear him accompany the Princess Camporeale of Naples in the final scene of *Tristan.*[40]

Saint-Saëns remained – for a time – an enthusiastic admirer and champion of Wagner's music, no easy matter in an atmosphere of mounting hostility that culminated in the riotous performances of *Tannhäuser* at the Opéra in 1861. It was an enthusiasm that was to fuel his own ambitions towards opera. But the downward spiral from the heights of mutual admiration was not long in coming, as the two men came to represent rival nationalisms, and the deterioration in their personal relations was to be in remarkable parallel with that in the political relations between France and Germany that was to have such disastrous consequences for the whole of Europe.

IV • TEACHER

SAINT-SAËNS MADE A DETERMINED EFFORT TO COUNTER PUBLIC INDIFFE-rence to his works by organising a concert, to include the piano quintet, the piano concerto and the C major violin concerto, at the Salle Erard on 10th April 1860. It may have helped make his name better known as a composer, but it did little to persuade musical societies that his works were worth playing. Adolphe Botte, reviewer for the *Gazette Musicale*, wrote of him that,

young as he is, he has composed for a long time, but having quickly won over the estimation of artists, he has hardly made headway in the opinion of the public. Everyone will tell you, having read or heard something about it, that M. Saint-Saëns is a serious, learned artist, but no one will play you his works.

Botte also made the criticism that was to be repeated over the years, that both his playing and his music lacked the emotional depth to engage his listeners.

If his music is always interesting, if it captures the spirit, it is rarely beautiful and emotional . . . If M. Saint-Saëns could combine with the qualities that shine in his style something of his secret thoughts, of his passion, of his nature, we will assuredly see, in place of the composer of merit, a great composer.[1]

This verdict from the age of high romanticism has been surprisingly little altered by the age of modernity.

As well as trying to promote his music, and perhaps because it was making so little headway, Saint-Saëns stepped up his search for a suitable opera libretto, with about as much success. The only tangible result in this direction was the setting of a scene from Corneille's tragedy *Horace*, for soprano and baritone, written during December 1860 but not performed until over five years later. Three songs also date from this time – 'Alla riva del Tebro', to Italian words, 'Extase', a setting of Hugo, and 'Etoile du matin' – all of which show the twin influences of classical drama and romantic poetry. It was a blend in Saint-Saëns of the old and the new that was about to take on a wider perspective.

A bad bout of eye strain during the winter of 1860–61, an early sign of short-sightedness, made composition difficult, so the offer of a teaching post in March was all the more acceptable. It came from the Ecole Niedermeyer in Paris (really a reorganisation of an older school), founded in 1853 by the Swiss composer and teacher Louis Niedermeyer. The school had gained a reputation as a forward-looking institution after fixing its sights firmly on the remote past, as part of the movement for the reform of church music. Its declared aim was to train musicians for the Church by providing a thorough grounding in plainchant, polyphony and church music generally up to the early eighteenth century. This was a pioneering mission that appealed to musicians who were critical of the opera bias of the Conservatoire, who heard Delsarte expound the virtues of early music, who espoused the cause of 'serious' music in general and who wanted French music in particular to break the fetters of the Italian choral and operatic tradition. It therefore attracted teachers with progressive attitudes to music and music education, so that Niedermeyer's strictly antiquarian creed, which regarded anything written much after 1750 as unfit for the ears of his students, provided a foundation on which his staff began to build a much more broadly based curriculum. Here the harmonic theories of Saint-Saëns's teacher Maleden, rejected by the Conservatoire, were enthusiastically taken up. The academic atmosphere was well suited to the wide-ranging outlook and interests of Maleden's former pupil, who saw Niedermeyer's passion for old forms as a force for change, because the further back in time a composer delved, the more radical was his approach to the music of his own time. He wrote of the founder that he set out to apply the ancient modes to modern harmonic norms, "a fruitful if daring idea, preserving the character of plainchant while opening new vistas to harmony".[2] It was an approach that was to influence Saint-Saëns later in his own attempts to blend the modal characteristics of oriental music with conventional western harmony.

Niedermeyer died on 14th March 1861, and it was his son and successor, Alfred, who asked the twenty-five-year-old Saint-Saëns to teach piano at the school. He was not entirely new to teaching, for he had already a number of private pupils, for both piano and composition, but, as Pauline Viardot noted, he was "very fussy" about whom he taught.[3] He accepted pupils only of exceptional promise (and, usually, wealth). These included Marie de Reiset, the Viscountess Grandval, to whom he dedicated his *Oratorio de Noël* and several of his songs. Already a talented singer, she became under his guidance a versatile and prolific amateur composer whose operas enjoyed some success in their time. She had also known Chopin, and so, like Mme Viardot, was able to give Saint-Saëns valuable accounts of his playing style and technique. Although he was to continue to teach privately at different times for much of his life, other work allowing, the Niedermeyer professorship was the only public teaching post Saint-Saëns ever held and was relatively short-lived, lasting just four years. This was not because he was a bad teacher, or even because he disliked teaching. It was rather because a salaried position obliged him to devote valuable time and energy to pupils of varying ability, when he was interested only in the very gifted ones. Besides, he already had salaried obligations at the Madeleine, and the two positions proved too much of a tie as concert activity increased and the impulse towards composition was renewed.

Nevertheless, he seems to have been a popular teacher at the Niedermeyer.

He was still a young man, not much more than ten years older than most of his pupils and as such was someone to whom they could relate. His youthful zest and lively intellect were welcome antidotes to the school's gloomy surroundings and austere regime, under which reveille was at 5.30 a.m. and the only physical recreation was a long walk on Thursday afternoons. He taught the basic piano repertory of Haydn, Mozart and Beethoven with the same strictures against distortion and exaggeration he had been given as a child: "Above all, no emotion" was his chief advice. But he also introduced extra-curricular pieces by Chopin, Schumann, Wagner and Liszt, daringly contemporary works which gave his pupils a sense of adventure and discovery and which they would never have heard at the Conservatoire. One of his pupils recalled:

Apart from the technical matters on which he was very strict – purity of execution, care for sonority, quality of sound, pianistic colour, phrasing, accentuation, and the style appropriate to the composer – he liked to open our minds to all that was worthy of interest, even outside music, and stimulated our imagination by leading us on to the other arts and arousing our curiosity about everything.[4]

He amused them too, with his impersonations of opera singers (usually female) and by writing short farces in which they could act and write incidental music. This was a side of his teaching activity that was also to be the unexpected source of his first complete stage work, a comic opera (unpublished) called *Le Château de Roche Cardon ou Les Cruautés du Sort.* Another project he considered for his class was a series of musical portraits of animals – but the idea was shelved for lack of time.

Many of his pupils, as well as hearing him play the piano during lessons, would go to the Madeleine outside school hours to hear him on the organ, and in those who showed exceptional promise he took a strong personal interest that was to continue into their adult lives. Eugène Gigout, who became a professor at the school and later professor of organ at the Conservatoire, remained a lifelong friend, and Albert Périlhou, after he became organist at St Séverin, would often surrender the keyboards to his old teacher when he paid a visit. The early death in London of Edouard Marlois at the height of his powers as pianist, organist and conductor was the cause of much grief, while the success of André Messager's light operas in later years was a source of much satisfaction. Messager was not in Saint-Saëns's class at the Niedermeyer but received extra coaching in piano and fugue from him after leaving the school, so struck was the teacher by the boy's musical intelligence. Saint-Saëns took great pride in Messager's subsequent career as organist and composer and, as with most of his ex-pupils, helped to advance it when he could. In particular, he applauded Messager's skilful, sensitive handling of the French language in his stage works, "not the least of the attractions of his delightful *Véronique*", he observed,[5] seeing it as doing much to correct a widespread abuse of prosody which he blamed to a large degree on the influence of Meyerbeer.

Out of all the personal ties born from his years of teaching, the strongest was that with Gabriel Fauré, the school inspector's son from southern France who was so musically gifted that Louis Niedermeyer had accepted him as a pupil without payment at the age of nine. The paternal friendship between teacher and pupil that was to last a lifetime probably began in the spring of 1862, when the former was twenty-six and the latter approaching seventeen. In the summer of that year Saint-Saëns, with his mother and great-aunt, visited Fauré at Tarbes, near the Pyrenees. He made such a considerable impression that Fauré's parents came to look on him almost as one of the family, constantly urging him through their son to visit them again, and frequently sending him parcels of food – perhaps because they had heard how bad the food was at the Ecole Niedermeyer. (Fauré was equally well treated gastronomically during his Sunday visits to the Saint-Saëns household, which, he recalled, made a welcome change to school meals.) During his stay in Tarbes, Saint-Saëns was taken on long walks to local beauty spots, and got on so well with friends of the Faurés that months later, his pupil assured him, they were still "dazzled" – though he seems to have alienated one young woman, perhaps with one of his caustic remarks. Fauré wrote: "People talk to me about you to such an extent that it might become boring if ever it were within my power to tire of hearing your praises sung" but there was an "ill-wind towards you" from a certain Mlle Henriette. Writing back, Saint-Saëns sent his regards to various friends and, with an exclamation mark, to "the beautiful Henriette". He thanked his pupil for his hospitality by dedicating to him his piano transcription of Bach's Cantata no. 28, a "little nastiness" as he called it, of which Fauré was very fond.

These earliest letters between teacher and pupil are already full of the familiarities and jocularities that might be expected only in a longer established friendship, so that it was hardly necessary to "break the ice", as Saint-Saëns implored Fauré to do in September 1862.[6] But amid the playfulness and bonhomie is a strong paternal tone on the teacher's part, in frequent pieces of advice and even reprimand. Perhaps because he had as yet no family of his own and seems to have had no experience of or interest in women (indeed, he was somewhat contemptuous of them) his pupils became the object of a developing fatherly instinct, particularly in Fauré's case. The paternal aspect of the friendship was to become even more marked over the years, well after Fauré had become established as a respected composer and teacher in his own right. In the meantime, Saint-Saëns used his growing influence and contacts in high places to help further the career of Fauré, who in turn looked to his friend and mentor for guidance and practical help.

In later life Fauré acknowledged the debt he and others owed to their teacher, for introducing them to the beauties and subtleties of what was then the new music at a school where Chopin and Schumann were "not considered suitable for young people",[7] and for the guidance he gave them on their own compositions, which, although he was officially professor of piano, he examined "with a curiosity and care which only masterpieces would have deserved".[8] Saint-Saëns introduced him to Victor Hugo's poetry, and Fauré recalled with pride that his first song, 'Le Papillon et la Fleur', a setting of Hugo written "in the school refectory among the smells from the kitchen", was first played by his illustrious teacher, who put his own imprint on the manuscript in the form of a cartoon of the butterfly making a rude gesture to the flower.[9]

The pianist Marguérite Long, who knew Fauré in his later years, was told that "discipline was strict, comfort unknown" at the school, but that both teacher and pupil had fond memories of the place. Fauré believed that discipline encouraged "deep thought", but as it was school practice to teach in what would nowadays be called an open plan arrangement, so that as many as fifteen instruments were being played at once in the same room, it also produced in him a habit of withdrawing into himself.[10] This may be useful at times for a composer, but Saint-Saëns was constantly having to nag his pupil out of it, warning him that his persistent lethargy and singular lack of ambition were his greatest enemies. Fauré was especially grateful for this "sustained encouragement, which prevented me from going to sleep completely".[11] Saint-Saëns "rescued me from stagnation", he wrote in 1922. "He kept me working and saw to it that I sent him my earliest efforts as and when I wrote them."[12] In fact, Fauré continued to send him his new works for advice and comment well into his adult life. He valued this advice because Saint-Saëns's teaching, Marguérite Long was given to understand, "was generous and without prejudice", an attitude Fauré saw as being in welcome contrast to what he believed he would have encountered at the Conservatoire.[13]

On his frequent visits to Saint-Saëns's home in the Rue du Faubourg St Honoré, as much for some welcome home cooking as for musical guidance, like most guests Fauré was naturally regaled with the wonders of astronomy and invited to inspect the stars through the treasured telescope. An idea of the sort of evening that lay in store can be judged from an invitation Saint-Saëns sent to the directors of the Ecole Niedermeyer, couched in typically whimsical language. There will, he says, be a "modest repast" at which

ceremonies will be replaced by lively, animated dialogue. The nourishment will be healthy, if not abundant, and dessert will consist of an eclipse of the moon, and novas. A magnificent achromatic telescope will be at the disposal of the directors for observing the phenomena.[14]

Saint-Saëns visited London for the first time in the late summer of 1862.[15]

The purpose of his visit is not known and he seems to have forgotten about it in his old age, telling a friend that he first went to London as a refugee from the Paris Commune of 1871. If it was for an engagement in an increasingly busy schedule as a concert pianist, it would predate the concert usually cited as his London debut by nine years. He was certainly giving frequent concerts in the German states as well as in his own country, which, in conjunction with his duties at the Madeleine and at the Niedermeyer, makes his work-rate little short of phenomenal, especially for a man of delicate health. This perhaps helps to explain the relative dearth of new works in the two years to 1863, but he was always an efficient user of time, and thereafter composition too began to crowd in on his day. The only work of any significance from the earlier period is the suite for cello and piano, which marks Saint-Saëns's first appearance as a composer of real individuality, with a voice and personality of his own. It is also one of the earliest examples of the revival of the classical suite which was to be taken up by later romantics such as Tchaikovsky and Grieg, and developed further by twentieth-century neo-classicists. The 1862 suite puts new wine in old bottles: although forming a series of dance-like pieces, as in the baroque suite, the five movements do not correspond to baroque types. Romance and serenade are titles in vogue in the eighteenth century but not usually associated with suites, while scherzo is a name that belong to the nineteenth century. As for the content, there is a more rounded, more satisfying shape to the themes and a greater assurance in the handling of the material generally than in the sometimes rougher-edged works of the productive period of the late 1850s, suggesting that the fallow years between 1861 and 1863 were a time of gestation. The suite has many of the hallmarks of his mature style, beginning with the staccato effects that accompany the cello's chattering perpetual motion in the prelude, and continuing with a harmonic inventiveness throughout. The perfumed atmosphere of the languid serenade surrounds a meandering theme that here and there takes on a delicate sweetness of the kind that was to flavour many of Saint-Saëns's more extended melodies. Another such melody begins the romance, the most memorable piece in the suite, a theme of haunting beauty that is at once comforting and uncanny. It gives way to a more impassioned middle section, then takes flight on a series of chromatic key shifts before returning to the calm of the opening. The finale, a sturdy fugue, shows Saint-Saëns revelling in his contrapuntal powers, and closes in his favoured cyclical style by recalling the swirling continuum and staccato accompaniment of the prelude. Nearly sixty years later, in one of the last acts of his life, the composer orchestrated the piano part,[16] substituting a gavotte for the scherzo – a belated concession to the eighteenth century – and a tarantella for the original finale.

The suite for orchestra, written soon after the cello work, gives a firmer nod to eighteenth-century forebears by including both a gavotte and a sarabande.

The overall character of the five movements is one of rustic charm, rather like a French pastoral scene of the old school, painted in fresh, clear tones, in which romantically inclined melody and harmony are tempered by classical precision and sobriety. The bucolic mood is set by the prelude, built on a series of answering phrases, and continued in the dreamy sarabande. The gavotte strikes a more vigorous note, and has a remarkable central passage for woodwind over a dominant pedal note. After a fourth movement elegy of great warmth and feeling, the energetic finale shows that the Schubertian influence was still an active force at this time.

The orchestral suite was written in 1863, a year which saw Saint-Saëns returning to composition with renewed energy. During this year he also composed the *Spartacus* overture, the first piano trio and the Introduction and Rondo Capriccioso. The overture, inspired by a tragedy of Alphonse Pagès, is another example like the *Scène d'Horace* of a continuing interest in classical subjects. Like the *Urbs Roma* symphony, it was entered for a competition of the St Cecilia Society of Bordeaux: it won first prize and a performance in the city on 26th November 1863. It may have been intended as the start of a complete opera, for the subject – the hero crushed by circumstance – strongly appealed to Saint-Saëns, as was to become apparent in many later works. It can also be seen as a forerunner of the symphonic poems to come. But he was not satisfied with it, and it remained unpublished.

He worked on both the piano trio and the Introduction and Rondo Capriccioso for violin and orchestra while on holiday in the Pyrenees during the summer. The trio in F again shows, like the two suites, a stylistic advance on the works of the previous decade. He has thrown off some of the heaviness and textural thickness of the quintet to appear in lighter garb, with a fluency of language that speaks of youthful optimism and spontaneity, as if he is delighting in the gifts, material and artistic, that nature and life had bestowed on him. Sometimes he is a little too carefree, for the work has its weaknesses, chiefly a lack of variety in the two outer movements. The allegro vivace is dominated by the syncopated rhythm of the opening theme, which, pleasant though it is, is stretched beyond its means over the whole sonata structure, its syncopation wearing thin under repetition. And while the last movement, with its touches of whimsical humour, does have a contrasted second subject, it is in the home key in both exposition and recapitulation, finding its way to a related key only halfway through. The two middle movements are perhaps the most successful. If the spirit of Mendelssohn hovers over the quintet, the trio owes something of its character to Schumann, and this is most evident in these two movements, in the double-dotted figurations of the andante – which give way to a beautifully expressive middle section of flowing lyricism – and in the breezy scherzo built on two main ideas, whose rhythms are marked respectively by Schumannesque tautness and buoyancy. The trio was first heard at one of Saint-Saëns's Monday soirées, played by the composer, Sarasate and the cellist Jules Delsart, a mutual friend. It was published later in the decade.

The Introduction and Rondo Capriccioso is dedicated to Sarasate, a tribute not only to his powers as a performer but also to his volatile character and the lively seriousness of his homeland. The contemplative theme of the short introduction is characterised by a downward leap that anticipates the falling movement of the rondo's main subject. The brilliance and clarity of the solo writing, which confirms the break from the thick sonorities of the Liège school begun in the A major violin concerto, has made the work a favourite among violinists, but it is not a mere virtuoso showpiece. The rondo form is used to create a kaleidoscope of moods, from exuberance to tender passion, and the work's appeal lies in the way these elements can be enjoyed both in themselves and in the way they are placed and controlled within the overall framework. The rhythmic insistence sometimes becomes positively fiendish, a quality heightened in the orchestra by Saint-Saëns's favourite staccato rattles. The combination of this with a haunting lyrical sweetness, a heady mixture that was to reach new heights in the *Danse Macabre*, is at times quite exhilarating. Yet nothing is overstated: with all these ingredients, Saint-Saëns never loses his sense of proportion. It is as if the work breathes through the turbulence and tenderness of the South the clear, sober mountain air in which it originated.

There is a degree of maturity and mastery about the Introduction and Rondo Capriccioso that indicates Saint-Saëns's growing confidence in his powers as a composer, but while these were coming to be recognised in Germany, they were still largely unrecognised by Parisian audiences. Another concert of his works which he organised at the Salle Pleyel in March 1863 again had little success. Botte, who had before complained about lack of emotion in the music, was this time annoyed by "surprises and coquetries" in the harmonies, another aspect that was to alienate the composer from established opinion.[17] The obstacles to recognition, in the form of hostility or sheer indifference, were still formidable.

Music was certainly reaching a wider audience, thanks largely to Pasdeloup's Concerts Populaires at the Cirque Napoléon (later renamed the Cirque d'hiver), which took over from the Society of Young Conservatoire Artists in 1861, but even here, although the avowed aim was to introduce new works, programmes remained largely traditional and Beethoven still topped the bill. "Failure then, for us young Frenchmen, was synonymous with death," Saint-Saëns said of the period. "Even success did not ensure a second hearing."[18] When new French works were played the performance was usually half-hearted and unsatisfactory. When Bizet's Scherzo was introduced at a Concert Populaire in January 1863, Saint-Saëns reported that it was "badly performed and badly listened to, falling on inattention and general indifference". Many of the audience are said to have threatened to cancel their subscriptions.[19]

Saint-Saëns came to regard Bizet as a "brother in arms"[20] in this state of affairs. Their friendship was cemented a week after the fiasco of the Scherzo when they shared the platform at a concert of the National Society of Fine Arts (Société Nationale des Beaux Arts), another group aiming to encourage young composers which, probably for that very reason, did not long survive. Bizet conducted his Scherzo and Saint-Saëns conducted two movements of his A minor symphony. The Scherzo seems to have been preferred, the *Revue et Gazette Musicale* critic declaring that Bizet's music was "not at all distorted and far-fetched as is that of M. Saint-Saëns". The latter's conducting was not well received either: it "could hardly have been more hesitant, duller or more uneven".[21] He later conducted his suite for orchestra in a concert series organised by Henry Litolff at the Opéra, and his conducting was to improve with experience over the years.

Both Saint-Saëns and Bizet had the strength of character to shrug off criticism, which, as well as strengthening the bond between them, seemed to make them more determined than ever to succeed. They greatly admired each other's works: Bizet made a piano arrangement of the Introduction and Rondo Capriccioso, which at least allowed it to be heard in drawing rooms, and Saint-Saëns was one of the few to praise *Les Pêcheurs de Perles* when it failed on its première in September 1863. The opera proved to be of practical value too when he travelled to Le Vesinet to visit Bizet at his cottage. According to Bizet's friend and biographer Edouard Galabert, Saint-Saëns arrived in the village uncertain of the address so he stood in the main street and sang the aria 'Je crois entendre' at the top of his voice. Sure enough, Bizet heard it, went to investigate, and the visitor had found his man.[22]

The friendship with Bizet was of long-term significance for Saint-Saëns in that it helped to stimulate his own aspirations towards opera. His interest in vocal music, constantly exercised by duties at the Madeleine, had never flagged. As well as the *Scène d'Horace*, the early 1860s saw a continuing output of solo songs, including more settings of Hugo. In the meantime he had seen his other friend Gounod firmly established as an opera composer after *Faust*. In 1864 he helped launch Gounod's latest opera *Mireille* by playing the harmonium in a run-through of the score in the composer's drawing room, with Gounod singing and Bizet on piano.[23] Saint-Saëns was to give, again with Bizet, private performances of Gounod's incidental music to Legouvé's play *Les Deux Reines*, which was banned for political reasons and not seen on the public stage until after the fall of the Empire. More theatre work came from Berlioz, who had been asked to direct Gluck's *Armide* at the Opéra and turned naturally to Saint-Saëns for help because of his shared enthusiasm for and knowledge of Gluck's scores. This was not their first collaboration in the Gluck revival: they had both worked with

Pauline Viardot on her preparation of *Orphée* (in which she was to sing the title role) for production at the Théâtre Lyrique in 1859. In this pioneering project Viardot and Berlioz sought to be as faithful as possible to Gluck's intentions, scorning the hybrid versions that had been mounted in Germany (some of which had horrified Saint-Saëns when he saw them). There were considerable difficulties to overcome on two fronts: first, the opera was Gluck's own reworking for the French stage of his earlier Italian opera *Orfeo ed Euridice*, with additions, omissions, rescoring and the conversion of the principal role from castrato contralto to high tenor; second, the Lyric's Mauritian-born director Léon Carvalho, husband of the singer, demanded 'improvements' to meet contemporary tastes in drama and spectacle. Viardot and Berlioz resisted these demands in their search for authenticity, with some success, but Saint-Saëns was not entirely happy with the result, recalling with some bitterness that "we were persuaded to interfere with a work whose author deserved no consideration".[24] Nevertheless, the 1859 *Orphée*, with its principal role changed to mezzo-soprano, has become the standard version. Its immediate success helped to overcome Saint-Saëns's reservations, especially when Berlioz's production of *Alceste* at the Opéra two years later seemed to confirm that Gluck was being restored to public esteem. Yet the Opéra clearly had second thoughts about the box-office potential of *Armide*: shortly after Berlioz and Saint-Saëns had begun work on it they were told that the project had been cancelled.

Saint-Saëns hoped that his presence in the highest society might advance his own plans to join the operatic elite. He was encouraged in this hope when Princess Mathilde, cousin of the Emperor, secured for him exemption from military service, a privilege enjoyed in practice, if not in theory, by most sons of the well-off. He had also been invited into her select literary salon – which included Flaubert, Dumas father and son, and other literary giants – at her house in the Rue de Courcelles and at her château at St Gratieu. But he was to find that his musical gifts and aims made little impression on such august patronage. At the suggestion that she might help promote his operatic ambitions, the amazed princess declared to Carvalho that Saint-Saëns should be satisfied. "He plays the organ at the Madeleine and the piano at my house. Isn't that enough for him?"[25]

It was not enough. He knew that no matter how many orchestral works he wrote he would never be taken seriously as a composer in France until he had written and staged an opera. "I was a writer of symphonies, an organist and a pianist, so how could I be capable of writing an opera?" That was the position as he saw it. Pianists were particularly despised in the theatrical world, and that was why Bizet, he recalled, "who played the piano admirably, never dared to play it in public".[26] With no chance of a commission, he had to take the initiative, but a suitable subject still eluded him. He turned again to *Macbeth*, with

Mme Viardot in mind as the female lead, and approached Carvalho with the idea. But Carvalho was not interested, and produced Verdi's version of the story instead, in April 1865: it was, Saint-Saëns noted, with the slightest hint of satisfaction, "a terrible flop that cost him 30,000 francs". The stage door seemed firmly closed, not only to new French opera but also to new French ballet. He proposed to the Opéra a ballet about Cleopatra based on a novel by Théophile Gautier and with a scenario by Jules Barbier, but it was declined. He noted with indignation that when the Opéra directors "consented to order a ballet from Delibes, they did not dare to trust him with the whole work but let him do only one act and gave the rest to a Hungarian".[27]

Exclusion from the theatre, combined with neglect in the concert hall, prompted the twenty-eight-year-old Saint-Saëns to compete again for the Prix de Rome. It was an astonishing move on the face of it because, if successful, he would have had to give up his respected positions as organist and teacher to take up residence in Italy and Germany. It was clearly as a composer that he was determined to make his mark. He saw the prize as a means of gaining wider recognition as a composer and of removing a lingering sense of social insecurity. But this second attempt was as ill-fated as the first: before submitting himself to the stipulated seclusion he fell ill, probably from overwork. He wrote to a friend from his cell that he had been in bed "until yesterday morning, then transported to the Conservatoire, where I was imprisoned to take part in the musical competition vulgarly called the Prix de Rome. I am still very unwell. I shall be free only on 5th July".[28] Despite his illness he duly emerged on that date with his cantata *Ivanhoé*, to a set text as usual, and it was sung to the examiners by Célestine Galli-Marié, who was to become the first Carmen. The committee, chaired by Auber and including Berlioz, voted it down. They awarded the prize to one Victor Sieg, who, like the 1852 winner, never rose above obscurity, complaining in later life that his only claim to fame was to have beaten Saint-Saëns in a major competition. According to the composer-critic Ernest Reyer, he won the prize because he had a German name. But Saint-Saëns's vigorous championing of both the baroque and the vanguard, which aroused disapproval among the musical establishment, could not have helped his cause, and neither could his age. The judges probably considered him too old to benefit from the award, just as he was too young before. If at sixteen he lacked experience, at twenty-eight he lacked inexperience, as Gounod once told the young man – a phrase which, ironically, has come to be used as evidence that Saint-Saëns came by success too easily.[29]

Whatever doubt Saint-Saëns may have had about his standing in the musical world, it was high enough for the result of the contest to cause quite a stir. Perhaps by way of consolation, Auber, who had long urged him to write an opera, finally took a hand and asked Carvalho to offer him a libretto. The impresario obliged, but the piece was far from promising. *Le Timbre d'Argent*, a joint effort by Jules Barbier, librettist of *Les Contes d'Hoffmann*, and Michel Carré, librettist of *Les Pêcheurs de Perles* and *Mireille*, had already been turned down by at least three composers. The Faust-like story, originally in five acts, concerns a painter named Conrad who is offered a magic bell by the evil Dr Spiridion. If he rings it he will have anything he desires, but someone close to him will die. Conrad is betrothed to Helen but is infatuated by Fiametta, a dancer, and to win her makes himself wealthy by using the magic bell. A friend dies; when Fiametta still rejects Conrad he rings the bell again and his closest friend Benedict dies. Horrified and torn between the entreaties of Helen and the temptations of Dr Spiridion, Conrad smashes the bell and awakens to find it was all a dream. This rather easy ending is not only unnecessary – the preceding action is no more fantastic than that of many operas – but also destroys what dramatic power and emotional engagement the whole piece might otherwise have had. The theme of good versus evil had already been treated successfully in operas such as *Tannhäuser* and *Faust* with no such anti-climax. But it may have been something else that attracted Saint-Saëns sufficiently to accept the piece: the theme of men ruined by the seductive charms of a woman, which was to dominate many of his operas and the symphonic poems. There is no doubt that he disliked women, except those who possessed exceptional artistic talent. The fact that they so often appear in a destructive capacity in his works suggests that Saint-Saëns felt the prospect of a relationship with a woman to be a threat to his role as the artist-hero. It was an instinct that was to prove strangely and sadly well-founded, for the perceived threat was to turn into real tragedy and the greatest personal failure of his life.

After persuading the authors to make certain changes to the libretto, Saint-Saëns, as he recalled, "retired to the heights of Louveciennes and in two months wrote the score of the five acts".[30] The long, frustrating search for a libretto was over, but an equally long and difficult progress towards an operatic debut had only just begun.

V • PIANIST

IF SAINT-SAËNS BELIEVED THAT A CAREER AS A PIANIST MEANT EXCLUSION from the opera house and therefore from public acceptance as a composer, he did his cause no good by building a formidable reputation on the concert platform. An increasingly busy concert schedule on top of regular duties at the Madeleine made it impossible for him to continue teaching at the Ecole Niedermeyer, and he gave up his post there in 1865. Among his engagements as a pianist that year were a series of chamber recitals with Sarasate and a concert in Dijon in April to raise funds for a monument to Rameau in his birthplace. But the event that had the most impact came in October when he played his piano concerto in Leipzig, where his A minor symphony had already been performed. German audiences, always ready to recognise achievement in the forms of symphony and concerto, were now coming to regard him as France's most significant young composer, a recognition he could hardly have hoped for among his own, opera-orientated countrymen.

As with his editing, he approached his playing with the primary objective of being as faithful as possible to the composer's intentions, freeing the music from the impositions both of 'feeling' and of performance fashion. Equipped with a powerful technique imparted by the Kalkbrenner method as taught by Stamaty, he rejected the expressive intensity which the method was designed to achieve, the continuous legato which was expected of pianists regardless of the style and period of the music they were playing. Such indiscriminate expressiveness, he insisted, destroyed the character of classical works: without it, he was told, he "would never get a really fine effect – to which I was entirely indifferent".[1] His playing, therefore, was marked by a combination of technical brilliance and emotional reserve, in character with his self-effacing manner at the piano. This indeed often created an image of indifference. The short, business-like figure would walk smartly to the piano stool and begin to play apparently without any mental preparation whatever; he would play with the minimum of bodily movement, his face expressionless, with none of the wild contortions audiences had come to expect. At the end a brief nod would acknowledge the applause, with the same slight regard with which he had been brought up to treat any kind of praise or criticism.

It was a style that was to vary hardly at all throughout his long playing career. As late as 1906, the *Musical Times* noted that his playing "is not only remarkable for its unalloyed beauty, but furnished a welcome contrast to the noisy poundings of young and unrestrained virtuosi".[2] And Marcel Proust wrote that it had none of those "pianist's writhings, shakings of the head and tossing of the hair which spoil the purity of the music with sensuality . . . his playing was regal".[3]

But although it was an approach starkly at odds with the flamboyance and showmanship that went with the age of the virtuoso, it must also be seen in the context of the French style of playing in general, which tends towards elegance, precision and the tonal clarity that comes from finger strength. These were qualities which Saint-Saëns's boyhood acquaintance Francis Planté was now demonstrating in an illustrious career. Saint-Saëns's own style naturally stemmed to a great extent from his character and philosophy, from the principle of "no emotion" taught by his great-aunt, which he passed on to his own pupils with the instruction: "Avoid all exaggeration and strive to maintain the entirety of intellectual health."[4] But it also had much to do with the physical training of the Kalkbrenner school, in which the playing came almost entirely from the fingers and not from the arms, the result of Stamaty's iron bar. There was no need for arm movement: the fingers did all the work.

The technical power and emotional detachment were still there in old age: Claudio Arrau, who heard the veteran Saint-Saëns in Berlin, said he played "with incredible ease the most even scales you can imagine, and great power in the fingers", but with a sound that was "ice-cold".[5] He used the pedal sparingly. Earlier, Adolphe Botte called the playing "cold and dry"[6] while Leopold Mannes described it as like "a dry well".[7] But in place of emotional warmth was a purity and clarity of sound which the pianist Isidor Philipp said imparted to the piano "the charm and persuasive accent of the human voice".[8] The critic Michel Calvocoressi listed the qualities as "purity, perspicacity and ease",[9] while Romain Rolland – referring more to the composer, although the verdict applies equally to the pianist – wrote that "he is not troubled by any sort of passion; nothing disturbs the clearness of his reason".[10]

With the pearly brilliance of the sound went a fine tonal shading, which some mistook for a lack of dynamic contrast. As early as 1849 Henri Blanchard urged him to vary the tone more,[11] and as late as 1906 the *New York Times* criticised "restricted limits of dynamic contrast and tonal colour".[12] Another critic, Gaston Knosp, commented that it was because his playing was "always simple, noble and classically perfect in every respect" that it was labelled "cold and unfeeling",[13] but this commonly held view stemmed more precisely from this quality of subtle tonal gradation. And the playing was not, in fact, always "perfect". A tendency to fast speeds, as if matching the speed of his speech and thought, sometimes led his fingers to run away with the music, so that it was not always accurate. At a concert he gave at the Carnegie Hall in New York in 1906, "he seemed at times to be carried away by the impetuosity of the music; the phrasing was now and again slighted, to the detriment of the rhythm", the *New York Times* reported.[14] The occasional sacrifice of accuracy was one of the criticisms made by Clara Schumann in her damning verdict on Saint-Saëns's playing – made rather ungraciously in view of his championing of her late husband's works, something of which she seemed to be unaware:

He achieves his results through industry alone, and even technically he is only a circus rider, offering not a single instance of tonal beauty. His playing is all octaves, with interchanging hands, arpeggios over the whole keyboard (always blurring the finish), enormously powerful hands, trills in thirds with two hands, etc. This really ceases to be piano playing and becomes a tightrope walking act.[15]

Clara Schumann represented an entirely different school of playing, which put poetic sensitivity and breadth of vision above fiery brilliance. The contrast must have been well demonstrated when she appeared on the same programme with Saint-Saëns at the Conservatoire Concerts Society on 27th April 1862: she played Beethoven's 'Emperor' concerto, he the same composer's Choral Fantasy. Her dismissal of his playing as empty showmanship applied also to that of his ally Liszt who was once, in her youth, the object of her starry-eyed adoration. She played none of Liszt's original works, only his transcriptions, to show that, while she disapproved of his style, she was perfectly able to match his virtuosity. She was in good company, it seems, at least among her counterparts in France, for Liszt complained that "all the best known French pianists – with the exception of Saint-Saëns – have not ventured to play anything of mine except transcriptions, my compositions being considered absurd".[16] Liszt recognised his young friend as an ally and declared that "the only two people left in Europe who know how to play the piano" were Saint-Saëns and himself.[17]

But it would be a mistake to regard the two men alike as pianist-composers. For Liszt, one of the greatest pianists of all time, the piano was of course his primary medium of composition, whereas Saint-Saëns regarded it as just one of a large family of instruments. He even came to view it with some hostility in later years when, amid the excesses of the Wagner imitators, he denounced it as "the damaging tyrant of music" which had made possible "heretical harmonies".[18] When the Queen of Italy told him that her sons were learning the violin and cello he heartily approved, claiming that "the exclusive devotion to the piano these days has been the death of chamber music and almost of all music".[19] It will be shown that he regarded the piano not as the monarch of instruments, to which status the nineteenth century had elevated it, but as one among equals.

Saint-Saëns's programmes as a pianist – and it must be remembered that programmes of the period often consisted of a mixture of concerto, chamber and solo works – were wide-ranging and innovative to reflect the broad sweep of his musical knowledge and interests. They included the more advanced works of Schumann and Liszt and pieces of his own as well as the early keyboard giants Bach, Rameau and Couperin. He gave the Paris première of the Schumann concerto in 1865. He was also an enthusiastic advocate of Mozart's keyboard works, especially the concertos, at a time when – with few exceptions – they were little valued and not often played. His concerto series at the Salle Pleyel in 1864–65, which also included some of the sonatas and trios, was a milestone in the nineteenth-century rediscovery of Mozart, featuring at least nine of the concertos with players from the orchestra of the Théâtre Italien.[20] The concertos were a revelation to English audiences too when he gave a similar series in London in later life, to be hailed as a pioneering Mozart interpreter. *The Times* described his playing as "of the most finished kind" showing "a profound knowledge of and sympathy with Mozart's music".[21] "He neither vulgarises the music nor treats it like a precious curio. We get from him an impression of the virile personality of Mozart."[22] As well as performing the concertos he also wrote cadenzas for K.482 and K.491, and for the concerto for two pianos K.365. But that the programmes of the young pianist could sometimes be a little too innovative for 1860s Paris is suggested by the fact that a further series planned at the Salle Pleyel in 1865 was abandoned after one concert because of a row with the management over the choice of works.[23]

The pianist, free of regular teaching commitments, had also returned to composing, and in December 1865 completed a setting of Psalm 18 (in the English Bible, Psalm 19, 'The Heavens declare the glory of God'). Like his earlier religious settings, the Psalm combines scholastic accomplishment, period knowledge and contrapuntal brilliance with imaginative harmonic flights and orchestral colouring. The rhythmic pattern that dominates the short orchestral prelude continues into the first chorus – a simple, almost child-like rejoicing – which reappears to close the work. Among the notable sections are an elaborately woven motet for two sopranos, contralto, tenor, baritone and bass, in which the balance and contrast between the vocal parts is handled with exceptional skill; and the beautiful soprano aria 'Domine, adjutor meus', with its striking cello counter-melody. An unusual feature is the quartet for baritones, said to have been written to make use of some good baritones which the Madeleine choir boasted at the time. The Psalm was sung at the church during Midnight Mass. Another unusual combination is that of the serenade for piano, organ, violin and viola or cello, dedicated to the Princess Mathilde and played, with the composer at the organ, at one of her soirées in January 1866, when the guests included Auber and the Prussian Prince Hohenzollern. A public performance followed in February, and on 7th March the *Scène d'Horace* was played by Pasdeloup at the Cirque Napoléon, with the soprano Anne Charton-Demeur, Berlioz's first Beatrice and Dido. In April Berlioz and Gounod were among the audience at the Salle Pleyel to hear the serenade and the cello suite.

In August Saint-Saëns wrote the *Trois Rapsodies sur des Cantiques Bretons* for organ, inspired by a visit to Rennes, in Brittany, where Fauré was newly installed in his first organist post. He travelled with some artist friends, including the painter Henri Regnault, and sketched the rhapsodies while on a pilgrimage with them and Fauré to Sainte Anne-la-Palud, on the Gulf of Morbihan. He dedicated the pieces to his host and former pupil: together with the *Rapsodie Bretonne* for orchestra, written soon after and based on the first two of the organ pieces, they are the first examples of works incorporating the folk idioms of particular localities and countries that were to form a major part of Saint-Saëns's later output. He came to hear a selection of Breton folk tunes in the unlikeliest of circumstances, during a boat trip in the region. He recalled the captain, "a very young man, almost beardless, bronzed and thick set, with large blue eyes whose sweetness could not hide their vigour. He was extremely polite and reserved". When they set sail, the captain disappeared into the hold, and his passenger assumed he had gone to sleep.

Several minutes later a fine, rough sound was heard along the flanks of the boat. The captain was playing the oboe! During the whole crossing he played the tunes of his country, those airs of a character at once so savage and so charming, that are such a welcome change from our too refined music, and refresh the soul like a salty breeze.[24]

Fauré, feeling lonely and isolated in Rennes, must have welcomed the company that descended on him that summer. He owed his job to the recommendation of Gustave Lefèvre, Louis Niedermeyer's son-in-law who had become head of the Ecole Niedermeyer in 1865, but had neglected to thank him. Saint-Saëns was most indignant when he found out, and wrote to Fauré in January 1867 in tones of a scolding schoolmaster: "you have committed a serious offence which you really must rectify as fast as you can". He talks of an informal concert where "we made a real racket in the house . . . why weren't you there?" and the paternal tone is continued in news of "a publisher I have in mind for you". This was Choudens, who was to publish most of Fauré's early songs.[25]

The organist-composer Charles Widor was another promising young musician whom Saint-Saëns helped, using his influence to secure for Widor at the age of twenty-one his first major engagement as organist at the International Exhibition in Oporto in 1865.[26] Four years later he took Widor on as his assistant at the Madeleine, where the apprentice organist perfected his craft under the maestro's influence, example and guidance, before taking over at the church of St Sulpice in 1870, a position he held for sixty-three years.

But for all the help and advice he was able to give younger musicians, Saint-Saëns was not able to advance his own cause in the field of opera. *Le Timbre d'Argent* remained in the drawer for two years after he wrote it. Opera managements, as he wryly noted, could not take a concert pianist seriously.[27] The only consolation was the production of *Armide* at the Théâtre Lyrique in the autumn of 1866. After the Opéra cancelled its commission from Berlioz, Carvalho stepped in to rescue the venture – somewhat to Berlioz's surprise, knowing the impresario as he did and thinking that the opera would "hardly suit his commercial world". The revival of the project seemed to give the ailing composer a new lease of life, blotting out the neuralgia and stomach pains that had so often confined him to bed. He was able to get up every day "just like other people" to open the door to Mme Charton-Demeur, who was to sing Armide, and Saint-Saëns, "a first-rate musician who knows his Gluck almost as well as I do".[28] "An extraordinary thing has happened to me", he told the younger man one morning, "I am not in pain".[29] Berlioz knew that his soprano was new to Gluck, but after considerable uncertainty in a particular passage, she would suddenly find its dramatic potential, and "Saint-Saëns and I could only clasp hands in silence; we were breathless. Never did a human being find such expression".[30]

Co-operation on *Armide* brought Saint-Saëns closer than ever to Berlioz. He even managed to convert him to Bach, which, as Berlioz's music was anything but contrapuntal, was something of an achievement. "I always remember his astonishment and delight at the performance of a chorus by Sebastian Bach which I made known to him one day", Saint-Saëns recalled. "He could not get over the fact that the great Sebastian had written such things; and he confessed to me that he had always taken him for a sort of colossal thematic power house, made of very learned fugues but devoid of charm and poetry." Work on *Armide* had temporarily diverted attention from the veteran composer's failing health, but it soon had to be faced again. Saint-Saëns, accompanying him on concert tours, was dismayed by the way he ignored his diet, prescribed to counter stomach cramps, and instead "ate whatever he pleased". Sitting next to him at a dinner, his young companion "did all I could to oppose coffee, champagne and Havana cigars. It was all to no avail and next day the poor man was writhing in the usual agony."[31]

While *Armide* reached the stage at last, Saint-Saëns's own progress towards the footlights was painfully slow. After much pestering, Carvalho agreed to hear *Le Timbre d'Argent,* two years after it was written. He invited the composer to dinner, after which Saint-Saëns played the opera on the piano to the director and his wife Marie Miolan, who seems to have been comfortably unaware of their guest's celebrated mimicries of her singing. Carvalho gushingly declared the work a masterpiece and said he would certainly stage it, insisting only that his wife should sing the principal part. This condition began an extraordinary sequence of twists and turns in the history of *Le Timbre d'Argent.* The principal part was not for a singer but a dancer, Fiametta, to whom the singing role of Helen was subordinate. This was obviously not good enough for Mme Carvalho, so Barbier and Carré were asked to rewrite the piece, building up the part of Helen, the composer making the necessary alterations to the music. This they did, but the director was not satisfied. Instead, "he tormented us for a long time to make the dancer into a singer on his wife's account". Saint-Saëns relates that Carvalho's demands then became ever more outlandish. First he wanted a second dancer, then wild animals to heighten the dream aspect, and on further reflection, a pool into which Mme Carvalho's Helen would dive to recover the fatal bell. Later still he wanted to change the period setting, then suggested that all the music should be cut except the choruses and the dances, with the rest played by actors. Saint-Saëns accused him of being obsessed by the idea of collaboration. "Even a work hallowed by time and success had to bear his mark."[32]

The wrangling over the opera – which also saw it reduced from five acts to four – took up another two years, but was to some extent offset by a triumph in the concert hall on 4th April 1867, when Sarasate premièred the A major violin concerto at the Salle Pleyel. "Saint-Saëns has never before soared to such heights", said the *Revue et Gazette Musicale.* "The violin was treated here as if the composer were a Joachim" – a tribute to his grasp of the technicalities and expressive power of the instrument. The concerto was followed by the Tarantella which had so charmed (and deceived) the guests at Rossini's soirée ten years before: it was played by its dedicatees Louis Dorus (flute) and Adolphe Leroy (clarinet), and was encored, the *Revue* critic enthusing: "Here one can sense a master's hand. The piece is founded almost entirely on a ground bass that is repeated by the various instruments in a most original way."[33] The concerto was performed again on 27th April, conducted by the composer, boosting his fame in the concert hall but at the same time weakening his claim to recognition in a country devoted to opera, a paradox built into the musical situation in the France of the period.

The disregard in which he was held by the country's musical establishment was graphically illustrated in the summer of 1867, in the extraordinary affair of the International Exhibition, an event designed to show to the world the industrial, commercial and cultural progress of the Second Empire since the exhibition of 1855 (itself inspired by the Great Exhibition in London). Plans included a competition for a hymn of peace and a cantata in honour of the exhibition, to be performed in the Hall of Industry. A prize of 1000 francs was offered for the poems chosen for each piece, and 936 poems in all were submitted. The winning hymn of peace was a joint work by one Gustave Chouquet and the then little-known Parnassian poet François Coppée, later to achieve popularity for his sentimental stories of the poor and to become a staunch defender of the establishment during the Dreyfus affair. The winning cantata poem was by a seventeen-year-old, Romain Cornut, who entered, along with his brother, only because his father wanted him to do so. His piece was called *Les Noces de Prométhée*, in which the stealer of celestial fire is wedded to Humanity, thus producing human endeavour and creativity. The Paris correspondent of *The Times* dismissed both works as "among the feeblest efforts of the French muse".[34]

The musical side of the competition attracted so many entries that the hymn of peace (823 submitted versions) was abandoned. There were more than 100 submissions for the cantata prize of 5000 francs plus a medal, among them settings by Bizet and the as yet little known Jules Massenet. Saint-Saëns, worn out by concerts and the complications over *Le Timbre d'Argent*, was ill when the competition was announced, and hurriedly composed his setting just in time for the closing date. Like the finale of the E flat symphony, it calls for large orchestral forces, including saxophones and four harps, to convey the message of human triumph. Berlioz and Verdi were among the judges, as well as – on paper at least – Rossini, Gounod and Auber, but these three were clearly bored by the whole business. Rossini was president of the selection committee but never present, Gounod made his excuses and left his job as committee secretary and Auber was asleep at most meetings.

Among the anonymous entries Bizet did not make the final four, Massenet was a runner-up and Saint-Saëns was declared the winner. When his identity was revealed Berlioz could hardly contain his delight, heightened perhaps by a sense of relief that his young colleague had not been rebuffed again after the Prix de Rome disappointment. Here at last was the major prize he had predicted for his friend. He rushed to Saint-Saëns's home to tell him the news, but no one was in. Instead he wrote to an acquaintance the same day, 11th June:

We heard 104 cantatas and I have had the very great pleasure of seeing the prize unanimously awarded to my young friend Camille Saint-Saëns, one of the leading musicians of our time . . . he is an astonishing pianist. Now at last somebody has done something sensible in our world of music.[35]

Bizet wrote that "it was a very fine fugue with two choruses" that won the prize for Saint-Saëns, for whom "I am delighted", but suggested also that he had submitted his entry on foreign manuscript paper and that this had fooled the judges into thinking they had safely chosen a German composer, perhaps even Wagner.[36] "They were disagreeably surprised," according to the composer Emile Paladilhe, "when they opened the envelope and found the name of Saint-Saëns."[37] But the winner always denied that he had used foreign paper in an attempt to mislead the selectors, insisting that he now had no need to obscure his identity because Auber, as well as Berlioz, was – contrary to popular belief – well disposed towards him, especially after the Prix de Rome failure. In view of Auber's minimal involvement in the judging, this benevolence hardly seems relevant. Neither is it entirely certain: although Auber declared that Saint-Saëns had shown himself to be "a symphonist so confident in his method, so far removed from drudgery, of such an attractive manner, that I cannot name his equal among us",[38] even such a verdict on a "symphonist" can only be qualified praise from someone so sure of the superiority of opera.

Terrified of failing and of being seen to have failed, Bizet went to great lengths to conceal the fact that he too had competed, even from someone who regarded him as a loyal friend. In congratulating the winner he was guilty of a blatant deceit – of which Saint-Saëns seems to have remained unaware – when he wrote to him: "I regret not having competed. I should then have had the honour of being beaten by you." Elsewhere Bizet referred to the cleft stick of French musical life which meant that even such a triumph as the exhibition prize would go against the victor, writing of the prevailing opinion that "Saint-Saëns's work is very remarkable, that it gives evidence of outstanding musical gifts, while at the same time proving that its composer will never be a man of the theatre".[39]

Sure enough, the musical establishment, embarrassed by the competition result and swayed by the strong anti-Berlioz faction from advancing the cause of his ally any further, backed away from having the cantata performed. Saint-Saëns was told that the subtleties of the work would be lost in the Hall of Industry's acoustics. The organisers were spared having to pay him the 5000 francs prize money when Rossini, once his jovial champion, who had done nothing to help in judging the competition, persuaded the Emperor to have his own bombastic *Hymne à Napoléon III* "and his valiant people" played instead. There was outrage amongst the musical public at this injustice. A journalist, Hippolyte Prévost, reported Saint-Saëns's grievances on 16th July and was told by the committee's new secretary that the cantata was "too long" for the occasion. The composer reminded the Commissar-General of the promise contained in the competition conditions to make available all necessary resources for the performance of the winning work: he was told that all the money for musical performances had been spent and, on further protest, that "the promises of the musical committee are not binding on the Imperial Commission". Saint-Saëns related this interview to *Le Figaro*, and, fearing a public outcry, the authorities at length grudgingly paid him 2500 francs – half the prize money, after the press insisted that he "had the right to the highest respect as a man, a prizewinner and a long-esteemed artist".[40]

Les Noces de Prométhée was belatedly given a makeshift performance at the Cirque de l'Impératrice on 1st September 1867, with the Belgian singers Marie Sasse and Victor Warot, and the French baritone Jean-Baptiste Fauré. Saint-Saëns played the march from it to inaugurate the new Cavaillé-Coll organ at Notre Dame the following year, and finally received full compensation when the complete cantata was performed again at the Industrial Exhibition of 1878, under a different political and musical regime.

With work on producing *Le Timbre d'Argent* at an impasse, Saint-Saëns was at least encouraged by comments on the work by Bizet, who made the piano-vocal score in 1867 and wrote to the composer: "I am enchanted by the third act. It has an exquisite tenderness and purity. The end of Helen's lovely song is indescribably glowing." Elsewhere Bizet called it "charming, true opéra-comique, slightly tinged with Verdi. Of Wagner, of Berlioz, nothing."[41] But with a production seemingly as far off as ever, Saint-Saëns was contemplating other vocal projects, notably an oratorio based on the biblical story of Samson and Delilah, suggested by a guest at one of his Monday soirées. After sketching the broad outlines of the text he asked for a libretto from a distant in-law, a young Créole from Martinique named Ferdinand Lemaire, two of whose poems he had set to music. Lemaire suggested it should be an opera rather than an oratorio, a bold idea as operas based on biblical texts were rare and likely to be frowned upon by theatre managers ever conscious of audience (and censor) sensibilities. Despite the prospect of having a second unperformable opera on his hands, Saint-Saëns accepted the suggestion, and set about creating a Delilah that would be the perfect vehicle for the bittersweet mezzo-soprano of Mme Viardot.

His readiness to tackle the subject can best be explained by the nature of the story, which clearly aroused in him sympathies strong enough to outweigh the apparent disadvantages of the project. As in *Le Timbre d'Argent* the theme is a man's destruction by a woman, but here it is no dream, and has the added weight of biblical authority, with the physical and moral strength of the hero making his fall much more terrible. That this theme struck a deep chord in the composer is evident in the fact that the second act seduction scene, in which Samson finally succumbs to Delilah's charms, was the first part of the opera to be written. Delilah's famous arias 'Love, come help my weakness' and 'Softly awakes my heart' were first sung to an invited audience at Saint-Saëns's home in 1867, the composer providing the as yet unwritten accompaniment on the piano. He never forgot the "stony silence" with which they were received. "I had not the faintest acknowledgement, even of mere politeness."[42]

Among the guests at that discouraging event was Anton Rubinstein, on his annual escape from the Russian winter. Saint-Saëns fondly recalled:

We often played piano duets, submitting to rough ordeals the pianos that served as a battlefield, without pity for the ears of our listeners. We had a good time, making music with passion, simply for the joy of it, and we never had enough. I was so happy to have met a true artist, without the pettinesses that sometimes, sadly, follow most great talents!

Rubinstein planned a series of eight concerts in Paris, to include his own works, and Saint-Saëns reluctantly agreed to conduct them, believing himself too inexperienced for the task. It gave him the experience he felt he lacked, for "during those concerts I acquired my education as a conductor". The Russian virtuoso did not make it easy for him.

At rehearsals Rubinstein brought me scribbled scores in manuscript, full of erasures, cuts and doodles of every kind. I could never get him to let me see the music in advance; it was too amusing, he said, to see me getting to grips with all the difficulties. Moreover, when he played he did not concern himself at all with the orchestra that accompanied him; you had to follow him, a little haphazardly, and sometimes such a cloud of sonority arose from the piano that I heard nothing else and had no other guide than the view of his fingers on the keys.

After the last concert, in April 1868, Rubinstein pointed out that he had not yet conducted in Paris and asked his colleague to arrange it. After making inquiries Saint-Saëns told him that the nearest date was three weeks away, at the Salle Pleyel – and that he would use the time to write a piano concerto for the occasion, which he would play himself. By this time the two men were almost inseparable, and Saint-Saëns recalled with some amusement that they made an incongruous pair, "he athletic, tireless, colossal of stature as of talent, me frail, pale and slightly consumptive", a contrast, he mused, similar to that of Liszt and Chopin, adding modestly that he resembled the latter only in delicate health.[43]

Meanwhile, *Le Timbre d'Argent* was making some progress. Mme Carvalho, still dissatisfied with her part, had withdrawn, another soprano had been engaged to sing Helen, and rehearsals were at last underway at the Théâtre Lyrique. Then, on 6th May, while Saint-Saëns was working on the concerto, news came of Carvalho's bankruptcy, dashing all expectations. This calamity, and the disappointing response to the fledgling *Samson*, seemed to confirm the mutually exclusive domains of opera house and concert hall: for while success in the one seemed farther off than ever, it was about to hit new heights in the other. On 13th May, exactly a week after Carvalho's downfall, Saint-Saëns gave the first performance of the G minor piano concerto, under Rubinstein's baton, in a programme which also included the first piano concerto and the Tarantella.

It was a less than polished première. The composer complained of tiredness and insufficient rehearsal because of the short time he had had to write the work. And, apart from the scherzo, it was not well received, partly perhaps because of the quality of performance. Saint-Saëns wanted Liszt's verdict and sent a printed copy of the score to Henri Regnault in Rome, to take to the master. The painter called at the Villa Medici, where Liszt was staying, and was at first told that no one was at home, but he persisted and was able finally to hand the score to the illustrious tenant. Soon after, Liszt wrote to Saint-Saëns that, in the concerto, "you keep just account of the pianistic effect without sacrificing anything of the composer's ideas, an essential rule in this type of work," adding that "it pleases me greatly" and predicting its success.[44] He was not wrong: the concerto was quickly taken up by other pianists and, given wider currency by Bizet's transcription for solo piano, it soon established itself as a standard work in the repertory, a position it has never lost.

Though not now quite so frequently played as it once was, the G minor piano concerto remains one of the most popular and best-known of all Saint-

Saëns's works. That it took just seventeen days to write has impressed commentators, but it is probable that its ideas had been germinating for some time. Stegemann, in his study of the concertos, has argued that it was Saint-Saëns's habit to keep musical ideas in note form or in his head until such time as they could be used in a given context. The apparent period of composition was considerably shorter than the real period, and was almost entirely taken up by the mechanics of writing down what already existed as ideas. These ideas were often altered in shape or rhythm before taking their final form – as his sketches testify.[45] It has been argued that Mozart composed in the same way, creating the impression of incredible facility. Saint-Saëns had certainly had the principal theme of his concerto's first movement for at least three years: it was not his at all but was written by Fauré for a choral piece he planned to write during his student days at the Ecole Niedermeyer. As he was not happy with it for this purpose, his teacher asked to have it, promising to make good use of it in the future. And indeed it suits well the solemn mood of the concerto's opening andante.

The oft-repeated joke about beginning with Bach and ending with Offenbach[46] has tended to belittle the work's merits, and familiarity to cloud the bold originality of its design – a slow movement followed by a faster and then a still faster, hurtling towards a brutally dismissive end, like one long accelerando. The movements are self-contained and, unlike in earlier works, there is no thematic cross-reference between them. But each movement is in itself hardly conventional. The novice listener cannot fail to be arrested by the opening solo prelude in the style of Bach which, in a subdued form, also heralds the end of the movement without a reprise of the second subject, a tender, plaintive melody of great feeling. Albert l'Hôte in *La France Musicale* thought this andante sostenuto to be a piece "of the kind that tends to defy analysis", being more like "a brilliant improvisation",[47] and indeed Saint-Saëns later revealed that it was the result of an improvisation while playing the organ at the Paris church of St Augustin.

The sylph-like allegro scherzando brings us out of the chapel into the brightness of a spring day, in the Mendelssohnian terms of razor-sharp orchestration and melodic *bonhomie*, and with Saint-Saëns's favourite device of the light orchestral staccato chord on the off-beat. The finale's energetic tarantella suggests a swarm of bees, one of which leaves his company and, in the form of a trill-based figure, hovers up and down the keyboard buzzing around a soft chant in the orchestra to form a central section, before rejoining the swarm, which brings the work to its hectic close. The piano writing, as Liszt points out, strikes a subtle balance between the expectations of virtuosity and the working out of the thematic material, and shows a significant advance on that of the D major concerto, with a greater clarity, lightness and freshness.

The considerable, if slightly delayed, success of the concerto helped to advance Saint-Saëns towards the position of France's leading symphonic composer, an advance that seemed to be confirmed when he was made a Chevalier of the Légion d'Honneur on 15th August. The decoration, news of which was brought to him at the Madeleine by a delighted Abbé Deguerry, was however in response to another work, a cantata – written in haste – for a festival at Versailles to mark the centenary of the birth of General Hoche, a military hero of revolutionary and Napoleonic France. It was performed below a statue of the general, but was never revived.

Encouraging as all this was, it could do nothing to improve his prospects in opera. A few weeks after the fall of Carvalho at the Théâtre Lyrique, the Opéra, under Emile Perrin, offered to take *Le Timbre d'Argent* but in a modified form to suit the larger stage and the available cast. The librettists, however, not surprisingly refused to change it yet again and Perrin lost interest, though he valued contact with Saint-Saëns enough to invite him on to the jury considering entries in a competition for a new work for the Opéra in 1869. The anonymous entries included works by Bizet and Massenet, both of them unsuccessful, though Massenet was second: the winner was a nonentity. Saint-Saëns's only opportunity to write for the stage was one he would rather not have had. His old friend Gounod had been commissioned to write a ballet for a new production of *Faust* at the Opéra but was reluctant to oblige because a resurgence of religious scruples at the time prevented him from working for the theatre. He asked Saint-Saëns to write the ballet, much to the latter's embarrassment. At his home in St Cloud, while playing cards with a visiting cleric, he listened in silence as Saint-Saëns pleaded that music by someone else would not fit in well with the opera. Gounod merely nodded and carried on playing cards, and to Saint-Saëns's great relief said nothing more about the ballet. He wrote it himself and it was highly praised.[48]

Meanwhile, Mme Carvalho had left Paris for a concert tour of Brittany after the collapse of her husband's reign at the Lyrique, and Saint-Saëns, remembering Fauré at Rennes and ever on the lookout for work for his protégé, arranged for him to be her accompanist. As for himself, he embarked on another exhausting concert tour of the German states, further enhancing his reputation there as both composer and pianist.

Despite the operatic setbacks, his interest in vocal music was as alive as ever. Among several songs written in 1868–69 were two settings of Hugo and one of Legouvé, 'Maria Lucrezia', which he dedicated to his pupil the Viscountess Grandval. In all, nine of his songs are dedicated to her, perhaps indicating something more than a teacher's affection. It is impossible to assess his feelings accurately, as affairs of the heart were a matter he generally avoided in his letters and reminiscences. The unsuccessful proposal of marriage he is believed to have made to the daughter of a rich and influential family may have had more to do with a need for social advancement and respectability than with a yearning for female companionship, but he was not impervious to a combination of physical beauty and artistry. Like many young men he fell under the spell of Augusta Holmes, whose musical gifts were as great as her physical charms and were to make her a successful composer of symphonies and symphonic odes. (Her family added a grave accent over the 'e' of their surname to give it the pseudo-French appearance of Holmès.) Born in Paris of Irish parents and twelve years Saint-Saëns's junior, she was idolised by the ardent poets and painters who were his companions, joining them on summer picnics at Versailles and Fontainebleau, and singing to them at her flat in the Rue Mansart. The painter Georges Clairin described the twenty-year-old Augusta as "tall and well-built, majestic and serene, with fine golden hair that fell in a sheet down her back, and green eyes that made us imagine the sea of Ireland. She was not so much a woman as a goddess."[49] Clairin rented a studio with Regnault in the Boulevard St Michel at Versailles, and recalled a night when, in semi-darkness, Saint-Saëns began to play Gluck on the piano (a "bad piano" rented by the month). Then,

in the moonlight, whose pale rays, filtered through the stained glass windows, spread through the studio a pallid and mysterious light, Augusta comes forward like a goddess and, with her arms raised to the sky, unloosens her hair with a sudden movement and begins to sing, exciting us to ecstasy and to arms . . .

Regnault too charmed the circle with his fine tenor voice, which Saint-Saëns described as "exquisite . . . of entrancing tone, irresistible seductiveness, like his profound looks and the whole of his personality".[50] Arthur Duparc, who was to edit Regnault's letters, remembered evenings grouped round the piano

listening to a Beethoven sonata or a Wagner score played in masterly fashion by Saint-Saëns; we joined in singing one of the big chorus scenes from Gluck's Orphée, *or kept silent to let Regnault, in his sweet penetrating voice, utter some new song or Italian cavatina.*[51]

For Saint-Saëns, in his early thirties, such occasions, which he called "veritable orgies of youth, art, music and poetry",[52] were the delights of what seemed like an Indian summer of youth, in what were to be the last years of the Second Empire. They were the happiest years of his long life.

As he was the only professional musician in the group, it is fairly certain that he coached Augusta Holmes in composition, at least on an informal basis, before she came under the tutelage of César Franck. Her intoxicating good looks, her warm, vibrant voice and her musical abilities were enough together to break down even his avowed antipathy to women. He fell in love and proposed to her. He himself, to judge from one of the few portraits that exist from this period, cut a rather more dashing figure than the rather bookish young man of ten years before: almost handsome, the head slightly too large for the body but with a fine mane of dark hair and neatly trimmed beard, impressively earnest, knowledgeable eyes and an intense expression of burning inquiry. But he was only one of many admirers and she turned him down, determined to pursue a musical life of her own. "We were all of us in love with her", he recalled philosophically. "Literary men, painters, musicians, any of us would have been honoured to have had her for a wife." He remained on friendly terms, and came to dedicate some of his works to her, but with the passing of romantic possibilities he relapsed into his natural misogyny. And it was typical of him that Holmes's later success as a composer (under the pseudonym of Herman Zeuta) confirmed him in this attitude. It was not meant as a compliment when he wrote: "Like children, women do not recognise any obstacle and their will overcomes all. Mlle Holmes is very much a woman . . ." As such, she proved that women "are curious when they take up art seriously: they seem preoccupied above all with making us forget they are women by putting on an overflowing virility, not imagining that it is exactly this preoccupation which discloses the woman." This, he argued, applied equally to Holmes's music, which he declared to be full of grotesque exaggerations, effects overstated to the point of absurdity and orchestral sounds subjected to "a system of forced growth" – qualities which were anathema to his own musical aesthetic.[53] Exaggeration is not art, he was to declare, in contradiction of the sculptor Rodin; "it kills art, on the contrary".[54]

A note of sadness was struck in those halcyon days by the death of Berlioz in March 1869. A few weeks earlier Saint-Saëns had called at the lonely room in which Berlioz was on his death bed, and was shocked by the sight of the wasted figure, who, upon seeing him, held out a fevered hand. Knowing Berlioz's sensibility and strong imagination, the visitor at first declined to clasp it. "It was cold outside and my hands were like ice . . . I thought my cold hand would seem to him like death." When he at last gave in and took the hand, he found he was not mistaken, for the dying man "gave a grievous cry, turned to the wall and spoke to me no more". Saint-Saëns was for ever grateful for having worked with Berlioz, for his support and inspiration, and spoke of "private qualities which I found, entirely opposed to his reputation in the world, where he appeared arrogant, hateful and spiteful. He was a good man, on the contrary, good to a fault."[55] The pitiful circumstances of his death must have brought home to Saint-Saëns the neglect and hostility Berlioz suffered in life, and the continuing disregard of French composers generally in their own country. What was needed, he felt, was an organisation solely for the performance and promotion of new French music, in France. The time was not far off when he was to help found the National Music Society (Société Nationale de Musique).

For the present, concert engagements were taking him more frequently than ever to the great German centres of music – although he accepted them with a certain uneasiness about leaving his great-aunt, who was now in her eighties.

His standing there was confirmed when Liszt asked him to take Berlioz's place as the honorary French member of the Association of German Musicians. In Munich he was regarded highly enough to be invited to conduct the first performance of *Das Rheingold*, which was being mounted at the impatient insistence of King Ludwig and against the wishes of Wagner, who wanted it performed only as part of the as yet uncompleted *Ring* cycle. Probably for that reason he declined the invitation, although he was also not confident enough of his conducting skills to take on such an awesome task. He could not, though, resist attending the première – to Wagner's annoyance – on 22nd September 1869, in company with Augusta Holmes, the poet Catulle Mendès and his wife Judith, daughter of the poet Théophile Gautier. He then set about preparing for a first performance of his own at the Gewandhaus, Leipzig, that of his third piano concerto, on 25th November.

The new work had a generally hostile reception. There was a heated argument in the audience that nearly came to blows, over what were considered outlandish tonalities at the start of the slow movement. The *Allgemeine Musik-Zeitung* thought the concerto "trite" – though it approved of the finale's "terse form" and "fiery vitality" – "Occasional eloquent beginnings do not deliver what they promise" and the work represented "a combinatory talent rather than genuine creativity".[56] The spirit of Liszt is certainly very strong, most notably in the cadenza-like passages in the first movement. As in the previous concerto there are three movements, without thematic recollection between them, but the last two are linked. In fact, the third concerto is more classically conceived than the second, with a conventional fast-slow-fast format and the first movement closer to a strict sonata form in that the second subject reappears. But as in the previous work, the piano is heard first, this time creating a swirling mist over which a theme of lofty grandeur is given out by the horns and woodwind and becomes the principal subject, declared in bold octaves by the soloist. After a turbulent subsidiary passage the piano toys with the second subject, a theme of rhythmic rather than melodic interest with its triplet interjections. The brilliantly inventive development, which at one stage goes through a kind of wild dance, is both opened and closed by quasi-cadenzas, before the recapitulation is announced by a solo flute over tremolando strings.

The andante, whose opening off-key wanderings – repeated halfway through – caused such a fuss, is a piece of tender melancholy and nostalgia, into which the ardent Wagnerian weaves a reference to *Tristan und Isolde*. This is appropriate, for both love and death mingle in the delicate atmosphere built up around two main themes, the second of them announced by left hand octaves to orchestral accompaniment. Amid the tenderness, and some delicious interplay between piano and orchestra, a ghostly menace lurks. But the resulting uncertainty is swept away by the tremendous energy of the finale, which bursts in with a muscular, upwardly striving main theme. This alternates with a second theme of great warmth and humour, and the concerto ends with a long coda of exhilarating vitality.

The E flat concerto was better received at its Paris première, given by the composer in the spring of 1870 (after a two-piano version played at the Salle Pleyel on 17th March). Adolphe Jullien of *Le Ménestrel* wrote that "the passionate admirer of the great German masters is recognisable in every measure of this glowing music".[57] To him, it seems, a "combinatory talent" was no bad thing. However, apart from the Lisztian passages and the quotation from Wagner, it is difficult to discern anyone else in this music but Saint-Saëns, both in the thematic material and its treatment. Of all the neglected works, it is particularly undeserving of neglect. Among its outstanding features are the strongly dramatic developments, and although they are contained so as not to disrupt the overall structure, the German critic's complaint about eloquent openings not delivering remains curiously wide of the mark.

Another of the third concerto's achievements is the fine balance between soloist and ensemble, perhaps even finer than in the second concerto. The piano has plenty of virtuoso display while at the same time partnering the orchestra on equal terms – and here is a clue to one of the great mysteries of Saint-Saëns's life and work, that of why this great master of the piano wrote relatively little of worth and substance for the keyboard alone. Apart from the studies, six of them for the left hand, written at different times later in his career to explore technique, the bulk of his output for piano solo consists of the suite of 1891, the *Thème Varié* of 1894 (a stern test piece for the Conservatoire), the Six Fugues from his last year and the Allegro Appassionato in C sharp minor. The rest are short, lightweight trifles. It is remarkably little for such an otherwise prolific composer, even when taking into account the two main works for two pianos, the Variations on a theme of Beethoven and the Scherzo. Viewed against this, the masterly combination of piano and orchestra displayed in the second and third concertos suggests that Saint-Saëns's perception and handling of the instrument were essentially orchestral, that he was best able to write for it only in the context of other instruments. This would explain both the otherwise startling and incongruous appearance of the piano in the mature C minor symphony and, in a way, the irreverent inclusion of pianists as a breed in *Le Carnaval des Animaux*.

Saint-Saëns wrote that Liszt tried to introduce orchestral effects into his piano writing; for instance, by making each hand range more widely over the keyboard to recreate the opulence of orchestral sound. This is why much of Liszt's solo music falls awkwardly under the hands and is by no means – as is often supposed – 'pianist's music'. But if Liszt's aim was to "introduce the orchestra into the pianoforte,"[58] Saint-Saens's was to introduce the pianoforte into the orchestra. His view of the piano as an orchestral instrument is expressed in the qualities of playing he valued – articulation, tonal strength, clarity, brilliance, percussiveness – and those he avoided – expressive legato, poetic sonority. That this lay behind his comparative neglect of the solo repertory can further be demonstrated by contrast with Fauré, who at first emulated his teacher's style. "Here's a style you can't disown", Mme Pochet de Tinan, a mutual friend, wrote to Saint-Saëns of Fauré's playing in 1874. "The clarity, the simplicity, the gentleness, the charm, it's your playing to the life."[59] However, Fauré later moved away from the sparkle and simplicity towards greater legato, intensity and intimacy – and his works for solo piano are his crowning glory.

The integration of soloist with orchestra sought – and achieved – by Saint-Saëns has been seen as indicative of a classical outlook which has in its sights the early eighteenth-century type of solo concerto. Although he by no means shunned virtuosity, which he saw as "a powerful aid to music, whose range it extends enormously",[60] the element of classical unity which he applied to the romantic concerto was at odds with the nineteenth-century cult of the virtuoso, of the soloist as hero (or heroine), to the extent that it could shock and infuriate. One critic, hearing the third concerto in Paris in 1876, condemned it, for all its pianistic bravura, as "sacrificing" the solo part to orchestral effect and even of signalling "the death of virtuosity".[61] That this work could be seen at the time as setting a dangerous precedent gives it a significance in the development of the twentieth-century concerto, with its emphasis on balance and restraint.

By the time of the concerto's debut, Saint-Saëns had virtually abandoned work on *Samson et Dalila.* A second attempt at his home to arouse interest in the fragments so far written, with Augusta Holmes singing Delilah, Regnault as Samson and Romain Bussine, Regnault's music teacher, as the High Priest, again met with indifference, and the manuscript was put away in a drawer with that of *Le Timbre d'Argent.*

Samson's hour lay in the future but its partial composition at this time nevertheless marks an important stylistic departure, in the evocation of its eastern setting. The oriental touches that accompany Delilah's arias are among Saint-Saëns's first essays in this genre, taking up a thread that runs through French art from the early years of the century. Among those pursuing the theme were people close to his experience: Ingres in painting, Hugo in poetry (his *Les Orientales* was published in 1829), Félicien David in music and Bizet (with *Les Pêcheurs de Perles*) in opera. Its treatment in art was to become more strongly developed as the century progressed and the French overseas empire expanded, creating a growing interest in and fashion for what were imagined to be the exotic sounds, perfumes and colours, and other sensuous delights of the East.

Later, Saint-Saëns was able to use authentic eastern melodies collected on his travels as a basis for certain compositions, but at this relatively early stage, when he had not yet travelled outside Europe, he had of necessity to rely on second-hand material and his own imagination. Turning from *Samson*, he explored oriental styles instead in a piece for military band, *Orient et Occident* in which, as the title suggests, they are contrasted with themes of a more familiar western shape. Otherwise, his oriental works for orchestra date from the 1880s onwards, when he began to collect and study eastern and North African folk melody at first hand on a regular basis. From the late 1860s he was concerned mainly with creating an oriental atmosphere for sung texts that specifically required it, as in the superb *Mélodies persanes* of 1870, six songs to poems by a minor writer, Armand Renaud. They mark the crowning point in a vocal output that began in the 1840s and was soon to come to a temporary halt as he became almost exclusively concerned with larger forms. These delicious songs, inhabiting a world of gorgeous palaces, scents, spices, luxuries and wild, opium-induced fantasies, imbued throughout with an aura of dark mystery, are each dedicated to a different friend or acquaintance. 'La brise', an invitation to the dreamer, belongs to Pauline Viardot, and Regnault's song is a sabre-rattling evocation of the bloodthirsty intentions of a conqueror, in declamatory style. The song dedicated to Augusta Holmes – perhaps with suggestive intent – is a song of unrequited love, in which, after a central section in $\frac{7}{4}$ time, the lonely girl declares her fate to be bound up with that of the brave young hunter who is the object of her passion. But perhaps closest to the composer's soul is the sentiment expressed in the especially beautiful song of love and death, 'Au cimetière': he who has loved carries the memory of it into death, but he who has not feels only the emptiness of a lost life. The song has a gentle, lilting pathos, from a man in his mid-thirties who had still not known a steady relationship and may have wondered if he ever would, or indeed was capable of one. Again, as in the slow movement of the third piano concerto, the tender passions go hand in hand with darker thoughts.

Fascination with the Orient is further expressed in another song of the period, 'Désir de l'Orient', to Saint-Saëns's own words. However, one of the last products of the first great songwriting period which ended in 1871 shows the composer also indulging a taste for another part of the world. The duet 'El Desdichado' is one of the earliest works to sing of Spain, a country with which Saint-Saëns was to have a long love affair, fostered in part by his association with Sarasate and also by his own travels. Like Bizet, and later other French composers, he was to write a number of works of a Spanish flavour, and in 'El Desdichado' this trans-Pyrenees axis, as it were, is neatly reflected in the use of both French and Spanish words, and in the fact that it was written for Claudie and Marianne Viardot, whose celebrated mother was Spanish.

The year 1870, destined to end in national disaster, began promisingly enough. As so often in Saint-Saëns's early career, encouraging developments came from the German states, where Liszt was organising performances of *Les*

Noces de Prométhée in Weimar and Jena, writing that rehearsals were going well but that "we shall have to see about the four harps, saxophones, etc".[62] Saint-Saëns joined Liszt in a two-piano recital during the Beethoven centenary festival in Weimar, and afterwards casually mentioned that he was writing an opera about Samson and Delilah, but that no one was interested. Liszt urged him to finish it, promising – without having heard a note of the opera – to have it performed in Weimar, where he had been court music director for eleven years and still wielded considerable influence.[63]

At home, more encouragement to persist with *Samson* came from Georges Hartmann, publisher of several of Saint-Saëns's early works and a rare supporter of new music. There was, too, a new approach for *Le Timbre d'Argent* but this soon looked like another false hope. Camille du Locle, Perrin's nephew, who had joined the management at the Opéra-Comique, made an offer for the work but then asked for changes to it which Barbier and Carré were again reluctant to make. To complicate matters, the librettists then quarrelled among themselves. With one living in Paris and the other in the country, Saint-Saëns spent much of the early summer travelling back and forth trying to get the two men to agree. Just when a breakthrough looked imminent, external events conspired to delay even further the long-sought operatic debut. A diplomatic row over the succession to the Spanish throne marked a new low in French relations with Prussia, and war was in the air.

VI • PATRIOT

APART FROM THE PERSONAL LOSSES, SACRIFICES AND DISRUPTION THAT war inevitably brings, the Franco-Prussian conflict of 1870–71 left its mark on Saint-Saëns in three distinct but interrelated ways. First, the accompanying burst of nationalistic fervour brought to a head his long-felt need – already sharpened by the death of Berlioz – to raise the status of French music and rid it finally of a sense of inferiority and indebtedness to both Italian and German culture. Second, the war left him with a dislike and distrust of Germany and the Germans that was to intensify into his old age but was by no means shared by most other French musicians. It was a sad irony that this antipathy was thus to alienate him both from many of his own countrymen and from the nation that had premièred some of his works, had early appreciated his worth as a composer and was in many ways his spiritual progenitor.

Third, and on a more personal level, the war soured relations with Wagner. These had already taken a downward turn when Saint-Saëns attended the première of *Das Rheingold* in the autumn of 1869 and that of *Die Walküre* the following summer, neither of which had been authorised by Wagner, who did his best to persuade his friends to stay away from them. He was clearly angry at those who ignored his pleas, and Saint-Saëns's declaration that he counted himself privileged to be alive to hear two such great works did little to help the situation. Relations were already delicate, therefore, when he set out with other French Wagnerians, including Catulle and Judith Mendès and the young composer Henri Duparc, to visit the house at Triebschen, near Lucerne, where Wagner was living with Liszt's daughter, von Bülow's estranged wife Cosima. They arrived on the evening of 19th July 1870 – hours after France declared war. Because of the political situation Wagner had tried to put the visitors off, and Cosima (who was to marry him a month later) agreed that "to see a Frenchman now would be very unpleasant". But they could hardly turn them away. "Feelings of great embarrassment, though the dear people are friendly", Cosima wrote in her diary after their arrival.[1]

The embarrassment was compounded by the fact that the French minister announcing the declaration of war was Cosima's brother-in-law Emile Ollivier, who, in his own words, took responsibility for the coming conflict "with a light heart". Conversation on the whole steered clear of politics, and Wagner kept his bitter anti-French diatribes for later occasions, but Cosima could not help having her say about what she felt was the injustice of the French action. She does not mention Saint-Saëns by name in her diary entries for 19th–20th July: the conductor Hans Richter remembered that the visiting composer accompanied Wagner "very well" in act two of *Die Walküre,* parts of *Siegfried* and the Norns scene from *Götterdämmerung.*[2] It was the last time the two men were in harmony, for their friendship, already undermined, was soon to be irrevocably broken on the wheel of rival nationalisms.

Saint-Saëns left for home the next day, encountering some delay at a border on full alert. Life in Paris in the early days of the war went on much as usual, but news of one defeat after another cast a lengthening shadow as the national mood changed from heady optimism to sombre anxiety. In September, Napoleon III surrendered at Sedan, the Germans surrounded Paris, a republic was declared, and Saint-Saëns, following Bizet's example, joined the Parisian militia, the National Guard, ready to play his part in the defence of his native city. As a member of the fourth battalion, the Seine, his main duty was patrolling the ramparts and keeping an eye on the encircling enemy. When the Germans finally decided to bombard the city in January, the screams of passing shells provided him with the diversion of noting their musical pitch. Otherwise, with the requisitioning of most theatres for hospital use, music became a matter of morale-boosting and fund-raising for the war effort. He organised a concert at the Palais Royal in aid of Geneva Cross ambulances, and on 3rd November played the organ in Cherubini's Requiem. "As his concluding voluntary he played the *Triumphal March* [?] of Beethoven", *Le Soir* reported. "May this fine composition be the prelude to the impending success of our armies."[3] He had written a cantata, called *Chants de Guerre,* for a benefit concert organised by Perrin three days later, but it was rejected and he rewrote it for orchestra as the *Marche Héroïque,* giving the first performance, in uniform, in a two-piano version at a charity concert in the Grand Hotel. The march's flag-waving exuberance, tempered by an air of nobility, is interrupted by a slower, more reflective episode introduced (in the full orchestral version) by solo trombone. The slow, broad triple time of this interlude gives slightly too much weight to the centre of the piece, but this did not prevent the *Marche Héroïque* from becoming a popular concert item for years to come.

Saint-Saëns suffered his greatest personal loss of the war as the conflict drew to a close. He was at his billet in the Hall of Industry when Clairin brought the news that Regnault had been shot in the head while on patrol on the outskirts of Paris, where he was found, face down, by an ambulance team. The armistice was signed on 28th January, the day after Saint-Saëns played the organ for the funeral at St Augustin. He included the song 'Au Cimetière' from the *Mélodies Persanes,* and later dedicated the *Marche Héroïque* to Regnault's memory. The extent to which he was affected by the artist's death can be judged from the mystical significance he attached to it. In later life he told of two ill omens. He last saw Regnault, he said, "starting for drill with his rifle in hand", leaving an unfinished water-colour still wet on the easel. Just before going out, Regnault wiped with saliva a shapeless spot at the bottom of the picture and tapped it; the composer was astonished to see what looked like a lion's head emerge from it.[4] Later that day the composer was dining with comrades at an advance post when he heard an unearthly chanting of a theme he was later to use in his Requiem. He learned afterwards that Regnault had been killed at the very same moment. (He told this story years later to the astronomer Camille Flammarion, a student of the supernatural, who retold it after Saint-Saëns's death to illustrate his theory of 'spirit activities'.)[5]

The defeat of France brought about the final break with Wagner. The last straw was the notorious farce *A Capitulation*, written by Wagner in twisted celebration of the French defeat, in which he heaped ridicule on the French nation – whose soldiers are portrayed as cancan dancers – and on French artists, including Saint-Saëns's idol Victor Hugo. It was an outpouring of anti-French bitterness that undoubtedly stemmed from Wagner's past failures in gaining a foothold in the Parisian theatre, and in particular the fiasco of the *Tannhäuser* production at the Opéra in 1861, withdrawn after three performances because of the disruption led by the young, aristocratic and boisterous members of the Jockey Club. It can be argued that Wagner meant by the capitulation of the title not that of the French to the German army but that of German writers, artists and musicians to the delights and splendours of Parisian life. Saint-Saëns did not see it that way: *A Capitulation* was an insult to his country and he never forgave its author. Although he continued to recognise the musical genius he had been one of the first to champion, the personal relationship was over and he never shared in the starry-eyed worship that had so many Wagnerians in thrall. Disenchanted with the man and sickened by the philosophy, he was left with a clear-headed objectivity in appraising the music, with no illusions about the Wagner 'religion'. For his part, Wagner became ever more contemptuous of the Frenchman whose musicality and technique had so impressed him. His high praises of these qualities, quoted earlier, are deflated by one of the most withering putdowns ever penned by one composer about another: "I afterwards learned that his stupendous receptivity for all the technical material of a work was not accompanied by any corresponding intensity of productive power, so that when he tried to set up as a composer I quite lost sight of him . . ."[6]

In the wake of military defeat – its humiliation rubbed in by the Germans' triumphal parade through Paris on 1st March – came an urgent need to rebuild national pride, and Saint-Saëns played his part with a determined effort to set up at last a new society to promote the works of living French composers, to provide that ready platform so long denied them and generally to raise the standard of French music. He had before him the example of his Russian colleague Anton Rubinstein, who had helped found the Russian Musical Society in the 1860s, and ideas were discussed with interested parties at his now-resumed Monday evening gatherings. Final plans were drawn up in collaboration with the Conservatoire professor Romain Bussine, and the National Music Society was set up on 25th February 1871, at the house of Henri Duparc, the junior member of the group. Bussine was president, Saint-Saëns vice-president and the young composer Alexis de Castillon was secretary. Saint-Saëns had met Castillon at the home of a family friend – the same friend who had offered to play his childhood piano pieces nearly thirty years before. Other composers on the first committee included Fauré, Franck (though not yet a French citizen), Edouard Lalo and Ernest Guiraud, with the organist and choirmaster Théodore Dubois. 'Ars Gallica' was the society's motto, and however much the founding musicians may have differed in artistic outlook and aims, they were united in the cause of making the music of living French composers more widely known and appreciated. They were to act "in brotherly love, with complete forgetfulness of self", according to the constitution, which included the aim of encouraging "all musical endeavour, whatever form it may take, on condition that there is evidence of high, artistic aspiration on the part of the author".[7] This condition was to assume ever greater import for Saint-Saëns, as "musical endeavour", in his view, increasingly failed to satisfy it.

The ink was hardly dry on the statutes launching the new society when politics again overshadowed art, to delay the inaugural concert by nine months. In March left-wing battalions of the National Guard seized control of Paris, declaring the rule of the Commune and opening the prospect of a terror to match that of 1793. The capital was again surrounded, this time by troops of the unseated government based at Versailles. Although at first Parisian life remained largely unaffected by the revolutionary regime and the siege – far less so than during the war – Saint-Saëns, as a former member of one of the bourgeois, 'loyalist' sections of the National Guard, felt himself to be in some danger, and it seemed advisable to join those citizens already leaving Paris in their thousands.

He was reluctant to abandon his mother and great-aunt to possible danger, but they urged him to go, arguing hopefully that they would be spared any violence because of their age. As the political situation deteriorated, he wrote to London offering his services to concert organisers there and, with a heavy heart, finally took his leave of the two women. The very next day all roads and railways out of Paris were closed. Soon after the capital was bombarded and invaded by the Versaillais, the barricades were up, public buildings set on fire and more than twenty thousand people killed. They included the Archbishop of Paris and the Abbé Deguerry, Saint-Saëns's colleague at the Madeleine, held hostage and shot by the Communards. As war had fanned a forceful nationalism in Saint-Saëns, so the Commune, in addition to stories of the ruin suffered by great-aunt Charlotte's family in the terror of eighty years before, did much to shape his political conservatism, his distrust of left-wing movements and later his contempt for trade unionism.

He arrived in London with limited funds and no prearranged work, as his attempts to secure engagements had fallen victim to a disrupted post. At last, after several weeks of living off extra funds borrowed from fellow exiles, he was invited by the Musical Union to play in a matinée concert at the St James's Hall on 6th June. The programme included Mozart's G minor piano quartet, and several solo pieces: Chopin's F major waltz, a mazurka and a gavotte of his own and his transcription of the Dervishes' chorus and dance from Beethoven's *Ruins of Athens*, all played, according to the *Musical Standard*, "in a most finished style".[8] He was delighted to find that the Musical Union's principal cellist was fellow countryman Jules Lasserre, originally from Fauré's home town of Tarbes, who became principal cellist with Pasdeloup's Concerts Populaires and left for England at the end of the 1860s.

In fact, Saint-Saëns could take comfort from contact with a sizeable community of French expatriates, some of them old friends. Pauline Viardot was lodging at 30 Devonshire Street, where the traditional soirées and charades were resumed with gusto, Saint-Saëns extemporising suitable accompaniment on the piano and donning bonnet and blond tresses for his celebrated rendition of Marguerite's 'Jewel Song'. (He was able to refresh his memory of Mme Carvalho's singing for she too was in London.) There was also a double act with Turgenev as a surgeon, playing at dissecting the horizontal 'corpse' presented by the composer in flesh-coloured tights. Gounod, also in exile, was another regular providing music for these gatherings, which attracted a variety of literary and artistic figures, among them Henry James and C. E. Hallé, son of the founder of the Hallé Orchestra. Hallé relates that "Gounod and Mme Viardot would sing and improvise waltzes for four hands for the rest of us to dance to" and recalled one particular charade, of which

the subject was Daphne flying from the advances of Apollo, who rose in the character of the sun behind Mount Olympus. Mme Viardot was Daphne, Manuel Garcia (her brother), with his cheeks puffed out and the rays of the sun in gilt paper round his head, was Apollo. Turgenev, who was very large, was the mountain, and Gounod did the incidental music.[9]

Gounod allowed Saint-Saëns to make some money by agreeing to his writing a 'paraphrase' for piano of his cantata *Gallia*, one of the works that opened the new Albert Hall that spring. Gounod's cantata had been well-received, and Saint-Saëns, delighted that a French work could make such an impact at a time of national humiliation, wrote to his mother after the performance that "France is avenged!"[10] His piano version demonstrates his exceptional ability, noted by Wagner and others, to reproduce on the piano the essential character and quality of a work, with all its various nuances. Reviewing the piece, the *Musical Times* said that "the salient portions of the composition are displayed with such effect as to convey to the stranger a very good notion of the entire work . . .Were all 'paraphrases' as good as this we should have nothing whatever to say against this class of composition."[11]

He sold the Paraphrase on *Gallia* to Novello's together with two other piano pieces, and earned extra cash by writing songs, including a setting of Tennyson's 'A Voice by the Cedar Tree', which he sold to Boosey and Hawkes. Another performing engagement came from George Grove, founder of the musical dictionary, who, as a director of the Crystal Palace in Sydenham, invited him to play the organ there. His recital on 24th June included the *Trois Rapsodies sur des Cantiques Bretons*, and a prelude and fugue by Bach which was ruined, much to his annoyance, by an obstinate cipher on the instrument. The performance as a whole introduced English audiences to an unfamiliar style of organ playing. The *Musical Standard* reported that "M. Saint-Saëns possesses great command of the organ but some of his combinations sounded very strange to English ears".[12] The ten guineas he received for the recital made him feel positively well-off, so that on meeting Romain Cornut, the young poet of *Les Noces de Promethée*, similarly exiled but also penniless, he was able to treat him to lunch.

It is perhaps understandable that Saint-Saëns should have remembered the early summer of 1871 as the date of his first visit to London, rather than the autumn of 1862, because it was this latest visit that gave him the contacts that were to lay the basis of his fame and reputation in England. But in July, with links to Paris restored after the suppression of the Commune and the confirmation of the Third Republic, he headed for home, making his way among scenes of destruction to 168 Rue du Faubourg St Honoré, where, in a joyful reunion, he was relieved to find both his mother and great-aunt unharmed and in good spirits.

The high water mark of anti-German feeling in the post-war period did not immediately bring the long-awaited opportunity for French composers that might have been expected. Pasdeloup had revived his Concerts Populaires on 19th June with an announcement that he would not play another note of German music, but even the strongly nationalistic Saint-Saëns knew that this was "absurd and impracticable". The Austro-German classics continued to provide the staple fare in programmes, with only an occasional outing for French works, including the first orchestral performance of the *Marche Héroïque* on 10th December 1871. Only Wagner was banned, temporarily. Still, as Saint-Saëns appreciated, even an occasional outing was better than nothing: if Pasdeloup "was not able to make Beethoven responsible for the loss of Alsace, he was able to put his orchestra at the disposal of French composers".[13]

As a performer, Saint-Saëns's willingness to give concerts in the new German Empire was not likely to win approval amid the intensity of hatred for the former enemy. In the summer he appeared at Baden-Baden, where Mme Viardot had a villa, and for this was expelled from the Society of Authors, the professional body for writers and artists. Unruffled, he continued to perform wherever and whenever he could, subject to duties at the Madeleine and his concern for his ageing mother and great-aunt. In August he returned to London to help inaugurate the newly completed organ of the Albert Hall, his recital forming part of a series by specially-invited foreign organists, among them Anton Bruckner, whom he had first heard and praised in Paris in 1869. His programme included, in transcription, extracts from Gounod's *Faust*, the *March Héroïque*, selections from his *Oratorio de Noël*, and the *Trois Rapsodies*, as well as his arrangement of Liszt's 'St Francis Preaching to the Birds', in which, reported *The Orchestra* magazine, "with the rendering of the chattering and flitting of birds and the old prophet tones of the Saint, the effect was most marvellous". The journal hailed him as a foremost practitioner of a new, more colourful and varied style of organ playing that had been made possible by the technical innovations of Cavaillé-Coll, producing a wealth of sound which, as the *Musical Standard* had noted, was unfamiliar to English ears.[14]

But while he was always prepared to travel abroad to concerts, it was at home in Paris where, in the words of Jean Bonnerot, his first biographer, he "rediscovered his honour, strength and conscience".[15] He was beginning to be engaged as a soloist on a regular basis by the Conservatoire Concerts Society, but that bastion of conservatism was still, for the time being, less receptive to him as a composer. In the autumn he submitted a symphony "of modest proportions" (probably the A minor) and the vocal score of a cantata, of which, he modestly suggested, "some fragments will perhaps be able to find a place in one of the society's spiritual concerts". He explained that the cantata's "primitive orchestration" was designed for performance in church – it had, of course, been written for the Madeleine – so would have to be modified for concert performance.[16] Nothing seems to have come from this approach, but he had at least put his career as a composer on a more stable basis by signing a publishing contract with his old Conservatoire classmate Auguste Durand. The *Marche Héroïque* was the first of his works to be taken by the young firm; Durand also received the rights of those of Saint-Saëns's works already published by Hartmann, who had decided to develop his Massenet list instead. It was not always to be an easy relationship between the composer and his publisher. There would be many a row, with Saint-Saëns threatening to take his work elsewhere, but these were always resolved and he remained with the firm of Durand for the rest of his life.

As the opera houses reopened in the autumn of 1871, Saint-Saëns reminded du Locle about his interest in *Le Timbre d'Argent.* The director shrank from accepting a full-scale work, but suggested a one-act piece instead, and introduced the composer to a librettist who was to prove a valued mainstay over the next thirty years, a partner in the struggle for operatic honours. Louis Gallet, a hospital bursar, was a compulsive writer whose *Djamileh*, an oriental tale of love and deception, was being set at this time by Bizet. In him Saint-Saëns was convinced that he had at last found his ideal collaborator, "the sort I had always dreamed of meeting but never dared hope I would". Gallet "understood music and criticised with good taste". There was a bond of sympathy between the two men: they lived in the same street and met almost every day, the composer recalled, "bombarding each other with fanciful sonnets, whimsical stanzas and extravagant drawings". Like Saint-Saëns, Gallet had practical common sense while being "alert to everything unusual and interesting": in all he was to write some fifty opera librettos, as well as plays, romances, public speeches, memoirs, pamphlets and articles, as prolific in words as Saint-Saëns was in music. He was also a skilled painter, and helped to paint many opera sets. The composer appreciated the partnership with Gallet because, "drawing from a background of surprising richness, he added to the fantasies of my imagination elements of solidity without which they would have been deficient".[17]

Yet in hindsight, Gallet is now seen as being far from an ideal librettist, his work for the theatre lacking dramatic sense and action. Winton Dean, in his biography of Bizet, writes that "he thought more of poetry and atmosphere than of the stage".[18] It can be argued then that Saint-Saëns had misjudged his man, blinded perhaps by his sympathy, liveliness and productivity, and that Gallet, because of this static quality in his librettos, contributed to the composer's ultimate failure in opera.

For their first collaboration, the two men decided to take advantage of a taste for everything Japanese that had followed the first contacts of the West with Japan in the 1850s. The result was *La Princesse Jaune*, a light opera for just two singers that exploits to the full the popular perception at the time of Japan as a picturesque Pacific island of strange, exotic images and quaint, mediaeval customs. Kornélis, a Dutch scientist, is transported to this fantastic country in a drug-induced haze, and imagines himself in love with an oriental princess who in reality is a Japanese figurine. As in *Le Timbre d'Argent*, the story is finally revealed as a figment of the imagination, but here the light-hearted character of the piece softens the let-down. It appealed to Saint-Saëns's sense of fun, his taste for the bizarre and his growing interest in the oriental, and it afforded the new departure of specifically 'Japanese-style' music, as imagined by Western ears, thirteen years before *The Mikado*. He thought of incorporating the music for his recently written song 'Désir de l'Orient' but abandoned this idea in favour of a completely fresh approach, and produced a score that is full of dainty touches and an ethereal lightness skilfully created by understatement, and couched in orchestral colours that have all the lacquered finesse of painted porcelain. These qualities are notably demonstrated in the beautifully crafted overture, a masterpiece of delicacy and precision which, as so often with Saint-Saëns, seems to be exactly the right length with not a single superfluous note.

While preparations for *La Princesse Jaune* were set in motion at the Opéra-Comique, Saint-Saëns turned his attention to the interrupted proceedings of the National Music Society, which gave its first concert on 17th November, at the Salle Pleyel. The event, he declared, was "a great success".[19] The society at its inception had about 150 members – composers, performers and interested listeners – whose average age was just above thirty. This number quickly grew as more concerts followed, with Massenet and Bizet among the new recruits. Programmes were decided at Bussine's house on Sundays, where composers played their works in piano reduction. Performers gave their services free, and the Pleyel and Erard piano companies allowed the use of their halls. Concerts, at least in the early days, consisted chiefly of chamber works, stimulating a flowering of interest in this medium that had been growing throughout the previous two decades. Thus was answered Blanchard's call of 1856, for French composers to take the opportunity afforded by this chamber music revival to unseat the German tradition, which he saw as having no living representative since the death of Mendelssohn (at the time, Schumann was a modern who could not be taken seriously, and Brahms was still virtually unknown). When Fauré's first violin sonata was played at the society in 1877, Saint-Saëns hailed it as a genuinely native work that had finally "defeated" the German school, and, looking back, recognised the chamber revival as the backbone of the resurgence of French music in the last third of the nineteenth century.[20]

His own debut at a National Society concert, however, was not with a chamber work but with an orchestral one, *Le Rouet d'Omphale,* a symphonic poem that marked the beginning of an astonishingly creative decade, even by his standards, and ushered in a new phase both in his own music and in that of his country.

VII • SYMPHONIC POET

IT IS MISLEADING TO SUPPOSE, AS IT OFTEN IS, THAT SAINT-SAËNS introduced the symphonic poem into France. The term was coined by Liszt to describe his fourteen orchestral pieces inspired by literature; but the type, which has its origins in the opera overture, was already present in France long before *Le Rouet d'Omphale*. Berlioz wrote his early orchestral fantasy on Shakespeare's *The Tempest* (later incorporated into the monologue *Lélio*) in 1829, and the individual movements of his programme symphonies could be regarded as prototype symphonic poems in their own right. Franck wrote an orchestral work, *Ce qu'on entend sur la montagne*, inspired by a poem of Victor Hugo, in 1848. These works are non-operatic expressions of a strong literary and pictorial undercurrent that runs through French music throughout the nineteenth century, but as the audiences hearing Saint-Saëns's work in 1872 were still largely ignorant of both Berlioz and Franck, let alone Liszt, they missed this deeper significance.

Le Rouet d'Omphale was first heard in a two-piano version at the Salle Erard on 7th December 1871, Castillon partnering Saint-Saëns after Augusta Holmes, to whom the work is dedicated, pulled out. Fauré was his partner for the National Society's Sunday evening hearing before the first orchestral performance in January. Audiences, however prepared they might have been for a new beginning in French music, did not know what to make of it. And those patrons of Pasdeloup's Concerts Populaires less committed to the national musical renaissance were quite baffled. Here was Saint-Saëns, the innovator and champion of the vanguard, taking another new and unfamiliar path. In time, *Le Rouet d'Omphale* won recognition in France for the symphonic poem as a form and, its antecedents largely unheard of, came to be regarded as the first of those descriptive works that constitute a staple commodity in French music of the late nineteenth and early twentieth centuries, a form developed by Franck, d'Indy, Chausson, Dukas and others, and taken further by Debussy.

The symphonic poem is one of the most characteristic creations of the romantic age, and in embracing it Saint-Saëns was taking another, more radical departure from his classical base. But just as he saw no contradiction in his admiration for both Hugo and Racine, so he saw none between this homage to Liszt and his upholding of classical values. In fact, his four symphonic poems, written in the six years to 1877 in a decade that saw the production of some of his finest works, are very much cast in his own distinctive mould. They are not mere imitations of those of his hero but modified in design and language according to his acute sense of proportion, line and taste – with varying degrees of success. He defined the Lisztian symphonic poem as "an ensemble of different movements depending on each other, proceeding from a fundamental idea and connected together in one piece. The plan of a musical poem thus understood can be varied indefinitely."[1] His own works in this form are much more concisely crafted, following his tendency towards compaction already demonstrated in the concertos. Of his symphonic poems only the last, *La Jeunesse d'Hercule*, is longer than fifteen minutes; the rest are under ten. The material is generally less diffuse, more tightly constructed, than in the Liszt works, and the transformation of a theme to express different poetic ideas and characteristics, a principal feature of the Lisztian model, is less evident than a more conventional variation or development.

Le Rouet d'Omphale is in a straightforward ABA form, the agitated struggle of the central section providing a contrast with the playfulness on either side. Its subject has a personal as well as a musical significance. In choosing the legend of Omphale as retold by Victor Hugo, Saint-Saëns returns to the theme, already approached in *Samson et Dalila*, of the hero laid low by feminine wiles, and there is an almost mischievous irony in the dedication to Augusta Holmes, whose beauty, tantalisingly out of reach, seemed to make a mockery of all his intellectual accomplishments. Hercules is the fallen hero here, sold as a slave to the Queen of Lydia, who becomes his lover on condition that he dresses as one of her waiting women and joins them at her feet spinning thread.

Saint-Saëns read the story in Hugo's *Contemplations*, and was reminded of it when he saw, first, a spinning wheel in a friend's house and, later, a painting in an artist's studio of a voluptuous Venus. The result was a brilliant piece of orchestral writing in which the queen's coquettish charms, represented mainly by woodwind, are intertwined with the silken swiftness of the wheel as played on the strings to weave a pulsating web of seductiveness. The music has a relentless forward drive that carries the spell into the middle section, ever present as, on the brass, the muscular exertions of the strong man to break free from his degradation increase in desperation and despair. They give way to a mocking parody on the oboe as Omphale laughs at his efforts, and the spinning resumes, subsiding at last in a beguiling diminuendo which leaves the violins, alone, high in the upper register.

Saint-Saëns described the idea behind the work as "feminine seduction, the triumph of weakness over strength". Yet, ever practical and down-to-earth, he does not here allow extra-musical ideas to override purely musical considerations. His approach to programme music was to use literature as a starting point: once it had served its purpose in prompting orchestral patterns, the finished work stood or fell according to strictly musical criteria of form and colour. The spinning wheel, for instance, was "chosen only for the sake of rhythm, and to give a special character to the piece".[2] He was not a man to be unduly swayed by poetry and drama: he could not be struck as by a thunderbolt, as Berlioz was by Shakespeare. He considered that Berlioz was "too fond of Shakespeare" for his own good, and, unlike many nineteenth-century composers (including Liszt) had no interest in the Bard from the point of view of purely instrumental music (leaving aside his earlier flirtation with *Macbeth* as an opera), preferring instead to draw inspiration from classical antiquity. The wide-ranging, epic nature of Shakespeare's dramas made them entirely unsuitable for translation into musical forms that satisfied Saint-Saëns's instinct for shape and proportion. Otherwise he saw no reason why suitable literature should not provide a basis for composition as long as the result was good music. In the controversy that raged at the time about the relative merits of programme and 'absolute' music, he could not accept that the former was necessarily inferior. "Many things have been written on this subject which I find impossible to understand. Is the music in itself good or bad? Everything lies there. Whether it has a programme or not, it will neither be better nor worse."[3] *Le Rouet d'Omphale* could be heard with or without knowledge of the story behind it. Interviewed many years later by the American critic Philip Hale, the composer asked: "Do you hear Hercules groaning in rage? You are welcome to the pleasure, if you hear him. Is the oboe the mocking voice of Omphale? It is as you please." And Hale adds: "He smiles as he speaks; if one cries out against his cynicism he smiles the more."[4]

Just over a week after the first orchestral performance of *Le Rouet d'Omphale* on 18th January, Saint-Saëns's first teacher and 'second mother' died at the age of ninety-one. Great-aunt Charlotte was active and alert almost to the end, and he was unprepared for her loss. It was a shattering blow. From his birth she had been his guide, his advisor, his mentor, one of the twin pillars of his domestic and working life. Her death made him more dependent than ever on the other pillar of emotional and material support, his mother. Now sixty-three, she began to accompany him more frequently to his concerts as well as continuing to play hostess at his Monday soirées. He cancelled all concert engagements for a month after Charlotte's death but then took on a punishing work schedule to take his mind off his grief. There was work as organist at the Madeleine, work for the National Society, work as pianist at recitals and concerts. On 10th March he gave the first performance of Castillon's piano concerto at a Concert Populaire under Pasdeloup, a riotous affair as the piece was greeted with boos and catcalls almost from the beginning. Pasdeloup wanted to stop, but Saint-Saëns signalled to him to continue and soloist and conductor carried on through the mounting din to the end, Saint-Saëns throwing the audience black looks along the way and shouting to them in his shrill voice that the players were determined to finish the performance whatever the protests.[5] The experience was proof that in the aftermath of war Paris audiences outside the National Society were not necessarily disposed to be more sympathetic to new French works.

Composition was another natural means of solace. Saint-Saëns's only published work for the cello as a solo instrument since the childhood lessons with Franchomme had taught him its richly lyrical potential had been the suite of 1862. His feeling for the cello, with its deep, dark tone and capacity for both dignified and impassioned utterance, was now rekindled by the melancholy that set in after his bereavement. Prompted also by his acquaintance with Auguste Tolbecque, professor of cello at the Marseilles Conservatoire, and with Jules Lasserre, it resulted in the C minor sonata and the A minor concerto, written within a short time of each other. It is even possible that he worked on them at the same time, but although both works are in minor keys their form and character are quite distinct. The sonata is a mainly turbulent work, suggesting feelings of unease and intimations of insecurity that can come with the loss of a close relative, while turbulence is only incidental to the concerto, whose overall mood is one of calm reflection after the opening squall. The three-movement sonata is conventional in form while the concerto is another essay in condensation on the lines of the A major violin concerto.

The story of the composition of the cello sonata shows the strong influence that Mme Saint-Saëns had over her son. The new work was tried out on guests at a Monday evening soirée, and was enthusiastically applauded. But the composer's mother had other ideas: the finale was "worthless", she told him. He wished her goodnight, said no more of the sonata, and for the next ten days shut himself away, appearing only for meals. He then played his mother a new finale, which she approved: and this is the one that has been played ever since. The original was destroyed. The conventionality of the sonata is almost severe, with its outer movements both in strict sonata form – quite a reaction against previous experiments in telescoping. There is also a reaction against a previous lightness of texture: thick, heavy chords and striding triplets abound in a mood of passionate grandeur, emphasised by firm closes in the minor key. (The concerto in contrast ends in the major.) It is as if the insistence on a rigid structure is a device to counterbalance these outpourings and contain them within a formal discipline. Frequent chromatic juxtaposition heightens the conflict. The first movement's second subject is a contrasting soft passage of piano chords hovering over the cello's broken fifths in the bass, but its first appearance in D flat major, a chromatic shift up from the home key, makes it an uneasy calm. The genuine respite comes in the andante tranquillo, in the relative major. The chorale-like theme is taken in turns by piano and cello over staccato accompaniment and there is a sombre reminder of C minor in a subsidiary theme, again carried alternately by the two instruments. A central episode toys with the main subject in semiquavers before the piano restores it in shimmering broken chords.

If the chief hallmark of the sonata is dramatic tension, that of the concerto is melodic abundance. Wealth of melody combined with a lack of formal correctness of the kind imposed on the sonata gives the concerto the character more of a concert fantasy, and it is no surprise that it came to be referred to – like that earlier experiment in abbreviated form, the A major violin concerto – as a concert piece. Formal analysis is of a single movement in three sections: an exposition and development, an allegretto, and a finale which recapitulates the opening theme but substitutes new material for the second subject. The ritornello-style passage that closes the exposition – a curiously starchy episode in marked contrast to the melting lyricism around it – returns to signal the end of the whole work, which is rounded off by a coda in the major.

From this purely formal point of view the concerto appears somewhat unbalanced, as the last section is twice as long as the two previous sections combined. The listener has the impression less of shape than of a succession of themes and moods, a kind of musical tableau. If the cello sonata displays an unusual degree of emotional intensity, the cello concerto, with its rich lyricism, provides an unusual case of content outweighing form. But that does not prevent it from being one of Saint-Saëns's most appealing works. He achieves a satisfying balance between soloist and orchestra and the haunting otherworldliness that characterises so many of his melodies is here strongly felt. The second subject, which reappears in the development virtually unmodified and in the same key, and which does not survive beyond the first section, seems to rise from the depths, as does the second new theme of the finale, an ascending succession of crotchets. The upward movement of these two melodies contrasts both with the downward rushing triplets of the principal subject and with the drooping melancholy of the finale's other main theme.

The allegretto, which in piano reduction came to be a favourite salon piece in its own right, is a delicate minuet on muted staccato strings that suggests a ghostly evocation of an eighteenth-century drawing room, rather like the slow movement of the A minor symphony but with the composer commenting on the scene from across the years in the form of a counter-theme by the soloist. If Saint-Saëns was here thinking of his beloved great-aunt and the oft-recounted days of her youth, it is a touchingly dainty tribute to her memory.

That the concerto was first performed at the Conservatoire Concerts Society, on 19th January 1873, shows the influence which the National Music Society was beginning to exert. The Conservatoire orchestra was now prepared to break from tradition to give a contemporary French work. A few months earlier Saint-Saëns had played his second piano concerto with the orchestra, but it was a singular honour to be granted a première – even though the conductor Edouard Delvedez tried to play it down by telling the composer he had programmed the cello concerto not for his benefit but out of respect for the veteran soloist, Tolbecque, then in his eighties.[6] The National Music Society had been demonstrating the worth and viability of programmes of French works, and Saint-Saëns dated the consolidation of the national musical revival to a concert midway through the society's first season, 1871–72, when the audience included, by invitation, prominent figures in French musical life. He recalled that "the effect of this concert was amazing":

The distinguished audience did not seek to hide its surprise. So it was possible then to make up an interesting programme with new compositions by French composers! Such a concert was not only possible but fascinating, even for the most difficult and biased listeners. It can be said that on that date the aim of the society was achieved and from then on French names appeared on concert programmes on which no one had previously dared allow them. The barriers had gone. The rest followed naturally and without effort.[7]

French chamber music also had additional platforms in other concert series that sprang up alongside the society, like the Daube concerts and the oddly-named Mozart Concerts, which played very little Mozart.

Pasdeloup at first remained impervious to this growing tide of national music making, and the hostile reception given to Castillon's piano concerto was hardly likely to convert him to the cause. Saint-Saëns played his second piano concerto with him on 13th December 1872, but on the whole contemporary French works remained on the sidelines at the Concerts Populaires in the first two years of peace. As well as the generally unadventurous programming, Saint-Saëns also criticised Pasdeloup's conducting, claiming that his concerts were well-regarded only because the blurring acoustics of the Cirque d'hiver covered up his inaccuracies and because there was little competition.[8] But even Pasdeloup could not ignore forever the progress being made by the National Music Society, and competition finally arrived in the forward-looking Concerts Nationals, established by Hartmann at the Odéon under the conductor Edouard Colonne. Saint-Saëns played his second piano concerto and accompanied Pauline Viardot in a Schubert song at the inaugural concert on 2nd March 1873. In response Pasdeloup began to boost the French content of his concerts – but at the same time blotted his copybook in the eyes of the nationalists by reintroducing Wagner. His performance of the *Tannhäuser* overture caused violent demonstrations, as did most subsequent Wagner performances throughout the 1870s, when the composer was still strongly associated in the popular mind with Prussian militarism. Saint-Saëns accused Pasdeloup of gross insensitivity, and even of being a German agent.[9]

Perhaps more than most of his colleagues in the National Society, he saw the musical renaissance in fiercely nationalistic terms, as a stick with which to beat what he saw as the continuing German influence on French musical life. He now had a new, powerful weapon in his armoury – journalism. From April

1872, he wrote a regular column, under the pseudonym Phémius, for a journal called *La Renaissance littéraire et artistique*, founded by a friend, Emile Blémont. Here, and elsewhere after the journal closed in December 1873, he expounded his enthusiasms and antipathies, justifying Rameau, championing Liszt, defending Bizet, and generally supporting young French composers of promise. These included Massenet, whose sacred oratorio *Marie Madeleine* was first performed on Good Friday 1873 and was described by Saint-Saëns in print as an "audacious experiment . . . full of life, love and melody".[10]

Journalism was a perfect outlet for his wide-ranging interests and intellectual independence. He produced mountains of prose about music, science, philosophy, literature and art in general, from a mind never at rest, always exploring and entirely indifferent as to whether his views won him friends or enemies. There is a lightness, clarity and wit about his writing that to an extent parallel qualities in his music and reflect his character and the high-pitched, quick-fire chatter with which he bombarded friends and colleagues. The critic Georges Servières remembered these verbal onslaughts for their "keen animation, diabolic mischievousness, railing irony and agility in leaping from one subject to another with a sprightliness of fancy that equalled the mobility of his features, which were animated at one and the same time by the most contrary expressions". Servières described the composer at this time as "of short stature. His head is extremely original, the features characteristic, a great brow, wide and open, where, between the eyebrows, the energy and tenacity of the man reveal themselves, the hair habitually cut short, a brownish beard turning grey, a nose like an eagle's beak, underlined by two deeply marked wrinkles starting from the nostrils, eyes a little prominent, very mobile, very expressive."[11]

Saint-Saëns's compulsion to work following the death of his great-aunt set a pattern for the future: work was to be his usual panacea for ills to come. As well as adding journalism to his workload, he sought also to branch out into more conducting. In May 1872, a month after taking up the pen on a regular basis, he aimed to do the same with the baton, applying for a conductorship with the Conservatoire Concerts Society. Nothing came of this, but he was to serve frequently as a competition juror in the Conservatoire's piano class and, from July 1874, for the Prix de Rome.

The greater opportunities open to French orchestral and chamber music in the 1870s were not matched in opera. There was as yet no Wagner in French theatres, but Saint-Saëns and his contemporaries still had to struggle against conservative prejudice and the lingering influence of Meyerbeer. Bizet's *Djamileh* failed at the Opéra-Comique in May-June 1872, with Saint-Saëns one of the few to leap to its defence, describing it in a sonnet to the composer as a pearl cast before swine.[12] In June came Saint-Saëns's turn for failure. On the 12th his long wait for an operatic debut finally ended when the Opéra-Comique staged *La Princesse Jaune* in a triple bill with *Djamileh* and Paladilhe's *Le Passant*. The two singers were Paul Lhérie, lately returned to the company after a quarrel four years earlier, and Alice Ducasse. During its preparation, du Locle, fearing that an all-Japanese set would be too startling, modified the design to place Kornélis in more familiar Dutch surroundings for part of the time. This concession to taste failed to save the piece: it lasted five performances, after which it disappeared from the repertory for many years.

Not for the first time, Saint-Saëns had bewildered his audience with novelty, this time by using eastern-style themes and adapting them to accepted western notions of harmony and rhythm. The line of a melody in oriental style is essentially at odds with major and minor scales, having more in common with plainchant and the ancient modes. Saint-Saëns was fascinated by this similarity, but was faced with the problem of how to create an oriental melody while providing it with a harmonic base that would be acceptable to contemporary western ears (a consideration unlikely to bother most of his modern successors). The irregular rhythms of eastern music also had to be adapted to nineteenth-century western concepts. The result is not so very startling to present-day listeners used to the oriental exoticism of the romantic era (and of the Hollywood epic) but it disconcerted the 1872 audiences for *La Princesse Jaune*, leading one critic to complain that it was impossible to tell in what key or in what time some of the music was written. The composer recorded that "this innocuous little work was received with the fiercest hostility" and denounced as incoherent and bizarre.[13] He was also at something of a disadvantage in this immediate post-war period in that he was still seen as an ardent champion of Wagner at a time of prevailing hostility to Wagner's works, when critics ever on the lookout for the faintest traces of Wagnerian influence, saw it in anything remotely strange or unusual. One of the few critics to give *La Princesse Jaune* at least qualified praise was Ernest Reyer, who called it "fine, elegant, colourful", its instrumentation "full of pretty details, ingenious couplings of sound and imitative effects that could not be done better". Far from sharing in the general bewilderment, he could see in the opera no trace of "a bold, innovative genius".[14]

Reyer was clearly in a minority, for Saint-Saëns had undoubtedly again identified himself with the vanguard, not with any imagined Wagnerisms but with the oriental elements in his opera. Orientalism was seen as a powerful source of change in music because of the challenge to conventional tonality posed by its modal basis. The Lydian mode appears in the *Breton Rapsodies*, causing *The Orchestra* magazine to observe that new departures were afoot in both playing and composition, and that "amidst all this change there is constantly turning up not so much the snatches of the old church chant as the recall to a still older period, the time of the Greek and Oriental".[15] Saint-Saëns too realised the implications for the future. Writing in 1879, he makes the assertion, bold for its time, that:

the tonality that afforded a basis for modern harmony is dying. The major and minor scales reign no longer unchallenged; the ancient modes are reasserting themselves, and then the oriental modes, in infinite variety, will invade art. All this will bring new elements to exhausted melody and a new and fertile era will open. Harmony will undergo changes; rhythm . . . will develop, and thus will a new art be born.[16]

Once again in his experience, the future of music was inextricably bound up with its past, evolving from established methods. This conviction helps to explain his fierce opposition in later years to what he saw as the revolutionary break with the past made by the impressionists and atonalists, the "infuriated boars rushing through beautiful gardens and playing havoc with the most delicate flowers",[17] even though the modal style of Debussy in fact fulfilled his prophecy about a new art, and the old tonality breathing its last.

The failure of *La Princesse Jaune* deepened the sympathy between Saint-Saëns and Bizet. Mindful of the new opportunities for orchestral music, he urged his "brother in arms", as he called him, to give up trying to make a name in the opera house, where "they don't want us", and "take refuge" in the concert halls. Bizet, however, knew his destiny: "I'm not made for symphonies, I need the theatre. I am nothing without it", a reply that points to the essential difference in outlook between the two men. Saint-Saëns loved the theatre, but needed it as much for reasons of professional advancement in a wider world of music as for reasons of artistic compulsion, and he certainly was "made for symphonies", that is, music of symphonic construction. He fondly recalled his friendship with Bizet as being based on a mutual tendency to brutal frankness about likes and dislikes, as well as to a common experience of setbacks. "Otherwise we differed completely and pursued different ideals. He sought passion and life; I ran after purity of style and perfection of form. Our friendly discussions had a liveliness and charm that I have never again found with anyone else."[18] He remained convinced that the barriers against native opera composers that stayed up well into the 1870s were a disaster for French music. "The policy imposed on Bizet and Delibes certainly deprived us of several works which would now be among the glories of the repertory at the Opéra and Opéra-Comique. That is an irreparable misfortune, one which we cannot sufficiently deplore." He suggested that the great operas of Mozart might never have been written had he had to wait so long for a first production, and "we should never have known the great days of the Italian theatre if Rossini, Donizetti, Bellini and Verdi had had to undergo our regime".[19]

In the face of this latest operatic disappointment, Saint-Saëns turned briefly to the solo song; he was drawn to the oriental and occult themes of the minor poet Henri Cazalis, a doctor by profession, who wrote under the name of Jean Lahor. His two settings of Cazalis are among the very few songs written in the decade from 1872, the second of them a bizarre piece about a churchyard at midnight where skeletons are summoned from their graves and set dancing by Death playing a fiddle. It was called 'Danse Macabre' and would eventually be transformed into the third of the symphonic poems. For his second symphonic poem, *Phaëton*, he stayed with Greek mythology, this time combining his love of classical literature with his passion for astronomy in an ancient space adventure story. Phaëton implores his father Helios, the sun god, to be allowed to drive his fiery chariot. He gets his way, but in his over-confidence loses control of the horses and comes close to colliding with the Earth. Zeus prevents a cosmic catastrophe by striking him dead with a thunderbolt. While the story produced some of the most dazzling orchestral writing Saint-Saëns ever penned, *Phaëton* is an ultimately disappointing work, the least satisfying of the symphonic poems, from the point of view of form and in part of content. He seems as carried away by his subject as Phaëton is by his horses.

The scoring is for a large orchestra, including a gong and two pairs of kettle drums. After a blazing opening on the brass, combined with a bracing upward sweep on the strings in the grand Lisztian manner, Saint-Saëns launches the chariot on its celestial ride in an extraordinarily vivid piece of imaginative writing that conveys the dizzy exhilaration of the young man on his first flight through the ether. Things then start to go wrong, for musical rather than for narrative reasons. A slow section, announced by a disappointingly weak theme on the horns, seems to serve the purely functional role of putting the breaks on the tempo, as if the chariot has suddenly stopped in mid-air. The excitement is revived in an agitated section evoking the youth's vain struggle to regain control, culminating in the thunderbolt, a triple forte for full orchestra. The work ends quietly with a rather limp valediction, softly recalling the confidence of the start. The listener is left with a feeling of anti-climax, of having been short-changed. If the rule is that the literary idea should not upset the balance of the structure, the composer comes dangerously close to losing sight of it. It is as if he has fallen between the two stools of musical story-telling and formal consistency: the result is a lop-sided work that is saved only by the heady intoxication of its opening.

Phaëton was written in 1873 at a time when Saint-Saëns's health was under mounting strain from his self-imposed workload following the death of his great-aunt. Over a year of an almost unbroken schedule of concerts and composition, as well as duties at the Madeleine, writing and private teaching began to produce alarming symptoms of the latent tuberculosis that had been a threat throughout his childhood. On medical advice he took the boat to Algeria, where it was hoped the climate would help his breathing. He spent October and November at Pointe St Eugène, just outside Algiers, at first relaxing and recuperating in the warm Mediterranean air and reviving a boyhood hobby by examining the plants in the botanic gardens. Later came walks in the countryside, where he was captivated by the "clear, transparent sky of a blueness unknown to us", by the orange trees heavy with fruit, by the distant "multi-coloured mountains" of a land where "everything breathes life, abundance and fertility".[20] It was to become a favourite place of sojourn throughout the rest of his life, affording escape from the hectic musical and social round of Paris, and the solitude he came increasingly to crave. And it was where he was to die.

He wrote poetry in this idyllic convalescence, rejoicing that "nothing happens in this place, no hostile voices to disturb the silence and its divine hymn".[21] And, after a while, he wrote music. Mindful of Liszt's promise to have *Samson et Dalila* staged at Weimar, he set to work on sketching the third act, inspired by the sights and sounds of a land so lately part of the Turkish Empire. Here for the first time he was able to hear music of an eastern culture at first hand, and from a prominent leader of the Arab community he acquired the big tune for the Philistines' bacchanal.[22]

At the end of November he returned to Paris, and what now seemed the petty squabbles of musicians and critics. *Phaëton* was given its first performance by Colonne at a Concert National on 7th December and, like *Le Rouet d'Omphale*, left its audience puzzled and divided. It was later taken up by Pasdeloup, and Saint-Saëns was fond of recounting an incident during rehearsal that neatly illustrated the veteran conductor's erratic approach and his stubborn conviction that he could do no wrong. When the composer interrupted to point out that he was taking the music too fast, Pasdeloup turned to his players and said: "Gentlemen, don't you know you are taking it too fast?"[23]

While *Phaëton* caused controversy and confusion, Saint-Saëns took satisfaction in advancing the career of his favourite protégé, Fauré, now working as a choirmaster in Paris. He had already introduced him to the influential Viardot family and from January 1874 invited him to deputise at the Madeleine during his increasingly frequent absences on concert tours. His detailed instructions as to the daily service are full of his irrepressible wit: "At the Orate fratres the organist thinks seriously of finishing. When the children in the choir fidget, the organ stops. The organist wipes his hands . . . the organist goes to lunch at Richard Lucas (a nearby restaurant)" and so on, until "after the final psalm, definitive exit". The letter is headed by a cartoon of a man at an organ that has a large rocket in place of the pipes.[24] Fauré's mother was still sending Saint-Saëns parcels of food from the countryside – in a poem fairly reeking of hyperbole he tells his young friend of a paté whose promised delights were "akin to the golden robes of the glorious Emperor of China"[25] – while Fauré was no less appreciative of Mme Saint-Saëns's cooking on his visits to 168 Rue du Faubourg St Honoré, where he was, as always, invited by her enthusiastic son to inspect the stars through his telescope.

One of the engagements that took Saint-Saëns away from the Madeleine was a London (later Royal) Philharmonic Society concert on 13th July 1874, the first of many appearances with the society. At first he offered to play one of his own concertos, but conscious of the unease his reputation for 'modernity' might cause (a reputation that *Phaëton* had done much to bolster) conceded: "If my own concerto alarms you, I shall play Beethoven." In deference also to what he thought would be English sensibilities as to the piano, but with an eye to getting his own way, he added: "I esteem Broadwood, I prefer Erard." In the event the audience at the St James's Hall heard him play Beethoven's fourth concerto – on an Erard.[26] As a composer he was to do further homage that year to Beethoven with his Variations for two pianos on the trio theme from the third movement of Beethoven's Piano Sonata op. 31 no. 3. Skilful and inventive, the Variations soon became a regular item in recital programmes, which commonly included two-piano works among string quartets, trios and other chamber combinations as well as instrumental and vocal solos. Perhaps the Variations' fall from fame has as much to do with the demise of the mixed-media chamber concert as with the general neglect suffered by most of Saint-Saëns's music.

With the interruptions of war, bereavement and ill-health behind him he was back in full flow, both in work and in the socialising that formed an integral part of his life. Evenings not pre-booked by concerts or organ duties were invariably spent at musical gatherings at the homes of the rich and famous, and these included royalty. He was one of a group of musicians and painters, who also included Liszt and Vieuxtemps, invited to the Netherlands to spend two weeks at the country house of King William III at Het Loo. No women were allowed, except the actresses and dancers of the royal company who performed every evening after dinner.[27] Among musical gatherings in Paris were those at the home of Gustave Doré in the Rue St Dominique. The celebrated engraver, famous for his illustrations for Dante's *Inferno* and of the London slums, was a keen violinist and an intimate friend of the composer, who "became the confidant of his secret sorrows and his innermost griefs".[28] Liszt often played the piano at Doré's studio and listened while Saint-Saëns and a friend performed a two-piano version of *Les Préludes* and extracts from the *Dante* symphony. There were the soirées held by Victor Hugo, then in his seventies, an exile from the Second Empire who had returned to France in 1871 a literary legend. Saint-Saëns still held him in awe and was thrilled to be under the same roof as this "hero of my youthful dreams" although he came to be somewhat cynical about the poet's ardent republicanism after the Emperor of Brazil, no less, called on him "and the next day he could not stop talking about it". His visits to Hugo's house came to a temporary halt when the poet hinted that he would like him to set his *Esmeralda*, a piece the composer considered entirely unsuitable, so that "I never dared go there again".[29]

Pauline Viardot still kept house, attended by the infatuated Turgenev and other literary giants such as Flaubert and George Sand. Saint-Saëns accompanied her singing, as well as improvising everything from solemn contrapuntal pieces to lively waltzes to which everyone could dance. But there was also a more private occasion, when singer and composer expressed their shared enthusiasm for Bach by performing one of his cantatas, Saint-Saëns playing the Cavaillé-Coll organ that had been installed in a basement gallery. Bach was still too obscure for salon company, and the only audience was Saint-Saëns's mother and Mme Viardot's son Paul. "I cherish the memory of that day as one of the most precious in my musical career", the composer wrote.[30] Upstairs there was lighter fare: as well as the waltzes and the sketches he supplied for the guests' amusement, there were the games, the charades and the operatic parodies in makeshift costume. He had lost none of his capacity for biting humour, and enjoyed telling funny stories, according to Servières, "adjusting on his nose with both hands, in a way peculiar to him, his eye-glasses, behind which his eyes sparkled with malice".[31] This malice was always ready to boil over into outright rudeness, for Saint-Saëns was easily irritated, especially by incompetents and favour-seekers, and more especially if they were women. At one of his own Monday evening gatherings, a female guest repeatedly asked him to accompany her two daughters in a vocal duet. He grudgingly agreed, but the two girls, who could barely keep in tune, were so out of time, both with each other and with the piano, that an exasperated host turned to their mother and snapped: "Which of your two daughters, Madam, do you wish me to accompany?"[32] His impatience and irascibility occasionally spilled over into his letters, like the one in reply to repeated requests for him to attend a Conservatoire meeting, referring also to a failed appointment at his house: "It is absolutely impossible for me to come to the Conservatoire this evening as you ask me. As for M. Gailliard, if he did not find 168 Faubourg St Honoré it is because he did not take the trouble to look for it."[33]

One result of his continuing friendship with Pauline Viardot was an unexpected airing for *Samson et Dalila*. The singer, now retired from the stage and settled into a life of composition, poetry, play-writing and painting, had not forgotten that the part of Delilah was written for her, and was all too aware that the likelihood of her ever singing it on stage was receding with every year it remained unperformed. She took the initiative in trying to create interest in the opera by arranging a private performance of the second act in the garden of a friend's house at Croissy, by the Seine west of Paris (she mistakenly remembered it as taking place at nearby Bougival). She invited Olivier Halanzier, director of the Opéra, and the event went ahead on 20th August 1874. Saint-Saëns arrived to play the accompaniment and was astonished and delighted to find the performance dressed with home-made scenery and costumes. He was quite taken with Viardot in her oriental robes, belying her fifty-three years and the declining power of her middle register with a convincing portrayal of the seductress. Still the theatre bosses were not convinced: Halanzier thought it dramatically flawed and too advanced, with its "simple lines", for the grand opera tradition, and remained wary of its biblical subject.[34]

Saint-Saëns shrugged off the slight as just another example of establishment hostility, but he was to respond more positively to criticism in another quarter. Augusta Holmes, whose impersonation of Don Giovanni was scandalising the respectable and amusing the broad-minded in the Parisian salons, was also impressing her many admirers with her masterly interpretation of the song 'Danse Macabre'. She was in fact one of very few singers who could tackle it, as most complained that it was too difficult. Saint-Saëns answered the criticism by turning the song into his third symphonic poem. The orchestral version is a model of precision and proportion, within whose bounds the representation of morbid mayhem passes through several shades of mood and emphasis. As the most tightly constructed of the four symphonic poems, it is perhaps the most successful, and comes closest to the Lisztian model, being built on two main themes which pass through various transformations, from frenzied to forlorn, before they are combined on full orchestra at the climax. A notable innovation is the use of a xylophone to suggest the clacking of dancing bones, its first appearance in mainstream western music since its arrival in Europe from the Far East, by way of Africa, some three hundred years before.

The quirky nature of the piece is established at the outset, for the midnight chimes, sounding strangely muffled on the harp, as though heard through a fog, are on the dominant (a detail that irritated Wagner), while soft chords on violins emphasise the stillness of the scene. Death breaks in on the calm, playing diabolic diminished fifths on his out-of-tune violin to launch the macabre waltz, a dance which mixes with malevolent intensity an intense sadness, a sickly-sweet submission to its all-embracing leader. The combination grows out of the two main themes, the first holding the germ of the work's contrasting moods in its chromatic juxtaposition of G minor with A flat major. The second contains those modal elements that so attracted Saint-Saëns and perplexed his listeners, and which here lend themselves to pliable mood transformation as well as providing a source of dizzy disruption and uncertainty. It becomes the subject of a fugue, and from it also grows a mocking parody of the Dies Irae chant, that favourite of nineteenth-century composers. The rhythmic drive is relentless, between the opening chimes and the oboe's cock crow which dispels the skeletal dancers at the cold light of dawn, in a tremolando shiver on the strings of the kind first used in the D major piano concerto sixteen years before. In its quieter moods, the work calls to mind one of those ornate Victorian tombs surrounded by low iron railings, but its concentrated energy makes it a virtuoso orchestral showpiece whose popularity has survived the derision heaped on it by 'educated' musical opinion.

Danse Macabre, with its slick orchestration and its combination of the fantastic with formal neatness and elegance, is one of Saint-Saëns's most typical works. Opposition to it has a long pedigree, but while for the most part it has been attacked as a piece of old-fashioned nonsense, in the beginning it was attacked as being outrageously novel. With it, the composer of the symphonic poems seemed to have reached new heights of bizarre idiosyncrasy, leading one critic, Adolphe Jullien, to call it "either an aberration or a hoax".[35] That it was well-received by the audience at its Concert National première early in 1875 was thanks largely to the hard work of Colonne in driving his players to overcome the technical difficulties of the piece – indeed in getting them to perform it at all, as many of them complained that it was unplayable. The composer reported to Durand that it was "magnificently played" and encored.[36] In less capable hands it was likely to have a very different effect. When the veteran Pasdeloup conducted it in October 1875 it was greeted by a storm of boos and catcalls so noisy that the composer's aged mother fainted with shock.

Although the contrast with the first hearing suggests it was Pasdeloup's performance rather than the work that caused the rumpus, Saint-Saëns was still regarded as an advanced composer, associated with controversy, with a peculiar quality of musical imagination of which the symphonic poems are succinct, concentrated examples. Servières wrote that "there was always something of the fanciful even in his most academic works, so that I didn't need a programme to recognise something by Saint-Saëns".[37] The writer Hermann Klein thought his music had "a strange, exotic ring",[38] and the American composer Arthur Foote, who, at Boston in 1876, played in the first performance in the United States of the Beethoven Variations, remembered that "Saint-Saëns's music came to us as a stunning novelty".[39] For the Saint-Saëns of the 1870s is not the Saint-Saëns of later years, the conservative theorist asserting the supremacy of form over content. To the younger man form was an important consideration, but only as a springboard from which the musical imagination could take flight. Music needed to stretch its wings if it was to have life, and its expressive content was as vital an ingredient as its formal base. Expressive grandeur was one of the characteristics he admired in Liszt. "It is by the justness and intensity of expression that Liszt is really incomparable. His music speaks . . . "[40] And in another comment on Liszt that can be applied equally to the music of his own early maturity, Saint-Saëns declared: "How much greater is the charm when to the purely musical pleasure is added that of the imagination coursing without hesitation over a determined path."[41] Once the structural basis, apparent or implied, is in place music can soar to the expressive heights. Yet with this imaginative soaring goes a directness and clear-headedness in the handling of the material that saves it from obscurantism. Another observer, Maurice Emmanuel, wrote after hearing *Le Rouet d'Omphale*: "The orchestral style of M. Saint-Saëns is all fullness and clarity. With superior skill he treats the instrumental voices like a painter of frescoes treats in colour the various designs of his decorative art: it is always honest, and always simple."[42]

It was while composing the *Danse Macabre* that he decided to make a fresh attempt at marriage. This time his proposal was accepted. Marie Laure Emilie Truffot was the younger sister of a private pupil of whom he thought highly and to whom he dedicated his Caprice for piano on ballet airs from Gluck's *Alceste*. One day late in 1874 – according to one account, at the swimming baths[43] – Saint-Saëns suddenly and unexpectedly asked Jean Truffot, in a humorously off-hand way, if he would like to be his brother-in-law. His pupil indignantly replied that such an idea was no matter for jest, but later Saint-Saëns confirmed that he was making a formal offer for Marie's hand to her father. She was a girl of no serious artistic ambition, and as he had been rejected by Augusta Holmes on the grounds of artistic rivalry, he may have viewed this fact as a major qualification in a wife. At nineteen, she was less than half his age, but because of his professional and financial security there were no parental objections, and at the northern town of Le Cateau, where the Truffot family lived, Saint-Saëns was married on 3rd February 1875. That the wedding occurred at the same period as the appearance of the *Danse Macabre* is of darkly ironic significance. Love and death, already linked in such works as *Le Timbre d'Argent*, *Samson et Dalila* and the *Mélodies Persanes*, and hinted at in the third piano concerto, had come together again, and this time the link was to prove prophetic of real-life tragedy.

VIII • HUSBAND and FATHER

THE NEW MME SAINT-SAËNS ENTERED INTO AN UNENVIABLE DOMESTICITY, with a husband dedicated to his art and to his mother. There could be no separation from the woman who had guided and supported him all his life; after the wedding he brought his young bride back to Paris to live in the family home with an in-law who, there is no doubt, strongly disapproved of the marriage and resented this outsider coming into her home to claim the affections of a genius she had reared and fostered over forty years. It is unlikely, indeed, that she would have considered any woman good enough for him, let alone this young slip of a girl with, in her view, very little knowledge or appreciation of high art. At the same time, Saint-Saëns's career left him little time for his wife. There was no honeymoon and concert engagements were soon to take him even farther afield, to Russia and Austria. With a husband often irritable, mostly absent and in an intellectual world of his own, and a disapproving mother-in-law out to find fault at every turn in household matters, life for the young Marie must at times have been intolerable. She took an interest in her husband's work and had a genuine love of music, but although he played new compositions to her it is doubtful that he had any regard for her views. His mother was the dominant influence here, as the incident of the cello sonata had shown, and although his wife insisted that "there was never the slightest disagreement between us" about music,[1] that was probably because she felt there would have been little point. This was never likely to be the perfect marriage. Nevertheless, the first year of Saint-Saëns's marital status proved to be a particularly fruitful one: besides the composition of several major works, his first son was born.

On 6th March 1875, the newly-married composer organised and took part in a concert of his works at the Salle Pleyel with Charles Lamoureux, assistant conductor at the Conservatoire Concerts Society, soon to emerge as one of the great figures of late-nineteenth-century Parisian music-making. The programme included the third piano concerto and a new work, the B flat piano quartet, which attained considerable popularity during Saint-Saëns's lifetime. It combines classical and romantic elements on a broad scale, beginning conventionally enough with a self-contained sonata movement and ending with a complex rondo in which preceding material is recalled and refashioned. The sunny opening, with its distinctive rhythm marked by acciaccaturas on weak beats, is contrasted with a second subject of flowing triplets, the material combining in a serene coda. The andante alters the mood from warm optimism to frowning contemplation, in which the piano's prickly staccato sequence becomes the accompaniment to a severe chorale on the strings; the two elements are combined in various ways, rising to an angry climax. The playful scherzo in D minor begins a long journey back to the home key; interrupted by recitative-like passages and a central section in duple time, it provides some light, if sardonic relief, its triplets whirling away into nothing before the finale, still in D minor, announces the gruff rondo, reminiscent of Mendelssohn. As the music struggles to regain the light of B flat, it takes in references to the andante chorale and the first movement's acciaccaturas, before the quartet's opening theme shines like a beacon in a condensed recapitulation. The second subject then combines with the chorale in a fugue, leading to a triumphant conclusion in which the rondo themes reassert themselves. The skill with which Saint-Saëns achieves a feeling of unity from disparate elements helped to make the piano quartet, in its time, one of the best known works in the medium.

Another new work from what was to be an extraordinarily productive year was the brief Allegro Appassionato for cello and piano (the accompaniment was later orchestrated), written for Lasserre. This sprightly piece, in which the soloist has all the glory, shows Saint-Saëns in full lyrical vein, each melodic turn seeming like a natural progress, with here and there those dark edges that haunt so many of his melodies. March also saw the first performance of *Carmen*, perhaps the most famous example of the hostility faced by young French opera composers at the time. Saint-Saëns could not attend the première, at the Opéra-Comique, and by the time he did see *Carmen* the following week it had already been condemned as obscene and tuneless. The epithet Wagnerian, then still a derogatory term used to describe anything that deviated from the lyrical norms of Italian opera, was also applied to it. Saint-Saëns, however, was overwhelmed by *Carmen*, and was one of a small band of enthusiasts who leapt to its defence. "I found it marvellous, and I am telling you the truth", he wrote to Bizet, who, badly in need of moral support, much appreciated the comment and wrote back: "Those three lines, signed by a master, by a man of honour like you, console me immeasurably for all the insults . . . You have made me proud and happy."[2]

A few days later, on Good Friday, 26th March, Saint-Saëns himself experienced the frustrations of French opera composers, when Colonne conducted a concert performance of the first act of *Samson et Dalila*, again to general disapproval. The critic Henri Cohen wrote:

Never has a more complete absence of melody made itself felt as in this drama. And when to this lack of melodic motives is added a harmony at times extremely daring and an instrumentation that nowhere rises above the ordinary, you will have some idea of what Samson *is like.*[3]

This latest condemnation deepened the affinity Saint-Saëns felt with Bizet in what he saw as their comradely struggle to achieve success on the French stage, but it is not apparent that Bizet, though he valued Saint-Saëns's support, felt any such bond with a composer who had already made his name on the concert platform. He fell ill after the failure of *Carmen* and died in June, aged thirty-six. Saint-Saëns was at the Madeleine when a mutual friend, the composer Henri Maréchal, brought him the news. He was devastated, and for a long time could only sit in silence. Of all the many deaths of friends he was to grieve over, that of Bizet had the most lasting effect: to a deep sense of loss was added a lifelong readiness to champion Bizet's music and defend its integrity against unscrupulous and insensitive editors and producers. This may also help to explain his determination to continue his own fight for operatic recognition and his later persistence in writing operas in preference to symphonies, a preference which has puzzled some observers as much as his earlier preference for symphonic music over operas. Of course, he was motivated by his well-known rivalry with Massenet, but perhaps there was also a kind of homage to Bizet's memory, a feeling of carrying on the work he had begun. For the present he turned his scholarly knowledge of opera to use in editing the works of Gluck, a task bequeathed to him by a wealthy spinster, Fanny Pelletan. An admirer of Berlioz, she had been inspired by his championing of the eighteenth-century master to dedicate her remaining years to producing a complete edition. She asked Saint-Saëns to help her in this in 1875 and when she died a year later he took sole charge of the project, which took some thirty years to complete.

After the piano quartet Saint-Saëns produced another, more startling essay in the adaptation of symphonic form to new modes of expression in the fourth piano concerto in C minor. One of the most accomplished works in the repertory, it shows him at his most masterful in combining formal elegance and classical restraint with poetic feeling and technical brilliance in a unified structure, and has been called a "perfect union of classic intellect with the structural freedom of romanticism".[4] In contrast to the familiar three-movement design of his earlier piano concertos, the fourth is laid out in two movements, each divided into the elements of sonata form in such a way that the whole represents both a single symphonic movement and the four movements of a complete symphony. (A similar plan was to be used for the third symphony, also in C minor.) The first and second subjects, which provide the underlying idea of questioning and resolution, act as opening allegro and slow movements respectively, and the development doubles as a scherzo before the recapitulation of the second subject, transformed into a triumphant finale.

The first subject, a curiously angular theme in crotchets, sets a mood of cautious inquiry and uncertainty with its chromatic slides, despite its almost nonchalant announcement by the strings without introduction – one of the most unusual and quietly arresting openings in all concerto literature. The first part of the theme is repeated by the piano in block chords, then the second part is similarly alternated, and this pattern applies in the variations that follow. A cascade of octaves on the piano ushers in a transition involving a downward shift to A flat and a sequential passage, swaying mysteriously on a turbulent undercurrent. A shaft of sunlight breaks through the swirling clouds to reveal the second main subject, given softly by the woodwind, that promises in its chorale-like rectitude the certainty of a benediction after the doubts and queries. The piano answers with a meditation that becomes virtually a subsidiary theme though clearly derived from the second subject, carrying the music into the slow movement, where the material is varied with both delicacy and intensity.

The second movement proper is launched by the cascade of octaves heard earlier, ushering in a scherzo in which earlier material is developed further, the prickly first subject mockingly turned into a plaything and alternated with a jocular new theme, in contrasting compound duple time and characterised by a repeated note. Some increasingly fantastic convolutions suddenly give way to a mysterious return of the meditative subsidiary figure of the first movement, treated fugally on muted strings, which in turn gives way to the all-conquering version of the second subject. This appears in simple triple time which, because it has not previously been used in the work, gives the feeling of having cleared the air. After dismissing some angry protests in the piano's depths, the concerto soars with mounting exhilaration to its victorious conclusion.

Saint-Saëns played the concerto, with Colonne, at the Châtelet theatre on 31st October. Cohen noted the integral relationship between piano and orchestra: Saint-Saëns "makes the piano an instrument of the orchestra . . . instead of reducing the orchestra to the subordinate function of accompanist". He was put off, however, by some aspects of the work which to him reinforced the composer's reputation as a disturbing innovator – what he calls "aberrations of modern style".[5] The concerto made a greater impression in Germany, and it went on to rival and sometimes surpass its G minor predecessor in popularity.

The fruitful year 1875 also saw the composition of the oratorio *Le Déluge*, which many regarded as one of his greatest works, though it had a stormy reception at its première and was rarely performed even in Saint-Saëns's lifetime. Its origins can be traced to a letter to Durand suggesting a three-part choral work, either a biblical oratorio on the subject of Jerusalem, a lyric poem, a cantata "or I don't know what". The composer was not at first enthusiastic about the oratorio idea, regarding the form as "pleonastic" but he was encouraged in it by the apparent successes Massenet was having in the genre, which suggested (falsely as it turned out) that oratorio, for long unfashionable in France, was making a comeback. Abandoning the subject already considered, Gallet instead supplied a text based on the Old Testament story of Noah. With it Saint-Saëns created one of his most vivid pictorial representations, that of the cataclysmic rise of the waters, which Camille Bellaigue later described in *Le Figaro* as the symphonic equivalent of Niagara.[6] For this he uses a full orchestra including five trombones and four low saxhorns as well as chorus, yet the overwhelming nature of the subject is conveyed less by dynamic force than by subtle understatement. Stylistically, the oratorio includes elements of classical austerity as well as romantic picture-painting: it uses fairly conventional recitatives, and there are three fugues, the first of which, on a subject reminiscent of Bach in one of his sombre chromatic moods, introduces the orchestral prelude, the only portion of the work to achieve wide currency. Suggestive of elemental beginnings and primeval innocence, the prelude also includes a melody for solo violin whose gently rocking melancholy anticipates Rachmaninov. The delicate scoring serves to heighten the effect of the later tumult, so that when played as a self-contained piece, out of context, it loses a great deal. The first part describes the degeneration of the human race, God's decision to destroy it (an agitated chorus in canon) and His instruction to Noah to build the ark. Noah is represented by a short phrase, derived from part of the 'innocence' theme of the prelude, that suggests his straight-forward morality – and it is regrettable that its first appearance should be answered immediately by the chorus with a close of the utmost banality. The weakest section of the work, the first part ends with a resumption of the chorus of God's anger, the canon giving way to a fugue. After the flood, the second part ends pianissimo, portraying the resulting desolation, and gives way to a strongly chromatic chorale-like theme that dominates part three, in which God and Man are reconciled. The flight of the dove is a piece of tone painting that anticipates *Le Carnaval des Animaux*, the 'innocence' theme is recalled and the oratorio ends with the sturdy third fugue.

While Saint-Saëns was at work on *Le Déluge*, his first child André was born on 6th November. Deprived of paternal affection in his own childhood, the composer now had a son of his own to cherish, on whom he could bestow those fatherly affections hitherto lavished on young friends and pupils. Such loving attention was, however, bound to be curtailed by professional demands. Less than three weeks after André's birth, his father left home for Russia, for a series of concerts in St Petersburg and Moscow. From the point of view of his health, the tour was a risky business. Only the year before, he had exchanged the Parisian winter for the sunnier climes of Algeria because of physical fragility; now he was preparing to exchange it for the much more severe Russian winter. But the prestige the tour promised was too great to turn down. His first Moscow concert was on 13th December, when he played his Beethoven Variations with Nikolai Rubinstein, founder and director of the Moscow Conservatoire and brother of Anton. Tchaikovsky heard this performance and was much impressed, as he was also by the *Danse Macabre* given at a Russian Musical Society charity concert five days later. He also heard Saint-Saëns play his third piano concerto and conduct *Le Rouet d'Omphale* (which he liked rather less), and was confirmed in his view that the visitor represented the "progressive element" in French music, tempered by a feeling for classical methods. "He combines most successfully the style of Sebastian Bach – for whom he has an evident affection – with national French elements, of which the characteristically piquant rhythm makes itself clearly felt." The ardent Francophile, Saint-Saëns's junior by five years, added that "all the most sympathetic characteristics of his nationality – cordial sincerity, warmth of feeling, intellect – make themselves felt in every note of our guest's compositions. They are further illuminated by his artistic interpretation of them, which shows much distinction, much thoughtful and careful phrasing, without a trace of affectation."[7]

As well as making his music known in Russia, the tour greatly boosted Saint-Saëns's confidence in his conducting ability. From his hotel he wrote to Durand: "I have as conductor an aplomb of which you have no idea, and which stupefies me when I think of it." In style the conductor mirrored the pianist, undemonstrative and eschewing flamboyance, with a distaste for 'virtuosi' conductors. He was to lament the custom of the conductor turning to the audience to receive applause – introduced into France by Lamoureux – and thought it absurd when Italian opera conductors went on stage to bow. "There is nothing more laughable than to see him, as the last note of an opera dies away, jump down from his stand and run like mad to reach the stage in time." Such men "are not subservient to the music but the music to them", he wrote later. "What constitutes an orchestral conductor's worth are the excellence of execution he obtains from the musicians and the accurate interpretation of the composer's intentions."[8]

While in Moscow, Saint-Saëns also went to see a production of *Faust* with Tchaikovsky, who found him congenial company, delighting in his lively conversation, good humour and sense of fun. His brother Modest wrote that the visitor "had that touch of individuality that Peter always found attractive in people and also a certain knack for instant friendship".[9] A mutual enthusiasm was pantomime and dance, and it is to Modest that we owe the details of an impromptu ballet danced by the two men, accompanied by Nikolai Rubinstein on piano, in an otherwise empty hall at the Moscow Conservatoire, with Tchaikovsky as Pygmalion and Saint-Saëns, in customary female role, as Galatea. Always anxious to help younger composers, Saint-Saëns advised his host to give a concert of his works in Paris, suggesting Colonne's Concerts Nationals orchestra as the best to approach as it would not be too expensive.[10] According to Modest he even offered to conduct *Romeo and Juliet* himself, out of consideration for Tchaikovsky's pathological fear of taking the rostrum, but this appears to have been a misunderstanding. Saint-Saëns was always ready to help promote Tchaikovsky's music in France: in 1881, for instance, when Adolf Brodsky tried to introduce the violin concerto into Paris concerts, he accompanied at auditions. But he never conducted it.

The Russian tour served its purpose of spreading Saint-Saëns's fame and reputation, winning him many new admirers, but from it also sprang a mutual hostility between him and that wild, gruff, bibulous member of the Five, Mussorgsky. Saint-Saëns regarded him as a madman and his music as rough and uncouth, while Mussorgsky dismissed him as a purveyor of bonbons, a "framer of miniatures," and was one of the first to argue that his brilliant orchestrations cloaked "tiny little thoughts".[11] But by bringing back with him to Paris the vocal score of *Boris Godunov* – presumably out of a perverse curiosity – Saint-Saëns unintentionally advanced the cause of the music he so deplored, because it was seen on a visit to his apartment by the organist Jules Brayer, a former colleague at the Ecole Niedermeyer. Brayer, at that time manager of the Lamoureux concerts, studied it and launched a small circle of enthusiasts, later to include Debussy, through whom Mussorgsky's music was to grow in influence in the West.

While Saint-Saëns was in Russia, prospects were revived of a production of *Le Timbre d'Argent* at the Opéra-Comique, only to vanish again on his return. Du Locle had included the opera in his schedule for October 1876 but, as before, it was hit by petty squabbles. The lead tenor decided the part was not grand enough and pulled out in a huff, and du Locle once more began to lose interest when, in March, his reign at the theatre ended in bankruptcy. As well as these latest operatic trials, Saint-Saëns's attention was also engaged by rehearsals for *Le Déluge*; the controversial first performance was conducted by Colonne at the Châtelet on 5th March. Part two, with its swirling flood waters, could barely be heard above the uproar it caused, loud protests clashing with counter-demonstrations of loud applause, and it was a brave decision of Colonne to play the section again from the beginning, this time bringing it to a firm and audible conclusion. Although the clash of opponents and supporters was fairly even, there were few critics in favour. Bonnerot came to regard *Le Déluge* as "one of the most perfect, purest works of the master" and Bellaigue preferred it to *Samson et Dalila*, but it was mostly condemned as 'descriptive music', still regarded as an inferior type. *Le Ménestrel* called it the work "of a great musician, but a musician nevertheless who has gone off the rails". It was played again a week later, by which time the shock value had worn off, leaving only a lukewarm response.[12] It had to wait until 1891 to be accepted by the Conservatoire Concerts Society, but was rarely revived, apart from the 'innocence' theme from the prelude, which became a favourite recital piece of violinists.

Saint-Saëns was not at the second performance of *Le Déluge* on 12th March; he was in Lyons, playing his E flat concerto in a concert held by the impresario Aimé Gros, on the way to a tour of Austria-Hungary. During this stop he met Modest Tchaikovsky, and was somewhat put out when he spoke about the alleged offer to conduct *Romeo and Juliet* in Paris. Not surprisingly, Modest – who raised the matter expressly against his brother's wishes – found him "evasive".

His brother was so embarrassed at hearing this that when he visited Paris later in the year he did so incognito, taking particular care to avoid Saint-Saëns. Later still, in December, Saint-Saëns met the pianist Taneyev, who had studied composition under Tchaikovsky, and repeated the advice that the Russian composer should give a concert in the French capital. Taneyev duly relayed the advice to his former teacher, who replied that he could not raise the 2000 francs needed. The two composers thereafter became, in Modest's words, "as strangers" until they met again seventeen years later.[13]

The Austrian tour in March 1876 included several concerts in Vienna, and although Saint-Saëns's quotation of a newspaper report that "the *Danse Macabre* has electrified the public" needs to be balanced against his obvious interest in putting a favourable interpretation on events, the series undoubtedly helped to strengthen his reputation in one of the great centres of musical tradition.[14] On 30th March he wrote to Durand about arrangements he had made for a performance in Vienna of *Le Déluge* the following winter, and gleefully recorded that the critic and champion of Brahms, Eduard Hanslick, placed "my quintet above the sextet of Brahms, which was played in the same concert". During the tour he made a brief visit to Budapest where, before an invited audience, he played the organ at the synagogue, the only good organ in the city, he was told. He wanted Liszt to be present, but the messenger sent with the invitation was told that the master could not be disturbed as he was sitting for his portrait.

Duties on the Prix de Rome jury recalled Saint-Saëns to Paris, but concert work soon took him abroad again. On 7th July he played the Beethoven Variations with Marie Jaëll in a Musical Union concert in London, and two days later gave a recital of his works at the St James's Hall with Lasserre playing the serenade from the cello suite and Edouard Marlois, his former Niedermeyer pupil, joining in the two piano version of the *Marche Héroïque*.

An engagement of a different kind was to lead into a controversy that would surround Saint-Saëns for many years to come. On 21st July he was made music critic of the evening paper *Le Bon Sens* (later *L'Estafette*), founded by the writer Léonce Détroyat, whose wife had been a childhood friend of the composer. His first major assignment was to cover the first Bayreuth Festival, being launched by Wagner that summer. He approached the Bayreuth phenomenon detached from the fevered adoration of the Wagnerians, not only by his distaste for the new German nationalism it represented and his dedication to the cause of French music but also by his reverence for the music of the past, of Bach, Gluck and Mozart. It was fitting, therefore, that he travelled to Bavaria in August from the Rameau Festival in Dijon, where he joined the flautist Claude Taffanel in recitals of instrumental and keyboard works by the eighteenth-century master.

From Bayreuth, where he attended the second performance of the complete *Ring*, he sent Détroyat seven long articles containing a balanced assessment of the operas which, at a time when it was becoming impossible not to be either violently for or violently against, infuriated supporters and opponents alike. He wrote with some foreknowledge, having already seen the first two operas in Munich and knowing the last two from the score, but with the first experience of the whole cycle he was able to see the grand sweep of the vast concept, writing that "from the heights of the last act of *Götterdämmerung* the entire work appears in its almost supernatural immensity, like the chain of the Alps seen from the summit of Mont Blanc". Some parts of the *Ring* he praised highly: the Siegmund-Sieglinde scene in act one of *Die Walküre*, for instance, was "the theatre of the future; neither opera nor non-lyrical drama will ever produce such an emotion in one's soul". Other parts he found weak and far-fetched, and while he commended the orchestration throughout he condemned the vocal writing as putting an intolerable and unnecessary strain on the human voice. The singers he heard were no match for the demands placed on them: indeed, "singers worthy of the name are rare in Germany . . . Most of them taking part in the *Ring* shout instead of singing".[15] But his scorn was chiefly directed against those who saw Wagner as the beginning and the end of art. The one-time champion of Wagner in France acknowledged a debt to all the great masters of the past as well as of the present and thus found himself increasingly at odds with those who turned their admiration into idolatry, who would have no other gods before Wagner. Such adulation could be almost embarrassing, as in an incident he recalled at Wagner's house, where a female admirer begged Wagner to play a certain chord she had heard in *Siegfried*. "But it's the chord of E minor", he told her. "You could easily play it yourself." She insisted, and when he finally obliged at the piano, she sighed and fell into a swoon on the sofa.[16] Saint-Saëns was to attack the Wagnerians in stronger terms in his book *Harmonie et Mélodie*, published in 1885 at the height of the Wagner boom in France. He was also to denounce the aggressive nationalism of the Wagner philosophy, but in 1876, despite the insult to France from *A Capitulation*, he was more equivocal on the subject. "Richard Wagner detests France, but what is that compared with the worth of his works?" Later he says it is absurd to say that Wagner is an enemy of France: "He hates only those who don't like his music".[17]

While in Bayreuth Saint-Saëns played the piano at a reception at Wagner's house on 24th August, and apparently even he was not entirely immune from the craze for Wagner souvenirs. A story is told that he engaged in a tussle with an amateur musician of Dutch origin called Benedictus for possession of Wagner's silk handkerchief, which its owner had left in the pocket of a coat he had wrapped round the shoulders of Judith Mendès. Benedictus won the contest, and Wagner, when he heard of it, declared: "Ah, the flying Dutchman!"[18]

Saint-Saëns's own operatic fortunes took a step forward when the Théâtre Lyrique – which, under Carvalho, had first commissioned *Le Timbre d'Argent* twelve years before – made a new offer for the work. This time it was the government that made the decisive move. The theatre had lately been revived, helped by a small subsidy from the Ministry of Fine Arts, which was "kindly disposed" to the composer and made the grant on condition that the theatre produce his long-ignored opera. Still the project was plagued by bickering. Saint-Saëns found a tenor to sing Conrad, but was then told that he would be engaged for only four nights, which suggested that the director, Vizentini, planned only four performances. As time went on Saint-Saëns began to have the strong impression that the theatre hated the opera and resented its obligation to stage it. The government's intervention was proving a two-edged sword. Another tenor was finally engaged, a "perfect singer but no actor", cuts were made against the composer's wishes, and he had to contend with a surly stage manager and ballet master, who both brushed aside his "most modest suggestions". "Some stage settings I requested for the prologue were declared impossible – I have seen them since in *Les Contes d'Hoffmann.*" The orchestra complained that the music was unplayable, and "I had to pay the cost of extra musicians in the wings myself". Finally, two advance notices "were intended to pave the way for the failure of my work".[19] These venomous items appeared in a journal called *L'Ordre*, which on 29th November protested: "Truly, we cannot avoid M. Saint-Saëns and his Bell . . . Ah! who will deliver us from M. Saint-Saëns?" It later returned to the attack, dismissing the composer as "notoriously unpopular and incontestably bereft of talent," and adding: "Assuredly we shall not escape . . . The public will judge the poor work of this person. The staging of the Bell will be his punishment and our vengeance".[20]

The première was scheduled for 15th January 1877 but the delays pushed it back to 23rd February. In the meantime Saint-Saëns had fared little better with his latest orchestral work, *La Jeunesse d'Hercule* – the fourth, last and most extended of his symphonic poems – which Colonne conducted at the Châtelet on 28th January. This elegant work returns to the formal regularity of *Le Rouet d'Omphale* but portrays an entirely different hero from Omphale's emasculated sex slave. Here is an idealised Hercules, whose moral strength survives the blandishments of sensual pleasure to win immortality. There is a rarefied atmosphere of refinement, appropriate to such a lofty idea, which is introduced by soft chords on the violins, suggestive of childhood innocence. The hero is represented in two aspects, the first of noble piety embodied in a theme, beginning with a rising semitone, which Saint-Saëns was to use again twenty years later when he again portrayed Hercules in the incidental music for *Déjanire*. A more passionate second theme introduces a physically stronger, more assertive trait before a flighty third subject brings the strong man to the temptations of feminine charms. This leads to a central section which turns up the heat of desire and revelry to culminate in a pulsating bacchanalia, at the height of which the hero stamps his foot and rejects the pleasures thus presented. The return of the piety and assertion themes in virtually unaltered form indicates that the noble youth is untouched by vice. An extended coda develops these characteristics until, after a final farewell to earthly delights, the hero stands triumphantly on the threshold of the gods in a blaze of arpeggios on the brass, a piece of Lisztian bravura in which Saint-Saëns tips his hat to the acknowledged master of the symphonic poem. Liszt, indeed, greatly admired *La Jeunesse d'Hercule*, which deserves a high place among descriptive orchestral works for its melodic aptness and imaginative ingenuity contained within a clear, logical framework.

The shift away from the hero destroyed by female allure towards the hero unscathed by it perhaps indicates the maturity of the married man, for whom sexual relations no longer threatened hidden dangers. *Le Rouet d'Omphale* had been dedicated to Augusta Holmes; Saint-Saëns may therefore have thought it appropriate to dedicate *La Jeunesse d'Hercule* to his wife. His motive in doing so seems honourable if the work is seen as demonstrating the triumph of virtue over vice; quite perverse if seen as an assertion of the superiority of male chastity. Was it a hint to his wife that he could quite well do without her, and that he sought immortality in a man's world of intellectual achievement? Whatever the case, Marie daringly declined to accept the dedication, saying she wasn't satisfied with the piece and asking for *Le Déluge* instead. Saint-Saëns gave the symphonic poem to Henri Duparc; as for *Le Déluge,* if he did ever consider inscribing his wife's name on it he soon changed his mind. Not one of his works is dedicated to her.

La Jeunesse d'Hercule left its audience as much puzzled and divided as its predecessors in the form, the critics repeating their opposition to programme music and declaring that it was incapable of representing moral sentiments. The reaction to *Le Timbre d'Argent* was similarly mixed. Some praised its lyrical qualities; others called it tuneless. One described it as "a nightmare in four acts that lasts five hours".[21] Servières was more charitable, declaring it "not entirely devoid of melody" and praising the ballet and the "ravishing" chorus that opens act three, saying "it was not bad for a first opera".[22] The muddled thinking that the Wagner phenomenon had brought about in musical criticism was also well illustrated in press comments, some of which denounced the opera as 'Wagnerian' while others complained that it was not. (Bizet had said, approvingly, that there was "nothing of Wagner" in it.) The habit of viewing new works in this distorting mirror Saint-Saëns found "stupid and annoying": "If a musician composes serious music, it is Wagner; if another writes light music, fine, it is not Wagner; if a locomotive whistles, again Wagner."[23]

He regarded the first performance of *Le Timbre d'Argent* as a success, especially as the baritone Léon Melchissedech as Dr Spiridion had to encore several numbers. Melchissedech, though, like the leading tenor, was no actor, and Caroline Salla was a dramatic soprano singing a part that had been rewritten years before to suit the light, high soprano of Mme Carvalho. "They concluded, therefore, that I didn't know how to write vocal music", the composer recalled with some bitterness.[24] Gounod was in the first night audience following the score and was delighted by the opera, as Bizet had been. He wrote to Saint-Saëns: "It is because I have to work day and night that I have not told you of all the charm which I find in hearing your work. Like everything that comes from you, this holds the attention, and provokes a lively and ardent interest in your old and faithful friend."[25] Gounod is a strong influence on the work, which inhabits the fantastic world of *Faust*. But to the seriousness of *Faust* is added the light-heartedness of the fantastic as evoked in *Les Contes d'Hoffmann*, which was still to come. All three operas are by the same librettists, Barbier and Carré, and it may be significant that Offenbach began considering *Hoffmann* during the initial run of *Le Timbre d'Argent*. Saint-Saëns's work is of uneven quality, a not unusual feature of a first opera, with all the freshness and faults of youth. It is pulled in different directions by a mixture of styles, which include a Neapolitan song and a Viennese waltz: as Saint-Saëns himself said in later years, "there is in this work everything from the symphony to operetta by way of lyric drama and ballet".[26] There are some striking stage effects too, and the overture at least is worth the occasional outing.

Le Timbre d'Argent received eighteen performances from February 1877 after which it disappeared from the repertory, reappearing only briefly in Brussels two years later. Despite the disagreements over the Paris production Vizentini remained on friendly terms with Saint-Saëns, and planned a revival of the opera when, some years later, he took over the Opéra-Comique, but nothing came of it and the work was rarely heard again.

In the spring Saint-Saëns resigned as organist at the Madeleine, ending the nineteen-year tenure that had been a mainstay throughout his formative years. Royalties from compositions and editions, private teaching, journalism and the large concert fees he could now command made the parting possible, and the demands of his other activities made it also mutually acceptable to him and his clerical employers, among whom he had no real friends since the death of Deguerry in 1871. In any case he now played there only for the grandest occasions, while the Madeleine clergy looked askance at the appearance of his name in concert programmes and elsewhere, and were uncomfortable with what was looked upon as his austere style in church music. Dubois, his colleague in the National Society, was promoted from choirmaster to succeed him, and the new choirmaster, on Saint-Saëns's recommendation, was Fauré.

Leaving the Madeleine coincided conveniently with the expiry of the lease on the apartment in the Rue du Faubourg St Honoré, and Saint-Saëns, no longer tied to a particular place of work, was free to transfer his family to a larger home across the Seine, nearer his birthplace. The choice of 14 Rue M. le Prince was influenced by a friend, the postmaster Albert Libon, a wealthy music enthusiast who was a regular guest at Saint-Saëns's Monday soirées and to whom *Le Timbre d'Argent* is dedicated. Libon's nephew, the colonial governor Armand Rousseau, already lived at the premises and Libon thought it would be nice if Saint-Saëns lived there too, so that "I should then be able to see both of you every day".[27] When the fourth-floor apartment became vacant the composer took up the suggestion and moved in, believing also that the air would be better for the baby André.

The family had barely settled in at their new home when Saint-Saëns was off on tour again, to South West France, Lyons and Switzerland, writing to Durand from Geneva that the *Danse Macabre* "makes its accustomed effect".[28] From Switzerland he travelled to Antwerp to oversee rehearsals for *Le Déluge*, and went on to London for a concert at the Musical Union. On his return at the end of May he was told that Libon had died during his absence, leaving him 100,000 francs to support his career as a composer. A condition that he should in return compose a Requiem to be performed on the first anniversary of Libon's death had been revoked at the last minute, but Saint-Saëns was intrigued by the request and did not dismiss it. There were, however, more pressing obligations. Liszt had at last sold the idea of producing *Samson et Dalila* to the Weimar court opera, whose director was now the Danish conductor Edward Lassen, and Saint-Saëns was busy putting the final touches to the score in readiness for the long-awaited première in December. He resigned his regular seat on the Conservatoire jury to give himself more time, for he was also working on a new opera. This latest commission had come from Aimé Gros for his Grand Theatre in Lyons, and the subject was a hero of French mediaeval history, Etienne Marcel, leader of a popular revolt against the Dauphin in the Paris of 1358. Marcel was in vogue in the 1870s as, during the rebuilding of the capital after the ravages of the Commune, he was widely regarded as a forefather of Parisian municipal life.

Saint-Saëns had for some time wanted to treat a subject from French history – another outcome of post-1871 nationalist feeling – and he set to work with Gallet in putting together a libretto which kept as close as possible to historical facts, a task undertaken "with difficulty but with infinite jest".[29] As well as appealing to the nationalist in the composer, the subject also provided ample scope for colourful pageantry, large crowd scenes and big choruses, contrasted with more intimate scenes involving the hero in a fictitious love story – in short, it allowed for all the ingredients of a grand opera in the Meyerbeer tradition. It is ironic that while Saint-Saëns was planning to renew the assault on the foreign-dominated French stage by adopting a tried and tested formula, the battle was being won by another Frenchman with a distinctive voice of his own: Massenet's *Le Roi de Lahore* (to another libretto by Gallet) was performed at the Opéra in April 1877 and won for its composer an eminence in French opera which he was to hold for the rest of the century and beyond. Saint-Saëns's greatest operatic triumph, meanwhile, was destined for Germany.

Leaving his wife heavily pregnant with their second child, he embarked, as a prelude to the *Samson* première in Weimar, on a punishing concert tour of German cities, beginning in Leipzig on 2nd November with the fourth piano concerto, three Bach transcriptions and Liszt's piano transcription of the *Danse Macabre*, for which he was presented with an illuminated address by students of the Leipzig Conservatoire, "to thank me for the pleasure which my compositions have given them". It was then on to Weimar, Berlin, Schwerin and Breslau before returning on the 27th to Weimar, where it was now "Delilah before everything!"[30] He wrote to Durand asking him to let his family know he was well, but he was clearly taxed by the tour, telling his publisher that "my intention is to do nothing more this winter".[31] He was happy with the male leads for the opera, the Hungarian tenor Franz Ferenczy having "everything of the neck and shoulders" to play Samson. "They find my music easy!" For Delilah Liszt had proposed Marianne Brandt, a "German Viardot," who had sung in the first *Ring*, but she was unavailable, and the role was taken by Mlle Müller, a young mezzo making her operatic debut. The première was given in the presence of the Grand Duke on 2nd December, and Saint-Saëns attended in company with Fauré, whom he had invited partly for his musical education but also to take his mind off his broken engagement to Pauline Viardot's daughter Marianne. After a shaky start, the performance (sung in German) proceeded in masterly fashion under Lassen, and the applause was tumultuous. The composer was called to the stage after the second act and again after the finale, and decorated with laurels. It was a far cry from the doubts and indifference the opera had met with in his own country, where news of its triumph passed almost unnoticed. Again it was Germany that had paid him the greatest compliment of recognition, and soon the opera was being taken up by opera houses all over the country. France was not to hear it for another thirteen years.

The qualities that so impressed that first audience have gone on impressing audiences ever since. The reasons why *Samson et Dalila* has retained a place in the repertory, the only one of Saint-Saëns's twelve published operas to have done so, are not hard to find. The central theme of fateful infatuation, so unconvincing in *Le Timbre d'Argent*, is here set in a real historical world, fraught with ethnic rivalry and conflicting loyalties, the two central characters swept along on a tide of tragic inevitability, and portrayed in a score spiced with oriental tones yet as lucid and clear as a Mediterranean sky.

The story, taken from the Book of Judges, is divided into three acts: the first shows Samson as the victorious leader of the Hebrew rebellion in Gaza and his first meeting with the Philistine maiden Delilah; the second, Delilah's seduction and betrayal of the hero; the third, the blinded Samson's destruction of the temple at the height of the Philistine celebrations. As may be expected in a work written at difference times over a period of nearly ten years, there is some patchiness, reinforced by the use – in contrast with the more passionate, intimate scenes – of a severe, almost Handelian technique for some of the choruses: a reminder that the work was first conceived as an oratorio. These disparate elements are, however, counteracted by a subtle use of recurring themes and by the then unusual format of lyric scenes instead of separate numbers. Perhaps it was this that von Bülow had in mind when he commented, on hearing the opera in Hamburg in 1882, that "Saint-Saëns is the only contemporary musician to be left untouched by the Wagnerian doctrine, but who has drawn from it a salutary lesson".[32]

Most striking at the time must have been the absence of an overture, the opera beginning with the Hebrews bemoaning their subjection in a chorus whose contrapuntal formality is strongly suggestive of oratorio. The grim severity of the Hebrew choruses and the declamatory style of Samson's call to arms and of the Philistine priest's curses serve to heighten by contrast the seductive beauty of Delilah's music, which establishes her fatal charms by the end of act one in the lovely invocation to the spring. The storm that rumbles in act two, an effect which Saint-Saëns confessed to having borrowed from Rossini's *Otello*,[33] symbolises Delilah's malevolent intent as she begins her voluptuous assault on Samson. The seduction scene, of which the well-known (and much abused) 'Softly awakes my heart' forms only a part, is the core of the opera, the dramatic high-point whose emotional intensity gives it its lasting appeal, the crucial moment in the central theme of weakness triumphant over strength that had so haunted the young composer.

The power of the scene is further reinforced by what follows, the plaintive despair of the blinded Samson in the dungeon, the frivolity and exuberance of the Philistines, notably in the popular bacchanalia, and above all the taunting of the prisoner by his captors, led by Delilah and the High Priest in mock-classical canon, their amusement emphasised by the use of a glockenspiel in the orchestra.

The strongly anti-German Saint-Saëns of later years played down the opera's early success in the Second Reich, but at the time it helped to soften the German phobia he had harboured ever since the war of 1870. The goodwill thus generated was shown to be fragile, however, by an embarrassing misunderstanding at the celebration supper after the first night, when the composer made a speech praising "the man who has led us all out of obscurity", who was "the heart and soul of music today". He meant Liszt (who was not present) – but did not mention his name. Fauré recalled: "To our astonishment no one applauded. Our German neighbours were shooting furious glances at us." After an awkward silence, a member of the Weimar theatre stood up and said: "We are surprised it should not have occurred to Saint-Saëns to thank Liszt." Saint-Saëns then had to make another speech explaining the first.[34] The incident, if it was reported to Liszt in Budapest, did not affect his admiration for his fellow composer, for a week after the performance he wrote to the Baroness Meyendorff: "I know of no one among contemporary artists who, all things considered, is his equal in talent, knowledge and variety of skills, except for Rubinstein."[35]

Saint-Saëns stayed in Weimar for a week or so to see subsequent performances of *Samson*, and clearly enjoyed deputising for the chorus master when he was taken ill during the third act. Conducting in the wings, "I parted the waves", he told Durand, taking charge in the emergency so naturally that "I was like a fish in water".[36] The triumphant composer returned to an indifferent France in buoyant mood, receiving a further boost on 13th December when his second son, Jean François, was born.

In gratitude for Liszt's promotion of *Samson* in Weimar, Saint-Saëns set about organising a concert of the Hungarian master's orchestral works in Paris, where they were still virtually unknown. This was no easy task, as theatre managements and orchestras were mostly hostile to music they were certain no one would want to hear. He persisted, despite Liszt's reticence about having his works performed in public. "Saint-Saëns's idea is very noble and friendly, but I should beg him not to pursue it further," Liszt confided to Baroness Meyendorff in January 1878.[37] Saint-Saëns finally engaged a reluctant Théâtre Italien for the concert, and faced not only the ill will of the management but also an insubordinate orchestra and a chorus who demanded more pay for singing this strange music. "It would be hard to imagine all the opposition I had to overcome", he recalled.[38] Cosima Wagner told Judith Mendès that she thought it "truly brave" of him to champion her father's works in this way.[39] The concert eventually went ahead on 18th March and included the *Dante* Symphony – its first performance in Paris – the andante from the *Faust* Symphony and excerpts from *Christus*. Saint-Saëns's conducting was not up to the mark and the concert was panned by the press. That it had taken place at all was no mean achievement, but its promoter, knowing Liszt's attitude to the project and his desire for 'anonymity', tactfully refrained from writing to him about it.

His own music continued to gain ground. Strasbourg, since 1871 part of Germany, heard him in the fourth piano concerto and conducting the Romance for horn and orchestra, at the end of March. He received an ovation, which may not have been entirely unconnected with nationalist sentiment. The public, declared the local press, was familiar with "his masterly works and the eminent position he occupies at the head of the French school, as much as a pianist as a composer". As a pianist he represented "a vigorous school of playing which unites the percussive style of Franz Liszt and the suavity of Frédéric Chopin". As a composer he "has his eyes on the style of the great classical models, but draws from them, with an entirely personal touch, new and adventurous ideas and harmonies". The reviewer also drew attention to the way in which Saint-Saëns integrates the piano into the orchestral texture, so that the concerto "is more of a symphony in which is enshrined some replicas of the piano".[40] At the same time *Samson et Dalila* went from strength to strength in Germany, and it appeared that its success would spread to Brussels, when a concert performance was given there on 5th May before the Belgian king and queen. The royal couple expressed a wish to see it staged at the capital's Théâtre Royal de La Monnaie, but any hopes that their influence might bring this about were dashed by sceptical theatre directors who liked to keep their principal tenor, Lafarge, for Wagnerian roles. Brussels had to wait another sixteen years to see *Samson,* longer even than Paris.

From Strasbourg Saint-Saëns went to Berne to find solitude in which to compose the Requiem for Libon, the anniversary of whose death was approaching. Although the posthumous commission had been revoked, he felt he owed it to his benefactor to make this tribute to his memory, and set to work at a furious pace, sending Durand sections of the work as he wrote them and finishing the whole in just eight days. "The paper disappears as if by magic, because I work with an ardour that is unequalled", he told his publisher in an accompanying note.[41]

The Requiem, for four soloists, chorus and orchestra, follows in the style of the early Mass and *Oratorio de Noël* in that it presents a relatively simple, direct treatment of the text, foreshadowing the better-known Requiem of Fauré in its gently shifting harmonies and the impassioned inflexions of some of its melodies. The emphasis is on pity and consolation rather than the loud apocalyptic visions of a Berlioz or a Verdi. Only in a few short outbursts does the dynamic rise to a double forte. The harmonies can sometimes seem a little naïve, as in the tame perfect cadence that follows the opening pangs of grief, but at times, notably in the Oro supplex, they are strikingly chromatic, in a mood of troubled but tender pleading. There is sometimes a matter-of-fact feel about the music that betrays the hurried circumstances of its composition, especially in the extreme brevity of the Hostias and Sanctus, which seem to end almost as soon as they have begun, but the final Agnus Dei rises to a much greater intensity, repeating a funeral march-like theme built on a sequence of suspensions, and incorporating earlier material to give a sense of unity and inevitability to the whole.

Saint-Saëns returned to Paris to rehearse the new work and to indulge in a little music-making in lighter vein: to write the finale, virtually overnight, of a comic opera called *Nina Zombi,* to which eight other composers had contributed, and which was performed to riotous applause at a salon evening on 17th May. On the 22nd he conducted the Requiem at the church of St Sulpice, two days after the anniversary for which it was written, with Widor at the organ.

The original request for a mass for the dead, made in unusual circumstances, turned out to be as fateful as a similar request had been for Mozart.

Death followed it, and although Saint-Saëns continued living, something in him also died. On 28th May, just six days after conducting the Requiem, he returned to his apartment in the evening to be told by a visiting cousin that his son André was dead. At about three that afternoon, the child was waiting for his mother to take him out when he heard through an open window the voices of his playmates, sons of third-floor neighbour Armand Rousseau. While his mother was busy in the next room, his grandmother dozed and the servant washed linen in the kitchen, the two-year-old, attracted by the shouts of his friends, climbed out on to the window ledge, slipped and fell four floors to his death.[42] The tragedy was the beginning of the end of Saint-Saëns's marriage, for mixed with the shock and despair was his conviction that it was his wife's fault. It confirmed in him what seems to have been a growing prejudice against her, undoubtedly fuelled by his mother, and an impatience with what he considered her lack of competence. That very evening he is said to have refused to speak to her, instead giving her a note with the single word "Farewell" written on it,[43] but the couple stayed together for the time being, and there was to be another cruel stroke of fate before the final parting.

A concert engagement in London on 15th June helped to take his mind off his grief. The invitation had come from Wilhelm Ganz, conductor of the New Philharmonic, and Saint-Saëns felt sufficiently confident now of his English following to play his G minor concerto rather than playing safe with Beethoven, as he had done before. He was not disappointed: each movement was applauded and the scherzo had to be repeated on demand. As for his playing, *The Times* thought "his phrasing is excellent and his technique unerring; only his touch is a little wanting in delicacy, a circumstance not surprising in an artist whose favourite instrument is the organ". As an encore he played two "charmingly quaint" pieces by Rameau.[44] From his lodgings at 2 Carpenter Street, off Berkeley Square, he wrote to Durand: "I have been honoured with the word 'triumph' in the papers, which are not always kind, as you know. I played my trio with Wieniawski and Lasserre and also my quartet, which Wieniawski didn't know and which made a great effect on him . . ." He also reported hopes (which proved unfounded) of an operatic debut in London, with Carl Rosa, director of the English Opera company, considering either *Le Timbre d'Argent* or *Etienne Marcel*: whichever he chose, "the other will be for Covent Garden". He was to continue hoping in vain for a London opera debut for many years to come.

Back home, Marie was so distressed by the death of her son and the uneasy feeling that she had been blamed for it that she could not feed the baby Jean François, and he was taken to be looked after by her mother in Reims. The baby sickened and died on 7th July. It was not in Saint-Saëns's nature to pour out his grief in public. His only known reference to these events is in a postscript of a letter to a friend mainly about the practicalities of concert planning. Thanking the correspondent for his words of sympathy, he adds: "I have just lost two children in the space of a month and can assure you that my gaiety is notably restrained."[45] Fauré wrote in October that Saint-Saëns's mother was doing her best to keep up the family spirits and that they would not have pulled through "that trying time" without her. He notes, though, that Marie "appears to be suffering a reaction to the distressing events of earlier in the year".[46] In fact, she was having to cope not only with her own loss but also with the growing animosity of her husband and his mother (though she did not yet realise the full extent of the latter's ill will).

Marie had nothing left but an increasing sense of isolation and loneliness, whereas her husband could take refuge from grief in his work, as he had done before. This included settings of two Chansons of Victor Hugo, for soloists, chorus and orchestra, and rehearsals for *Les Noces de Prométhée* at the Industrial Exhibition in the autumn, when the cantata at last received the official recognition denied it in 1867. At the distribution of prizes, the exhibition also heard *Orient et Occident* conducted by Colonne. In November were concerts in Brussels and Liège, but soon the work began to tell on his health, and he turned down an engagement in Wiesbaden to take a rest in Geneva, complaining of palpitations and fainting fits. Nevertheless he accepted a commission for a new choral work from the Birmingham Festival, for performance the following August. Until his old age, and to an extent even then, it was extremely rare for him to turn away invitations either to play, to compose or merely to socialise: as he once told Durand, "I cannot refuse engagements without seriously damaging my interests".[47]

As well as the shattering personal loss he had suffered in 1878, came a blow to his professional ambitions when he competed with Massenet for membership of the Academy of Fine Arts at the Institute, the dome of whose building had been a symbol of artistic goals since his childhood. A successful application would have put a seal of official recognition on his achievements as a musician. Gounod supported his candidature, but Massenet, his junior by seven years, backed by Ambroise Thomas, his former teacher at the Conservatoire, was elected by a majority of five votes. His credentials were impeccable: he had just been appointed professor of advanced composition at the Conservatoire, and, more importantly, had a stage success at the Opéra; while Saint-Saëns held no academic post and his operatic endeavours seemed destined for lesser, or foreign, glory. Massenet, much given to flattery and an excessive desire to please, wrote to his rival that the Institute had made a great mistake in its choice, to which Saint-Saëns, with characteristic bluntness, replied: "I entirely agree." What made the election even more galling was that on the first ballot Saint-Saëns led Massenet by one vote, with thirteen; Massenet then gained six votes from other candidates in the second ballot while Saint-Saëns's vote remained the same. At a reception at the home of fellow composer Edouard Lalo, where the victorious

Massenet was the centre of attention, Saint-Saëns studiously ignored him. Asked by his host to make friendly conversation with the man of the moment, he replied: "Why? I've said all I wanted to say." The relationship between the two men was one of professional respect but personal dislike. Saint-Saëns had long supported the other's works and used his influence to have them performed in Germany, but when Massenet heard about the success of *Samson et Dalila* in Weimar he began to suspect the motives behind such friendly gestures and Saint-Saëns was hurt by his ungrateful attitude. "I never intervened again", he wrote. Massenet made it plain to him that he could not be on friendly terms "after a confession he made to me one day";[48] but he had his students at the Conservatoire study his rival's works, and told Liszt, entirely unprompted, that he considered Saint-Saëns the most important French musician since Gounod. For his part, Saint-Saëns praised Massenet's ability "to combine modernism with respect for tradition" and admired his phenomenal productivity – he once saw him ill in bed turning out pages of orchestration while in "a most uncomfortable position". He also defended his music for its "charms and smiles" against those who criticised it for not being profound. "The artist has a perfect right to descend to the nethermost depths and enter into the inner secrets of the soul, but that right is not a duty." Perhaps with fond recollections of the sunny days of his own youth, the lover of comedy and light opera warned young people against demanding music that was all "gloom and boredom". "They may live to regret, too late, the lost hours which they might have spent in gaiety."[49] On a personal level, however, he grew increasingly envious of and irritated by Massenet's operatic successes and his unerring instinct for satisfying public taste. Many years later, it is said, a journalist asked Saint-Saëns's opinion of Massenet: superficial, all sugar and water, he replied. Massenet was then asked his opinion of Saint-Saëns: a great master, the pride of France, was his verdict. Confused, the journalist told Massenet of Saint-Saëns's opinion of him, to which he replied: "Never mind, my friend, perhaps we are both mistaken."[50]

Etienne Marcel opened at Lyons on 8th February 1879, conducted by Alexandre Luigini, composer of the famous *Ballet Egyptien*. Saint-Saëns attended the première, after postponing for three days another engagement scheduled for the same night to conduct the *Danse Macabre* and *Le Déluge* at the Paris Hippodrome. In the opera, the provost of merchants leads Paris in revolt against the Dauphin Charles, but loses popularity and agrees to open the gates of the city to the royal troops. For this he is killed by the demagogue Maillart. Meanwhile his daughter Beatrice is in love with the Dauphin's equerry Robert and is torn between him and her father. The opera ends with the triumphant entry of the Dauphin into Paris, an outcome that would have appealed to Saint-Saëns's royalist sympathies. As a piece of national political pageantry it had its contemporary models in *Boris Godunov,* which Saint-Saëns had, almost unwittingly, introduced to

France, and in the historical operas of Verdi. But although it contains the pomp and spectacle that would have appealed to contemporary taste – and the crowd scenes are its most effective feature – there is, instead of the bombast of grand opera, a kind of controlled power creating subtle evocations of the moods of the volatile Paris populace in the Middle Ages. The ballet music, which contains some appropriate archaisms but also the anachronism of a waltz, was particularly well received and went on to appear occasionally in concert programmes. The Lyons press was enthusiastic: "The unity of the drama is so full of life that you would believe the score to have been written in a day, it is so homogeneous, the different pieces linked under the influence of a uniquely logical and consistent mind."[51] It is this impression of smoothness and correctness, outweighing any dramatic and emotional appeal, that perhaps explains the opera's lack of staying power. It was performed five years later in Paris, in the far from ideal conditions of the Château d'Eau, with its restricted stage, when Aimé Gros took over there. This was an ill-fated venture: Gros had no money to pay the chorus, who carried on only out of respect for the composer, and the corpulent tenor's struggle to get up after singing his love duet with Beatrice at her feet caused gales of laughter. The company declared itself bankrupt after only five performances. The opera, however, was well received and was more successfully staged at Rouen, where Saint-Saëns was called to the stage after act two and presented with a huge bouquet. He caught his long nose in it every time he bowed, until relieved of the flowers by a stage-hand. Yet despite this favourable reception *Etienne Marcel* was afterwards rarely performed.

Two days after *Etienne Marcel*'s Lyons première, *Le Timbre d'Argent* was performed at La Monnaie in Brussels, largely through the prompting of the king and queen. But the operatic elite of Paris had yet to be conquered. Saint-Saëns had now written four operas, none of which had been seen on France's principal musical stage: the Opéra had not yet embraced Wagner, but it was still dominated by the Italians, and especially Verdi. When the theatre staged the French version of *Aïda*, Saint-Saëns's resentment boiled over in a newspaper column in which he angrily predicted the work's failure in Paris and denounced Verdi as an enemy of France, insisting that "no French management should ever accept any composition signed by one so anti-French as the distinguished Giuseppe, whose *Les Vêpres Siciliennes* was adapted to a subject directly hostile to France". Hearing the polemic across the Atlantic, the *New York Times* pointed out that the libretto for *Les Vêpres Siciliennes*, about the Normans in thirteenth-century Sicily, was written by Scribe, adapting Delavigne, "neither of whom have [*sic*] been stigmatised as unpatriotic".[52] (The opera was in fact written for the Paris Exhibition of 1855.) Verdi himself merely noted that the Paris production of *Aïda* had caused some ill feeling in Saint-Saëns. There was more to the attack, however, than personal resentment and wounded national pride: underlying it was a deep-seated opposition to the whole Italian school and the supremacy of melody over harmony. In 1879 Saint-Saëns argued in print against the belief that harmony was a "secondary element" in music and "proceeds from melody; that melody is spontaneously conceived and is the outcome of genius, whereas harmony is the product of calculation and science".[53] He was later to develop the argument, asserting that, far from melody being "natural" and harmony "artificial" the opposite was the case: harmony existed in nature whereas melody was a creation of Man. Harmony did not proceed from melody, otherwise plainchant and folk song would gain by being accompanied, which they did not, but melody could derive from harmony, as Wagner had shown.[54] Thus Saint-Saëns's target was still the exaltation of melody; only after the Wagner mania had taken hold in France in the 1880s was he to cry out against the disappearance of melody.

The sense of exclusion from the artistic high ground of his own country was sharpened by more tours abroad in 1879. In February he left for Germany: at Hanover he played his fourth concerto and one of his Op. 52 Studies, and conducted the *Danse Macabre*; at the Leipzig Gewandhaus he conducted the A minor symphony. From Hanover he wrote to Durand that "by sheer will-power I managed to raise the temperature of an audience that seemed determined not to be warmed out of its indifference", with the result that he had to encore the *Danse Macabre*. It was "one of those *tours de force* which, accustomed as I am to them, always take me by surprise". The visit brought a reunion with Hans von Bülow, who "is always talking about *Dalila*".[55] *Le Déluge* and *La Jeunesse d'Hercule* were acclaimed in Vienna, where he also played Beethoven's fourth concerto under Richter, and there were more successes in Switzerland before his return to Paris in April. In May he was giving concerts in Italy – where he also rejected a libretto about Alexander the Great offered to him by the publisher Giulio Ricordi. All Paris had to offer at this time was a post as music critic of a journal called *Voltaire*, and a slot in a benefit concert at the Opéra for victims of a flood disaster at Szegedin in Hungary. For this he conducted the *Danse Macabre* and a new *Rêverie d'Arabe*, later to be incorporated into the *Suite Algérienne*, in a programme shared with Gounod, Massenet and Delibes. There was also the embarrassment of being nominated, through a misunderstanding involving his publisher, for membership of a banking organisation: not surprisingly, he promptly withdrew his name when he realised what was happening, pleading "complete inexperience" of commercial matters and telling Durand: "I have never been known to take an engagement other than a purely artistic one, as my occupations and aptitudes do not allow me to take up any other kind. I profoundly regret this misunderstanding . . ."[56]

The dichotomy between Saint-Saëns's fame abroad and his more modest standing at home was further underlined by his relationship with English audiences. On 31st May 1879 he made another appearance with Ganz's New

Philharmonic, playing his fourth concerto and conducting the A minor symphony, and was engaged by the orchestra to return the following year (when the series was renamed 'Mr Ganz's Orchestral Concerts'). Just one month later he was back, playing his G minor concerto with the Philharmonic under William Cusins, with Bach's prelude and fugue in A minor on the organ as an encore, and appearing also at the Crystal Palace with the same concerto and *Le Rouet d'Omphale*. His increasingly frequent visits to England gave him a liking for the country that was a kind of personal precursor of the *entente cordiale*, at a time when Britain and France were still political rivals. Through the Philharmonic Society he met Sullivan, whose oratorios he admired and whose comic operas, making their first appearance about this time, he would certainly have appreciated.

While in London he usually took the opportunity to call on Pauline Viardot's father, the great singer Manuel Garcia, now on the staff of the Royal Academy of Music. Garcia lived in Bentinck Street, where he was neighbour to another acquaintance, the writer Hermann Klein, one of the composer's most consistent admirers and champions. On one visit to Klein's home, Saint-Saëns walked in on a terrible family tragedy that was a painful reminder of his own recent loss. Klein was out, and in his absence one of his younger brothers had accidentally shot himself in the head and died just a few moments before Saint-Saëns called. Amid the distress another brother tried to explain to him what had happened and the shocked visitor, thinking it was Hermann Klein who was dead, burst into tears. The writer met him later, after the true facts were revealed, and was taken into an emotional embrace by "this warm-hearted Frenchman", as he called him.[57]

Saint-Saëns's impressions of English musical life grew even more favourable after involvement in the Birmingham Festival, which brought him into contact with Max Bruch. Bruch had also been commissioned by the festival to write a choral work, and both composers agreed to attend rehearsals prior to the concerts in August 1879. Bruch set Schiller's *The Lay of the Bell,* while Saint-Saëns's contribution was *La Lyre et l'Harpe*, Victor Hugo's ode on the contrasting values of classical antiquity and Christian morality. Rehearsals for the ode were soured by complaints from the chorus about the English translation – what *The Times* called "an extraordinary example of involved diction".[58] The baritone Charles Santley, who as a composer of church music had a sensitive ear for lyrical directness and clarity, substituted his own version for his solo passages in the performance in the Town Hall on 28th August. The ode consists of twelve sections alternately singing the praises of pagan joy and sensuality, represented by the lyre, and the stern, uplifting virtues of Christianity, represented by the harp. The two instruments are not used in any literal sense to denote the conflicting cultures: the harp, indeed, often accompanies the ancient muse, while the organ is associated with Christianity. Instead, a short prelude makes a bald statement of the dichotomy with two contrasting ideas, a solemn theme in E flat minor on the organ, later identified by the contralto soloist with Christian austerity, and a shimmering tremolando, with modal shifts, on strings and woodwind, which later heralds a boisterous chorus celebrating the ancient gods. The first half ends with Christianity in the ascendant, as a tenor solo announces the spreading of the Gospel; his noble theme is taken up by the choir and rounded off with a triumphant fanfare. Particularly effective also are the second-half duet for contralto and tenor, 'Love divine', and the baritone solo 'Be joyful', with its obvious debt to opéra-comique, but the final reconciliation of paganism and Christianity, 'Say to Pindus's echo Carmel's hymn', is perhaps too glibly done, with its recollection of earlier themes. It is this thematic recall, limited though it is in scope, together perhaps with the orchestral chromaticisms of the second half's opening number and the superficial resemblance of the prelude's second theme to the first chords of *Lohengrin*, that led *The Times* to give the work the convenience label 'Wagnerian' and to describe its composer, erroneously, as "a faithful disciple of Wagner".[59] In fact, the score abounds with that combination of disciplined fugal writing, laced with chromatic spice, delicate orchestral colouring and distinctive melodic inflection that is Saint-Saëns's hallmark.

The tenor soloist at the festival performance was the musicologist William Cummings, organist at Waltham Abbey, who first used Mendelssohn's tune for the words 'Hark, the Herald Angels Sing'. Saint-Saëns was delighted by the performance, criticising only minor errors on the organ and harp, and after the final chorus was repeatedly called to the platform by prolonged applause. Yet he realised that enthusiasm was far from total. *The Times* thought the "contrapuntal subtleties" of the work were mostly lost on the audience – and there was to be little chance of becoming familiar with them, as *La Lyre et l'Harpe*, like *Le Déluge,* has been consistently ignored by English choral societies. That this should have been the case in the late nineteenth century is at first surprising, given the esteem in which Saint-Saëns was held in England, but becomes less so when it is remembered that the nation's musical taste demanded, not subtlety and refinement, but the rousing moral uplift of a *Messiah* or an *Elijah* and the blood and thunder of a Verdi Requiem.

Discounting this neglect of his choral works, Saint-Saëns was convinced by his experience at the Birmingham Festival that the continental perception of England as a land without music and of the English as unmusical was entirely false. The festival series impressed him by its scale and by the large resources of singers and orchestral players it could call on. He was particularly struck by the quality of the Birmingham choir, who, he said, should be heard by "everyone who has spoken of the unmusical English". "They have everything: intonation, rhythm, a fastidious tonal gradation and a lovely sound . . . you may, for example, require them in a moment to alter a particular expression or tempo and you will find that they will do what you want straightaway. Passages difficult to sing and perilous pianissimos in the top register are child's play . . . Choirs held to be more musical have not as yet attained this level of ability." This, after the grumbles over the English text of *La Lyre*. But then this sensitivity was likely to have enhanced his opinion rather than otherwise, in view of his own fine ear for the clarity and aptness of sung words.

He saw English musicality as being fed on a diet of oratorio, which he believed stemmed from a peculiar blend of the Catholic and Protestant religions, in which the Bible – especially the Old Testament – stood pre-eminent, "hence the appeal of such works as *Israel in Egypt*, *Elijah* and *Solomon*, the subjects of which would never mean as much in other countries". The apparent contradiction that the largely New Testament-inspired *Messiah* enjoys the greatest popularity of all he explains by a perception of the Gospel as part of this biblical tradition, which he apparently regarded as an odd nuance of religious thought, "something which the foreign visitor to England is acutely aware of, and which is peculiarly difficult to explain to other nations".[60] He saw as an illustration of this peculiarity the extraordinary success some years later of Gounod's devoutly Catholic work, the oratorio *Mors et Vita*. "On one of those days of awful black, rainy weather that London specialises in, I saw the vast auditorium of the Albert Hall filled to its upper galleries with a host of eight thousand people, silent and attentive as they listened devoutly."[61] Perhaps not surprisingly, he had little sympathy for the more extreme forms of Protestantism: the Salvation Army he thought "ridiculous"[62] and equally irksome must have been the strong puritan strain that kept *Samson et Dalila* off the English stage for thirty years. The Lord Chamberlain's ban on operas treating biblical stories, which, for example, had forced Verdi's *Nabucco* to be disguised and renamed for its London première in 1846, was not finally lifted until 1909, when *Samson* was staged at Covent Garden.

The determination of Saint-Saëns to build on the reputation he had won for himself and his music in England is revealed in a letter to Durand of 17th October 1879, making an earnest plea to be allowed special rights to sell his works (except songs not in English) to English publishers: "I have worked a long time to make a name for myself in London. I have made great efforts there." In December he was in London again to promote his interests, staying at 11 Ryder Street, St James's, and reporting on "one of the best performances I have heard" of *Le Rouet d'Omphale*.[63] In Paris his music was having a less comfortable ride. Pasdeloup opened the Concerts Populaires season on 11th January 1880 with *La Lyre et l'Harpe,* repeating it on the 25th, with indifferent results. On 1st February there was a rather different reaction when Saint-Saëns, encouraged by the favour his A minor symphony was now commanding abroad, conducted it at the Châtelet: after the adagio a fight broke out in the audience between supporters and opponents, which subsided only when Saint-Saëns began the scherzo.

Escape from the twin perils of indifference and controversy lay in another foreign tour, this time to the Netherlands and Germany in the first two weeks of February. The itinerary gives some idea of the tight schedule such tours involved: beginning in Brussels, it took him to Arnhem on the 16th, The Hague on the 18th, Rotterdam on the 19th, Amsterdam on the 20th, Utrecht on the 21st, Amsterdam again on the 23rd, Berlin on the 25th and 26th, returning to Lille on the 28th. And this in the days before high-speed travel. But even on this tour he was thinking of England. In Brussels he met Ernest Gye, director of Covent Garden, and pressed the case for *Etienne Marcel* to open the next London season. Gye promised to consider it, raising enormously (and falsely) Saint-Saëns's hopes both for his opera and for an English operatic debut, with the belief that "*Etienne* has more chance of success in London".[64]

He returned to England for the third consecutive summer in early May 1880, playing the first concerto and the Beethoven Variations at a Ganz concert. His stay in the capital was interrupted by another long journey, this time to Baden for two concerts in the Association of German Musicians festival, attended by Liszt, who had been making strenuous efforts to promote *La Lyre et l'Harpe* in Weimar. Back in London, he played his fourth concerto under Richter at the St James's Hall on 7th June, and gave recitals of his and Fauré's music at the Steinway Hall. He was also to have conducted the prelude to *Le Déluge* at another Ganz concert (its première in England) at the St James's Hall but for an accident that happened backstage as he was making his way to the platform. A trapdoor had been left open and he fell through it, seriously injuring his back, and Ganz had to conduct the prelude instead. For two days he lay in bed at his lodgings at 55 Brompton Square, counting himself lucky he had not damaged his fingers, but bemoaning the fact that "I have been able to see no one; it's unbearable".[65] He recovered in time to hear his English part-song 'My Land', written for the Musical Union, performed at the St James's Hall on 30th June by Santley and the Swedish Vocal Quartet (the piece was published by Boosey). But enforced idleness was irksome because it interrupted efforts to have *Etienne Marcel* accepted by Covent Garden. When Gye began voicing doubts about the opera, he urged him to see it at Brussels, where it was due to be performed in the autumn. "I am still trying for *Etienne Marcel* in England", he wrote to Durand on 2nd July, but even Queen Victoria was not able to sway the Covent Garden bosses.

Saint-Saëns was granted an audience with the queen at Windsor on 8th July. After hearing stories about her aloofness he was somewhat apprehensive about the meeting but was surprised to find that "she stretched out both hands to take mine, and talked to me with great cordiality". At her request he played the organ in the chapel, accompanied Princess Beatrice's singing teacher, daughter of the great bass Luigi Lablache (who had in turn taught the queen), played the piano and finally accompanied the princess herself in an aria from

Etienne Marcel, which she sang "with great purity of style and diction" even though she was terrified of singing in front of her mother for the first time. The queen was so delighted by the occasion that, unknown to Saint-Saëns, she asked Gye's wife, the soprano Emma Albani, if *Etienne Marcel* could be staged at Covent Garden. "Her wish was never granted", the composer noted after hearing of the approach.[66]

It was becoming clear that the only chance of reaching the London stage was with a new work. Carl Rosa offered a commission, and in response Saint-Saëns showed him another libretto by Gallet, about a courtesan in sixteenth-century Italy, called *Proserpine.* This too fell on stony ground, and *Proserpine* was to take shape only much later and under different circumstances. The double irony was that, after pinning his hopes on London, his next operatic breakthrough was to come, at last, from the Paris Opéra and with an English subject. He owed the commission to write *Henry VIII* to his old friend Gounod, who was given the task first but, mindful of the younger man's frustrated stage career and that of many another French composer, declined with the comment that "of all people Saint-Saëns has the right to a failure at the Opéra".[67] Gounod's motives in passing on the work were not entirely altruistic, as he did not really care for the subject. Saint-Saëns was not wildly enthusiastic either: he would have preferred to follow *Etienne Marcel* with another French historical opera – the Gallic hero Vercingetorix was considered as a subject – or, failing that, one with an Asiatic theme, in which connection Voltaire's tragedy about Genghis Khan, *L'Orphelin de la Chine,* and another work set in ancient Russia and Persia were both pondered and rejected. But the prospect of a production at the Opéra was too good to turn down, and while in London in 1880 he began some period research in the library at Buckingham Palace (to which he was accompanied by a friendly curator for just two hours once a week). There, as well as admiring a collection of Handel autographs, he found "an extremely beautiful melody buried under thickets of pointless ornamentation" in a volume of sixteenth-century manuscripts.[68] The tune, identified as the 'New Melody' from *Will Forster's Virginal Book,* now in the British Library, was to become a major theme of the opera.

As well as making new plans for opera, Saint-Saëns also produced several new orchestral works during 1880, the most important being the B minor violin concerto, which had been on his mind since at least the previous summer. From the outset he intended the new violin concerto to be his ultimate essay in the form – "it is certainly the last I shall write", he declared[69] – and that he took particular care in deciding on the material for it is suggested by the possibility that the work published in 1880 as a Morceau de Concert was originally conceived as the concerto's opening movement. Of Mendelssohnian grace and nimbleness both in the orchestral and solo parts, the Morceau de Concert is in sonata form complete with a short cadenza after the recapitulation. The fully-fledged concerto that finally emerged is in striking contrast to its predecessor of twenty-one years before. In place of formal condensation and integration are the conventional three movements, quite distinct and with almost no thematic cross-references between them. The main departures from traditional form occur in the first movement, and probably raised fewer eyebrows than the pianissimo discord that heralds the second subject, which makes its first appearance, unusually, in the subdominant major. This beautiful flowing melody for the soloist, one of the most extended Saint-Saëns ever wrote, ends in a tender sigh and is rounded off by gentle reminders from the orchestra of the first subject's opening crotchets. This first subject, with its insistent rhythms and declamatory style, provides the material both for the development and the extended coda, the second subject alone, again unusually, forming the recapitulation.

The middle movement, in the unrelated key of B flat major, is a lilting pastoral and "shows what can be done by a great musician when he imposes upon himself the simplicity which embarrasses the lesser man".[70] It is based on two themes, the first ending in a gentle arpeggio figure that achieves a distinction of its own at the end where the clarinet doubles with the solo violin playing harmonics to achieve a striking, organ-like effect. The more sweeping, more heart-felt second theme is interspersed with a demisemiquaver flourish, like a bird call, that provides the only instance in the concerto of thematic recollection as, transformed in character by the soloist, it serves as a stern introduction to the lively finale. Here three themes are grouped together: the first bouncy, tarantella-like, tripping its way over the violin's upper register; the second more sober, giving way to the long strides of the third, full of energetic confidence. Instead of a development there is a fourth, hymn-like tune which, after the repeat of the opening material in full, blazes out on the brass to herald a brilliant coda.

Throughout the work the dramatic and expressive aspects of the violin are given full rein but within the bounds of the main musical idea, to which virtuosic display, as in the piano concertos, is subservient, and in which the orchestra plays an equally important part. Despite its challenging opening, the overall mood of the violin concerto is sunny, sometimes genial, often exuberant, culminating in that blazing optimism that is a Saint-Saëns hallmark, though with a sprinkling of those characteristics associated with the darker side of his musical language, the shivering tremolandos, the discreetly placed, slightly sinister staccato chords, like little exclamation marks. The concerto is dedicated to Sarasate, who had lately premièred the early C major concerto, only just published. He played the new work with Saint-Saëns in piano reduction at one of the composer's Monday soirées and gave the first full performance in Paris on 2nd January 1881.

The *Suite Algérienne* is a memento of Saint-Saëns's stay in North Africa in 1874: in fulfilment of a long-held promise to Durand, it was written mostly while on holiday in Boulogne during July 1880. After an uncertain reaction to its first performance at the Châtelet on 19th December it soon established itself as one of his most popular works. Unlike the orchestral suite of 1863, it bears no relation to the classical suite but is rather a series of descriptive pieces, beginning with a prelude intended to evoke a sense of anticipation on approaching Algiers. There follows a Moorish rhapsody, a reverie said to have been inspired by the memory of a moonlit night in Blida, and, as a reminder of Algeria's colonial master, a French military march. The folk element is supplied by a sprinkling of native melodies and liberal use of sharpened fourths and flattened sevenths, but there is a curious lack of tonal contrast that gives the work an oddly anaemic quality. The prelude is an extended insistence on C major, which caused murmurs of protest at the first performance, the rhapsody opens with page after page of the dominant seventh of D, and the reverie never leaves A major. The suite's appeal lies in its vivid orchestral colouring, which saves the Arab melodies from monotony by dressing them in different hues at each repetition; in an easily identifiable melodic interest; and in the stirring, rumbustious march, long a favourite with brass bands.

A mark of Saint-Saëns's growing prestige at home was a government commission in September 1880 to form a committee for introducing the study of singing in schools. For this he called together Dubois, Bussine, Fauré and others, but further planning had to be put off because of a tour to Spain and Portugal in the autumn, in company with Paul Viardot. This inspired two more travel-orientated works for orchestra, the *Jota Aragonese* and *Une Nuit de Lisbonne* which is less of a local colour piece than a light mood picture inspired by a balmy evening among palm trees and baroque facades. The composer described it as "a little barcarolle", and it was played at the last concert in Lisbon, on 13th November. The gently lilting tune has a melancholy tinge in its downward sequences, but its delicate beauty is overstretched and cloys somewhat with repetition. Its dedication to King Luiz of Portugal indicates Saint-Saëns's growing favour among foreign royalty, and his stay in Lisbon was made even more pleasant by the popularity which the overture to *La Princesse Jaune* was enjoying there.[71]

While in Spain, Saint-Saëns heard of the death of Offenbach, and sent off an appreciation for publication in the *Voltaire*. He also met Léonce Détroyat, co-author with Armand Sylvestre of *Henry VIII*, and took the opportunity to discuss the planned opera with him, working out several modifications to the libretto, cutting several scenes to concentrate the action on the king's break with Rome and his love for Anne Boleyn, and toning down the cruelty and debauchery in Henry's character. Saint-Saëns began serious work on the music and became so involved with it that he turned down a second commission from the Opéra, offered by Auguste Vaucorbeil, Halanzier's directorial colleague. This was another work by Détroyat and Sylvestre, called *Inès de Castro*, which had already been offered to Verdi but had been declined because he was too busy with *Otello*.

Saint-Saëns considered taking it on but in March 1881 told Vaucorbeil that "a good spirit which visits me often" had advised him to apply himself to *Henry VIII.* "Music comes into my head only when I think of *Henry VIII,* not when I think of *Inès.*"[72]

As well as working on the opera he undertook a recital tour of Switzerland in March 1881, visiting also Nice and Strasbourg. The Nice recital included Liszt's 'St Francis on the Waters': "I put not the slightest emotion in it, and I have never played it so well in my life," he wrote to Durand.[73] The burst of creative activity in 1880–81 and the constant round of work of all kinds made his now childless marriage increasingly irrelevant and irksome to him. The shared grief had given way on his part to deep resentment, which Marie at first found hard to understand. All was revealed after the final parting. In July 1881 the couple, both in need of a health restorative, took the waters at the spa town of La Bourboule in the Auvergne. "My wife is always going red, apparently from the effects of the treatment, which she bears admirably . . . yet the doctor claims that I have more need of it than she does," he wrote to Durand, adding darkly that "life is full of sadness, but I shall never grow accustomed to it".[74] One morning he left the hotel and did not return, leaving Marie to make frantic inquiries as to his whereabouts. Alone, and in great distress, she finally discovered that he had gone home. Luckily, Henri Duparc was staying at the same hotel and offered to return with her to Paris, where she sought solace from her mother-in-law – only to realise from her reaction that "she was the one who had caused all the trouble". Saint-Saëns himself was not to be seen. Unknown to Marie, her husband's favourite cousin had also been blackening her name and poisoning his mind against her. She was handed a note from him formally declaring that he did not intend to return to her, whereupon she packed her bags and went back to her own family. There was no legal separation, but he never saw her again. She is quoted as saying in later years: "I suffered many injustices through the capricious nature of my husband, but he had good qualities too."[75] Anyone asking Saint-Saëns about his marriage in later life was invariably met with a steely silence. As one friend put it, "he guarded his secret with dignity".[76]

IX • THE IMMORTAL

SOME COMPENSATION FOR THE BREAK-UP OF SAINT-SAËNS'S MARRIAGE WAS afforded by a reconciliation with Victor Hugo, which came about through plans to put up a statue to the poet. The composer wrote a choral work to his own words for the unveiling, but public subscriptions for the statue fell below expectations and the project was abandoned. He instead conducted his *Hymne à Victor Hugo* in a series of concerts at the Trocadero, the new public entertainments venue built for the 1878 Exhibition. "The performance was splendid", Saint-Saëns wrote, "a large orchestra, the magnificent organ, eight harps and eight trumpets sounding their flourishes in the organ loft, and a large chorus for a peroration of such splendour that it was compared to the set pieces at the close of a fireworks display." The object of this gushing piece of adulation heard the performance and was easily seduced by its lofty praise of him as an embodiment of genius and immortal art. Dismissing the earlier rift, he asked Saint-Saëns to dine with him and his friends, a social engagement that became a regular event. They were "small gatherings", the composer recalled, that were "among the most precious recollections of my life",[1] spent in lively conversation about art, life – and death. At one of them the astronomer Camille Flammarion, founder of the French Astronomical Society, held a seance in which the assembled guests are said to have conjured up the spirit of Molière, who upset Victor Hugo by saying he did not think much of his poems.

This was the sort of company, delighting in speculation and debate, in which the former husband and father felt most at home, rather than the cosy domestic surroundings of the family man; after he had abandoned Marie, cultural circles came to play perhaps an even greater part in his life than in his bachelor days. And if Victor Hugo represented artistic immortality, as Saint-Saëns proclaimed in his *Hymne*, his musical admirer was himself to become an Immortal in a more literal sense.

Members of the Institute, elected for life and officially representing the highest level of cultural and scientific achievement in France, were long known as the Immortals. This sobriquet was said to derive from the seal used by the Institute's pre-Napoleonic forebear, the French Academy, with its laurel wreath decoration and the inscription "To Immortality". Having been rebuffed in 1878, Saint-Saëns finally achieved his ambition to join the Immortals in 1881. He was elected, in preference to Delibes, after the death of Reber the previous November left a vacancy in the Academy of Fine Arts, one of the Institute's five sections. His inaugural speech, by tradition, contained a long eulogy on his predecessor, and he was able to deliver it in all sincerity as he had long recognised the debt he owed to Reber for helping to shape his upbringing in the classical symphonic style. He had, after all, dedicated *La Lyre et l'Harpe* to him. He could not, however, resist drawing parallels between Reber's lack of success in opera and his own, in order to take a swipe at theatre directors. "Logic may rule the theatres but who can say what motivates theatre directors?" he asked. "For them Reber was not 'a man of the theatre'."[2] The comment was omitted when the speech was published in 1885 in *Harmonie et Mélodie* for by then Saint-Saëns had made some progress at the Opéra with *Henry VIII* and was anxious to remain on good terms with theatre bosses.

Many a Thursday afternoon was spent at the Academy, but membership of the Institute also gave him access to sessions of the other academies, enabling him in years to come to indulge his passions for astronomy, physics, metaphysics, biology, zoology, philosophy and classical archaeology, and to relate his musical experience to some of them. In 1886, for instance, he presented a paper to the Academy of Sciences on the need for a standard metronome, and in the same year published an essay on the theatrical decors of ancient Rome. This suggests an answer as to why buildings and scenery depicted in wall paintings at Pompeii seem to defy gravity and perspective; they are, he argued, probably representations of stage sets. Acoustics were another meeting point of art and science to which he turned his thoughts. Institute membership conferred on him an intellectual status through which he also gained acceptance as a contributor to various learned journals, and in September 1881 the magazine *La Renaissance de la Musique* published an article from him on the acoustic phenomenon of the multiple resonance of clocks. Although, as he admitted, his explanations were "hypothesis without any scientific pretence",[3] they nevertheless provided a basis for further study by others. (He later broke with *La Renaissance* over its enthusiasm for Wagner, rebuking its editor Edmond Hippeau for the journal's "erroneous ways".)

But it was as a practising musician that he gained from the Institute the official recognition for which he had struggled for so long. Younger musicians looked to him more than ever for advice and guidance, and for the career advancement that his influence in high places could secure for them. At the Conservatoire, tutors were more anxious than ever to show off their promising pupils to him on his visits. Now his name could appear in print with the impressive suffix "de l'Institut", giving him the satisfaction of having caught up with his rival Massenet in official standing. But while membership of the Institute greatly enhanced his prestige, it also marked his transformation from a representative of the vanguard into an establishment figure viewed with scorn and derision as out of touch and out of sympathy with new ideas by some among the younger generation. The tradition of regarding the Institute as a body of outdated conservatives would inevitably reinforce Saint-Saëns's changed image from that of innovator to that of reactionary, in the decade that opened with Franck's piano quintet and saw Wagner's operas attracting an increasingly fanatical following in France. Saint-Saëns's response to Franck's quintet was symptomatic of a deep-seated aversion to the new developments in music that were to gather pace during the 1880s, leaving him increasingly isolated, especially after the deaths of so many of his friends and champions, Liszt and Gounod in particular.

One of the major theatres of this process was the National Music Society. Franck's quintet, dedicated to Saint-Saëns, was given at a society concert on 17th January 1880, with its dedicatee at the piano. As he played, he felt a growing sense of horror at the sounds he was helping to make. Their unprecedented emotional fervour offended his firmly-held principles of taste, balance and proportion, and as soon as the last chord was played he walked off the platform in a huff, spurning the applause and pointedly leaving the manuscript, with its dedication, on the piano. Franck, greatly hurt by this rejection, changed the dedication. Saint-Saëns's view of the work was shared by the more conservative members of the audience – and, when he came to hear it, by Liszt – but it is often asserted, probably with good reason, that Saint-Saëns's hostile reaction had as much to do with his unrequited passion for Augusta Holmes as with musical principles. Since she began to study with Franck, who was now nearly sixty, rumour had it that the saintly church musician's feelings for her were rather more than those of a master for his pupil. ("Franck saintly? Go and ask Augusta Holmes", another of his students is said to have remarked.) Many who heard the quintet had little doubt as to the object of its manifestly erotic longings. Certainly Franck's wife flew into a rage at the mere mention of it, so it would not be surprising, in view of its associations, to find it touched a raw nerve also in a man who had proposed to Augusta and had instead been through a marriage that had proved both loveless and childless.

The quintet was an expression of a new musical intensity advocated by Franck's followers, led by Vincent d'Indy, in opposition to what they regarded as the superficiality of the French tradition. It was a development that was part of a wider movement in art and literature, profoundly influenced by Wagner, which was ultimately to undermine Saint-Saëns's position as a leading figure in French musical life. It is ironic that, as the young composer had been disadvantaged to some extent by association with Wagner's music when it was widely regarded with suspicion in France, so the established artist's independent views on the subject would similarly make him enemies when Wagner was all the rage.

Support for Wagner in France had always tended to come less from musicians than from novelists and poets attracted by his ideas of opera as a fusion of all the arts. Among the early enthusiasts in the 1850s were Baudelaire and Théophile Gautier, while opposition came from the music critics Fétis and Scudo, who ridiculed the very idea of a 'music of the future' (not Wagner's phrase but that used by his supporters) and attacked Wagner's music as subservient to theory and lacking all-important melody. Interestingly, these were the same grounds of criticism cited by Saint-Saëns thirty years later as Wagner began to dominate French musical life. But in mid-century the 'new music' hailed by a select artistic circle could make little headway in a country where orchestral concerts were dominated by the classical trinity of Haydn, Mozart and Beethoven and where the stage was held by Italian opera, Meyerbeerian grand opera, opéra-comique or the new lyric opera espoused by Thomas. Pasdeloup's inclusion of Wagner in his Concerts Populaires from 1861 was invariably accompanied by clashes in the audience between 'conservatives' and Wagnerians. The attempt to introduce *Tannhäuser* to the Opéra in 1861 was bound to fail before a house expecting to be entertained by spectacle and exotic dancing to hummable tunes. Hostility was also connected to politics, and was to remain so. As Wagner, once the dangerous revolutionary, found favour in imperial circles (Napoleon III had, after all, come to power on the back of the same revolutionary movement) so the disenchantment of radicals was added to the enmity of monarchists. The Jockey Club members who led the opposition to *Tannhäuser* were 'legitimists' acting as much out of dislike for the Napoleonic regime as out of affronted taste.

Thanks largely to the efforts of Pasdeloup, the circle of Wagner admirers grew throughout the 1860s to include Saint-Saëns's friends, the writers Catulle Mendès and his wife Judith, Gautier's daughter, so that by the end of the decade Bizet could write that "few people have the courage to persist in their hatred of Wagner".[4] Again it was politics that acted as a brake on the Wagner expansion, in the form of extreme anti-German feeling after the French military defeat and the siege of Paris in 1870–71, and publication of Wagner's satire *A Capitulation*. Pasdeloup's attempts to re-introduce Wagner to the Parisian concert hall sparked violent demonstrations throughout the 1870s. The tide began to turn back in Wagner's favour after the publicity and prestige surrounding the first Bayreuth Festival in 1876, so that by 1879 Pasdeloup could conduct the first act of *Lohengrin* to "unanimous enthusiasm".[5] The baton was taken up, as it were, by Colonne and by Charles Lamoureux, who founded his Nouveaux Concerts in 1881.

Wagner was also to win new allies in literature, with the advent of the Symbolist movement, which aimed to free art from what were considered to be artificial rules and conventions that stood in the way of emotional intensity, the baring of the artist's soul and the 'natural' evocation of sensations and impressions. The Symbolists, who included Mallarmé and Verlaine, hailed Wagner's music dramas as achieving this intensity and 'fluidity' (one of the movement's favourite nouns) by dispensing with the set pieces of aria and ensemble, breaking down the distinction between voice and orchestra, and generally avoiding every kind of barrier to the free flow of expression. D'Indy and later, for a period, Debussy were among the musicians closely identified with the Symbolist aesthetic.

It was the quasi-religious, missionary fervour of the new movement and its deification of Wagner that put Saint-Saëns on his guard. Reporting on the *Ring* from Bayreuth in 1876 he had sought to convey the beauty, intensity and grandeur of the music but had also criticised its *longeurs* and the subordination of the singer to the 'total' musical concept. And he was not going to give up the right to criticise as he saw fit in deference to what was rapidly becoming a cult. "I love liberty passionately and cannot bear to have admirations imposed upon me. Enthusiasms to order freeze the blood in my veins and render me incapable of appreciating the most beautiful works."[6] He thus reserved the right to be neither for nor against Wagner, and as if to demonstrate his even-handedness encouraged the Austrian impresario Angelo Neumann in his (unsuccessful) plan to bring a production of *Lohengrin* to Paris in 1881. In March of that year he wrote to Durand:

I see the great battle that is being prepared for next winter: Wagnerians on one side, anti-Wagnerians on the other. I find this deplorable and I do not want to be in the one camp or the other. Now I have taken a position, and I shall always be able to refer to this letter, which will have preceded the battle, when I am unjustly accused.[7]

But, as he foresaw, he came under mounting disapproval from the Wagnerians for opposing the influence of the new cult on French music and berating French composers for what he called their habit of "crossing the Rhine in their search for truth". "Nothing could be better than to go to Germany for masterpieces, but do not go there for theories", he was to write later.[8]

He stated his independent position unequivocally at the opening of this new era in French music with the septet for trumpet, strings and piano, whose formal neatness and conciseness, humour and overtly archaic idiom represent a reply, intentional or otherwise, to the Franck quintet. It was written for a chamber music society called La Trompette, devoted to the cultivation and practice of the trumpet. Saint-Saëns was a member for many years (as was the young violinist and future conductor Pierre Monteux) and he greatly valued the society's promotion of chamber music in general, writing in 1898 that it had become in Paris "an artistic jewel whose brilliance can be seen from afar".[9] It took some time for him to accept the society's request for a chamber piece to include a trumpet, a combination he at first considered absurd. To society leader Emile Lemoine he wrote: "I shall write for you a concerto for twenty-five guitars and to play it you will have to depopulate Castille and Andalucia; but a piece with trumpet? Impossible!"[10] Nevertheless he began it "in a moment of good humour"[11] early in 1880, playing the piano in the first movement at a La Trompette concert in January, and worked on it intermittently throughout the year, playing in the first complete performance on 28th December.

The septet's four movements – preamble, minuet, andante and final gavotte – echo the classical suite, but although it looks back to the eighteenth century in style and form, its unusual instrumentation gives it a distinctly modern ring that looks forward to the eighteenth-century pastiches of Stravinsky, so that at times it sounds as if it could have been written in the 1930s. In fact, unconventional combinations were not new to Saint-Saëns: the Serenade of 1866, for instance, combines organ with piano and strings, and the later Barcarolle is for harmonium with piano, violin and cello. Attention must also be drawn to the elements of the septet that stamp it firmly as of its time, the virtuosity, the warmth and chromatic tendency of some of the harmonies, especially in the minuet, and cross-references between movements. The preamble's main subject reappears at the close, and a distinctive rhythmic figure first heard in the preamble turns up again as the basis of the andante, which, lyrically as well as rhythmically, carries overtones of Schumann in meditative mood.

The septet soon established itself in the repertory, as some of Saint-Saëns's other works gained wider recognition. In October 1881 he was invited to Liverpool for a week by Max Bruch, then conductor of the Liverpool Philharmonic, and as well as playing the G minor concerto took the baton for *La Jeunesse d'Hercule*, before going on to give two well-attended organ recitals, which earned him £120. He was invited to dinner by Bruch and his wife Clara, and it was a pleasant reunion for the two composers after their first meeting at the Birmingham Festival two years before. *La Lyre et l'Harpe*, written for Birmingham, had been given its French première by Pasdeloup on 11th January 1880 to a less than enthusiastic reception, but when it was performed by the Conservatoire Concerts Society on 19th November 1882 it was highly praised. Early in 1882 it had been the main work in a festival in Saint-Saëns's honour at Mulhouse, one of the border towns annexed by Germany in 1871, during a tour of German cities in which the septet also featured prominently. At Mannheim he gave the piano recital which prompted Clara Schumann to her damning criticism of his playing. Little did he know of it: he felt honoured by her presence, writing to Durand that she was "much noticed; to thank her for coming I played two short pieces by her husband, which appeared to give her great pleasure".[12]

At Lille on 5th March he conducted *Le Déluge* and in Hamburg on the 14th conducted *Samson et Dalila* to such acclaim that he was moved to report to Durand that "I shall, alas, not have, like our friends Franck and Lalo, the glory of being understood only after my death!"[13] This was the performance that led von Bülow to declare that Saint-Saëns had been largely untouched by Wagner's ideas, and to praise *Samson* (not counting, presumably, Wagner's operas) as "the most important music drama which has seen the light of day these twenty years".[14] Later, in the summer, *La Lyre* was performed at the Magdeburg Festival, through the advocacy of Liszt, who greatly admired what he called "this remarkable work". (The performance had been postponed from the previous year because of delays in translation and choral rehearsals.) Bruch, who left Liverpool to take charge of the orchestra at Breslau, did much to promote Saint-Saëns's music there, conducting *La Jeunesse d'Hercule* in October 1883 and regularly performing the concertos, including the fourth piano concerto played by the composer.

While in Germany he looked on with amused contempt as the battle raged between the followers of Wagner and those of Brahms. Of the Germans, whichever side they favoured, he wrote that "our excellent cousins can no longer understand a simple, natural melody; that is too clever for them".[15] Already the tyranny of melody, enshrined in the Italian school, was becoming less of a target than the perceived disappearance of melody in Germany, as fanatical devotion to Wagner spread among French composers, among them d'Indy, Lalo and Chabrier. The Wagner boom was underway in France: new coteries of admirers were formed, like the 'Petit Bayreuth' and the 'Bayreuth de poche' of Judith Gautier (now separated from Mendès), the number of French visitors to Bayreuth was growing and for three years from 1885 the literary Symbolists had an influential mouthpiece in the *Revue wagnerienne*. More of his music was being played, notably under the determined Wagnerian Charles Lamoureux, and the religious awe that often attends Wagner performances, which forbids the slightest cough or whisper, let alone noisy demonstration, was already appearing, as Lamoureux made it plain that anyone interrupting would be thrown out of the hall. But a Wagner programme could still provoke riots in the street.

As before, opposition was inspired largely by politics and nationalism: the League of Patriots, founded in 1882, took an anti-Wagner stance, and Lamoureux's attempt to establish *Lohengrin* at the Opéra in 1887 was scuppered by the right-wing inspired threat to the Republic led by General Boulanger. There was just one performance, at which the riot police were on stand-by; it passed without incident inside the hall at least, except for one old man who stood up after the prelude and asked for the *Marseillaise*. He was told to leave. *Lohengrin* finally got its run at the Opéra in 1891, but even then, when Wagner polemics were losing their venom, it was not without violent demonstrations outside.

It had not been forgotten that Wagner had included *A Capitulation* in the complete edition of his writings, but for his devotees his works overrode any offence caused by his publicly stated hatred of France and its culture. Their position was summed up by Gounod when he wrote that "the insults of our national enemy are as nothing compared with the homage his works deserve".[16] Saint-Saëns noted that Wagner's admirers "have long known that his tactlessness is on a par with his talent. If I were to report what he said about a highly placed personage of the imperial court, there would be an exchange of diplomatic notes between France and Germany".[17] But whereas in 1876 he could accept that "the worth of his works" outweighed Wagner's Francophobia, he was now far less ready to overlook the anti-French rantings of *A Capitulation*. In the summer of 1882, he went to Bayreuth during the final rehearsal for *Parsifal* and called on the master at his house, Wahnfried, but only in deference to Liszt's wishes. He and Fauré had just visited Liszt in Zürich, and he felt obliged to carry out the request because "I owed him so much I could refuse nothing". At Wahnfried he told Wagner of the deep offence *A Capitulation* had caused. Wagner tried to make light of it, asking if he really bore a grudge "all because of a joke in bad taste". "It would have been so easy for you not to have made it", Saint-Saëns replied, to which there was no answer, and the two men took leave of each other for the last time.[18]

That summer Saint-Saëns completed his opera *Henry VIII* – except for the second act ballet – finishing the orchestration by the sea at Le Tréport, the Parisians' nearest bathing resort. There he rented a villa next to where the Durand family were staying, and the publisher's son Jacques remembered the composer as being very much in holiday mood. The forty-six-year-old was in spirits "as young as we all were", joining the junior Durand and his fun-loving friends at café concerts listening to the latest songs. Among the group was the twenty-one-year-old Albert Guinon, destined to become a dramatist of note, whom Saint-Saëns had engaged as his secretary. Guinon wrote a humorous 'complaint' about a store in the resort run by a Mme Jacob, where, it was said, holiday-makers could never obtain what they wanted and inquiries were answered with the most elaborate excuses. Saint-Saëns provided a tune for it, and the young Durand recalled that "we learned it by heart and sang it in front of the store, Saint-Saëns conducting. Mme Jacob took it in good spirit." Comic songs were a usual means of light relief for the composer, as Durand pointed out, but another light-hearted occasion proved to contain matter of more weight. While at the Durand villa he asked their grandmother if he could borrow her hat and coat. He put them on and, thus incongruously attired, sang a baritone aria, complete with gestures, with his fellow guest Guiraud at the piano. The windows facing the beach were open and a crowd of bathers gathered to listen. After the applause, another guest, a sculptor called Franceschi, went out to announce to the beach audience that they had just heard Saint-Saëns sing part of his new opera.[19]

As with his previous operatic ventures, *Henry VIII* met with a series of delays of various kinds, which caused the rehearsal period to be spread over several months. After preparations for production began at the Opéra in September 1882 Saint-Saëns was pestered by singers to build up their vocal parts, to the extent that he had to write a complete additional aria for Catherine of Aragon – it was dropped after the first performance because it held up the action. There were more cuts and reworkings, and the ballet had still to be written. In addition, there was a concert tour of Germany and Austria in January–February

1883, in which he conducted *La Lyre et l'Harpe* in Berlin and other cities throughout the two empires. The long-cherished goal of a production at the Opéra was finally achieved on 5th March, when *Henry VIII* was given a sumptuous première, with the Opéra's principal baritone Jean Lassalle in the title role, and with set designs based, like some of the music, on research in London. Choreography was by Louis Mérante, creator of the ballet *Sylvia*.

It was an event eagerly awaited by a public belatedly aware of the international standing of this newcomer to the Institute. One final hitch actually worked to advantage, when the tenor billed to sing the role of Don Gomes was taken ill and replaced by the much more suitable Etienne Dereims. Exhausted mentally and physically, Saint-Saëns left after the première to take a convalescence, on doctor's orders, in Algiers. From there on 12th March, he wrote to the Opéra conductor Ernest-Eugène Altès, congratulating him on the way the rehearsals had ended so successfully:

How did the sloppy and indecisive execution of the score become, first, the admirable execution and then the marvellous execution? How did the nymph become a soaring butterfly? I don't know. But I do know that the orchestra of the Opéra has proved once again to be the best in the world . . . The Concerts Society will not take offence at the praise I give, wherever it is merited. The Concerts Society and the Opéra: the god of music in two persons. As for you, my dear friend, how can I ever pay the inestimable price of your collaboration over all these days and months? Your care has been known to smooth out the least difficulty; I shall not forget it.[20]

The opera's libretto is a reworking of a play by the seventeenth-century Spanish dramatist Calderon, called *The Schism in England*, based only loosely on historical fact. It concerns the king's love for Anne Boleyn, his break from Rome and his attempt to uncover an affair between his young queen and the Spanish ambassador Don Gomes. His rejected first wife, the ailing Catherine, possesses a compromising letter which would condemn Anne, and which Henry sets out to obtain. He brings Don Gomes to see Catherine, just as the new queen also arrives aiming to retrieve the letter. In a dramatic final quartet, Henry declares his passion for Anne in a cynical attempt to arouse Catherine's vengeful instincts and prompt her to hand over the incriminating document but instead she throws it in the fire as she sinks to her death.

Catherine was sung at the first performance by the Austrian soprano Gabrielle Krauss, whose considerable acting ability brought out in full the tragic nobility of the role. Catherine is the opera's real heroine, its most sympathetic character, and is finely contrasted with the coquettish Anne, whose girlish, selfish ambition allows Saint-Saëns's misogyny full rein, especially in the act two love duet in which Henry tells her he wants her for his wife, not his mistress. Anne can only repeat with wide-eyed glee "I shall be queen" and all her previous scruples about Henry already having a wife disappear. The prelude to the four-act opera is based on the theme discovered at Buckingham Palace, and serves merely to set the period atmosphere, with no hint of the tragedy to come. The theme reappears at later points to emphasise the period feel, notably at the climax of the Synod scene, when the assembly declares its support for Henry in his defiance of Rome. As in *Etienne Marcel*, political conflict provides a framework for personal conflict, but here the element of confrontation is more marked. As well as Henry's challenge to the pope and the final showdown in Catherine's bedroom, it gives rise also to the death sentence on the Duke of Buckingham, and Catherine's unavailing pleas for mercy. In the final scene of act one personal tensions are dramatically played out against the offstage funeral chorus for the doomed Buckingham, as Catherine expresses her horror at Henry's ruthlessness and Anne sings of ill omens as the king assures her of his love. The display of conflicting emotions related to and sharpened by audible events offstage is strongly reminiscent of *Carmen*, and Tchaikovsky was to use a similar device in *The Queen of Spades*.

Among the notable set pieces are the king's love song in the first act, the confrontation between Catherine and Anne, and the duet of the dukes of Surrey and Norfolk sung over another piece of musical period setting, the repeated strains of a Tudor-style dance (anachronistically marked as in minuet time) which is supposedly going on in the palace gardens. Catherine's final act lament, in which she recalls the homeland she will never see again, is a poignant exercise in sorrowful reflection in which the irregular rhythm and harmonic clash between E minor and C minor bring out a sharp taste of bitterness and regret. The second act ballet, danced in Richmond Park as an entertainment for the papal legate, gives Saint-Saëns an opportunity to indulge in some local colour pieces – and here he falls into one of the traps set for continental artists treating subjects from British history. He includes a Highland dance, apparently unaware that Scotland was not part of Henry's kingdom. And the opening dance, based on the traditional English tune 'The Jolly Miller' (an anachronism as it dates from the seventeenth century), is confusingly called Entry of the Clans. To add to the cultural confusion, the ballet also includes a gypsy dance, giving Saint-Saëns an excuse to provide some oriental-style music! Only in the last piece are we reminded of where we are, with a lively English jig.

The central pinnacle of the opera is the second act love scene, as the seduction scene is of *Samson et Dalila*. Here though the subject is the real passion of man for woman instead of the destructive powers of woman over man. Nevertheless, love in *Henry VIII* is viewed in a cynical aspect, tied up with considerations of jealousy, ambition, power and wealth; and, in the character of Henry, with sheer cruelty. In this light it was bound to trigger a response in a composer whose own love life had been soured by bitter experience.

Inevitably the opera was variously called Wagnerian and not Wagnerian, while some hailed it as a triumph of the French school. Although it contains elements both of Meyerbeer, in its scenes of spectacle and sensationalism, and of Wagner, in its recurring melodic figures, it avoids imitating either. The spectacular and the sensational are integral parts of the drama, and not there merely for effect, as they tend to be in Meyerbeer, and the use of representative themes hardly amounts to Wagnerian intensity. *Henry VIII* shows Saint-Saëns taking an individual path which, if it must be compared, perhaps comes closest to that of his late friend and colleague Bizet, with its emphasis on clarity and lucidity. These qualities are perhaps not best suited to a subject involving a series of often violent emotional confrontations: his melodic style, as has been pointed out, tended to avoid confrontation. This was no doubt in Tchaikovsky's mind when he said that with *Henry VIII* Saint-Saëns had shown himself incapable of writing a great dramatic work. But then Tchaikovsky was having problems of his own in producing an emotionally convincing opera to follow *Eugene Onegin*. Much of the music in *Henry VIII* is extraordinarily fine, and although its initial run (complicated when both Lassalle and Krauss fell ill) did not extend beyond a few performances it returned to the Opéra the next season and was to become Saint-Saëns's most frequently performed opera after *Samson et Dalila* (though still far less often than *Samson*, and often in an abridged form). It helped to earn his promotion to Officier of the Légion d'Honneur in 1884, and by 1891 it had been played for the fiftieth time at the Opéra, in whose repertory it remained until 1919, after eighty-seven performances. Frankfurt was to hear it in 1887, Milan in 1895, Moscow in 1897, London in 1898, Antwerp and Prague in 1900 and Monte Carlo in 1908.

The breakdown in Saint-Saëns's health after the opera's première was more serious than he first supposed. He suffered a dangerous relapse on his return to Paris from Algiers, and had to resume his convalescence, first at Cauterets in the Pyrenees, from where he travelled west to take the salt water treatment at Salies-de-Béarn, and then in Provence. He was able to resume concerts in the autumn, but the winter forced him to warmer climes again, first to Italy and then to North Africa, where he spent his time in complete relaxation. Work resumed on his return to Paris, where he conducted his *Hymne à Victor Hugo*. Composition began again too, with two choruses and two works for piano and orchestra, the Allegro Appassionato and the *Rapsodie d'Auvergne*, the latter built on a tune he heard sung by a washerwoman in a mountain village in the region. Along with the *Rapsodie Bretonne*, it is one of his very few works based on folk melodies of his native country.

Saint-Saëns wrote the *Rapsodie d'Auvergne* in Toulouse, where he was supervising rehearsals for a production of *Henry VIII*. The opera's progress was encouraging: it had enjoyed a second season in Paris, and Gounod had published a long pamphlet praising it in every detail, concluding that it had "earned the most signal honour for French art". Declaring Saint-Saëns to be "one of the most astonishingly gifted men I have ever met" who "knows his business thoroughly", Gounod points to the independent line he takes in his work, belonging to no party or clique, and never posing as a reformer. He is never afraid of not making an effect, so that he "never exaggerates; thus he is never far-fetched, nor violent nor over-emphatic. He uses every combination and every resource without abuse . . . He writes as he feels and as he knows." He never imitates, says Gounod, any of the musical styles in his huge store of knowledge: this is not quite true, as has been seen, but when he does imitate he does it in his own way and to serve a specific artistic purpose. Gounod does, however, point to the fact that Saint-Saëns stood aside from the new moves towards greater emotional and spiritual intensity in the wake of the Wagner phenomenon and their more exaggerated manifestations. There is "no solemnity, no transcendentalism" and his music "keeps time . . . without perpetually dragging out over those silly and detestable pauses which make any proper musical construction impossible".[21]

An illustration of the divergence between Saint-Saëns's aesthetic of regular lines and classical sobriety and that of the Wagnerians came when he visited the Weimar Festival in May 1884. There he saw a new opera, *Sakuntala*, by Felix Weingartner, one of Liszt's students. He was moved to ask why love was such an agonising affair for the Germans that it always had to be accompanied by dissonances, prompting Liszt to advise his young pupil to "keep it simple, and round off your melodies in four-bar phrases".[22]

Yet Saint-Saëns was still a prophet of a new music. In a lecture in 1884 to fellow Immortals he returned to the subject he had broached a decade earlier, foreseeing a time when the ear would no longer be satisfied with tones and semitones, a system that could not achieve "musical truth" but only an "approximation". When this happened, he said, "another art will be born and music as we know it today will be like a dead language whose masterpieces survive but which is no longer spoken".[23] It is ironic that in that same year he was on the committee that awarded the Prix de Rome to Claude Debussy. For Saint-Saëns, the compositions which the young man produced during his tenure of the prize turned the subject of the new music from a speculation into a spectre, from a matter of distant possibilities to a reality too close for comfort, and he almost certainly helped to write the official report condemning them. No longer regarded as the dangerous innovator, he came increasingly to represent to his admirers an island of sober tradition in a sea of wild modernity. For his critics, who saw him as an enemy and, ultimately, an irrelevance, the tide was rising and the island was doomed to be submerged. Musical history has tended to favour the critics. Yet, a century after the controversies, passions and mud-slinging, hindsight suggests that the view of Saint-Saëns as a stern reactionary is only part of the picture. What we see is a fifty-year-old composer consolidating and developing further his own individual style, along lines laid out over the previous twenty or thirty years, long before the advent of what he came to attack as the formal anarchy and stylistic excesses of the Wagnerians. There was the same striving for a balance of form and content and, to that end, the same readiness to experiment with structure and technique.

The D minor violin sonata, for instance, adopts the unusual formal plan of the fourth piano concerto. Two movements are subdivided into the constituents of a regular four-movement sonata, but there is also here a greater sense of maturity and calm assurance underlying the work's vibrant energy. Stylistically, the sonata owes more to the third violin concerto in its darkly restless opening (possibly the "little phrase" that so fascinated Proust) and the easy-going nature of its central repose. The adagio into which the first section leads is a peaceful, meditative conversation between violin and piano, the two instruments then playing, by way of contrast, with a touching, charmingly simple sequential figure, before repeating both sets of material in modified form.

In view of Liszt's comment about Saint-Saëns's preference for four-bar phrases, there is a certain irony (possibly deliberate) about the sonata, both in its opening theme's ambiguous rhythm, with groups of nine quavers interrupting six-quaver bars, and in the equally ambiguous phrase structure of the third movement allegretto. These irregularities add a little spice to the fare, but the allegretto is marred somewhat by the constant repetition, bar after bar, of one rhythmic pattern, to which the song-like interlude provides little respite as the same pattern goes on in the accompaniment. It comes as some relief when the finale's breathtaking perpetual motion bursts in, a piece of waspish humour characteristic of Saint-Saëns the man (when in impish mood, he would unexpectedly increase the speed while accompanying, to the consternation of the poor violinist). The chattering semiquavers, a musical equivalent perhaps of the composer's rapid speech, constitute the principal subject of a sonata movement more regular than that of the opening, the impassioned second subject appearing, conventionally, in the dominant and later in the tonic. The 'big tune' of the first movement then makes a surprise entry to launch a lengthy coda, and goes on to suffer rather badly from over-repetition, a fault which tends to upset the balance of an otherwise satisfying formal layout. Two elements in the sonata were to find fuller expression respectively in two works that were to follow soon after. The playful humour of the finale was to be given freer rein in *Le Carnaval des Animaux*; and a distinct strain of bitterness detectable in parts of the violin's melodic line was to find its way into the symphony in C minor.

Saint-Saëns wrote the sonata for the Belgian violinist Pierre Marsick (a fellow performer in the first performance of the Franck quintet), with whom he embarked on a concert tour of Switzerland, conducting *Le Déluge* in Geneva on 4th November. Later he premièred the *Rapsodie d'Auvergne* in Marseilles. Music was beginning to flow from him again, and from 1885 he began to write songs with the same frequency as in the period to 1871. These later songs show him increasingly concerned with the technicalities of word setting, often at the expense of poetic feeling, and the atmosphere is more restrained, more refined than in the earlier songs. Again, this should be regarded more as a development of a long-held regard for correctness in the musical treatment of words rather than as a specific reaction to the overblown emotionalism of the Wagnerians. One of the first songs of this later phase is 'Une flûte invisible', to words by Victor Hugo. It proved to be a farewell to the poet, as Hugo died the same year, 1885. The funeral was a state occasion. Saint-Saëns was in the procession following the hearse as it carried the body from the lying in state under the Arc de Triomphe to the Panthéon for burial. Along the Champs-Elysées, lined with crowds, a gap appeared in the line of followers. Saint-Saëns found himself exposed to the onlookers, along with a fellow member of the Academy and Ferdinand de Lesseps, builder of the Suez Canal. There was a burst of applause as the three men passed, clearly intended for the famous de Lesseps, as yet untainted by the Panama Canal scandal and, as the composer pointed out, "at the height of his glory". Saint-Saëns was amused therefore when his Academy colleague "leaned across and whispered in my ear, 'Evidently they are applauding us'."[24]

His next important engagement took him on his first visit to Yorkshire, to take part in a concert in Leeds and to hear the Sacred Harmonic Society perform *La Lyre et l'Harpe* on the same evening, 18th November, at the Leeds Coliseum. The chamber concert consisted mainly of his own compositions, the piano quartet, the violin sonata (with Otto Peiniger), the Romance and Allegro Appassionato for cello (with Charles Ould), piano solos including the *Alceste* caprice, and solos played on the newly installed organ. Such versatility impressed the audience, but after all this new music conservative tastes were reflected by the *Yorkshire Post* reviewer, who described the early Beethoven string quartet with which the concert ended as "the treat of the evening".[25]

In *La Lyre* an otherwise praiseworthy performance was spoiled by what Saint-Saëns called "an indescribable charivari" in the clarinets. "I said afterwards, at supper, that the clarinets deserved to die! These animals . . ."[26] He followed the Harmonic Society, under its new conductor William Cummings (another acquaintance from the Birmingham Festival), to London for a performance of his setting of Psalm 18 at the St James's Hall. Cummings came in for criticism from *The Times* for not giving to the work enough light and shade, and that "finesse of rhythm and accent" seen as characteristic of French music. The reviewer thought the climax of the motet "very modern in its harmonic and orchestral colouring" (the word 'Wagnerian' was not used), and the Psalm, unfamiliar to London audiences, showed Saint-Saëns to be a "consummate master".[27] But it earned him respect rather than acclamation.

At least his reception in England was rather more polite than that awaiting him in Berlin in January. He had already felt the "cold water between me and Germany" following publication of his collection of essays, *Harmonie et Mélodie*, which includes his detailed appraisal of the *Ring* together with a more scathing attack on the growing Wagner cult and the new German nationalism the *Ring* appeared to represent. Whereas in 1876 he had written that "Wagnermania is a pardonable absurdity, Wagnerphobia an illness",[28] in 1885 "Wagnerphobia has lost its force and Wagnermania has developed – in France at least – in the most disturbing way . . . Those who were accused in 1880 of being too Wagnerian are now accused of not being Wagnerian enough."[29] He objected to Wagner's absurd claim to have fashioned in the *Ring* a German art, as if there was not one before, and warned of an aggressive nationalism that pervaded Wagner's work. Hans Sachs's paean to 'holy German art' at the end of *Die Meistersinger*, a phrase adopted by the patrons of Bayreuth as their motto, was "the cry of pan-Germanism and war on the Latin races", and "German music now brings us not only music but also German ideas, the German soul".[30] He contrasts this narrow nationalism with Beethoven's universality, and left no doubt as to which he regarded as the greater of the two. It was no longer possible, he wrote, to separate questions of art from matters foreign to it, but was confident that

pan-Germanism will pass away; art will not. Music, being a kind of indefinable universal language, is the mouthpiece of universal brotherhood, not of the domination of one race. And because Beethoven sang of universal brotherhood, because his spirit, instead of being merely a German spirit, is the human spirit, he remains the greatest, the only true great.[31]

Not surprisingly, *Harmonie et Mélodie* provoked outrage among German musicians and the German public. Saint-Saëns was due to conduct the Berlin Philharmonic in his suite for orchestra, "which no one wants to play in Paris", and other works – and there was already a hint of trouble to come at the rehearsal. "It was feared that there would be some opposition from certain members of the orchestra", he reported to Durand. "It was decided not to applaud me, to avoid provoking a counter-demonstration; the orchestra would instead simply stand and salute me. But after I had played the work, worse luck, they applauded me all the same!"[32] The opposition finally erupted into violence at the concert on 22nd January, in which Saint-Saëns had been billed by the Berlin papers as the man who hated German art and music. As soon as he stepped on to the platform there was an uproar of insults and whistles, and the

1. The 10-year-old Saint-Saëns at the time of his first public recital. *L'Illustration*, 1846. ROYAL COLLEGE OF MUSIC

2. Saint-Saëns in the 1860s. BIBLIOTHÈQUE NATIONALE DE FRANCE, PARIS

3. Marie Miolan-Carvalho. Saint-Saëns's mimicry of her in the role of Marguerite in *Faust* was a favourite party piece. ROYAL COLLEGE OF MUSIC.
4. Léon Carvalho, her husband, the theatre director who commissioned Saint-Saëns's first opera, *Le Timbre d'Argent*. BIBLIOTHÈQUE NATIONALE DE FRANCE, PARIS.
5. Gabriel Fauré, Saint-Saëns's pupil and closest musical ally. ROYAL COLLEGE OF MUSIC.

6. Pauline Viardot, mezzo-soprano and close friend of Saint-Saëns, for whom he wrote the part of Delilah. By the time the opera was first publicly performed she was too old to sing it on stage. ROYAL COLLEGE OF MUSIC.

7. Saint-Saëns in his forties, at about the time of the first performance of *Samson et Dalila* in Weimar. ROYAL COLLEGE OF MUSIC.

8. Exterior of the Paris Opéra in 1905. Only lately had *Samson et Dalila* become part of the established repertory there. ROYAL COLLEGE OF MUSIC.

9. Interior of the Paris Opéra, with the stage set for *Samson et Dalila*. ROYAL COLLEGE OF MUSIC.

ABOVE, 10. The fire at the Opéra-Comique in 1887, in which 131 people were killed. In it perished also the sets for Saint-Saëns's opera *Proserpine*, seriously damaging the chances of the work's survival. ROYAL COLLEGE OF MUSIC.

LEFT, 11. The composer of the 'Organ' symphony – Saint-Saëns in his early fifties. ROYAL COLLEGE OF MUSIC.

12. Nellie Melba in the role of Helen, in Saint-Saëns's 'poème lyrique' *Hélène*, his tenth opera. From a photograph in *Musica*, 1904. ROYAL COLLEGE OF MUSIC.

13. Sibyl Sanderson as Phryné, photographed in *Musica*, 1910. ROYAL COLLEGE OF MUSIC.

14. Saint-Saëns (centre) in Béziers at a rehearsal of *Parysatis*, 1902. ROYAL COLLEGE OF MUSIC.

15. The veteran composer at the height of his fame. ROYAL COLLEGE OF MUSIC.

16. Saint-Saëns at the Gloucester Festival of 1913 for the first performance of his oratorio *The Promised Land*, with Elgar (right) and Drs. C. H. Lloyd and A. H. Brewer. ROYAL COLLEGE OF MUSIC.

17. The 'last concert' at the Salle Gaveau, in a performance of Mozart under Pierre Monteux, 6 November 1913. ROYAL COLLEGE OF MUSIC.

police had to intervene to prevent a full-scale riot. Several demonstrators were ejected, while Saint-Saëns stoically carried on conducting, and went on to play his fourth piano concerto. Satirical magazines portrayed him leaving the hall under a hail of over-ripe fruit. Far from being intimidated, he revelled in the storm, to judge from his letter to Durand. "Excellent adventure! Now there is a Saint-Saëns question here, as there is a Wagner question in Paris. Some have drunk to my health in these quarrels." At a concert he gave with the violinist Emile Sauret, at that time teaching in Berlin, he was simply ignored. There was "no opposition: everyone looked away from me", while Sauret played the finale of the violin sonata "like a god".[33] Concert hall managers in Cassel, Dresden and Bremen all refused to allow him to appear, after the Leipzig musical press urged theatre bosses to ban the "French insulter", but Saint-Saëns remained confident that his works would go on making progress in Germany despite the fuss. "The Germans, a race of iconoclasts, make music with fervour, regardless of all strictures . . . As for me, I am in a delightful swim in this sea of injustice." He later complained, though, that the row was causing him to lose weight – and height. "The crucifixion has had a strange effect on me. My trousers have become too long and my girth too narrow. If this continues I shall become as finely shaped as an antique."[34]

Von Bülow, Hanslick and Neumann were among the few to come to his defence in the press. When in February he moved on to Prague, where *Henry VIII* was due to be given, he was told that the Austrian Emperor Franz Josef had serious doubts about allowing the opera to go on, fearing it might cause trouble. Neumann, manager of the Prague theatre and a noted Wagner interpreter, pleaded Saint-Saëns's cause, citing the composer's support for his attempt to take *Lohengrin* to Paris. Saint-Saëns wrote to his publisher on 14th February that some Germans in Prague had warned Neumann of a catastrophe if he went ahead with *Henry VIII*, while others had demanded to hear it. In the end caution prevailed: "It is thought wise to wait and I have asked him to postpone." It was a long postponement, for the opera did not reach Prague until 1900.

But Saint-Saëns was able to give concerts in both Prague and Vienna. He was also writing what would become two of his best-known works. In a letter to Durand of 9th February he refers both to a symphony and a humorous composition for a Shrove Tuesday concert at La Trompette, *Le Carnaval des Animaux*. "I have only the finale still to write. Fourteen numbers! You will tell me I should do better to work on my symphony. You are right, but it is so amusing!" He adds that this "amusing" piece will not be for publication, but "will be one of my posthumous works".

Le Carnaval des Animaux was a surprise gift for the veteran cellist Charles Lebouc, whose playing of the section evoking the smooth, graceful motion of a swan made a deep impression on the audience at the *mardi gras* concert in

March. The whole work represents that quirky, eccentric side of Saint-Saëns's art and character that can be traced back at least as far as the early song setting of La Fontaine's 'La cigale et la fourmi': while the ant sings his cynical advice, the grasshopper in the piano's top notes plays a popular folk tune, 'J'ai du bon tabac'. This satirical mood found further expression in the charades and play-acting of his social life, in the witty cartoons scribbled on letters and manuscripts, and in the comedies improvised for pupils at the Ecole Niedermeyer, where the idea of a 'zoological fantasy' was first conceived. Among other musical jokes written for private amusement were *Les Odeurs de Paris*, a series of imitative effects on such items as a bagpipe, tin whistle, bird warbler, bass drum, pistol and humming top (the drolleries of Satie, Ibert and other twentieth-century Parisians were nothing new), and the Italian opera parody *Gabriella di Vergy*, written with Jean Bonnerot and performed at the home of Jules Barbier in 1884 and at a more public showing in the Horticultural Hall in March 1885. To these, *Le Carnaval* was a worthy successor.

Animals were a lifelong source of fascination, amusement and speculation for Saint-Saëns, from the collection and observation of insects in his infancy to the companionship of dogs and cats in his old age. He was interested from childhood in the capacity of an animal for individual intelligence as opposed to common instinct. Overcoming an aversion to spiders, he would spend a whole week patiently training a spider to accept without fear a dead fly from his finger. Once, in the forest at Fontainebleau, he put his finger in the middle of a busy group of ants and noted the different speeds at which they retreated, "indicating different degrees of fear". He was astonished to find that one ant resolutely refused to budge, and on his repeating the experiment actually prepared to charge the finger with its mandibles. "I withdrew, overcome by the prodigious courage of the insect. Where would you find a human being with the audacity to withstand a giant taller than the Eiffel Tower?" He professed a horror of any form of cruelty to animals, condemned hunting,[35] by "sportsmen who kill for the pure pleasure of killing", and greatly regretted the introduction – and success – of bull-fighting in the arenas of southern France, "a school of barbarism which makes a pleasure of the sight of death and dishonours the glorious land of Spain". His love of animals led him to denounce Christianity for abandoning them "to any brutality" on the grounds that they were made for man's benefit, and to approve of the Buddhist idea of the transmigration of the soul at death into another species, which "affords the animal a wonderful degree of protection".[36]

Le Carnaval des Animaux is scored for chamber (or full) orchestra and two pianos, and ranges from sheer buffoonery to tone painting of remarkable brilliance and ingenuity, as the animals portrayed range from the ridiculous to the sublime. Berlioz's *Danse des Sylphes* becomes the dance of the elephants when played on double basses; pianos and strings create the watery world of the aquarium. The tortoise moves to an absurdly slow version of Offenbach's *Orphée* galop; a virtuoso flute paints a vivid picture of the diving and soaring of birds in flight. The mule is mimicked in a piece of conciseness that anticipates the brevity and sparse textures of the twentieth-century experimentalists, and an extra touch of wit is the inclusion of pianists practising scales, a breed to which Saint-Saëns belonged and which, he suggests, can hardly be regarded as human. The fossils' dance has a double link with the *Danse Macabre*, in its use of the xylophone, here given the starring role, and in its main theme, derived from that of the symphonic poem.

Because of the work's whimsicality and craftsmanship, it is easy to overlook its melodic and harmonic interest, 'the Swan' notwithstanding. Here Saint-Saëns is at his most inventive, as well as demonstrating some typical characteristics. There is the slightly acidic brand of melancholy, and the use of modal elements which give rise to the explorative harmonies of 'the Cuckoo' and, through their association with his oriental style, make the entry of the lions sound almost like an oriental march. And 'the Swan', despite all the hackneyed versions and variations it has been subjected to over the years, surely remains one of the most beautiful melodies ever written. Yet Saint-Saëns, aware of *Le Carnaval*'s potential for popular appeal, was worried about the damage it might do to his reputation as a serious composer. As with his previous musical jokes, he stuck to his intention of withholding it from publication in his lifetime, with the exception of 'the Swan' which went on to become a phenomenal money-spinner in publishing terms. When the complete *Le Carnaval* was published, a year after his death, it confirmed his fears by becoming his most famous work, largely through its use as an introduction to 'classical' music for successive generations of primary school children.

A lesser-known chamber work from 1886, combining solo piano and strings, is the Valse Caprice. It was written as a wedding present for the pianist Caroline Montigny-Rémaury, when she married Franck's pupil Louis de Serres, an occasion which led to the piece being called 'The Wedding Cake'. This nickname is unfortunate because it trivialises what is in fact a well-argued miniature demonstrating in microcosm the concertante style of the composer with its finely-balanced interplay between soloist and ensemble. It is more of a scherzo than a waltz, in which snatches of melody emerge through a kaleidoscope of virtuosity, leading to a consolidation of the main theme by the soloist. Critics have been too ready to overlook these qualities of conciseness and balance, dismissing the piece as a worthless trifle. The more malicious held it up as an example of the superficiality and triviality which they alleged in all Saint-Saens's work, rather like those who dismiss Tchaikovsky's music as empty noise because he wrote the *1812* overture.

Perhaps Saint-Saëns had the Valse Caprice, or even more likely *Le Carnaval*, in mind when, in conversation with Francesco Berger, secretary of the Philharmonic Society in London, he pointed out that a composer did not always make his name by his greatest works: his reputation could be made by an "unconsidered trifle" trotted out casually that happened to be a hit with the public. Berger, the son of an Austro-Italian merchant who had settled in London, was an accomplished composer, pianist and teacher. He was impressed, as so many were, as much by Saint-Saëns's personal characteristics as by his outstanding technical ability. He described the composer at this time as

of middle stature, square-set, with a finely chiselled nose and a wonderful pair of alert, penetrating eyes. He has a remarkable speaking voice, loud and very shrill, and he talks so rapidly that it is difficult to follow him – his words flash from him like sparks from an anvil. I always speak French with him, but he understands Italian, German and English.

On one of Saint-Saëns's visits to his house, he played Berger's Suite in G at sight "so perfectly that I can only describe it as astonishing".[37]

Berger had taken up his post with the Philharmonic Society in 1884, and it was he who proposed the commission from Saint-Saëns that produced the symphony in C minor. The composer was already contemplating a return to the form he had neglected for over twenty-five years, since the unpublished symphony in D of 1859, perhaps prompted by the fact that two of his former pupils had written substantial works in this medium, Messager in 1877 and Fauré in 1884. In August 1885 he went to Antwerp to help Fauré prepare for a performance of his symphony at a French festival there, in the face of petty obstacles with which he was all too familiar and which Fauré blamed on "a German faction, tenacious and crafty, which wants to wreck the French festival". (The performance went ahead, under d'Indy's baton, but Fauré was not satisfied with the work and eventually destroyed it.)[38] As has been seen, Saint-Saëns was at work on his own symphony by February 1886, laying aside a promise to his publisher to write a new piano trio. Durand seemed especially anxious for him to finish it, but the composer, aware that he was writing something extra special, would not be hurried.

You ask for the symphony: you don't know what you ask. It will be terrifying . . . there will be much in the way of experiment in this terrible thing, and I shall certainly have to make changes after the first performance . . . After the symphony will come the trio which I have long promised you.[39]

He intended to dedicate the symphony to Liszt, and when his aged hero visited Paris for the last time in April, Saint-Saëns played him the draft of the new work. Within a month it was finished. Saint-Saëns wrote to Berger that he was looking forward to conducting it in London, adding some tongue-in-cheek comments about "this imp of a symphony" and the size of orchestra it required, quite apart from the organ and piano. "You asked for it; I wash my hands of the whole thing."[40] And after a rehearsal he wrote to Durand from his rooms in Upper Baker Street reiterating his conviction that he had produced something exceptional. The symphony "is truly terrible; I was right. Happily I am dealing with a first class orchestra . . . I have a few small retouches to make, but that's a small matter. The coda of the finale is really extraordinary."[41]

He conducted the symphony on 19th May at the St James's Hall, as well as playing Beethoven's fourth concerto under Sullivan, and was afterwards introduced to the Prince of Wales, patron of the Philharmonic Society. Critics noted a nervous excitement in him throughout the evening, especially in the concerto, his playing of which was described by the *Daily Telegraph* as "full of fire without being exaggerated".[42] They were less sure about the symphony, one calling it "more grandiose than great", another "more a rhapsody than a symphony".[43] The *Telegraph* called it a "symphonic fantasia" that defied discussion in terms of the accepted norms of musical architecture. "We should as soon think of a serious dissertation on the Brighton Pavilion." The inclusion of piano and organ was particularly perplexing:

We cannot describe the effect as happy. The pianoforte was a profitless tinkle and the overwhelming personality of the organ dwarfed everything else . . . Some of the melodies are noble, and their treatment is masterly; the orchestra keeps up a continuous display of beautiful colour.

But in the finale the composer's imagination "runs away with him". The symphony was received respectfully rather than enthusiastically, but it showed that the fifty-year-old composer could still ruffle feathers with the novelty of his utterance, and it set the seal on his reputation in England as his country's most forward-looking composer, "a maker of experiments in music", said the *Telegraph*, "one of the order of art pioneers who make clear the way to a land of Goshen or into the desert. Every art needs such men."[44]

The symphony is directly linked to Saint-Saëns's fourth piano concerto, in key, form and to some extent style and mood. As in the violin sonata also, there are two separate halves containing between them the usual four movements. The symphony, though, is exceptional in the whole of Saint-Saëns's vast output for its length: it is by far the longest of all his purely instrumental works, its structure the most ambitiously expansive. It is no longer than a symphony by Beethoven or Brahms, but viewed in the context of Saint-Saëns's tendency towards brevity and conciseness, it is gargantuan. Yet even here he does not lose sight of the overall design: for the opening allegro he reverts to a stricter sonata form to provide an element of stability, and its first subject is used at various points throughout the symphony in various forms and guises, to give a sense of unity. This first theme opens with two three-bar phrases, again, as in the violin sonata, belying his reputation for regular measures, and has been likened to that of Schubert's 'Unfinished' Symphony, with its uneasy murmurings in the strings. The comparison is given some weight by the fact that Saint-Saëns originally planned his symphony in B minor. It is perhaps even more like the opening of Wieniawski's *Légende* for violin and orchestra, but such similarities are superficial, and the comparisons worthless (as Brahms had cause to point out after the première of his first symphony), because each work has a character and purpose of its own. Saint-Saëns's symphony can be seen as a summation of his life and work to date. The prominent part given to the organ is clearly intended as a reminder of his main occupation for most of his career, an occupation that gave him the most happiness and esteem, and the poco adagio in which it first appears is redolent of nostalgia for a golden time remembered. The inclusion of a piano (played by four hands in the finale) is perhaps a reference to another lifelong activity. Although both instruments are an unusual feature in a nineteenth-century symphony, there were precedents for their use in symphonic works: Berlioz includes a piano in his fantasy *The Tempest*, and Liszt introduces an organ into his symphonic poem *Hunnenschlacht*.

Stylistically, the most notable characteristics of Saint-Saëns's earlier works are here writ large. Troubled, chilly waters subside before a triumphalist finale, which becomes a magnificent kaleidoscope of mood, texture (often contrapuntal) and tone colour whose excitement never flags. The work abounds in piquant harmonic juxtapositions and chromatic shifts, notably in the first movement's memorable second subject, which may seem like an influence from Franck but are in fact of the kind Saint-Saëns had first learned as a child from Boëly, "the imagination coursing over a determined path" that had been a guiding principle in the symphonic poems and other works. But most striking of all is that the hints of bitter irony found in so many of the earlier works are here fully blown into a bleak intellectual despair, as deep as the night sky he so loved to contemplate through his telescope. It makes its mark at the outset, in the slow ethereal chords of the brief introduction, and is reinforced throughout by frequent references to the doom-laden 'Dies Irae', derived from the turbulent opening theme. It is a profound, sometimes menacing, sometimes anguished pessimism not unusual in a nineteenth-century mind given to scientific inquiry, which brought with it the loss of religious certainty and a sense of isolation, of being alone in the universe. Coupled with it is perhaps an anxiety stemming from a consciousness of age, the deaths of friends and contemporaries, and an uneasy awareness that the chief companion and support of the composer's life, his mother, was now well-advanced in years. This feeling of insecurity, both intellectual and personal, so pervades the symphony that all the storming victories of the finale are not enough to dispel it. D'Indy was one of the first to sense this when he wrote of the symphony that "the final impression remains one of doubt and sadness".[45]

To the composer himself the symphony was a crowning achievement. "I have given all that I had to give. What I have done I shall never do again."[46] And this was indeed the case. It was his last symphony, and although he continued to compose for the rest of his long life he never again attempted anything on such a scale. Liszt, who had done so much to encourage and inspire him, died on 31st July, before it was published, so that the score is now dedicated "to the memory of Franz Liszt".

The work soon established itself in the English and French repertories, but in Germany its progress was delayed by the continuing furore over *Harmonie et Mélodie*. Its first French performance was at the Conservatoire on 9th January 1887, prompting Gounod to call Saint-Saëns 'the French Beethoven' – meaning that he had brought symphonic music into the mainstream of French musical life. It went on to a third performance at the Concerts Society, an unprecedented honour for a living French composer which did much to set the society more towards playing new works.

But the movement towards a greater earnestness in French music, for which Wagner was the model and the inspiration, was gathering pace, and Saint-Saëns found himself under increasing attack at home as well as in Germany. His denunciation of the Wagnerian influence on French music left him increasingly out of touch with the aims and ideals of the rising generation of French composers who regarded him as too set in the past. Their attitude towards him was most strongly expressed by the critic Georges Jean-Aubry, who, looking back some thirty years later, wrote of how Saint-Saëns was seen by younger musicians in the last years of the nineteenth century and later. He "has too often proved how little an appreciation he has of French music apart from his own. It has pleased him to take up a scowling and aggressive attitude towards young musicians. He had the right to adopt it; we have the right to take no notice of it."[47] In 1917 he wrote that "during the last forty years, while the most admirable musical development ever known since the sixteenth century was taking place, Saint-Saëns assumed more and more a frowning countenance, and was either clearly hostile or simply indifferent towards younger musicians".[48] This was not entirely true, as will be seen, but it illustrates the light in which Saint-Saëns was coming to be viewed.

One of the main theatres of opposition to him was the National Music Society which he helped to found. The kindly, self-effacing Franck, who remained wary of Wagner's influence and had written the word 'poison' on his copy of *Tristan*, found himself the reluctant and somewhat bemused figurehead of the new movement, which was increasingly influential in the society. Saint-

Saëns, who had replaced Bussine as president, saw the 'Franckists' as a threat to the society's original aim, the cultivation of a distinctively French musical style that would stand alongside the central European tradition and be independent of it. "I began to be aware", he wrote many years later, "of the underground work going on with a view to sapping my influence and substituting for it that of Franck and his pupils", who, at society meetings, "formed an exclusive circle, plotting in low voices in dark corners".[49] In the autumn of 1886, in the wake of Saint-Saëns's triumph in England, the 'Franckists' decided to act. In November d'Indy put forward a resolution to include foreign works in the society's programmes, and had no trouble in getting it passed. Saint-Saëns, who in any case attended meetings of the society less frequently than before because of his growing disenchantment at "petty annoyances," resigned along with his co-founder Bussine, and went off to give some concerts in London. Franck succeeded him as president, with d'Indy and Chausson wielding the power as his secretaries. D'Indy's worship of his hero led him into an amusing error in later years, misdating the Paris première of Saint-Saëns's C minor symphony by a year in order to present Franck's D minor symphony as breaking new ground with the form in France. Saint-Saëns's symphony was first heard in France in 1888, he wrote (by mistake or design), by which time Franck had virtually completed his symphony and so could not have been influenced by it. In fact, Franck sketched the D minor symphony in the summer of 1887, well after the 'Organ' symphony was performed in Paris.

Saint-Saëns regarded the decision to perform foreign – that is, mainly German – works at the National Society as an act of betrayal, denying to native composers valuable performance time and turning the clock back to the bad old days when French music took second place. Looking back on the 1886 coup, he wrote: "From that moment on the Césarian and Wagnerian party had imperial power, and the society became, what it is now, a closed shop, whose values and aims I know nothing of but which is entirely out of touch with the intentions of the founders."[50] While he honoured the great works of the German school, including the operas of Wagner, the enthusiastic acceptance and emulation of Wagner's ideas and methods was to him as dangerous as it was absurd, a view in some way justified by some of the pseudo-Wagnerian effusions that were to come from d'Indy, Chabrier and the rest of 'le petit Bayreuth'. Strangely, Wagner, as distinct from the classical and early romantic Germans, was hardly ever played at the society under the new regime. But his spirit reigned there. Although by 1910 "the society seems more exclusively French than ever," wrote Romain Rolland, he adds that "the influence of Vincent d'Indy and the school of Franck is predominant".[51]

The irony could not have been lost on Saint-Saëns that in the 1880s he, the younger man by thirteen years, was regarded as an outdated reactionary while Franck, in his sixties, was hailed as the beacon of the vanguard. Not surprisingly, he felt increasingly bitter towards his venerable rival, as his public and private comments make clear. The bitterness was no doubt compounded by the fact that Augusta Holmes numbered herself among Franck's pupils. It was certainly greater because of the recollection of the help and encouragement he had given Franck in the early days of the National Society. He claimed, for instance (though his claim is disputed), that when Benoist retired from the Conservatoire organ professorship in 1872 he was offered the post but declined it in favour of Franck in order to give him a position on which he could build his reputation as a composer. Saint-Saëns would not in any case have been inclined to accept the offer because it came at the time of his great-aunt's death and because he was simply unwilling to take a regular teaching post, and some biographers who are hostile to him have attributed Franck's appointment to the recommendation of others.[52] But there is really no reason to doubt his sincerity in view of his undisputed readiness to support struggling musicians. At the time he genuinely believed that Franck had the makings of a great composer and needed only the opportunity to develop, but the music he was to write soon changed his mind. Many years later he told Francis Poulenc: "It was made out that this great talent amounted to genius. I entertained no such notion."[53] And even when, in old age, he was finally reconciled to Vincent d'Indy, his view of Franck remained unaltered. In a letter of 1917 to d'Indy he wrote: "Apart from rare and happy exceptions I find his music graceless and charmless; it bores me."[54]

Never one to conceal his views, Saint-Saëns frequently ruffled the feathers of his fellow musicians where Franck was concerned. It was with a noticeable lack of grace that he attended Franck's funeral in 1890 (which, incidentally, d'Indy did not attend because of musical commitments), and in 1898 there was outrage when he refused to join a committee planning to erect a monument to Franck after suggesting that his influence on French music had been "disastrous". A letter to *Le Monde Musical* clarifying his position was hardly likely to calm the waters. "What I had written was that his influence on the French school was not a happy one, and I have nothing to add to that except that a statue to Rameau, Méhul or Hérold would seem to me much more appropriate."[55] Later he declared that Franck was "more of a musician than an artist; he was not a poet", added that his music was technically flawed and suggested that he was also lacking as a teacher. A pupil (probably Henri Duparc) called on Saint-Saëns for advice on orchestration after finding that Franck was unable to help.

Three series of painstaking consultation lessons enabled him to bring out the only orchestral composition by which he is known to the public [Duparc's Lénore*?]. All the same, he did not advertise the fact and, in the eyes of the world, he remained César Franck's pupil.*[56]

War sharpened this tone of bitterness. In 1915, his anti-German feelings having reached new heights, he accused Franck, born in Belgium of German stock, of cynically adopting French citizenship solely to be eligible to join the National Society, so that his works, which "were then mostly unheard", would be performed and he would "emerge from the shadows of obscurity". At the society he was "welcomed with open arms".[57] With Massenet, Saint-Saëns disliked the man but frequently defended his music; with Franck, he disliked both the man and the music. By the mid-1880s, disillusioned with the National Society and its aims, and perhaps feeling that he had now made a significant contribution to the French orchestral and chamber repertory, 'the French Beethoven' was turning with renewed determination to that more traditional branch of French musical life, opera.

X • MAN of the THEATRE

THE ENTHUSIASTIC RECEPTION GIVEN TO THE C MINOR SYMPHONY SEALED Saint-Saëns's unusual position in French music, as a composer whose reputation rested almost entirely on his orchestral and chamber music and hardly at all on his operas. *Samson et Dalila* had still not been professionally staged in France or anywhere else outside Germany, *Henry VIII* had scored only a moderate success and his other operas to date had largely disappeared from the repertory. Despite all his achievements in raising the status of French symphonic music, and the public honours bestowed on him because of them, he still felt insecure in a land so devoted to the visual and the dramatic, where the supreme temple of music – indeed, the official Academy of Music – was the Paris Opéra. At least he had the consolation of knowing that, in the matter of operatic struggle and neglect, he was in good company. In 1886 he penned for his own amusement a short 'autobiography' of a celebrated composer who tries for glory in opera, "where he saw so many mediocrities", but fails. It was about Rameau, who was well into his fifties before he finally achieved recognition in the theatre.[1]

From 1886 Saint-Saëns took up in earnest his long campaign to establish himself in the field, and within six years had written three operas. Four more were to follow, and his stage work was to extend also to incidental music, ballet and even plays. But it was the vocal form of theatre that was his prime concern, and it is no coincidence that his growing preoccupation with it followed his resumption of songwriting in 1885. He regarded the voice as having irresistible appeal because of its existence in nature and its basic humanity. "The public prefers vocal to instrumental music . . . because the voice is the only natural instrument", he observed. "It is even the one eternal instrument so far as human things can be eternal. Instruments pass and have their day . . . but the human voice remains." To him, it was not simply a question of the opera composer supplying a popular demand in order to make ends meet, though it was not surprising that "musicians instinctively turn to the kind of music that will enable them to earn their living". Writing for the voice was a natural impulse in a composer, and he pointed out that Wagner, who was almost exclusively concerned with opera, could hardly be accused of writing for financial profit, given that it brought him many years of poverty.[2]

From this appreciation of the natural appeal of the voice comes the purity and clarity of the vocal line and of diction which are a major feature of Saint-Saëns's operas, and which put them very much in the French classical tradition, set apart from both Wagnerian music drama and Italian bel canto.

As such, they form a significant part of the late-nineteenth-century French musical renaissance. Despite their use of recurring themes, and their tendency towards 'lyric scenes' and away from big arias, they are outside the Wagnerian mould in that the orchestra objectively underlines the action on stage rather than being emotionally and scenically involved to the extent that the voice has to function almost as an orchestral instrument in itself. This form of integration, Saint-Saëns believed, placed an unnatural and unnecessary strain on the human voice. In the balance between orchestra and singers he is closer to Verdi than to Wagner, but his style is more restrained, tempered by the lightness and delicacy of a Gounod and his own inclination towards moderation and controlled emotion. Whatever the demands of the drama, he tried to avoid taxing the voice unduly, testing the singer's stamina or putting up formidable technical obstacles. He is perhaps best compared to Bizet, his "comrade-in-arms" in the struggle for recognition, who would almost certainly have applauded his work, as he had once applauded *Le Timbre d'Argent*. It is a pity, in view of the fact that Bizet's early death is so much lamented, that the operas of his great admirer and survivor in the cause have been comparatively so little considered.

In pursuing, in opposition to the Italians, a balance between melody, declamation and symphony, "the god in three persons of lyric drama",[3] Saint-Saëns came to view Wagner as having sacrificed the first to the last, the voice to the orchestra. "He would even have liked to suppress the art of singing altogether . . . as though the human voice were not itself the finest of all instruments!"[4] Gounod, he believed, had achieved a more satisfactory synthesis, and had also been an important influence in correcting the abuses of French word setting. Of Gounod he wrote:

To the system of melodic independence, of melody sought after for itself and to which words were made to fit as far as they could be, he preferred, like Gluck, that of melody born from declamation, moulded on the words and setting them in relief without losing anything of their due importance, so that the two elements grow one by the other instead of being in conflict.[5]

The matter of French word setting is one of the ways in which Saint-Saëns's operas most directly rebel against the Italian school. From his earliest songs he had, through love of his native literature, been concerned to set the language to music that was sensitive to its rise and fall, that allowed its special rhythm and metre to flow naturally. The robustly melodic Italian style, which had dominated French opera for so long, suited the regular metrical patterns of the Italian language. However, it was entirely inappropriate when applied, as in the operas of Meyerbeer, to the more pliable sonorities of the French language, whose accents, Saint-Saëns pointed out, were more irregular and "almost imperceptible". In this it differed from German and English as well as Italian. His praise of Messager's settings has already been mentioned, but he himself poses as determined a challenge to the dominance of Italian lyricism as Rameau, Gluck and Méhul had done in the eighteenth century, and he attacked composers who murdered verse to fit in with "what they modestly call their inspiration".[6] His operas are a bid to return to the perceived tradition of French opera as drama set to music, in which the melodic line allows rational action and linguistic clarity, and singing is closely allied to declamation. "It is impossible to speak without singing", he noted, "not only in verse but also in prose."[7] His operas are thus opposed to the Italian tendency to melodic predominance and the supremacy of the aria over dramatic expression and logic, as well as to the Wagnerian attempt to integrate voice and orchestra.

Yet for all their balance and linguistic correctness, none of his twelve complete published operas, with the single exception of *Samson et Dalila*, achieved lasting success. His dramatic instincts often fail to meet his dramatic aspirations, and it is ironic, in view of his care for the literary side of opera, that the music so often outshines the drama. Messager wrote that "Saint-Saëns's ideas are of more musical than dramatic worth", and Debussy was to conclude that he would always be a concert-hall composer, never at home in the theatre, to which he had come "with the spirit of an unrepentant old symphonist".[8] The librettos, particularly those of Gallet, took a lot of the blame, and the choice of subject usually failed to grip the public imagination, but the operas as a whole were seen to err on the side of objectivity and understatement, possessing a certain poetic elegance and charm but lacking the emotional involvement to make the drama and the characters convincing. This view has persisted and opera houses have only rarely been prepared to risk a revival, testing public taste for any shift in receptivity.

The origins of Saint-Saëns's next stage work, *Proserpine*, can be traced back at least seven years previously, when he had tried, without success, to interest Carl Rosa in London in an opera based on the verse play by Auguste Vacquerie. The Italian Renaissance setting of the story, together with what he called Vacquerie's "classical refinement" and the "sonority" of his poetry, appealed to the composer.[9] When the baritone Victor Maurel planned to set up a new Italian theatre in Paris, Saint-Saëns put the idea to him, proposing to adapt the poem with Vacquerie's consent. Again the project was forgotten, but after considering several other subjects he came back to *Proserpine* and asked Gallet to produce a libretto. In July 1886 he travelled to Florence for some background research, returning by way of Berne, and settled in the countryside outside Paris during August and September to write the opera undisturbed – except, that is, for the friendly attentions of a young tabby that called regularly. He was amused by the cat's display of jealousy when a neighbour showed him their puppy. "I took it up and kissed it. The cat, seeing this, set her back up and walked away in a huff; it was three days before she returned." People who disliked cats did so, he believed, because they

regard it as beneath their dignity to be forced to win the affection of a superior being who is conscious of his worth and bestows his friendship only where he knows it will be appreciated. No animal could be more cajoling or more faithful than a cat, once you merit his good opinion, but he will not tolerate ill-treatment and he is excessively jealous.[10]

The cat's behaviour was strangely appropriate, for jealousy is a main theme of the opera Saint-Saëns was then writing. Set in sixteenth-century Italy, it concerns the unrequited love of a courtesan, Proserpine, for a young nobleman, Sabatino. He has turned his back on the life she represents and is engaged to Angiola, sister of his friend Renzo. Proserpine learns of the impending marriage and engages a group of bandits, led by Squarocca, to prevent it. Squarocca learns that Renzo is to accompany his sister from the convent at Turin to Sabatino, and with his followers intercepts them on their journey. He brings Angiola to Proserpine, who poses as a fortune-teller, warns her that her marriage will be a disaster and advises her to return to the convent. The plot fails when Angiola rejects the 'advice' and Squarocca's bandits are arrested. Proserpine confronts Sabatino at his house and when the bride-to-be arrives, lunges at her with a dagger. In the original version she is killed by Sabatino, but the ending was later changed so that she stabs herself after being restrained, which was considered both more dramatic and more morally correct.

The name Proserpine is a reference to the character of Greek legend, who is carried to the Underworld and is thus denied the warmth and brightness of the sun, just as the courtesan of the opera is denied the happiness of true love. What interested Saint-Saëns, apart from the scope for period and local atmosphere, was the contrast between the two principal women:

Angiola is day, Proserpine is night; Angiola is innocence, candour, pure love and virginity, Proserpine is damned; true love for her is the forbidden fruit. It is torture to touch it, but she is attracted to this torture and dies sooner than renounce it . . . The chaste love of the saintly woman seems a small thing next to the infernal passions of the courtesan.[11]

In setting Gallet's text, Saint-Saëns encountered a small problem in the sonnet in which Sabatino declares his love for Angiola. He altered it "for musical reasons", and threw Gallet into a fit of despair. He then reverted to the original verse and adapted the music instead, sang both versions to the wounded librettist, and when Gallet couldn't make up his mind as to which version was best, compromised by incorporating elements of both. In many ways *Proserpine* is Saint-Saëns's *Carmen*, with its rejected lover (in this case the woman) and its final fatal stabbing. The music abounds in melodic inflections strongly reminiscent of Bizet's masterpiece, there is the same blend of bubbly humour, tender passions and dark thoughts, and the Italian setting allows for splashes of local colour to match the Spanishness of the drama in Seville. Examples are the charming duet between Proserpine's guests Orlando and Ercole, set to a siciliana, and the tarantella that sets the scene for Squarocca's camp. Like *Carmen*, *Proserpine* has a representative theme that reappears in various moods and guises, though it is one more of bitter melancholy than sinister fatalism. Of slightly ambiguous tonality, it is announced straight away in the short, brooding prelude, which is soon dispelled by the bright sunshine of Proserpine's palace gardens. The tender complaints from admirers about her reluctance to bestow her amorous favours recall those of the soldiers that wait on Bizet's heroine, and the heady abandon of the chorus that closes act one, heralding mischief afoot, echoes the song of liberty sung by Carmen and the smugglers. But whereas *Carmen* was composed as an opéra-comique, with spoken dialogue, Saint-Saëns's four-act 'lyric drama' has continuous music within each act, and the musical elements are more subtly integrated, with fewer big numbers. The emotional high spots are extended dialogues between main characters rather than showstopping solos, notably in the first act between Sabatino and Proserpine, in which the nobleman declares he is not interested in her, and in their final scene.

The work was written for the Opéra-Comique, since 1876 under Carvalho's management. Preparations for the première on 15th March 1887 were comparatively untroubled after those of Saint-Saëns's previous operas, perhaps a sign of the greater esteem in which the composer was held, and he was not badgered into altering the score to suit fastidious singers. Reactions to the opera were mixed. The critic Emile Destranges thought it his best stage work after *Samson* and wrote a detailed analysis of its merits. Reyer too praised it highly: "You have covered *Proserpine* with flowers, and your praises have gone to my head", the composer wrote to him.[12] Others were not convinced, some condemning the libretto as dull and absurd, some condemning the opera as a whole for its supposed immorality. Servières was unmoved, singling out Proserpine's invocation and her fourth act duet with Sabatino as the only really dramatic points. *The Stage* thought Proserpine (sung by Caroline Salla) had "some superb passages which fairly bring down the house", but that the work as a whole lacked melodic interest, depending too much on "recitative" or declamation. It was "disfigured . . . by inequalities, which may mar its ultimate success".[13] The finale of the second act, a delicate piece of musical scene painting, in which Squarocca has infiltrated a group of beggars receiving alms in the convent, was wildly cheered and had to be repeated. However, the raw passions of the later scenes were considered too coarse, a reaction that casts some doubt on the received view of Saint-Saëns as cold and detached. He himself laid great emphasis on what he saw as the "inner emotion in the drama",[14] but it happened that

Proserpine had little chance to prove itself. Two months after the première, the Opéra-Comique burnt down during a performance of Thomas's *Mignon*. The fire killed 131 people, and the toll would have been greater but for the bravery of the baritone Alexandre Taskin, Saint-Saëns's Squarocca. He was decorated for his life-saving actions, but Carvalho was found guilty of negligence, fined and imprisoned, and served four years before being released on appeal. The fire also destroyed the sets for *Proserpine*, so that when the company transferred to the Sarah Bernhardt Theatre there was little chance of an immediate revival.

As if to confirm that he had *Carmen* in mind at this time, Saint-Saëns wrote the lovely Havanaise for violin and orchestra, his contribution to the dance form made famous by Carmen's habanera. It is in many ways one of his most typical as well as most appealing works, a short piece of Spanish exoticism which combines lyrical warmth tinged with melancholy, with passages of dazzling virtuosity. The main theme (said to have been prompted by nothing more exotic than the crackling of a wood fire in a hotel room in northern France) laces the duple time and dotted rhythms of the dance with triplets that create a gently swaying languor, and meanders in an easy-going way through those bittersweet inflections, suggestive of wistful nostalgia and even regret, that haunt so many of Saint-Saëns's melodies. A series of episodes making up the central section begins with an energetic perpetual motion for the soloist that abruptly discards the habanera rhythm, but it insinuates itself back into the music to lead to a reprise of the main theme. A shorter series of episodes follows, with the soloist in playful mood until, in the delicious final bars, a hushed orchestra reasserts the underlying rhythm, the violin softly rising and falling above it in a sweet, delicate apotheosis of this particular dance. Saint-Saëns dedicated the Havanaise to Diaz Albertini, a violinist who frequently joined him on concert tours.

Shortly after *Proserpine's* première Saint-Saëns embarked on his second visit to Russia, travelling through Denmark and giving concerts both there and in St Petersburg, where he delighted the orchestra at rehearsal by counting beats in Russian. Among his travelling companions were a flautist, an oboist and a clarinettist, and this prompted him to write the Caprice on Danish and Russian Airs, for that trio plus piano. The Tsarina, Marie Feodorovna, who was also a Danish princess, accepted the dedication, and the new work featured strongly in the St Petersburg concerts. A double set of variations with an introduction in cadenza style, it is coloured by a woodwind virtuosity that recalls that of *Le Carnaval des Animaux*.

The summer of 1887 brought Saint-Saëns to London again and a renewed acquaintance with Wilhelm Ganz, who conducted a concert on 18th June at the St James's Hall that was possibly unique in the annals of programme-making at the time, with the composer playing all four of his piano concertos, one after the other. "He played them all by heart, and when he had finished seemed as fresh as if he had done nothing at all", an astonished Ganz recalled.[15] *The Times* called it "a remarkable display of energy and musical genius", which required "the highest intellectual capacities" and was carried out with "unflagging verve and freshness . . . a triumph of modern French art, achieved by one of its foremost representatives".[16] The 'triumph', coming as it did on the anniversary of Waterloo, was wittily seen by observers as the French revenge for that defeat.

The concert, however, was not well attended. Saturday afternoon was never a popular time for concert-going, and London was in the grip of Golden Jubilee fever. Saint-Saëns lost heavily "but", Ganz noted, "he apparently did not mind in the least". He may simply have chosen to conceal his disappointment: Ganz would not have guessed, for he was too ready to accept at face value the composer's more tongue-in-cheek comments, an ingenuousness which Saint-Saëns impishly exploited in conversation. "Knowing what a brilliant pianist he is, I was much struck by his telling me once that he hardly ever practises", Ganz wrote. In fact, Saint-Saëns habitually practised at least two hours a day, his busy travel schedule and other commitments permitting. The conductor was surprised when Saint-Saëns opened a conversation with: "Don't talk to me about music, it doesn't interest me at all", and seems to have been even more surprised when, after a while, he talked about nothing else. When Ganz travelled to Dieppe to hear a concert of Saint-Saëns's works, the composer asked "if I had left England for good".[17] Saint-Saëns had long been aware of Ganz's apparently total admiration of him – "he is more and more infatuated with me", he confided, with some amusement, to Durand[18] – and was sure of his immunity to any amount of leg-pulling.

"Saint-Saëns is a most charming man", Ganz wrote, "and speaks English perfectly. In French he talks so quickly that it is difficult to follow him."[19] Saint-Saëns preferred to speak French among his foreign hosts and always corresponded in his native tongue except on very rare occasions, usually when he was in high spirits. There are a few letters sent from abroad in the language of the country he was visiting, including some in Italian, and he would sometimes sign off a long letter in French with "Your obedient servant" – in English.

That he retained his youthful mannerism of rapid movement and rapid speech is further attested by other acquaintances. Hermann Klein wrote of "speed in everything": "he talked, wrote, composed, read a thirty-line score, corrected proofs, got through rehearsals, walked on and off a platform, all at the same consistent allegro, yet without undue haste or a trace of carelessness." He liked fast express trains and loved London hansoms, but felt uneasy in Paris horse taxis "because he knew they were not safe" (mindful perhaps of the accident that led to Franck's death). Although polite, said Klein, he was often brusque and impatient, and when strongly disagreeing with anyone spoke in "a rapid, staccato jerkiness difficult even for the French to understand".[20]

His impatience sometimes gave rise to eccentricities that could bemuse whole companies on the grandest occasions, like the dinner at a festival given in his honour which he had at first declined to attend on the grounds that he was on a strict diet. Assured that he could be served with whatever the doctor had ordered, he asked for pig's trotters, and sat down to dinner with the other guests. It was not long before the contrast between his pig's trotters and the rich fare enjoyed by everyone else became too much: blazing with anger, the guest of honour stood up and insisted on leaving.[21] The diet also caused some perplexity one evening at Chabrier's flat in Paris, where Saint-Saëns was a frequent guest with his favourite party piece, his impersonation of Mme Carvalho as Marguerite. The composer of *España* recalled that "we gave him a chicken and steak with artichokes, but he hardly eats anything".[22]

Saint-Saëns's forceful intellect was another of his most notable characteristics. Klein noted the piercing eyes which seemed to penetrate to one's very brain and behind which was "the most versatile mind I have ever encountered in a musician".[23] Pierre Lalo, son of the composer Edouard, was also struck by the "lively, restless, piercing eyes", the bird-like face with its "sharply curved profile and hooked, beak-like nose" which made him "strangely resemble a parrot", the quick movements ("he strutted like a bird and talked rapidly, precipitately"), and the pronounced lisp.[24] The "eagle beak" was also commented on by the American critic Philip Hale, as was the sallow complexion retained from childhood and a constant reminder of delicate health. "He is of less than average height, thin, nervous, sick-faced, with a great and exposed forehead, hair habitually short, beard frosted. His eyes are almost level with his face." He was "a man that knows the world and sparkles in conversation, is fond of society, at ease and on equal terms with the leaders in art, literature, fashion". Hale also noted that, forceful as his views were, Saint-Saëns had an impish habit of arguing against himself in conversation, so that he appeared "whimsical, paradoxical, indulging in sudden changes of opinion". But he was always ready to help those of whom he was fond. "He is faithful to friends, appreciative of certain rivals, kindly disposed towards younger composers, zealous in practical assistance as well as in verbal encouragement."[25]

Jean-Aubry's sweeping judgement of Saint-Saëns as a scowling ogre contemptuous of young musicians, quoted in the last chapter, is also contradicted by Klein, who remarked how surprisingly affectionate, in view of his irritability and forcefulness, Saint-Saëns could be towards anyone he really liked.[26] As a boy, Jacques Durand was terrified of him, but "I later realised that he hid a heart of gold under this rather unbending look".[27] J. G. Proudhomme pointed out that he was always ready to help the families of musical colleagues fallen on hard times, and when his notoriously short temper caused him to use harsh words he was quick to try to repair any damage. His short temper, which he admitted, was not an evil temper.[28] A student pianist at the Conservatoire, Amina Goodwin, remembered a visit to his home during which an outburst of impatience drove her to tears. "He at once patted my head and apologised for his nastiness. His disposition was impulsive to a degree, but he had a great sense of humour and wit, a charming, childlike nature allied to deep sincerity and depth of character."[29]

He seems to have been a shrewd judge of character, for the friends he made from boyhood, who came from all walks of life, tended to be friends for life. Rarely if ever was there a serious quarrel that was not soon forgotten, and he remained unswervingly loyal. The friendly encouragement of young composers and poets was less often bestowed in later years, as he found himself increasingly out of sympathy with modern tendencies, so that Stravinsky called him "that sharp little man" and Sir Thomas Beecham remembered him simply as "a very irritable man". Yet in the 1880s he was still taking a friendly interest in many aspiring young musicians such as Messager, who was then on the threshold of a glittering career as a composer of light operas. In 1885 his former teacher asked the Opéra director Vaucorbeil (to whom he had dedicated *Henry VIII*) to commission a ballet from the rising young star. The result was *Les Deux Pigeons*, produced the following year. His kindly intervention, Messager noted, would not have surprised those who knew him, for beneath the brusque, surly exterior was "a lively sensibility" that showed, amid a variety of spontaneous moods, "an excellent heart".[30]

It was the irritable man who first confronted the young Paderewski, who had just given his concert debut in Paris in 1888 at the age of twenty-eight, and took his piano concerto to Saint-Saëns for comment and advice. The composer rasped that he had no time to see him, and when the young man suggested he might come back at a more convenient time Saint-Saëns exploded: "I have no time – ever!" He then grudgingly agreed to hear the concerto and was, Paderewski recalled, "quite enthusiastic". From then on they were on friendly terms, so that Paderewski too was struck by the contrast between the gruff, impatient exterior and the genuine affection that lay behind it. Saint-Saëns was always difficult to approach, he noted, but "to me was always kind and considerate". After performing a Saint-Saëns concerto the pianist would receive a photograph of the composer signed with expressions of gratitude and affection. These "I prize very highly, because he was a man who never showed any sentiment".[31]

Among other performer-composers who were grateful to Saint-Saëns for help and encouragement was the Belgian violinist Eugène Ysaÿe, whom he praised for his "beautiful tone". Ysaÿe, who became professor of violin at Brussels in 1886, always appreciated Saint-Saëns's friendship. Another was the organist Charles Widor, Franck's successor at the Conservatoire from 1890, who, as has been shown, was first helped in his career by Saint-Saëns in the 1860s and wrote of him that under the "dry exterior he concealed an ardent soul and great warm-heartedness".[32] In 1887 Leopold Godowsky, then only seventeen, arrived in Paris from his native Poland and asked Saint-Saëns to teach him. The young pianist-composer, now known chiefly for his phenomenally difficult transcriptions and reworkings of the Chopin studies, clearly made a strong impression on the fifty-two-year-old, who explained that he did not give regular lessons but would be pleased to hear him play. Saint-Saëns was to spend many a Sunday over the next three years lying on a couch, sipping endless cups of drinking chocolate, and crying "Bravo, bravo!" as Godowsky played. The pianist recalled that he arrived early and left late, and that the whole day, apart from lunch and an afternoon walk, was spent at the piano. He played in the morning, receiving advice on how to improve his compositions, and in the evening Saint-Saëns played his own works to him. He stresses that, during all that time, he never received a formal lesson – "it was all encouragement and no criticism" – but conceded that his mentor did provide him with a daily routine that helped to structure his hitherto disorganised approach to work, as he had done for Fauré. Godowsky seems to have brought out in Saint-Saëns those paternal instincts that had once shaped relations with his Niedermeyer pupils, and that had been so shatteringly frustrated by family misfortune. He enrolled the youth at a gymnasium for fitness training, to get him into shape for the arduous touring life ahead, and seems to have come increasingly to regard him as a son to replace the two he had lost. In his memoirs, Godowsky relates that Saint-Saëns eventually proposed to adopt him – on condition that he changed his family name to his. He was furious when the young man refused. "Much as I deplored the fact that I had to appear ungrateful, it was my name and I wanted to keep it." Nevertheless, Saint-Saëns continued to lend his protection and favour to Godowsky's career, insisting that he join La Trompette and contribute to its programmes, and helping to secure concert engagements, including one conducted by Tchaikovsky.[33]

But it was Fauré who was the main substitute for a family, especially after his marriage to Marie Fremiet and the birth of their sons Emmanuel and Philippe. Saint-Saëns was a father figure to all of them, taking an interest in the progress of the children and enjoying conversations with Marie about astronomy, a subject in which she shared a lively and knowledgeable interest. This was something that gave her a feeling of personal worth: otherwise, she once confided to Saint-Saëns, she was a "zero figure" in the Fauré family,[34] especially when her sons began to earn laurels respectively as a promising biologist and talented sculptor. To Fauré himself, Saint-Saëns was variously father, teacher and friend, helping to further his career, offering serious and authoritative advice, and still calling him "my fat cat", "my big wolf" and other jocular names in letters. He was always ready to encourage as well as advise. In January 1887, shortly after the Paris première of the C minor symphony, he wrote to Fauré, in reply to the latter's praise of that work, about an (unnamed) admirer, a "fanatic" who "intends to buy all your music – he's just written to me that you've put Chopin completely in the shade". He himself was growing to admire Fauré's piano pieces more than ever. "The more I look at them the more I love them, especially the Nocturne in B major, which I find absolutely entrancing", he told him, adding whimsically, "I shall ask you for a lesson some time."[35]

It should be remembered that this readiness to encourage young musicians extended only to those Saint-Saëns regarded as having real talent. It was a favour genuinely and sincerely bestowed on people who, he sincerely believed, genuinely deserved it. "When I give compliments, they can be taken seriously", he wrote. He had no time for mediocrities and incompetents, and especially "the pretentious, who want to know everything without taking the trouble to learn it, who presume to make the rules for themselves. They can never do any good." He deplored flattery. "Beginners must not be led to believe too much that they have produced masterpieces. They must be taught, on the contrary, that if something is well done, they must strive to do even better."[36]

In contrast to his interest in and help for younger musicians, Saint-Saëns's envy of Massenet's operatic success was growing, fanned throughout the 1880s by the triumphs of *Hérodiade*, *Manon* and *Le Cid*. Perhaps in consequence, he was quick to defend the integrity of his own stage works, and refused to alter *Henry VIII* when the Opéra asked for a shortened, three-act version, suggesting instead that the third act could simply be omitted in its entirety. (In the end the opera was staged without the ballet, and later productions involved other modifications; not until 1909 was it heard again at the Opéra in its original form.) After the fire at the Opéra-Comique had put an end to *Proserpine*, he had another chance to outdo Massenet when the Paris Opéra asked him for a new work. For this he decided, from among several subjects suggested by Gallet, on a libretto about the sixteenth-century sculptor Benvenuto Cellini, already the subject of an opera by Berlioz. The idea was accepted by the theatre on 26th September 1887. The text was adapted from a play, *Benvenuto Cellini*, by Paul Meurice, a name from the composer's childhood. Meurice was the husband of Mlle Granger, the infant daughter of Saint-Saëns's neighbour at Rue du Jardinet. This personal acquaintance made it easier for him to approach Meurice about making alterations to the piece, which the author had created from an earlier romance with the help of Alexandre Dumas senior.

Saint-Saëns at first kept the title of *Benvenuto* but later changed it to *Ascanio*, the title of the original romance, to avoid direct comparison with Berlioz's work. The story too is different, with a love triangle that ends in tragedy, a series of complications and changes of heart far-fetched even by operatic standards.

Colombe, daughter of the Provost of Paris, is loved by both Cellini and his apprentice Ascanio. Cellini's admiration for the woman whom he sees as embodying his ideal of eternal beauty arouses the jealousy of his Italian admirer, Scozzone; Ascanio is loved by a French duchess. The rivalry of the two men ends when Cellini gallantly stands aside in favour of his pupil and, realising that Colombe is in danger from the two rejected women, hides her in a reliquary he has made for some Ursuline nuns. He arranges for her to be carried in it to the safety of the convent. The Duchess learns of the plan and causes the reliquary to be diverted to her house, intending its occupant to suffocate in it. However, Scozzone, at first in league with the Duchess, is conscience-stricken and takes Colombe's place. Cellini, meanwhile, secures the king's consent to the marriage of Colombe and Ascanio as a reward for his latest masterpiece, but the opera ends with the Duchess in dismay at finding that Scozzone has died in Colombe's place and Cellini in despair at the death of his admirer.

At first sight it is difficult to see what attracted Saint-Saëns to this unpromising material, other than the opportunity it provided to recreate the sixteenth-century French court. It is likely that the contrast between female treachery and Cellini's noble self-sacrifice also appealed to the misogynist in him. But the finished work strongly suggests that what struck the most responsive chord was the sculptor's fatherly interest in and concern for his young apprentice, a relationship that mirrored his own strong paternal instincts: the music he was to write for the scenes between Cellini and Ascanio is arguably the most effective in the opera.

Nevertheless, the play was to prove obstinately unsuited for operatic treatment, a fact that was to undermine the opera's chances of success, and Saint-Saëns confessed that he and Gallet adapted it "with considerable difficulty",[37] despite Meurice's approachability. Still he remained convinced of its worth, and there was the added incentive, held out by the Opéra, of a prestigious opening to coincide with the Paris Exhibition of 1889, marking the centenary of the Revolution, for which the Eiffel Tower was already being built. It was perhaps as well, in view of the time and effort the new opera was to take, that nothing came of a project to write an oratorio for one of the English festivals. Hermann Klein had written for him a text on the subject of Moses, something he had wanted to set since his student days. After modifying it according to the composer's suggestions, Klein submitted the planned work for future performance at the Norwich Festival, after hearing Saint-Saëns's Psalm 18 sung there in the autumn of 1887. Saint-Saëns replied to his report of that performance on 18th October: "Nothing could be more agreeable than the news you give me of my Psalm. I cannot console myself for not having gone to hear it; I was detained in Paris by some business at the Opéra. When you were in Paris I was compelled to leave hurriedly for Boulogne . . . Should the oratorio be arranged for Norwich, I should be very glad." He wanted Novello to publish the oratorio, which "will probably be my last work. It must worthily crown my career!" The festival organisers, however, were unwilling to commit themselves to what they regarded as an unknown quantity. Klein then approached the organisers of the Leeds Festival, who also refused.[38] It says something about the lack of success of *Le Déluge* and *La Lyre et l'Harpe* in England that the Leeds committee was able to come to the curiously erroneous conclusion that Saint-Saëns was new to oratorio, and that it could not therefore take the responsibility of accepting his proposal. Hearing of these rejections, and learning also that Rubinstein was writing an opera about Moses, Saint-Saëns gave up the idea of an oratorio and returned the text to Klein.

So he was free to concentrate on *Ascanio*. In November 1887, fearing the effects of the Paris winter on his health, he left for Algiers, where he began work on the opera almost as soon as he arrived. He wrote to Gallet: "Today, 17th November, I began *Benvenuto*. It is terribly difficult."[39] Soon, though, he was finding it "very amusing to do," breaking off in the evenings to listen to the café concerts in the port area of the city.[40] One of the main problems he encountered in the composition was that the casting of the statue – the climax of Berlioz's opera – came after Cellini had already been singing for some time, "and this scene with its violence seemed certain to exceed the strength of the most valiant artist".[41] Ever careful to keep the demands on the voice within reasonable bounds, he decided, in consultation with the author, the librettist and the Opéra, to cut the scene altogether. By February 1888 he had completed the second of the five acts and remained so engrossed in the opera that he turned down an invitation to write a piece for a choral competition being held that summer. Still in Algiers, he announced in a letter of 18th March to Jean-Baptiste Weckerlin, the Paris Conservatoire librarian, that "I have today finished the draft of my third act". His North African hibernation had now lasted five months, but he intended to extend it to beyond April, perhaps mindful of the relapse he had suffered on returning to France in the spring of 1883. The only consideration weighing against an extended absence from home was his mother, who was now seventy-eight: he told Weckerlin that he would return only if his mother was ill, "and I am hopeful that will not happen, because she bears up marvellously well. Next winter I shall not leave Paris, and if, as I hope, I am more resistant than I was this year to the effects of the cold, I shall be able to pay my respects in person."[42]

He returned to France in early summer and by September had finished the whole opera apart from the ballet, which he later composed, in piano score, while staying at St Germain-en-Laye (Debussy's birthplace, incidentally), incorporating into it some original sixteenth-century melodies he had found in the Bibliothèque nationale in Paris. With the opera at last completed after nearly a year, he felt an overwhelming need for rest. "I have finished", he wrote to Gallet.

"I feel immensely lazy."[43] He dedicated the opera to Pauline Viardot. As planned, he stayed in Paris as the winter came on and was managing to survive the cold quite well when the season proved traumatic in a way he could not have foreseen. His mother, who had borne herself "remarkably well" in her old age, caught a chill which quickly developed into pneumonia. After only a few days, she died on 18th December, aged seventy-nine. Of all the many deaths of friends and relations that touched Saint-Saëns deeply throughout his life, including those of his sons, that of his mother was the most shattering. It was to have a profoundly significant effect on his personal philosophy and indirectly on his music. The same evening he sent a brief note to Fauré, whose mother had died the year before: "My dear Gabriel, I too lost my mother this morning at nine o'clock. Not much point in saying more, is there? Not much point either in coming to see me, I am receiving only my relations because I cannot do otherwise – unless you would like to see her for the last time."[44] The bereavement, which, as with great-aunt Charlotte, had come so suddenly and unexpectedly, left him numb to the world, in a mood of indifference and resignation. "I arrived on 18th December at a complete nirvana; it's all the same to me."[45] The anxiety and pessimism that haunt the C minor symphony had been exorcised at the price of a terrible grief that was to give way to atheism.

After his mother's funeral and interment in the family vault at Montparnasse, Saint-Saëns, unable to remain in the apartment that had now seen two deaths in the family, took doctor's advice and travelled south, to the resort of Tamaris, near Toulon. Letters he wrote to Durand during January 1889 try to be reassuring and businesslike, but there was no hiding the desolation.

I see everything very coldly, asking only to be quiet . . . soon I shall get back to work. I shall return at the end of the month with my ballet all orchestrated . . . I am placed here like a cock in paté, in the midst of flowers, with the sea air and every comfort one could desire. The house is melancholy and dull, and that is precisely why I know no pleasure there, and shall not know any either . . . Sleep and appetite are not yet very brilliant, but I have already been able to take a long walk . . . After having put all my affairs in Paris in order at the beginning of next month, I shall – if the Opéra doesn't call me back – go I don't know where, to the sun, until the summer . . . Say to the gallery that I am well and that I am staying here to rest and not to be looked after. I do not have a debilitating illness, it is now this, now that. My general state is bad, that's certain. I am, however, in the best possible circumstances, in every way.[46]

His true state of mind is revealed more clearly on 28th January: "I began to work again today. Will better times come? I can doubt it. *Tristis est anima mea usque ad mortem* (my spirit is sad unto death)." By February he was giving way more completely to his depression, complaining that lack of sleep, lack of appetite and of all physical energy had forced him to stop work, but adding philosophically that "perhaps the worst is passed, for everything passes in this world". He was no better the next day. "This is a terrible time. I have a horrible dread of returning home . . . "[47] Durand was so concerned that he visited the stricken composer at Tamaris later that month, and found him quite unable to face Paris and the melancholy business of putting all his affairs in order. Instead he went to Algiers in March, under the assumed name of Charles Sannois, but by the end of April he could put off his duties in Paris no longer. Rather than stay in the capital he took accommodation at St Germain-en-Laye.

His mother had left him everything, but he knew he could never again live among the family heirlooms and the memories they evoked, especially her paintings and the little piano on which he had received his first lesson from his great-aunt. He sent them, together with most of his own possessions – including the telescope – to his cousin in Dieppe, where they were to form the basis of the collection that was to become the Saint-Saëns museum. After joining his former Niedermeyer pupil Gigout to play the organ at Jacques Durand's wedding, there was little to keep him in Paris. He called on Fauré, only to learn that he was in the country. As for his opera, he was in no fit state, physically or mentally, to deal with the lengthening delays and broken promises in its production. The Paris Exhibition was in full swing but *Ascanio* was not, after all, at the Opéra: the scenery had not even been commissioned, because of disagreements between the directors Ritt and Gailhard. There was also trouble in casting the role of Scozzone. The first choice was Hélène Richard, the first Anne Boleyn in *Henry VIII*, but she disliked the part, declaring it to be "without effect". She took particular exception to her main scene, in which she appears *en Bacchante*, first complaining that it would involve extra effort on her part to make it work and then threatening to ruin it deliberately so as to have it cut. Saint-Saëns refused to allow this, and became somewhat disenchanted with Mme Richard, ungallantly remarking to a friend that "her arms, which are not beautiful, and her figure, which is only slightly elegant, would not go well with the scenery".[48]

While the Opéra searched for another mezzo-soprano to sing Scozzone, Saint-Saëns withdrew to St Germain-en-Laye, leaving Durand, Gallet and also Ernest Guiraud, now professor of composition at the Conservatoire, who had taken an interest in the new work, to handle negotiations with the theatre. At St Germain he was able to share his grief with the violinist Diaz Albertini, whose own mother had died. He had little inclination to compose: apart from the ballet orchestration, a piano piece, 'Les cloches du soir', and an arrangement of a Bach sarabande for violin and piano were all he had produced so far that year. On 9th October, his fifty-fourth birthday, he set off for the south, having formally relinquished the apartment at M. le Prince. This time the hibernation was an escape from melancholy associations as much as from the northern winter. He wanted to be sure he would be left entirely alone, to think and to write as he felt inclined, and he left no forwarding address. To Gallet he wrote on the eve of his departure: "I am desolate at leaving without seeing you"[49] and explained that his aim was "to search afar, under other climes, for the means of making a new man of myself".[50] To Durand he declared his intention not to return until the spring, and explained that he had left instructions regarding *Ascanio* with Gallet. These allowed Guiraud charge of rehearsals and contained the specific instruction that not a note of the opera was to be omitted or altered without his consent – an instruction that was to be disregarded.

Adopting his pseudonym of Charles Sannois, he travelled through Spain, stopping first at Granada. Here he wrote a poem called 'Les Heures', which contrasts the bitterness and emptiness of life with the release offered by death: "All wound us, the last kills us", and yet these hours, "full of hope, dread or delight, are but an illusion, a dream without reality . . . a lie invented by man." They are ultimately futile, their "useless sounds lost in eternity".[51] The desolation lifted when he moved on to Cadiz, where he stayed for several weeks. There the climate and surroundings so delighted him that he felt able to write music again, completing the Scherzo for two pianos and beginning the fantasy for piano and orchestra called *Africa*. "Cadiz is an enchanting town", he wrote to Gallet on 30th November, "where everything charms the eye, where nothing is ugly or dirty, and such sun, such sky, such air! I intended only to pass through, but I stayed here, I refreshed my eyesight here."[52] On a visit to Seville he wandered in the gardens of the Alcazar, "delight of the Moorish kings", and was so impressed by the orange trees and the "thousands of oranges of special quality and exceptional smell" that he could not help picking one – and was caught in the act. "I paid the attendant – I have nothing to reproach myself for", he somewhat sheepishly recounted.[53]

In a letter to Ritt and Gailhard he put his absence down to health considerations: "Everyone who knows me knows that I can no longer bear winter in France . . . You must present *Benvenuto*, or *Ascanio*, without me, as *Lohengrin* was presented a while ago in Weimar without Wagner, and *Aïda* in Cairo without Verdi. I do not wish for *Benvenuto* a better fortune than that of those two celebrated works."[54] To Durand he wrote of plans to compose something for the Conservatoire Concerts Society, as well as the trio "for which you have waited so long . . . but I am at the mercy of the unexpected; I had no intention of writing a Scherzo for two pianos!"[55] This casual remark is interesting in that it strongly refutes the charge traditionally levelled against Saint-Saëns that he was a mere craftsman who had no belief in inspiration. Years later he was to tell an American interviewer that his inspiration was often sudden and unexpected: "Sometimes it comes in the middle of the night, sometimes in the daytime."[56]

In Cadiz he was undoubtedly in better spirits, but he was also in reflective mood. He began to write more poetry, much of which would be published in the collection called *Rimes Familières*. That he was thinking of absent friends is clear from those poems directly addressed to Viardot, Fauré, Gounod and others, praising their worth as artists. An ode to Augusta Holmes, found in her papers after her death, was written at Cadiz on 7th November, and refers to a "double ray" that "shines on your front" – the beauty of Astarte and the poetic genius of Sappho. In her choral works known as patriotic hymns (including one for the 1889 centenary of the Revolution), "the Republic, Art and Love have blended together their voices, guided by your powerful hand". To Viardot he says "hatred is the greatest homage: be proud that you have earned it," arguing (from bitter experience, it seems) that while everyone is ready to encourage the young artist, confident that he or she will never rise above the ordinary, their encouragement turns to hatred once they are proven wrong. To Gallet he spoke of his journey being in search of "nature's calm, forgetfulness, the father of happiness!" Another poem reflects on the nature of true friendship in general, proving that the saying "out of sight is out of mind" is false because "serious friends" do not betray each other after parting. Distance rather makes the heart grow fonder, just as we cherish the mythology and literature of classical antiquity across the centuries.

When the winter cold finally arrived in Cadiz he moved on to the Canary Islands, and on New Year's Eve booked into a Las Palmas hotel as Charles Sannois, "businessman". For the next four months – while *Samson et Dalila* was at last performed in France and *Ascanio* had its première in Paris – he was able to lead a life of peaceful contemplation, and blissful anonymity, in the tropical climate he found so congenial. Poetry began to pour from him, some of it wistfully contrasting the desire for tranquillity with the vanished ardour of youth, and much of it expressing an indignant and often angry atheism. Religious faith is "the poison of falsehood" which "takes for its ideal an impossible rapture, falsifying nature and simple happiness". It worships a God who condemns man for indulging the passions with which He endowed him.

You well knew, Jehovah, that in his trembling flesh
Man, quick to bless and quick to blaspheme,
Hides a soul that is aflame . . .
You placed near his lips a fruit which he desires;
You say: it's pleasure, don't touch! Why?
Under our feet the sloping abyss draws us.
Who dug it? You!

Man, not God, is the measure: he "reigns a conqueror on the sublime earth / He lives: the gods are dead or are silent, weary. / His brow touches heaven, his foot ransacks the pit; / He alone, and that is enough."[57]

The poems of Saint-Saëns are in many ways in parallel with the music, in their technical regularity, the classical elegance of form and metre and their style, which abounds with that sardonic wisdom that underlies both the quirkiness and the other-worldly melancholy in his melodies. Irony is cloaked in an aura of sadness, within strictly observed, traditional rules, which Saint-Saëns regarded as a stimulus to high poetic utterance and a barrier to mediocrity (rather than the other way round). "My principle is very simple", he was to write many years later. "What is verse? Language subject to certain rules. If the rules are discontinued it is no longer verse."[58]

Wit, never far away from his more serious utterances, also had a place in this poetic outpouring. He was amused rather than repulsed to see a tapeworm floating in a jar at a pharmacist's and was even more amused to learn that its name was Botriocephalus (literally, bunch head). This became the title of a comic dialogue, in the manner of La Fontaine, between a faun and a fury, a piece of "antique buffoonery", as he called it, that was eventually staged.

Stories of Saint-Saëns's four-month retreat in the Canaries were mostly gleaned by newspaper reporters at the end of the period, and tended to be embellished considerably in the retelling. They centred mostly on the suspicions he aroused by his movements, his musical expertise and his inability to resist indulging his interests. Here was a "businessman" who conversed with authority on astronomy, who liked to sketch landscapes, and who was a regular at musical events – chamber concerts, café concerts and brass band concerts on the promenade. Rumours began to circulate as to the true identity of "M. Sannois", including a theory that he was really one of the many English holidaymakers on the island, one who happened to speak French. These rumours were fanned by his frequent attendance at a local literary circle, where his musical prowess was often in demand – as when a guest wanted to sing Mephistopheles's serenade from *Faust* a semitone down, and 'l'anglais' was the only one present who could transpose at the piano. At last, sensing the danger of discovery, he stayed away from the literary circle, but then inquiries began to be made at his hotel. Finally, so the story goes, a chambermaid, seeing the manuscript sketches of the *Africa* fantasy on his desk, drew sinister conclusions from them and reported it to the already suspicious hotel manager, causing the supposed spy and his coded messages to leave Las Palmas for less conspicuous lodgings outside the town. Reports of him thereafter under constant police surveillance are, however, almost certainly an exaggeration.

For the next month he explored the other islands, visiting Tenerife and Lanzarote, before returning to Las Palmas. There he checked into a different hotel, but almost immediately began to excite curiosity again, chiefly by his renewed attendance at concerts. According to *Le Figaro,* when an Italian opera company arrived with a production of *Rigoletto* he offered to sing the part of Monterone when the company's baritone fell ill. Not surprisingly the manager turned down this approach from a total stranger, who then asked the conductor if he could play percussion. This offer too was declined.[59] In the *Musical Times* version of the story, however, Saint-Saëns's offer to sing was accepted; he rehearsed, but the performance never took place because the company went bankrupt at the last moment. "It is quite refreshing in these mercenary days to know that there are eminent composers who will sing for nothing", the journal commented.[60]

Back in the musical capitals of Europe speculation was rife concerning Saint-Saëns's 'disappearance', as first *Samson* and then *Ascanio* reached the French stage and there was still no word of his whereabouts. Some said he was dead – there was even a claim on his estate – others that he had gone mad and was in an institution. It was known that he had left Cadiz for the Canaries in December. *Le Figaro,* strongly suspecting that he was still in the islands, kept a reporter in Tenerife on look-out, while reports came in of sightings in France, North Africa and even the Far East – Java was one place mentioned. The government too ordered its diplomatic service to keep watch for him. Gallet, who had not heard from him since November, had nevertheless to issue denials of death and insanity, adding only that Saint-Saëns had gone abroad to dispel "melancholy" brought on by "domestic troubles".

Meanwhile, *Samson et Dalila* had scored a sensational hit when it was produced at Rouen in the first week of March 1890, in contrast to the almost total indifference it had met with in France over the previous twenty years. The French première drew almost the whole of the Parisian musical world, with every hotel room in Rouen booked well in advance. The opera had been chosen for performance by a new Lyric Theatre company in the town, set up by a M. Verdhurt. This was due largely to the efforts of Fauré (who took the rehearsals), Chabrier and other admirers, who may well have been inspired by a largely amateur production given at Liège in November and December 1888 – probably the first complete stage performance outside Germany. Although the performance at Rouen, conducted by the Marseilles Symphonic Concerts conductor Gabriel Marie, may not have been one of the best in terms of singers, it had the effect of ensuring the work's future. A production was planned for later that year in Paris to launch a new opera company being set up by Verdhurt at the Eden theatre.

As the first night of *Ascanio* approached at the Opéra, speculation as to the composer's whereabouts reached fever pitch, upstaging the new work in the advance notices. *The Times* in London took a rather cynical view of it all: "It is to be feared that this mysterious disappearance on the eve of the production of his opera will be attributed by a portion of the public to a desire to get himself talked about."[61] His absence had left the opera open to alterations, in contravention of his strict instructions. Guiraud was pressurised into cutting the scene to which Mme Richard had so strongly objected. When she finally refused to sing Scozzone, the Opéra directors, unable to find a replacement mezzo for the troublesome part, also persuaded him to rewrite it for a soprano, in consultation with Gallet and Durand. The part then went to Rosa Bosman, with Ada Adiny as the Duchess and the American Emma Eames as Colombe, so that all three principal females were sung by sopranos. Still there were last-minute delays and the first night was postponed, from 14th to 21st March.

The première was a glittering occasion, "one of the most brilliant I have seen" declared the correspondent of *The Stage*, "all the social, political, literary and artistic notabilities of the day being in attendance, from President Carnot downwards".[62] Every effort had gone into the production to score the maximum impact. Yet the production had a hollow ring about it. *The Stage* called the opera "an erudite and heavy composition, showing remarkable industry on the part of both composer and librettist, but lacking in melody and dramatic interest", and predicted that "it will not take a permanent place on the stage".[63] *Le Figaro* thought the music grey and half-hearted, sensing a certain "embarrassment and scruple" in Saint-Saëns's approach, and seeing a deep gulf between the composer's "fine intentions" and the audience's receptivity.[64] However, the set pieces, especially the ballet and choruses, were generally praised and Scozzone's second act solo 'Madame, il est ici' and the fourth act quartet were encored. Most of the criticism was levelled at the libretto, which *The Times* called "mediocre", the characters of Cellini, Francis I and Charles V "three mountains bringing forth a mouse".[65] The critic of *Le Temps* thought that "M. Saint-Saëns's talent and the care with which he has followed the words only render more noticeable the faults of a piece in which I cannot see a good opera text".[66] The *Musical Times* condemned the play as lacking "vital interest" and its characters as "either uninteresting or repellent",[67] while the *New York Times* commented that the text "complicated the obscurity of the story".[68]

Of the principals, Lassalle was as formidable a Cellini as he was a Henry VIII, and rather overshadowed Emile Cossira's Ascanio. Emma Eames was not at her best, as she herself admitted. She was Saint-Saëns's first choice for the role of Colombe – he had seen her acclaimed debut as Juliet the season before – but in this, her second season at the Opéra, "I was less effective . . . and sang less well, not only on account of the constant intrigue which I encountered at the Opéra but also because of personal trouble and anxiety".[69] The intrigues were to force her out of the company later that year.

Among the opera's admirers were Gounod and the musicologist Charles Malherbe, both of whom wrote detailed appraisals. Its independence from both the Italian and Wagnerian styles perplexed some commentators but impressed others, like the *Musical Times*, which saw it as something of an operatic

had come to Las Palmas to forget that he was a musician. "On arriving here, I found a climate without equal. I felt myself a poet; I have passed my time writing verse, always verse . . . " He also mentioned that he had been "very ruffled" by news of the postponement of the *Ascanio* première.[75] Press interviews were an aspect of fame he found particularly irksome – "I hate talking to the public about myself", he once confessed – but a worse menace were the autograph hunters and relic collectors constantly trying to invade his privacy. There were people who wanted locks of his hair and an English couple who went so far as to cut bits off his coat. Later, a comb, brush and pair of braces went missing from his hotel room. Perhaps not surprisingly, he came to loathe the very sight of autograph books and would never sign them. Sir Henry Wood wrote in his autobiography that "whenever he came to Queen's Hall the mantelshelf in the artists' room was piled high with these books. He would look at them in positive hatred and sweep the whole lot on to the floor."[76]

In his letter to Gallet, Saint-Saëns spoke of his delight that the cast of *Ascanio* was being so well received. "As for Lassalle, I can see and hear him from here." But he complained that since his discovery he had had hardly any time to himself. He had even been called upon by two singers to write them a song each, a romance and a comic duo, and on one occasion "I had to use violence to avoid an ovation from the populace". A consolation was that he was shown the artistic treasures of the cathedral, including a "jewel" of a work by, appropriately enough, Benvenuto Cellini. He intended to leave the Canaries in mid-May and asked Gallet not to reply, as he would be changing his address in a renewed attempt to "lose myself" in the few weeks that remained.[77] But it proved impossible to escape the limelight, and by the end of April he was back in France, at St Germain-en-Laye.

In May he arrived in Paris and booked into an hotel, a traveller in his native city. There he found his music still being performed: Paderewski played the fourth concerto at a concert of his works given by Colonne at the Trocadero on the 31st, which also included Mme Krauss and Emmanuel Lafarge (the Rouen Samson) in operatic extracts, together with the *Oratorio de Noël*, and extracts from *La Lyre et l'Harpe* and the C minor symphony selected by the composer. News of the performances earlier in the year of *Samson et Dalila* made him less happy. While he welcomed the opera's belated arrival in France he was dismayed to learn that some parts of it had been repeated, thus upsetting the balance of the work. When Durand and his son called on him at his hotel he complained about these repeats while standing at the wash basin, his head covered in soap. But, recalled Jacques Durand, "his anxiety subsided when we told him that Fauré had been in charge of the performance".[78] (Durand mistakenly records that Fauré *conducted* the performances; whereas, of course, he had helped to supervise the rehearsals.) He was no doubt displeased also about the cuts and alterations to *Ascanio*. However, despite his reservations about the performances, both operas looked set to make further progress, with *Samson* heading for Paris in the autumn and *Ascanio* still playing at the Opéra. This time he intended to keep a close eye on them.

The respective fates of the two operas could hardly have turned out more differently, the one heading for fame, the other for obscurity. By June 1890 *Ascanio* had been given twenty times, the receipts increasing as the run continued, and there were to be another ten performances by the end of the year. It then fell into neglect, and the sets were destroyed in a fire at the Opéra on 6th January 1894. Abroad it had even less impact than *Proserpine*, and there was a brief and unconvincing revival at the Opéra in the last year of the composer's life. As with Saint-Saëns's other neglected operas it is impossible to assess it accurately without seeing the effect on stage. This could perhaps be argued for most operas, but it applies particularly to these works because of the very fine, subtle balance between the music and the text. Gounod, in his long appreciation of *Ascanio*, made the point that "some of the musical intentions find their verification, their sanction, only on the stage", adding that "the richness and constant interest of the instrumentation cast over the whole work an incomparable prestige and an indispensable complement to the dramatic expression".[79] It is a view that has made little progress with theatre managements over the years. When operas fail, it is often a temptation, particularly when the music is of high quality, to blame the librettist, and Gallet has been accused of lacking dramatic sense and movement. This, however, cannot account for the failure of Saint-Saëns's operas to texts by librettists other than Gallet. If they lack realistic characters and compelling action, the composer must take at least some of the blame. Yet in their day, as has been shown, the operas had their champions. One of those arguing strongly in their favour was Hahn, an opera composer himself, who studied with Massenet at the Conservatoire but had private lessons with Saint-Saëns. Hahn said of him that

he brought to his theatrical works the same care for form, the same intellectual control and – and this is his big crime in the eyes of many – the same refinement of taste as in his chamber or concert music. Moderation in feeling and expressive balance are, it seems, forbidden to a dramatic musician. It is necessary to be 'theatre', as they say, everything must be grandly emphasised so as to get across to the ignorant masses."

He criticised Saint-Saëns's preference for historical subjects. "But given this tendency, how can we not admire the correctness, the appositeness, the taste even, with which he surrounds his characters and makes them speak?"[80] Writing in 1935 for the composer's centenary, Hahn thought that, contrary to Tchaikovsky's verdict, a performance of *Henry VIII* would convince the sceptical that Saint-Saëns was indeed "a man of the theatre".[81]

With *Samson* and *Ascanio* not due for production again until the autumn of 1890, Saint-Saëns took the opportunity to spend a few weeks in North Africa in June. He told the press he intended to lose himself in the desert and plan a new opera, for which he had several ideas in mind. He was, however, due to return to France in July to attend the inauguration of the Saint-Saëns museum in Dieppe. The cousin to whom he had sent his musical and artistic treasures, together with his household effects, for safe-keeping after his mother's death had presented them to the town so closely associated with the Saint-Saëns family name. They had been stored in a town hall annexe while a permanent home for them was built. Saint-Saëns was at the opening ceremony – surely an exceptional honour for a living musician – on 18th July. Also that month there was a festival of his music in Boulogne, including a staging of *La Princesse Jaune*, and extracts from *Le Déluge*, *Ascanio* and the *Suite Algérienne*.

The ceremonies and festivities over, he retired to St Germain, to spend the rest of the summer correcting proofs of his poems (*Rimes Familières* appeared the following year) and also preparing for publication some essays he had written in the last weeks of his stay in the Canaries. These appeared as a series in a journal called *La Revue Bleue*, whose music critic, René de Récy, was a friend and admirer. As well as reminiscences, they included a discourse on the metronome in time and space, leading on to some philosophical reflections about the nature of the universe that were to form the basis of his later book *Problèmes et Mystères*. They show a calmer, more considered outlook than the often vitriolic outbursts in *Rimes Familières*. The indignant atheism of the poetry was already mellowing into the more dignified deism of the prose.

Autumn was to bring more pressing reasons to contemplate life and death, as work began to take its toll on his health. There were preparations to supervise in Paris for the two operas. It was not possible to restore the part of Scozzone in *Ascanio* to its original mezzo, as the same cast had been engaged for the autumn production, which opened at the Opéra on 19th September. There were still the usual difficulties to face with management, singers and producers – and *Samson* was still to come. The pressures and the approach of winter finally brought about such a severe tubercular inflammation that he thought he was going to die. He was still recovering in bed when the curtain went up on the Paris première of *Samson et Dalila* at the Eden theatre at the end of October 1890. Next day he felt well enough to attend the second performance and, besieged by admirers, went backstage afterwards to congratulate the singers and musicians. Unusually, the press was in agreement in its praise, although Servières thought the production was let down by the two principals, Jean-Alexandre Talazac lacking the stature and passion of the hero while the statuesque Rosine Bloch towered absurdly over him, showing none of the spirit and seductive warmth of Delilah.[82] Nevertheless, it played to packed houses every night, and the Opéra, which had for twenty years refused to consider the piece, had now to acknowledge that perhaps it was after all worth considering. Yet the country's leading opera house still refused to commit itself, much to the composer's disgust, while *Samson et Dalila* went on to be played at provincial theatres all over France.

XI • THE TRAVELLING PHILOSOPHER

WHILE *SAMSON ET DALILA* BEGAN ITS SPECTACULAR RISE TO FAME IN French theatres in the last quarter of 1890, its run at the Eden lasted barely a month. Verdhurt, the director, was led on by the opera's money-spinning potential to overstretch himself financially, and by the end of November he was bankrupt. Meanwhile, Saint-Saëns was on his travels again.

While he still sought a genuine and permanent triumph in the theatre, the composer sought still more an escape from the burdensome life of a celebrity. He was now an established, even an establishment figure, in the world of music and knew the price of fame, the constant demands on his time and attention, the favour seeking, the prying. It had been demonstrated only too clearly in the final days of his sojourn in the Canary Islands. His older colleague Gounod already had long experience of it, as he was to describe graphically in his memoirs:

My readers cannot have any conception of the innumerable and indiscreet requests to which a musician is daily exposed – the crowds of young pianists, violinists, vocalists, composers, poets (lyric and otherwise), teachers and inventors of various methods, systems and theories, editors of periodicals pestering you to take their publications; not to mention the requests for autographs, photographs, the albums of the fans, and what not, sent to you for your signature. It all amounts to a perfect nightmare, and the musician is turned into a sort of national property to which the public has right of access at any and every hour. Our houses are not in the street any more; the street is in our houses. Our whole life is devoured by idlers, inquisitive folk, loungers who are bored with themselves, and even by reporters of all sorts, who force their way into our homes, to inform the public not only as to our private conversation but also as to the colour of our dressing gowns and the cut of our working jackets![1]

Saint-Saëns had had respite from such pressures in a few blissful months of anonymity. It was an experience he desired to repeat with ever greater frequency, so that, while he continued to work for and champion the cause of national music, he was always seeking the delights of retreat to southern shores. The patriot was also the expatriate.

Besides, Paris was no longer home after the death of his mother. He had no permanent address there for the next fourteen years, staying in hotel rooms when his presence was required. Concert work took him away from the capital as well as temperament, of course, but his absences, particularly in the winter, were also very much to do with his delicate health. The blue horizons and sunbaked splendours of the Canary Islands and North Africa were a welcome, even essential, alternative to the city's stale air and busy streets as well as to its musical politics. This was especially the case for a man approaching his sixties and constantly reminded, by recurrent appearances of tubercular symptoms, that his physical constitution rested on weak foundations. "My enemy is the Paris sky", he told Gallet. "I fear the hackney carriages and the spiders . . . the water I drink only if I'm sure it's pure."[2] To another friend he wrote: "My absence is something to which you must become accustomed . . . Paris is no longer liveable for me for ten months of the year. To die for music is still a happiness, I know, but it is a happiness to which I prefer the unhappiness of living without it."[3]

This ever-present need to get away caused him to turn down several offers over the years of permanent posts, among them professorships and even the directorship of the Conservatoire, situations that would have been incompatible with the nervous impatience of his character. For travel also appealed to his restless, inquiring mind and it was as an amateur explorer and observer as much as a professional musician that he was to visit all the continents of the earth except for Australasia. The calendar of his life became an ever more bewildering catalogue of places, extraordinary in the age before air travel, the more so as it accompanied virtually ceaseless activity as composer, conductor, pianist, organist and writer. Such an intense lifestyle, coupled with the frequent bouts of illness brought on by overwork, make it easier to understand his increasingly irascible and impatient character which left such an indelible impression on many who crossed his path. However, he never lost his sense of fun and was always good company with friends, to whom he remained unswervingly loyal, and his wit could still sparkle on social occasions. But embittered by so many personal tragedies, frustrations and disappointments, he wanted for the most part to be left alone, to compose, pursue his non-musical interests and generally contemplate the higher things. He told Hermann Klein: "I must have solitude. I like good company, but I like hard work even better."[4] It was during this period too that he began to lay greater stress on form rather than expression as the essence of music, extending to his art the impersonal quality of the hotel rooms, ship cabins and railway carriages which had become his habitat. Almost the only personal touches in these surroundings were the portraits of his mother and his first son which he always carried with him. Servières commented: "I strongly doubt that he was a happy man."[5]

The onset of the Parisian winter in 1890, the prevarications of the Opéra over *Samson et Dalila* and the need for convalescence after his serious illness prompted him to embark on a cruise that would take him through the Suez Canal across the Indian Ocean to Ceylon. After serving, with manifest reluctance, as a pall-bearer at César Franck's funeral on 10th November he left for Spain to begin his voyage. He took with him an opera libretto, *Eviradmus* by Alphonse Pagès, based on a poem by Victor Hugo. Again he travelled incognito, for the most part keeping to himself. He did, however, strike up acquaintances with a colonial official named M. Jacquet who was based in what was then French Cochin-China, and with a young doctor named Félix Regnault, the surname no doubt prompting melancholy recollections of an earlier friendship. The three were sitting in the ship's lounge one evening when a woman sat at the piano and played an aria from *Etienne Marcel.* Saint-Saëns said nothing. The cruise, meanwhile, was furnishing him with a wealth of material that would ultimately result in a series of learned articles, including philosophical reflections on seeing the pyramids for the first time and theories to explain the phenomenon of mirages. These he witnessed, among several "surprising things", during a week's stop in the Suez isthmus when, he confessed, he much regretted not having a camera.[6]

In Ceylon he decided to abandon *Eviradmus* and instead made several revisions to *Proserpine,* working without a piano. As well as cutting some of the third and fourth acts and the symphonic prelude to the last act, he introduced a tarantella and chorus of gypsies into act three and altered the end so that Proserpine kills herself instead of being stabbed by Sabatino. But it was not all work. While exploring the island he was delighted to make the acquaintance of a young panther, to study the Hindu customs and to visit the ancient temples of Kandy, calling in on a Belgian planter he knew on the way. He was also excited by the sight of the Southern Cross in the night sky above Colombo. But at length his constitution and his stomach began to suffer from the heat and the food, and he was feverish when he rejoined the ship for the return journey. The sea air soon revived him and he felt in sufficiently buoyant mood to tell his two travelling companions who he really was. He sat at the piano and played – and was instantly recognised by the woman who had played from *Etienne Marcel.*

The passengers again disembarked at Suez, and Saint-Saëns stayed for a few days at Cairo, where he completed the *Africa* fantasy. 'North Africa' would be a more accurate name for this little gem of a work, inspired as it is by the sights and sounds collected in and recollected from his many sojourns on the southern shores of the Mediterranean and the islands off the Western Sahara. It is an expression of the sheer joy he felt in these surroundings. It is also a microcosm of key elements of the composer's art, most obviously the orientalism, but also the detailed observation in the creation of local atmosphere and mood, the sharp and insistent rhythms, the wealth of melody and the fine balance of piano and orchestra; achieved here partly by an orchestral treatment that gives individual instruments, especially the woodwind, a concertante role which puts them almost on equal terms with the soloist. There is a razor-sharp precision and even prickliness about the texture and much of the rhythm – often syncopated – that suggests the sharpness of outlines under a tropical sun, palm trees and mosquitoes. But this is in contrast with a lyrical richness and variety, concentrated within the limits of barely twelve minutes and proceeding, by thematic paraphrase, transformation or brief development, with a marvellous fluency that shows the accomplished skill of the mature master. The strongly syncopated opening is followed by a piano cadenza in oriental style which leads into a beautiful flowing melody of refreshing simplicity. There follows a thematic kaleidoscope of mood and colour, including imitations of crickets and exotic bird calls, and building up to a climax dominated by a robust Tunisian folk tune. The fantasy is dedicated to Mme Roger-Miclos, who gave the first performance at a Colonne concert on 25th October 1891.

Saint-Saëns reached Paris in March but left shortly after for the Canary Islands, moving on from there to Algiers. There he amused himself by writing a one-act comedy about the complications which follow when a woman writes a document for a friend who claims to be suffering from writer's cramp. He drew on his highly developed sense of craftsmanship and rich store of wit, as well as his knowledge of classical French drama, and *La Crampe des Ecrivains* was later produced at the Municipal Theatre in Algiers, to some acclaim. From North Africa he moved on to Naples, where he studied ancient musical instruments as depicted on vases and wall-paintings from Pompeii, and noted down observations of the smoking volcanoes of Vesuvius and Stromboli. He was fascinated by the way the smoke rose quickly to a certain height then levelled out to form an umbrella cloud: it reminded him of a similar effect produced by exploding petrol tanks during the siege of Paris.[7]

His visit to Naples was cut short by a bilious attack which forced him back to the more congenial surroundings of Algiers, where he spent most of the rest of the year and where he took over a modest residence in Moorish style. From a hotel at Pointe-Pescade he wrote to the publisher Lemoine on 1st November: "It will take another two or three days for my little Arabic palace to be ready. It will be as big as a hand, but delightful."[8] He left Algiers only for brief visits to Paris and Geneva. In Paris, Colonne asked him if he would write a version for soloists, chorus and orchestra of the *Mélodies Persanes*, and this was the main musical task that occupied him in the latter half of 1891. As well as scoring the original songs he added two new numbers from Renaud's verse – 'La Fuite' with tenor soloist and 'Les Cygnes' for contralto and tenor – and gave the whole work a new name, *La Nuit Persane*. Colonne conducted extracts from the reconstructed work on 14th February 1892, but a complete performance was not heard until five years later at the Conservatoire Concerts Society.

After *La Nuit Persane*, Saint-Saëns turned again to considering ideas for an opera, having discarded a number of suggestions. His renewed determination to make a fresh assault on the theatre was no doubt fuelled by news that the Opéra had finally decided to stage *Samson et Dalila*, but any expectations of another grand opera from his pen proved groundless. After writing three operas in succession on weighty, tragic themes he wanted to try a lighter vein.

He took up a libretto given to him three years before by a playwright friend, Augé de Lassus, which he had read with much pleasure. This was *Phryné*, a story set in classical times of a courtesan who reduces a pompous old magistrate to ridicule through his infatuation for her considerable charms. It was the kind of subject – feminine wiles, sexual temptation and the ironies of human weakness – that was able to elicit a creative response in him. The new opera was promised for the opening of another Lyric theatre planned this time by Léonce Détroyat. With the agreement of de Lassus, *Phryné* was cut from three acts to two, but Saint-Saëns delayed work on it to return to the more serious area of chamber music.

The second piano trio, for which Durand had been waiting for at least six years, was finally begun in the spring of 1892 at Pointe-Pescade and completed in Geneva at the end of June. Saint-Saëns's first major essay in the medium since the violin sonata of 1885 is dedicated to the friend of his youth and former pupil, the Viscountess Grandval. One of the main points of interest is the inclusion in the finale of material originally intended for a string quartet, one of the very few combinations he had not yet felt confident enough to tackle. Nearly thirty years separate the second from the first trio, and the second is a reflection both of stylistic development and the profound changes that had affected the composer's life and thought in that time. Succeeding the sunny, carefree mood of the F major trio is a much weightier, five-movement work of dark intensity which is the most direct expression of his feelings of loss and despair in the first years of his bereavement and of the philosophical questions that were occupying his mind. The trio begins and ends tragically: the opening movement plunges straight into the stormy seas of the piano's shuddering semiquaver chords, over which the first subject is tossed like a doomed ship. This sombre picture is only briefly lightened by the gentle lilt of the second subject and is dramatically reaffirmed for the recapitulation in a towering fortissimo. There is an obsessive quality about the treatment of the material which pervades the whole work: the prickly five-in-a-bar rhythms of the second movement allegretto are softened only by the flowing semiquaver accompaniment of the second theme, and the central slow movement is a meditation on a single rhythmic idea, whose restlessness is finally soothed away in a calm resolution. The main relief is provided by the disarming simplicity of the intermezzo-like fourth movement, though even here the semitone drop at the very beginning sounds like a warning that all will not be well for long. The finale is a concentrated piece of juxtaposition, arising from two contrasting themes followed by a tightly argued tonal fugue, which includes some striking chromatic harmonies. The fugue is then combined with the first theme and a new, subsidiary idea introduces the return of the second, before E minor is reestablished and the work ends in a furious rush of semiquavers.

While writing the trio, Saint-Saëns was much encouraged to hear that his

Requiem had been substituted for that of Brahms in the Conservatoire Concerts Society's Good Friday concert. His letter to Lemoine in response to the news illustrates his view of Brahms's music as being of a heaviness widely mistaken for profundity. The Concerts Society's change of programme was "extremely fortunate for its audience, as the Requiem of Brahms is a bludgeon of the first order".[9] More sombre news was that of the death of Ernest Guiraud on 6th May, on the eve of Saint-Saëns's departure from Algiers. He complained in a letter to Gallet that a mutual friend (unnamed) had not notified him personally of Guiraud's death, leaving him to read about it in the newspapers. "He did not want to trouble me; he was very wrong. I know how to endure the cruelties of life, I have experienced them . . . "[10] He had grounds for criticising Guiraud, his addition of recitatives to *Carmen* and his tampering with *Ascanio* among them (he had also taught Debussy), but nevertheless admired and respected his former colleague in the National Music Society. As a tribute to his memory Saint-Saëns proposed to complete his unfinished five-act opera *Brunhilda*, just as Guiraud, on a more modest scale, had completed the orchestration of *Les Contes d'Hoffmann* after Offenbach's death. This, he felt, would be less likely to attract accusations of presumption on his part than a tribute entirely of his own, such was his jaundiced view of the petty enmities and jealousies of the musical fraternity.

Guiraud had composed three acts of the opera, mostly in vocal score. These his pupil Paul Dukas agreed to orchestrate while Saint-Saëns composed the rest, in collaboration with Gallet. Saint-Saëns was, however, a little more wary now of the strains of overwork and, especially now that he was trying to complete *Phryné* in time for Détroyat's new company, of the pressures of deadlines. He told Gallet: "I ask only that I shall not be forced to work quickly, as at other times; the idea of sitting long months without moving, in front of an inkwell, fills me with dread. We shall come to an arrangement with the Opéra so as to leave me with the time necessary to carry this task to a successful conclusion without too much fatigue."[11]

Similarly, he undertook to reconstruct and edit Marc-Antoine Charpentier's incidental music for Molière's comedy *Le Malade Imaginaire* – but took twenty years over it. "I have rediscovered in the Bibliothèque nationale all the original music which is by Charpentier; it is charming and is going to be very amusing to arrange", he told Gabriel Marie in August 1892.[12] A request for incidental music to another Molière classic, *Le Bourgeois Gentilhomme*, he passed to Fauré. As it was, he was hard-pressed to finish *Phryné*, for rehearsals were looming for the long-awaited *Samson et Dalila* at the Opéra. And in August, a week in Sicily was essential – to see an eruption of Mount Etna.

Returning to Paris, he plunged heart and soul into preparations for what was to be his greatest operatic triumph. Rehearsals for *Samson* ran true to form, with all sorts of battles with artists and management. The composer insisted on the finest details, including the making of special cymbals to be used by the dancers in the bacchanalia. When the dancers failed to grasp a certain movement he wanted, he jumped on to the stage in a fury to demonstrate it himself, brandishing his umbrella to reinforce the effect. "It was a picture", Jacques Durand recalled, "comic at the time, but the ballet master, at last understanding what the master meant, put it in, to the advantage of his choreography and for the greater good of the famous bacchanalia."[13] A greater aggravation was the withholding of promised special effects, especially for the act two storm, which the Opéra wanted to reserve for its next production, *Die Walküre*. That Wagner should take precedence even in such a detail infuriated Saint-Saëns, who responded by asking Durand's cousin Choisnel to take charge of lighting. Despite all the obstacles the first performance in November, conducted by Colonne, was an outstanding success – except that Choisnel's lighting effects so dazzled the audience that they had to be toned down for later performances. The opera, unlike the rest of Saint-Saëns's stage works, established a regular place in the repertory, reaching its 100th performance at the Opéra within five years and being produced all over Europe and reaching America in the years to 1914. His orchestral music, too – already given wide currency at home by Colonne, Lamoureux and his assistant and later successor, Camille Chevillard – had an even wider hearing in Paris after Jules Garcin retired from the Conservatoire Concerts Society and handed the baton to Paul Taffanel, a close friend of the composer and a champion of his music. *Le Rouet d'Omphale* was in Taffanel's first concert as chief conductor of the society on 27th October 1892.

Meanwhile, Guiraud's death had left a vacancy in the composition department at the Conservatoire, and Saint-Saëns urged Fauré to apply. At the beginning of the year he had written a poem to his former pupil from Algiers, a novel New Year greeting, wishing success and glory but also hinting at his own state of mind in the wake of his mother's death. From his "solitary crag" he looks back over the past and finds there "more than one tear". "But one memory charms me, that of having nurtured you." Fauré, with that lack of confidence and ambition that Saint-Saëns sometimes despaired of in him, was reluctant to accept extra responsibilities at the Conservatoire and wrote to his mentor declaring himself unqualified and physically unfit to take on the professorship. "I am sure you will understand and that when I come to see you, you will not have too severe a look for me."[14] In any case the Conservatoire's veteran director Ambroise Thomas, now a reactionary eighty-one-year-old, was hostile to Fauré, regarding him as an intolerable modern – much as he had once regarded Saint-Saëns – and made it known that he would oppose his application. Dubois, Fauré's senior at the Madeleine, was given the post instead.

Exhausted by the *Samson* rehearsals and anxious to get away for the winter, Saint-Saëns left after the Opéra première for Algiers. There, over the next three months, he completed *Phryné* in vocal score. Working against the clock to fulfil his promise to Détroyat, he enlisted the help of Messager in orchestrating the first act, supplying him with instructions but also allowing him some freedom of judgement. "Don't call me master any more", he wrote, "you're one too." He had seen Messager grow up "with some joy and pride, having worked on your education, as Gounod once worked on mine", the only difference being that Gounod was not at first pleased to see his protégé grow up, as "he needed to himself . . . I am not of that nature".[15]

Gounod, who was the last survivor of that trio (with Berlioz and Liszt) of mentors and heroes who had done much to guide and shape the outlook of the young Saint-Saëns, was now in terminal physical decline and living in virtual solitude. He was in no state to accept an invitation in December 1892 from Charles Stanford in Cambridge, to represent France in a concert the following June marking the fiftieth anniversary of the University Musical Society and to receive an honorary degree. Saint-Saëns agreed to take Gounod's place at Cambridge and was also due to visit the United States later in the summer, to play at the world fair in Chicago marking the 400th anniversary of the discovery of America. For the present *Phryné* took all his attention. The rush to complete the opera may have seemed pointless when Détroyat's theatre project collapsed, but Carvalho, reinstated at the Opéra-Comique after a successful appeal against his imprisonment, stepped in with an offer for the new work and was soon badgering Messager for the finished product. Early in March Saint-Saëns, still in Algiers, received a telegram from his apprentice relaying Carvalho's impatience. He replied on the 11th that he had completed the second act but had not sent it "because I am going to orchestrate it myself, while you finish act one". He also suggested that Messager should score the finale as it consisted mainly of reprises from the first act, with only slight modifications. The tone of his letter is that mixture of paternalistic authority, friendly banter and encouragement that he showed towards Fauré. Messager's collaboration, he suggests, will put him in favour with the Opéra-Comique because of what he optimistically foresees as the new work's "happy destiny", which would compensate for the setbacks Messager was suffering with his own "ravishing" *Madame Chrysanthème*. He also reveals that he is practising hard for his projected concerts in "Hangleterre" and "La mère-Ique," adding that if only Columbus had been shipwrecked before reaching America "I should not now be forced to work at scales and octaves!"[16]

As soon as Carvalho had the score of *Phryné* preparations were underway for a production. On 24th May 1893, within only two months of completion, it was premièred, giving the American soprano Sybil Sanderson a personal triumph as the artful courtesan. The piece is in the best traditions of French comic opera, a blend of frothy wit, refinement, natural simplicity and passages of great poetic charm, such as the pagan hymn and Aphrodite's monologue on the riverbank. It has been seen as Saint-Saëns's reply to the dominance of Verdi on the Parisian stage and the appearance of Wagner's works at the Opéra from 1891. Jean Bonnerot called it "French music's revenge".[17] Its conventional format looked like a defiance of Wagnerism and modern trends in general, and not all the critics approved. Henri Bauer described it as "wilfully old-fashioned, without any trace of amusement, pleasant parody or ironic significance".[18] Nevertheless, it won considerable popularity in its time, with fifty-six performances in the next ten years, and it travelled to several European cities during the 1890s, Messager adding recitatives for performances in Italy. Today the bulk of the genre to which it belongs – in the English-speaking world at least – is, regrettably, a closed book.

A week after the première Saint-Saëns crossed the Channel for a Philharmonic Society concert in London on 1st June before going on to Cambridge, playing his second piano concerto and conducting *Le Rouet d'Omphale*. He was, said the *Illustrated London News*, "greeted as a friend of many years standing", and after the concerto was repeatedly called to the platform by "one of the loudest and longest ovations that has been witnessed lately in a concert room".[19] Joseph Bennett in the *Daily Telegraph* added his tribute to "a musician of whom not only France alone but all musical countries are proud".[20] Tchaikovsky also appeared in the concert, conducting his fourth symphony. It was the first meeting between the two men since Saint-Saëns's first visit to Russia seventeen years before. The evening ended with a lavish dinner at the St Stephen's Club, on the Embankment at Westminster, described by Tchaikovsky in a letter to his brother Modest as "very smart and luxurious; we sat down to table at seven and rose at eleven-thirty (I am not exaggerating)".[21] The Philharmonic's secretary Francesco Berger sat between the two guests as they conversed in French, the taller Tchaikovsky "more subdued" while the "more animated" Saint-Saëns spoke "with much gesture and vehemence". It was, he said, like a meeting of the "aristocratic" with the "democratic".[22] The Scottish composer Sir Alexander Mackenzie, Principal of the Royal Academy of Music, was at the same table and noted Saint-Saëns's "snappy manner of speech".[23]

Preliminary rehearsals followed in London for the concert in Cambridge on 12th June. The Musical Society's event was intended to mark not only its golden jubilee but also the progress of music as a serious academic study at the university. Stanford had invited a prominent composer from each of five countries to attend, receive honorary degrees and generally lend prestige to the occasion. In the event none of those originally invited accepted: Grieg was ill, and no other Norwegian representative could be found; neither Brahms nor Verdi thought it worth the journey and were replaced by Bruch and Boito respectively; Tchaikovsky stood in for the aged Rubinstein; and Gounod, as we have seen, surrendered his place to his younger colleague. Saint-Saëns was somewhat nervous about taking part in what promised to be a very public occasion, especially when obliged to forego the accustomed privacy and refuge of a hotel room. He at first refused the offer to stay at the home of the President of the Musical Society, but was forced to yield after receiving a note that "it is usual for our most distinguished guests to stay at our homes and our committee would indeed be hard put to find an explanation for allowing the French representative to be satisfied with the hospitality of an hotel".[24]

There was a final rehearsal on the morning of the concert, which was given in the afternoon at the Guildhall in, as Saint-Saëns wrote, "a beautiful room of the smallest dimensions, before a favourably disposed audience". He played his *Africa* fantasy – its first performance in England – with what the *Daily Graphic* described as "a verve and unfaltering dexterity which fairly brought down the house".[25] The concert also marked Stanford's last performance as conductor of the society. There was a reception at the Fitzwilliam Museum and a banquet given for 100 guests that evening in the hall of King's College. Saint-Saëns occupied the place of honour on the high table, by reason of "the melancholy privilege of age". (Stanford had based the order of precedence at table on age to avoid an "international incident," and was pleased that Saint-Saëns thus qualified for top place as he thought that France was the country "most likely to feel a slight".) His seniority among the guest composers obliged him to speak on their behalf, a prospect he dreaded, despite his famed eloquence in conversation, "partly from lack of practice, partly from a natural timidity". But he rose to the occasion, buoyed up by the friendly company (and no doubt the food and wine), by the reflection that "after a half-century of existence" timidity could hardly be taken as an excuse, and by his ever-lively brain.

I said everything that came into my head, mixing the serious with the sweet, the pleasant with the harsh, as is the custom in England, where talks are given on every occasion, without pretension or pedantry. My colleagues declared themselves satisfied with the speech I had given in their name.[26]

Next day came the degree ceremony.

It began with us being dressed up in ample silk gowns with broad red and white sleeves, and capped with black velvet mortar-boards with gold tassels; and decked out thus, we walked in procession through the town under a scorching sun. At the head of the group of Doctors walked the King of Bhownagar in a gold turban sparkling with fabulous jewels, and a diamond necklace. Dare I confess that, being an enemy of the commonplace and of the nondescript style of our modern clothes, I was delighted with this adventure?

The members of the retinue having taken their places on a dais, the ceremony began with speeches in prose and verse, English and Latin. Now and then a student would throw in an amusing pleasantry; people laughed, the orator patiently waiting for them to finish before resuming his speech. I have known the time when such things also happened under the dome of the French Institute at the prize distribution of the Academy of Fine Arts; this has been called to order, with no gain to the charm of the proceedings.

The cheering from the undergraduates in the gallery was somewhat muted for the foreign composers as each was presented, because the praelector had trouble in pronouncing their names, so that it was difficult for the audience to identify them. Each composer heard a speech in Latin in his honour: the speech to Saint-Saëns referred among other gifts to his "almost incredible memory" and to his travels. "Into how many corners of the earth, and to what a multitude of listeners has his fame gone out!" And it concluded that "the author of *Samson* has woven fresh flowers for his crown of praise from the story of *Phryné*". After the ceremony there was another banquet, "still in our robes", at Christ's College, and a walk through the college gardens, where "my more fortunate colleagues were able to relax and be entertained by charming ladies; while I was off to Trinity College Chapel to try out the excellent organ there". At Trinity an admiring audience heard him play Bach's Prelude in E flat, one of his own fantasias and several improvisations, including a fugue.

Saint-Saëns liked Cambridge, "a nest of pointed Gothic arches in green fields", but pointed out that only the rich could afford to be educated there. He was fascinated by college chapels, which he thought more like cathedrals, and the easy-going attitude of students singing divine service, whom he described as "jolly, lively *bon viveurs*". He found the religious character of English university life most curious and thought that French students would be "most uncomfortable with it." But then the Anglican Church set "a seriously artistic scene, not at all formidable in the way our Catholic Church is". The English church seemed like an extension of the English home, and the "perfect gentleman" was not much different from "the married clergyman, a family man leading a life of elegance and denying himself none of the joys of life". As on his visit to Birmingham in 1879, he was much impressed by the standard of choral singing, from which he again concluded that the idea that musicality began on the southern side of the Channel was mere prejudice. He had earlier written that the English love of music was characterised by English reserve, so that

they never tire of the most hackneyed works, seeing that they are time-honoured. On the other hand, they readily listen to new and even daring works, as keen to get to grips with them as any public anywhere in the world. If they do not understand a work on first hearing they content themselves with not applauding, without adding noisy expressions of hostility. In short they are not excitable. And they do not have that turbulence, that stormy aspect of continental crowds so dear to artists who like to live with danger and emotion.

The English way is not so bad, he concludes, considering that it gave rise to Handel and Gounod oratorios, Haydn symphonies and Weber's *Oberon*, works which without England would probably never have been written. His Cambridge experience also coloured his view of English hospitality. "Never obsequious, it surrounds you with attentions without embarrassing you . . . and you fell that you yourself are not an embarrassment."

But despite his liking for England, he could not help feeling that his own music was performed less often there than it might have been. He knew well that, contrary to what was believed on the continent, fame in itself was not enough to secure musical success with English audiences.

They are thought to applaud what is not important, insensible to the worth and performance of a piece, asking only two essential qualities of a work: that it is supported by good publicity and that it bears a famous name. Many an artist has found, to his cost, that it is nothing of the kind.[27]

He was particularly irritated by the fact that not one of his operas had been heard across the Channel: even the queen had not been able to interest Covent Garden in *Etienne Marcel*. Wilhelm Ganz was equally unsuccessful with the Carl Rosa company, even though he was a director. Saint-Saëns wrote to him: "I have the greatest desire to have my operas played in England, but so far it is a desire that England does not appear to share; if you manage to change this situation, be sure that I should be extremely grateful to you."[28]

The most he could look forward to was a concert performance in English of *Samson et Dalila*, which had been suggested as a way round the ban on stage representations of biblical stories. This was scheduled for 20th September as one of a series of promenade concerts conducted by Frederic Cowen at Covent Garden. The two principals engaged were Emmanuel Lafarge and Elena Sanz, and Saint-Saëns agreed to supervise the final rehearsals – a decision he was to have cause to regret. For the event was to prove another in a series of frustrations that dogged the summer and autumn of 1893, bringing him rudely down to earth after the congratulatory pomp and glamour of Cambridge. His planned visit to the United States had been cancelled, and when he arrived at Covent Garden he found a deplorable state of affairs that threatened to wreck any chances of operatic recognition in London.

Choral concerts were a new departure for the Covent Garden proms, but not in practice a good idea, as Cowen later acknowledged, as the on-stage chorus was too far away from the orchestra for a good ensemble. Saint-Saëns also found that the orchestra was seriously under-strength as many of its players were at the Worcester Festival, and neither it nor the chorus had had adequate time to learn the score. Worse, there was no rehearsal for orchestra and chorus together. Cowen took up the baton much against his better judgement, "knowing how well impossible it would be to do the work justice with a hurried preparation at the very end of the season", as he later recalled, although he was grateful to have Saint-Saëns's advice as to tempi and interpretation.[29] Lafarge blamed the conductor for the shambles, quarrelled with one of the promoters, a Mr Farley Sinkins, and walked out in disgust two days before the performance, never to return. This was the last straw for Saint-Saëns: suddenly remembering an important engagement, he followed the tenor back to Paris, leaving the concert to its fate with twenty-four hours to go. In desperation, Cowen and the promoters asked Mme Sanz to track down the absentees and try to persuade them to return, but had finally to postpone the concert by five days. After three days Sanz returned alone, then she too absconded, complaining about lack of rehearsal time and having to sing opposite an English tenor she did not know. "I have too much respect for M. Saint-Saëns's work, for the press and for the English public to sing under these conditions", she told the newspapers.[30] Not surprisingly, the performance that finally went ahead on the 25th was, as Cowen ruefully recollected, "about as bad as it could be". Although the orchestra was back to full strength, the Worcester Festival having ended, the reinforcements were naturally even less familiar with the score than their colleagues. *The Times* noted the occasional slip in their playing, condemned the chorus as "lamentably deficient" and declared the substituted principals, Bernard Lane and Edith Miller, inadequate.[31] *The Stage* was a little more charitable: the two singers had, after all, taken over unfamiliar roles at extremely short notice, being "brave almost to the point of foolhardiness", the chorus was "as efficient as could be expected", and some passages were even "admirable".[32] The audience applauded, said Cowen, "in a damp, flabby way that suggested a polite expression of boredom".[33] There were two more performances. To Covent Garden audiences who had seen the complete *Ring* for the first time the year before (conducted by Mahler), *Samson et Dalila* sounded strangely old-fashioned. Yet the performances of 1893, ill-prepared though they were, at least planted the seeds of an interest in England that were to grow, with further concert performances all over the country, and eventually to flower in full-blown acclaim. Twenty years later, after the opera had finally established itself in the Covent Garden repertory, Sir Frederic Cowen, as he then was, could say with pride that he had conducted the first performance in London – "but I take care to suppress all the details".[34]

After his flight from London, Saint-Saëns could at least take comfort in *Phryné* and its popularity on the continent, which he attributed in large measure to Sybil Sanderson's alluring creation of the role. In gratitude he wrote for her the song 'La Libellule' to his own words. He also sent a copy of the score to Gounod, who wrote back on 12th October: "Thank you for your delicious *Phryné*. I am going to hear it with my eyes, those two second ears of a musician, after being intoxicated by it through the ears, those eyes of music."[35] It was the last piece of praise Saint-Saëns was to have from his old friend: less than a week later Gounod died. A memorial service was arranged at the Madeleine for the 27th, and his widow asked Fauré, still Master of the Chapel there, if Saint-Saëns would play the organ. From Fauré's note to his old teacher it is clear that she would have liked him to play for the whole service, but "she understood that it was impossible to exclude Dubois", so both the former and current resident organists performed during the ceremony. Saint-Saëns included, again at Mme Gounod's request, a passage from the third part of the *Redemption* oratorio.[36]

In the meantime rehearsals were going on at the Comédie-Française of a play for which Saint-Saëns had written incidental music – one of the commitments that had prevented him from travelling to America. This was *Antigone*, a version of the Sophocles tragedy by Meurice and Vacquerie, for which Mendelssohn had written music as long ago as 1844. The present production was designed to recreate as far as possible the spirit of the Greek original – as imagined in the late nineteenth century – with classical facades and sung choruses commenting on the action. Saint-Saëns based his score on the research of François Gevaert into ancient Greek music and on his own studies of ancient instruments, and the whole exercise was another manifestation of his interest in authentic historical reconstruction. The simplicity and directness required to convey the words to the audience with the greatest impact suited his tendency to conciseness and vocal clarity – as he says in a preface to the score, the whole charm of the concept lies in its "extreme simplicity" – and the use of the ancient modes follows on from the modal style adopted in his earlier 'oriental' music. The choruses are in unison throughout, to avoid any suggestion of modern harmony, while the orchestration is dominated by flutes, oboes and clarinets, all regarded as having Greek ancestry, and by harps intended to recreate the sound of the lyre, as in *La Lyre et l'Harpe*. The instrumental element, however, is strictly subsidiary to the words and the action, as it was with the Greeks. The orchestral accompaniment to the first entrance of Antigone and the later exit of Queen Eurydice abounds in curious chromatic slides derived from Gevaert's interpretation of a fragment from Euripides, while another of the very few pieces of ancient notation to survive, the *Pythian Ode* of Pindar, provides the basis for the final chorus. One of the few concessions to a later age is the use of a popular song from Athens in the lovely 'Hymn to Eros'.

The opening of *Antigone* on 21st November 1893 marked a new departure for the composer, that was to lead him to further incidental atmosphere settings, both in the theatre and eventually in the new medium of cinema. At the time, however, it did little to dispel the melancholy that had descended in the wake of Gounod's death. Another part of his life had gone and it was in a profoundly philosophical mood that he set off for a winter sojourn in the Canaries. There, in surroundings conducive to peaceful contemplation, he wrote over the next few months a long discourse on the meaning and purpose of human existence that, together with his earlier philosophical essays, was to appear in print as *Problèmes et Mystères*. The book was published by Ernest Flammarion, brother of Camille, the composer's colleague in astronomy and a student of psychic phenomena. It marks a coming to terms with life and with the universe, a resolution of the emotional and spiritual turmoil of preceding years to a calm acceptance of things as they are. The dark, uneasy pessimism of the C minor symphony has mellowed into a gentle glow of faith in human advancement.

The philosophy which he argues in *Problèmes et Mystères* is in the tradition of nineteenth-century Positivism, based on fact and observable phenomena. The movement was established by Auguste Comte and was strongly influential in the academic circles in which Saint-Saëns moved in the first decades of the Third Republic. It also owes much to the writings of Hippolyte Taine and his treatment of art, history and literature in terms of scientific inquiry, and to the writings of Ernest Renan, with their faith in scientific progress and their denial of the Scriptures as divinely inspired. Drawing on years of observing animal and insect behaviour directed to the common good, Saint-Saëns concluded that the driving force of existence is intelligence, which is present in all animals, even the humblest, in varying degrees, but most of all in man. With intelligence thus placed at centre stage, it follows that the true purpose of life is the dual one of scientific inquiry and artistic creation, the natural results of the working of the intellect. Without them life can have no purpose. Science and art have the power – and the duty – to improve the lot of mankind, "so that those who follow us may be happier than we are . . . We shall then see that life is good" in "the aesthetic enjoyment of art, the sight of sufferings relieved".

The religious certainties of divine truth have no place in this programme of pragmatic progress. Saint-Saëns accepts the existence of God, or at least a god, largely on the grounds that to deny it is simply an excuse for "anarchists" to disregard all rules, "to have no other law than the satisfaction of the lowest appetites". But his deism goes no further: the Gospel is not a literal account of divine purpose but merely a "symbol", its teaching "anarchistic". The idea of revealed religion he rejects as producing only intolerance and fanaticism. Religious faith is destroyed by the exercise of reason. God may be there but is beyond the intellect and so is not worth discussing: it is pointless to contemplate the unknowable. "People have always been disappointed in the search for final causes. It may simply be that there are no such things." And it makes no difference whether there are or not. Man's intellectual qualities are demonstrable, his spiritual qualities are not, so all that matters is human activity as an expression of intelligence, "the only fact we can be reasonably sure of", which is not tied to any "supernatural revelation, and does not venture to affirm absolute truths". Everything else is "madness and illusion". This is the religion of Humanity, of the kind espoused by Comte and his *foi des sans foi.*

Saint-Saëns spoke of the positive nature of his loss of religious faith, stemming from the "nirvana" he experienced after his mother's death, in a letter to Romain Rolland of 1910. "It is peace and joy which I find on abandoning all belief; this need to believe, which torments so many people, seems to me idle. It has been replaced in me by a need to know."[37] Such a philosophy was bound to be of great comfort and satisfaction to someone endowed more than most with wide-ranging intellectual powers. It reflected also his serene attitude to death which, having been so close to it so often in his life, he viewed as a gentle and natural process. Yet there is something about this spiritual self-sufficiency that is vaguely depressing, and it is a strange paradox that one who put such faith in human intellect came to prefer the company of animals to that of men, to espouse the cause of animals, and to call the cat "a superior being". And the confident view of human endeavour leading to a better world, so typical of the late nineteenth century, was in any case soon to be shatteringly overthrown by the twentieth.

The innate conservatism of the Positivist philosophy found expression in the author of *Problèmes et Mystères* in his right-wing political outlook, his distrust of democracy and his almost obsequious attitude to foreign royalty. It also demonstrates his distrust of and distaste for any kind of cult, including the Wagner cult, which he saw as breeding the same kind of bigotry and intolerance as religion. In his book *Portraits et Souvenirs* of 1899 he poured scorn on both the claim that Wagner was the first since the ancient Greeks to aim for a synthesis of music and drama, and on the assertion that he had achieved this aim to produce the ultimate Art. The idea of opera as a perfect union of music, drama, dance and spectacle

has always been the basis of opera, ever since opera has existed. The way of setting about it may possibly have been wrong but the intention was there . . . Wagner's system has achieved in a new and powerful way a close union of the various arts which together make up lyric drama. That is so. But is this system definitive, is it The Truth? No, it is not, because it cannot be: if it were so, art would have reached perfection, which is not possible for the human spirit. Art would then be no more than a random collection of imitations condemned by their very nature as mediocre and useless. The different elements which make up lyric drama will always tend toward a perfect equilibrium without arriving at it, regardless of whatever new solutions are found to the problem.

To argue that Wagner's operas were the supreme manifestation of art was to reject the achievement of every opera composer before him, including Mozart, which was absurd. Such an artistic faith was, like religious faith, dogmatic, fanatical and authoritarian, producing a philosophy comparable to religious mysticism, that obscured rather than revealed the beauties of Wagner's works and their achievements in the expression of human psychology and emotion. "As soon as writers seek, in a word, to initiate us into all these beautiful things, a dense fog descends, strange words and incoherent phrases appear all at once, like devils out of a box; in short, to put it politely, one can understand nothing of the matter." Operatic masterpieces have certainly been created by "putting the drama in the orchestra", but "it is not the use of such or such a system which establishes the superiority of a work, but the worth of its inspiration". Wagner himself did not hold rigidly to systems – his works would not be what they are if he had always conformed to his theories – and even confessed that "when I reread my theoretical works I no longer understand them". In his letters Saint-Saëns writes that "in the realm of art, theories are a little matter; the works are everything", and that "theories in art seem to me to hold so small a place beside practice". Artistic faith, he insists, does not affirm absolute truths. "It has the right to persuade, to conquer souls, not to violate them."[38]

This strongly held view marks a clear break from the composer regarded as an incorrigible 'modern', the prophet of musical progress and the propagator of new forms. As late as 1887 he was arguing that opera would one day reach perfection. Shortly after the première of *Proserpine* he wrote in a theatrical journal that "I believe the drama is progressing towards a synthesis of different elements – song, declamation and symphony blending in an equilibrium which I seek and others will one day find". This equilibrium "would be the last word in dramatic art", though he adds, with a hint of the pragmatist to come, "if art can have a last word".[39]

As well as throwing light on his attitude to the Wagner question, the spiritual detachment to which Saint-Saëns had arrived in *Problèmes et Mystères* is also of significance in his music, which hereafter shows a greater tendency towards a parallel emotional detachment. Musical harmony was a manifestation of the rational order of the universe, like the harmony of the stars that so fascinated him, and a line of melody was a human response to this influence of reason, so that "the artist who does not feel thoroughly satisfied with elegant lines, harmonious colours or a fine series of chords does not understand art".[40] The first prelude of Bach's '48', he points out, is nothing but a succession of broken chords, and is also "one of the marvels of music".[41] It is from this period too that he places ever greater emphasis on form, as the essence of musical composition and of all art, because it appeals to the intellect, which is the driving force of life. Expression without regard to form satisfies only the "lowest appetites" and "is always the germ of decadence". "Art," he told Camille Bellaigue in 1907, "is intended to create beauty and character. Feeling only comes afterwards, and art can very well do without it. In fact it is very much better off when it does."[42] The Venus de Milo, he suggests elsewhere, does not "express" anything and yet is one of the greatest works of all time.[43]

Coupled with this increasing concern for form for its own sake is a heightened interest in the distinctive sounds of individual instruments as the embodiments of pure musical beauty. The two elements, form and sonority, are represented respectively in two works of the period, the three Preludes and Fugues for organ and the *Fantaisie* for harp. The Preludes and Fugues, he told Gallet, were "strung together" as an exercise in formal discipline he only now felt ready to tackle: they were "something I have wanted to do all my life without ever daring to try it".[44] The *Fantaisie* was the first of three pieces he was to write for the harp, showing a grasp of and sensitivity to its tonal colour that puts him at the forefront of the harp's revival (outside Wales) as a prominent chamber instrument.

This more dispassionate period of his musical style had, however, barely begun. He wrote relatively little new music in the year after *Phryné*, preoccupied as he was with literary and philosophical matters and determined to avoid bringing on illness through overwork. As for the task of completing Guiraud's opera, he intended to take his time. While writing *Problèmes et Mystères* he was "little disposed to music", he told Gallet, who was growing anxious about the opera. "Don't trouble yourself about it", Saint-Saëns urged him from Las Palmas, "I am too well here to move."[45] The two men finally got together on the project at St Germain-en-Laye in the spring of 1894. For the winter Saint-Saëns planned a long tour of the Far East so as to be able to write the music uninterrupted. As long as he was in France other duties pressed on his time. He wrote the *Thème Varié* for piano as a test piece for the Conservatoire: Lecocq called it "charming, very ingenious but jolly difficult" and pitied the "poor young people" who would have to play it.[46] He also began work on a new edition of Rameau in consultation with Malherbe, an authority on the composer; the first volume, of keyboard pieces, appeared a year later. In May he presided over the Institute's jury in choosing a successor to Gounod. One of the applications came from the young Erik Satie, his second attempt at election. When it failed (he was still under thirty and had as yet composed only a handful of pieces, including the famous *Gymnopédies*) Saint-Saëns received an open letter from him written in the most bizarre language. A member of the Catholic Rosicrucians, he declared that his candidature was "authorised by God":

I was deeply grieved to see vulgar preferences cause you to forget solidarity in art. You have acted like an outcast and brought Hell upon yourself. Your aberration can only spring from the weakness of your grasp on the ideas of the century and your misappreciation of God, the direct cause of aesthetic debasement. I pardon you in Jesus Christ and embrace you in the grace of God.[47]

As it happened, Saint-Saëns's own preference for the vacancy, Fauré, was voted out in favour of Dubois.

Departure for the Far East was delayed by rehearsals for a production of *Proserpine* at Toulouse. He did not leave France until late in October, just missing a courtesy call to his Paris address by Verdi, who left a note saying "I come with grief at not having met a man who honours art and whom I admire very much".[48] Again he travelled under an assumed name, beginning his journey in Spain. There, he wrote to Gallet, he enjoyed a pleasant stay in Valencia, "celebrated for its oranges", savouring the solitude, the sunshine and the local liqueur, and attending evening performances of the *zarzuela*, the traditional form of Spanish opera then enjoying a nationalist revival. He confessed that he was "a little afraid" of starting work on *Brunhilda*, which he promised to do when his ship reached Ismailia on the Suez Canal.[49] There he spent several days on the opera, his only distraction being to watch the "graceful manoeuvres" of a sea horse.[50] By the time he reached India he was still occupied with the opera, writing to Gallet that "I have brought the last act to the midst of the monkeys and the coconut trees". Crossing the Indian Ocean to Indo-China, he reported:

I have tackled our last act on the high seas. The sea is of a marvellously beautiful blue unknown in the North; it is choppy and yesterday I had to spend the whole day on the bridge reading a novel . . . It seems I shall arrive just in time to see a great Chinese festival which lasts several days.[51]

In March 1895 he reached Saigon where Rousseau, his former neighbour in the Rue M. le Prince, was now governor. At the colonial offices he was also able to renew his acquaintance with Jacquet, the fellow passenger on his previous Indian Ocean voyage, who took him on a tour of the islands in the Mekong delta. There he was able to finish the opera in between detailed examinations of the animal and plant life of the islands. The tropical climate restored a sense of well being that inspired him to a poem, included in later editions of *Rimes Familières*, in praise of the "gods of the sun", so preferable – and here there seems to be a dig at the world of the *Ring* – to the "gods of Scandinavia and the North, the horrible North and its abhorred cold". Life does not belong there, but under other skies, away from "rough climates".

Returning to France in May with the completed last acts of *Brunhilda*, he contacted Dukas and at St Germain collaborated with him on the orchestration of Guiraud's original, adding a ballet and renaming the work *Frédégonde*. Despite their efforts the work, a story of love and betrayal in Merovingian Gaul, could not disguise its hybrid character and would never be anything more than a curiosity. And far from honouring Guiraud's memory, it cast him in a poor light as comparisons were inevitably drawn between his portion of the opera and Saint-Saëns's. Some critics even hailed the latter's fourth act duo a masterpiece and declared the whole of the fifth act one of the finest pieces of French dramatic art. *Frédégonde* was heard at the Opéra in December 1895, in a charity performance for soldiers returning from duty in Madagascar. It had a warm reception and was performed eight times, but thereafter sank into oblivion, much to Saint-Saëns's distress. Work on it had taken a special effort at a time when he was reluctant to handle large-scale projects: now its neglect had turned the intended tribute to Guiraud into a slight.

A Conservatoire concert on 8th December showed that Saint-Saëns, after all his illnesses and travels, had lost none of his powers as a pianist. His performance of Mozart's K.488 concerto was praised by the Conservatoire secretary Arthur Dandelot for its "surety of execution, distinctness of rhythm and prodigious technique".[52] That winter took him to Milan for the Italian première of *Henry VIII*, and then to Egypt. In Cairo he wrote a piano piece, *Valse Mignonne*, for the Khedive's daughter, and the duo *Vénus* for tenor and baritone, to his own poem. He began a second violin sonata and, on returning to Luxor from a Nile journey south to Aswan and Philae, set to work on a piano concerto, his first for over twenty years. He completed it in Cairo in April 1896. The impulse to compose, sluggish in the period following *Phryné*, had returned. The painter Georges Clairin, who stayed with him in Cairo, remembered him making onion soup with his left hand while scribbling music with his right.[53] There was even the prospect of a new opera, when the Egyptologist Emile Amelineau offered him a libretto on the subject of Isis, but the project was dropped when the writer refused to allow it to be reworked by Gallet, as Saint-Saëns suggested.

The F major piano concerto, which because of its place of origin and the oriental character of some of its passages, has come to be known as the 'Egyptian', looks both to the past and to the future in the composer's stylistic development. Its colourfully exotic veneer is in the orientalist mould that reaches back beyond the *Africa* fantasy to *Samson* and *La Princesse Jaune* and there are some thematic echoes of those works. But there is also a limpid quality and an easy pleasure in pure sound that belong to the more impersonal style that was increasingly to shape Saint-Saëns's output from this time. The composer had come a long way from the previous concerto, with its struggle between dark and light within an exploratory framework. Here there is no arguing of opposites, only a desire to please the ear over three conventionally separate movements, two of which are in straightforward sonata form. It is as if Saint-Saëns is wiping the slate clean and beginning again with basic structures before venturing any further with formal experiments. The name is misleading, for outside the central movement there is little specifically Egyptian or even for the most part oriental about the fifth concerto. The opening allegro suggests rather a general feeling of well being under a warm, tropical sky. The simple chords and gentle conversation between piano and orchestra that make up the composite first subject flow effortlessly into the lilting relative minor of the second. The finale, far from being 'about' Egypt, is said to be intended to convey the sense of excitement and adventure of a sea voyage such as those Saint-Saëns had enjoyed, contrasting an imitation of the thud of ship's engines with a bold second subject of invigorating forthrightness. Even the so-called Nubian love song of the central andante which Saint-Saëns said he heard during his boat trip on the Nile has nothing eastern about it to western ears. The movement also contains those solemn chord progressions with a hint of the unearthly that are typical of the composer in his non-oriental guise, but otherwise it is constructed of exotic themes and effects which justify at least in part the Egyptian label. There are imitations of the croaking of Nile frogs and the chirping of crickets, but Saint-Saëns himself described the movement in broader terms: as a journey to the East and even to the Far East, as the soloist's Chinese-style tune is accompanied in the high treble by tinkling acciaccaturas. Particularly striking is a short modal passage of chords in the piano's upper register which creates a strange harmony by an unusual spacing of the triad, an effect that looks forward to Ravel, a keen student of Saint-Saëns's music, particularly the concertos.

The E flat violin sonata also marks a stylistic departure from the earlier, better known D minor sonata. As with the piano concerto, there is a much greater fluency than in its predecessor and it abandons formal integration in favour of a conventional layout. The archness of the first movement's straightforward main subject, announced without introduction by the violin, is in suitable contrast to the more pliant second subject which, both in the exposition and the recapitulation, is repeated a semitone higher. The second subject's first appearance in the distant key of C major, and a false recapitulation in the middle of the development are the movement's only obvious deviations from the norm. There is nothing here of the earlier sonata's troubled conflict between anxiety and assertion: the dark undertones have evaporated leaving a lightness that is at times ethereal and a smooth musical flow. This is most evident in the nimble scherzo, where Saint-Saëns revels in the violin's playful mood with the effortless nonchalance of a man who has come to terms with life. The sense of heightened delicacy is maintained in the andante, in the unrelated key of B major. Above ascending scales on the piano, the violin hovers in a beautifully wistful cantilena of great lyrical tenderness, resuming after a central scherzando and finally floating away into the rarefied atmosphere.

Formally, the last movement is the most unusual of the four, halfway between a sonata and a rondo, though not strictly a sonata-rondo. Two thematic groups in the normal key relationship are followed by a third theme in the unrelated key of D major. The material is repeated with a limited degree of variation rather than development, the third theme cheekily assuming the home key before the recapitulation, where it then appears in another distant key, C major, a coda then reestablishing the tonic. The finale is more earthbound in spirit than the rest of the sonata, reminiscent of Schumann in places, but still in keeping with the light, graceful character of the work as a whole.

In the spring of 1896 Saint-Saëns headed for Paris with the new sonata and concerto destined for inclusion in a concert planned to mark the fiftieth anniversary of his first public appearance as a pianist. On the way he stopped in Milan to hear the *Danse Macabre* conducted by Toscanini, making his La Scala debut with a series of four concerts. He was delighted with the performance, and congratulated the young conductor backstage, declaring that it was the first time he had heard the piece played at the correct tempo.

The sell-out jubilee concert on 3rd June was at the Salle Pleyel, the hall where as a ten-year-old, he had created such a sensation. This was a poignant reminder of the passing of the years for the sixty-year-old composer, now something of a national institution, at the end of a long road to recognition with all its professional setbacks and private griefs. With Taffanel conducting members of the Conservatoire Concerts Society, their presence in itself an indication of the esteem in which Saint-Saëns was now held, the programme began and ended with two works which had featured in that 1846 debut: *The Marriage of Figaro* overture and the Mozart B flat concerto with which, as a boy, he had won so many admirers. His performance, with its "youth, grace and gentle, almost artless feeling", recreated "almost miraculously the delicate, thoughtful child, troubled by nothing", wrote Theodore Lindenlaub in his review for the commemorative booklet. In between came a selection of Saint-Saëns's own works, beginning with the 'Egyptian' concerto, which left the greatest impression on the audience. Before settling down to play, the composer read out a poem he had written in rhyming couplets, recalling the boy, "delicate, frail, of sallow complexion, but self-assured, ingenuous, full of spirit and joy", who measured himself against Beethoven and Mozart. He paid tribute to the guiding influences of his mother and his teachers Maleden and Stamaty, and with a typically blunt honesty careless of the occasion, referred to that instinctive distaste for applause and congratulation, the sound of which was "like a mire". He spoke of the contrasting delights and torments of the artist's life: "Art is like the sea, changing, capricious. It takes us to hell; it shows us the heavens . . . we make the best of it; the enchanting muse consoles us all with one caress."[54] And after protesting that his fingers were not as nimble as they once were, he proceeded to dazzle the crowded hall with his playing, not only in the two concertos, but also in his Concert Paraphrase on Massenet's *Thaïs*, written the year before, and as accompanist to his old friend Sarasate in the second violin sonata.

He was seen as conductor too when, after the introduction to the second act of *Phryné*, he took the baton while Taffanel turned soloist in the Romance for flute and orchestra.

The evening was a personal triumph, sealing his fame in France as the 1893 concerts in London and Cambridge had done in England. It was a belated recognition in his own country that was noted by at least some critics (they were not specially invited because of the huge demand for tickets, but attended anyway). Louis de Fourcaud wrote that

Parisians have learned slowly to appreciate him, while already his name abroad has resounded among the famous. Acclaimed in Germany, Russia, England and even Italy, in Paris he still struggled for himself and others. That did not deflect him from his course. He has played a superior role in our musical evolution and rendered such services as will not be forgotten by posterity . . . He is at present the musician who does the greatest honour to his country and, even better, to his art. I have known in no other part of the world at this time a composer more complete than he.

Victorin Joncières took an ironic tone in describing the jubilee concert as "a rare sight" at which "a French composer was acclaimed, and received unequivocal tokens of sincere admiration mingled with national pride, a sentiment which, for a long time, seemed entirely extinct among us, at least in musical matters". And Samuel Rousseau saw him as the perfect embodiment of French music:

The French genius is made up of clarity, logic and form, three words which sum up admirably the entire work of Saint-Saëns. He knows how to retain clarity in the most daring combinations of voices and instruments. He has achieved immortality in his lifetime.[55]

But there were dissenting voices. Adolphe Jullien pointed to the apparent contradiction between Saint-Saëns's avowal of the French cause in music and his work in essentially Germanic forms, and asked how he could be regarded as a leader of the national school when he had just written another concerto. And Hugues Imbert, a previously hostile critic, wanted to "reserve judgement".[56] While Saint-Saëns's high standing in the musical world was to be confirmed and consolidated in the succeeding years, the tide of critical opposition flowing round the base of the pedestal on which he had so lately been placed was to undermine and eventually destroy it.

XII • REACTIONARY and ROYAL FAVOURITE

JULLIEN'S CHARGE THAT SAINT-SAËNS'S SYMPHONIC PEDIGREE PUT HIM ON the periphery of French music was a cutting reminder of the dilemma that had dogged the composer ever since his E flat symphony had delighted Gounod and Berlioz over forty years before. The jubilee concert, with his fifth piano concerto fresh from his pen and his pianistic powers – despite his protestations to the contrary – manifestly undiminished, confirmed his international standing. Yet at the same time it pointed to the fundamental weakness in his position at home, where no musician could feel entirely fulfilled without laurels gained in the opera house. The vicious circle, in which each concert hall triumph seemed to put stage success ever further out of reach, had not been broken. He had now to compete not only with Massenet, who enjoyed two further triumphs in the 1890s with *Werther* and *Thaïs*, but also with the Wagner boom in Paris theatres, in the wake of the 1891 production of *Lohengrin* at the Opéra. The dominance, as he saw it, of German opera in French theatres was a particular cause of resentment over the next twenty years, as the presence of Italian opera had once been. In a letter to *Le Temps* he complained that "eight weeks of Richard Wagner are in the repertory of the Opéra, which augments them with the *Salome* of Richard Strauss. Of late, the director of a provincial theatre wrote to me that he could not give, next season, any of my works because he had to put on *Die Meistersinger von Nürnberg* and *Hänsel und Gretel*."[1] Earlier he had written to a colleague: "Let us hope that the Wagnerian fever will pass, as everything passes in this world, and that a day will come when French music is played in France."[2]

The fact that *Samson et Dalila*, alone of his operas, was now firmly established in the repertory was not enough. Saint-Saëns had had other things to say as a man of the theatre since *Samson* was written a quarter of a century before, and it vexed him that none of his other operas appeared to be earning any degree of popularity, with the possible exception of *Phryné*. The contrasting destinies of the one opera and the rest may even have led him to resent *Samson*'s growing success. As the years passed he even felt he had become a slave to it, pointing out to his friend Pierre Aguétant in bitter tones: "I have written other things."[3] Pierre Lalo wrote that "I have often noticed that the fortune of this unique work seemed to annoy him".[4] The failure of *Frédégonde*, bound up as the opera was with the cherished memory of a friend and colleague, was the last straw. When in the spring of 1896 he agreed to write a ballet for the Folies Marigny he insisted that it was to be the "postscript" to his career as a composer, as he saw no reason to go on piling up unused scores in his drawer.

He was in retiring mood: after the jubilee concert he thought seriously about giving up the life of a travelling virtuoso too. But he soon found the impulse to perform too great to ignore – "working at the piano is not work to me but a necessary evil," as he once put it[5] – and he therefore considered that he might as well go on touring the concert halls while his health lasted. Similarly, the ballet *Javotte* turned out to be far from his last word as a theatre composer. Not only that, it also proved, with some irony in view of his operatic failures, to be one of his most enduring works for the stage.

He began the ballet at Aix-les-Bains in July 1896 and finished it two months later at St Germain, where he played it through after Sunday dinner to his collaborator J. L. Croze, secretary of the Marigny, and several friends. He had met Croze at Gallet's home and had already set three of his verses as well as his libretto for the cantata *Pallas Athène*, for soprano and orchestra. For the scenario of the ballet Saint-Saëns had suggested a story from Boccaccio, which Croze adapted mainly by turning the central aristocratic family into peasants, giving it the rustic flavour in line with the popular theatrical taste of the time. The story was shaped into three scenes, the first establishing the village setting and the love of Jean for Javotte, whose parents forbid her to see him. The parents go to the village dance, leaving their daughter to do the housework, but Jean climbs in through a window and the lovers escape. Javotte is judged Queen of the Ball but is recognised, and the lovers are caught. When Jean asks to marry her the parents finally agree amid general rejoicing.

Although *Javotte* is his only complete ballet, Saint-Saëns was of course no newcomer to the art. No opera composer in France would have been. The ballets in his operas had proved to be the most popular features of those works, and in the productions of them in which he was involved he was fastidious in specifying movements and direction. He had, after all, been a competent mover himself in the private charades that had played such a large part in his social life, with an instinctive feel for the requirements and practicalities of dance. The music he wrote for *Javotte* (the title was chosen by Durand) has all the heightened airiness of texture of his later style, abounding with delicate orchestral effects to reflect the lightness, wit and exuberance of the story. The choreography was by Mariquita, ballet mistress at the Folies Bergère. The prospects looked good, but *Javotte*, like most of the operas, was to face obstacles before reaching the stage. The Marigny went bankrupt, and the Théâtre Royal de la Monnaie in Brussels, after offering to take the new work, then went back on its offer. The project was saved by Vizentini, the director who had first mounted *Le Timbre d'Argent* nearly twenty years before, who was now in charge of the Grand Theatre at Lyons. It was there that *Javotte* made its debut on 3rd December 1896, the composer conducting the first two performances. Also on the bill was *Proserpine* (still in its original version) in which Saint-Saëns had the satisfaction of hearing the role of Angiola sung by Mme Duperret, whose singing he had heard and admired during his visit to Saigon. Still the opera failed to make its mark, but the ballet was enthusiastically received. The Monnaie renewed its interest and *Javotte* was seen in Brussels on the 18th. Three years later it was on at the Opéra-Comique in Paris (where Mariquita had lately become ballet mistress) and reached the Opéra in 1909, its charm ensuring a popularity that kept it in the repertory until well into the twentieth century.

Despite the warm reception for *Javotte*, Saint-Saëns appeared as if he would keep his word about it being his last work. For more than a year after completing it he avoided composition, concentrating instead on writing, editing and performing, as well as attending meetings of scientific interest at the Institute and the Astronomical Society. While in the Canaries he wrote an article on Gounod for the *Revue de Paris* and during May and June 1897 gave a series of organ recitals in the Netherlands. Later in the summer there were concerts to conduct in Stockholm and Copenhagen. Before leaving the Danish capital he played his *Valse Mignonne* to Queen Louise and her two daughters at their chateau at Bersdorf. As with Queen Victoria, he was nervous about this royal appointment, but when he finally met the eighty-year-old Danish queen, he found her "the most delightful old lady imaginable". With her slight frame and alert mind, she reminded him of his great-aunt Charlotte. Queen Louise had been told that he had asked to attend her court, and when he protested that he had done no such thing, it "appeared to amuse her greatly".[6] Saint-Saëns was a fairly regular guest of successive presidents of France but, a monarchist at heart, he was especially proud of his contacts with foreign royalty. And, with his growing fame, he was to rise even higher in royal favour. Honours were to come in the next few years from the courts of Madrid and Berlin, Queen Victoria was to receive him for a second time and he was to reinforce his links with the British monarchy by writing a coronation march for her successor, Edward VII.

The Spanish royal family showed its admiration when Saint-Saëns conducted three concerts in Madrid in November 1897 – and alienated some sections of the Catholic press when the Queen Regent's enthusiasm led her into what they regarded as an act of sacrilege. Maria Christina wanted to hear the visitor play the Cavaillé-Coll organ at the church of San Francisco but was advised that it would not be correct for her to attend church for anything other than divine service. She therefore arranged to go to the church in full ceremony, with the thirteen-year-old King Alfonso XIII, other members of the royal family, and ministers, their coaches heralded by trumpet-blowing horsemen along the route. Inside the church, instead of a service, Saint-Saëns was waiting to play the organ to his host. As the Queen Regent stood leaning her elbow on the instrument, her chin on her hand, he played a religious march he had written for the occasion, which he dedicated to her, plus the *Trois Rapsodies* and, at her request, Delilah's aria. "She seemed", he noted, "rapt in ecstasy."[7] She also attended the final concert, which Saint-Saëns conducted, wearing the Cross of the Order of Isabella which had been bestowed on him the day before. The programme included *Le Rouet d'Omphale*, the A minor symphony and, as an encore, the *Danse Macabre*, after which he was presented with a laurel crown by the Madrid Conservatoire. Although Maria Christina had led the prolonged applause, the Catholic journals, outraged by the charade at the church as well as by Saint-Saëns's published anti-religious views, prepared their hostile notices, seizing on the *Danse Macabre* to denounce the composer as a purveyor of "devil's music".

But the social invitations flooded in. Saint-Saëns had to refuse most of them, but he did accept one from a debating society, where he made his first faltering speech in Spanish, apologising for his rudimentary grasp of the language. He joined in a performance of his F major trio, and offered to play any one of Beethoven's thirty-two sonatas, answering a request for Op. 26, and adding an arrangement of sixteenth-century Spanish music and pieces by Rameau. The week ended with *Samson et Dalila* at the Madrid opera house.

Another engagement with royalty, this time nearer home, was also to be the first step towards fame for the young Pierre Monteux, destined to become one of the great conductors of the twentieth century. Monteux had met Saint-Saëns at La Trompette, where he had played viola in the septet and in *Le Carnaval des Animaux* with the composer at the piano. Saint-Saëns was asked by a princess to conduct *La Lyre et l'Harpe* at her palatial Paris home in the Boulevard St Germain, which boasted a large, ornate ballroom with a gold and white pipe organ. During the rehearsal the organist was flummoxed by the composer's nervousness and irritability, and made several mistakes, causing the furious Saint-Saëns to fling down the baton and ask if anyone present could conduct from sight while he took over at the organ. The eighteen-year-old Monteux duly obliged, and later recalled that the composer was pleased with the performance. Not so the princess, who had engaged Saint-Saëns specifically as composer-conductor.[8]

The impulse to large-scale composition had now lain dormant for well over a year. Its re-awakening was prompted from an unexpected quarter, and stemmed in part from Saint-Saëns's interest in classical literature and culture, the source and inspiration of so many of his vocal and instrumental works. At one of the social gatherings at his home in M. le Prince over a decade before, a discussion about Wagner had touched on the phenomenon of Bayreuth and its power to draw devotees from all over the world. Would it have the same effect, it was asked, if a French composer were to stage an opera in a small town in France? Saint-Saëns, with the failure of *Etienne Marcel* after its Lyons debut still rankling, made no comment. But the seeds of an idea had been sown.

After visits to the Roman antiquities of southern France he had long been interested in the possibility of reviving the open air theatre performances that had been such a notable feature of Roman provincial life. This possibility became reality in the 1890s when opera became an annual event in the ancient theatre at Orange (where operas are still performed today). It was an age of classical revivals, which had already seen Saint-Saëns's involvement with *Antigone* in 1893 and which, in another sphere, saw Baron de Coubertin's launch of the modern Olympic Games in 1896. Against this background, a chance meeting with a wealthy wine merchant, Fernand Castelbon de Beauxhostes, on the way to an organ recital at Béziers in southern France, proved decisive. Castlebon, an amateur musician, was an enthusiastic advocate of outdoor stage performances like those of antiquity, after conducting a concert in the arena at Valencia. New arenas were being built throughout southern France with a view to introducing bullfighting to the region (much to Saint-Saëns's disgust). However, the arena at Béziers had not been finished and a fire had left it derelict. Castlebon planned to refurbish it for music and drama and asked the composer for a work to launch the venture. The invitation was irresistible, a unique opportunity to try for theatrical honours in an entirely novel way.

For a collaborator Saint-Saëns again turned to Gallet, who soon shared the general enthusiasm. After visiting Orange to study open air theatre acoustics, the two men decided on a play with music and choruses, along the lines of *Antigone*. The result was *Déjanire*, a tragedy on the downfall of Hercules. Saint-Saëns began writing the music at Las Palmas in March 1898 and completed it two months later, after a visit to Béziers to help with preparations.

A further indication that the sixty-two-year-old composer was active again came when Colonne conducted his *Lever de soleil sur le Nil*, a cantata to his own words for contralto and orchestra. The sun seemed to be rising too on his stage career. As well as the Béziers project which was scheduled for August, his long cherished hope that one of his operas would be performed in London was finally realised in July when *Henry VIII* was given at Covent Garden. He attended final rehearsals and saw a sumptuously dressed production (in French) with Maurice Renaud, of the Paris Opéra, in the title role. The ballet was omitted as it was seen as inappropriate for English audiences: as *The Times* put it, "it taxes the imagination somewhat severely by presenting a troop of Highlanders in Richmond Park". As with the concert version of *Samson et Dalila*, the opera followed a *Ring* cycle at the theatre and struck an oddly old-fashioned note in contrast, with its clearly identified set pieces. The fixed smile maintained by Anne Boleyn throughout the four acts did not help, and the performance also had to compete with the enormous popularity then being enjoyed at Covent Garden by Nellie Melba in *Roméo et Juliette*. However, *The Times* praised the dramatic high points of *Henry VIII*, the finely drawn emotions and even the "excellent" libretto, declaring the final ensemble "as fine as anything on the French stage", and believed its merits outweighed its lack of modernity.

The many formal solos and set, concerted pieces, though they may seem a little old-fashioned to those accustomed to more spasmodic utterances, are not the less expressive, eloquent and appropriate because they are organically interesting and melodically beautiful.[9]

But the paper's critic thought these qualities would make the opera esteemed rather than loved, while *The Stage* summed up a widely held view that was to consign almost all of Saint-Saëns's operas to oblivion: "Absolute conviction is seldom reached, and true inspiration is hardly once to be traced."[10] For the moment it was a welcome boost to the composer's operatic reputation, and he was called to the stage to receive a prolonged ovation, returning a second time with the somewhat stage-shy conductor Luigi Mancinelli. But, after two performances, *Henry VIII* was not performed again at Covent Garden.

While in London Saint-Saëns also appeared at a Philharmonic concert and matinees at the home of the Duke and Duchess of Connaught. And there was an audience with Queen Victoria at Windsor, in company with the queen's favourite violinist Johann Wolff. The visitors waited in a reception room along with members of the royal family in full evening dress, and when the queen entered Saint-Saëns was at first dismayed by how she had aged since their first meeting nearly twenty years before.

I was heartbroken when I saw her, for she was almost carried by her Indian servant and clearly could not walk unaided. But seated at a small table, she was just as she had been before, with her wonderful charm, her simple manner and her musical voice. Only the white hair testified to the years which had passed.

She asked about *Henry VIII* and its performance at Covent Garden, and the composer told her the story of how he had found the sixteenth-century melody at Buckingham Palace. "The queen was very interested in music in general and seemed to be especially pleased by this discussion", he recalled. "His Highness the Duke of Connaught wrote to me that she spoke of it several times." Musical offerings then followed, including extracts from *Henry VIII*. The composer retained fond memories of Victoria's "special charm". "She seemed", he said, "the personification of England."[11]

Saint-Saëns appreciated genuine interest in his art from wherever it came, but, given as he was to royal name-dropping and to a certain obsequiousness in his references to kings and queens, he was nevertheless under no illusions about the general level of musical appreciation among most of the aristocrats with whom he mingled. He was once at a musical evening in Rome hosted by Queen Margherita of Italy, moving among heavily decorated courtiers and ladies dripping with jewels, and noted that, when listening to "terribly serious" music, "all these great people were victims of a boredom they did their best to conceal".[12] And although he knew how to show due deference, he could still be his usual biting self if anyone, no matter how exalted, showed ignorance of or disrespect for music or his own artistry. Even the king and queen of Italy were targets of his sharp tongue when they dared to exchange words while he was playing.

From his visit to London in the summer of 1898 he went in August to Languedoc, where the opening performance of *Déjanire* at Béziers on the 28th and 29th surpassed all expectations. On the first afternoon alone ten thousand people, sweltering in the heat, watched and heard a soprano draped as a Muse, carrying a small lyre and wearing a golden olive crown, sing a 'Salute to Béziers', written by Saint-Saëns to Gallet's words. The vast set was a recreation of an ancient city, and among its classical columns and facades unfolded the story of the last days of Hercules, the jealousy of his wife Dejaneira (making her grand entrance Rhadames-like in a horsedrawn chariot), the shirt of Nessus and the hero's death and funeral pyre. It was, in a way, a precursor of the epic film, but with live music conducted by the composer. Adding to the spectacle were the huge orchestra and chorus, including a "curtain" of eighteen harps – obtained with much trouble and expense – which the composer, after considering the acoustics of the arena, placed on an upper level to help contain the orchestral sound within the auditorium. The sound was further reinforced by the preponderance of wind instruments over strings, but any heaviness in the scoring was, by chance or calculation, counterbalanced by the open air setting, so that the overall effect tended towards that ethereal quality that is so distinctive in Saint-Saëns's later works. The two performances, followed by concerts in the arena of Saint-Saëns's music, made composer and dramatist instant celebrities in the town. Streets were named after them and they were showered with civic honours. For Gallet, though, the glory was short-lived. Ill and almost deaf, he died just two months after seeing (but not hearing) his work so magnificently staged and so wildly acclaimed. Saint-Saëns, his exact contemporary, had survived yet another much-loved friend and colleague.

Comparisons were inevitably made between the Béziers festival and Bayreuth: the question that had been asked during that evening conversation at Saint-Saëns's former home had been answered. As Bayreuth celebrated a German cultural identity by drawing on German history and mythology, so Béziers celebrated the Latin heritage of France's ancient past. But the comparison was superficial: the Béziers festival remained a source of local rather than national pride, was not devoted to one composer and never approached the level of international following attracted by its Bavarian counterpart. Saint-Saëns himself saw it in more limited terms, as a revival of the traditions of the French grand theatre of the seventeenth century rather than as a quasi-mystical national shrine, an idea that would have been anathema to his essentially practical and pragmatic mind. And although he remained for a while associated with the festival, he was to make only three more contributions to it.

Delighted by the success of the first festival, Castelbon asked Saint-Saëns to write for it again but the composer instead referred him to Fauré, partly as a way of advancing his former pupil's career but also because he was finding the business of composition increasingly irksome on top of all his other obligations. "Music is such a tyrannical mistress", he wrote to Emile Renaud, organist at Versailles, complaining that work left him no time for social visits.[13] Fauré, now in his mid-fifties, had finally succeeded as organist at the Madeleine and was now also professor of composition at the Conservatoire. That did not alter the pupil-teacher relationship with his elder colleague, who had helped him to the Conservatoire post and was still advising and even giving orders in matters of composition as well as musical politics. The result of his recommendation to Castelbon was Fauré's first full-scale stage work, the lyric drama *Prométhée*.

Although he was to be less sympathetic to his later works, Saint-Saëns was coming more and more to regard Fauré as a rare light in a general gloom, a beacon of beauty and civilisation among what he condemned as the barbarities being inflicted on the old tenets of form and harmony. Fauré also shared with Saint-Saëns a qualified admiration for Wagner, regarding the *Ring* as "stuffed with philosophy and symbols".[14] In France the 'barbarians' were the post-Wagnerians, inspired chiefly by d'Indy, and Debussy with his disregard for traditional form and the conventions of harmonic progression. Although Saint-Saëns saw the tendency as Europe-wide it was France that was at the forefront, by virtue of the national musical renaissance which he himself had helped to create. His alienation was made all the more acute by the fact that his own work had been moving in entirely the opposite direction, towards greater formal austerity and an emotional detachment which he thought could only be achieved by adhering to long-established principles. Form and 'impersonal beauty' were, by tradition, the exclusive aims of instrumental music, he declared in *Portraits et Souvenirs*. In that book he looked back over his life and music and assessed the great personalities he had known – Berlioz, Liszt, Gounod and Wagner – relating their achievement to what he disparagingly referred to as modern art, where young composers made up their own rules without any regard for what had gone before. Each of those nineteenth-century greats, he admitted, had rebelled against the past in some way, but they also, in their different ways, had worked within and were conscious of musical tradition. This was in contrast to some of their followers, "rash souls, whom no exaggeration can frighten, treating the symphonies of Beethoven, with the exception of the ninth, as old boots". Berlioz had an instinct for regular as opposed to "heretical" harmonies, and his belated conversion to Bach was a source of pride to Saint-Saëns, who claimed the credit for it. Liszt, like Berlioz, was concerned with expression rather than form, yet "where would you find purer forms than in the second movement of *Faust*, in the Purgatory of *Dante*, in *Orpheus*?" Gounod felt compelled to try his hand at quartets and symphonies, and Wagner "was steeped in the tradition of Bach," bending it to his own ends.

The trouble with Wagner was that he went too far down the path of harmonic evolution, drawing from it "the most extreme consequences", and his influence was largely malign, both on compositional technique and on attitudes to music, creating anarchy in the one and a snobbish pseudo-intellectualism in the other. In his preface to *Portraits et Souvenirs*, Saint-Saëns, the lover of clarity and directness, ridiculed the "amateurs" with a passion for the obscure and incomprehensible, who turned their noses up if the instruments of the orchestra "do not run in all directions like poisoned rats". In vocal music "a simple, natural accompaniment causes them to shrug their shoulders". Both solo song and opera, in which he had once joined the opposition to the "tyranny of melody" in favour of greater integration of melody and harmony, had, he said, gone too far to the other extreme: "a simple song, accompanied naturally, is seen as contemptible, and in compositions devoid of this element it is pretended that melody is 'everywhere'." Fifteen years before, when the Italian school still held sway, he had criticised "not melody as such but the exaggerated importance then assigned to it". Now he lamented what seemed to be its total disappearance, before the onslaught of the Wagnerian music drama, with its abolition of the aria and its treatment of the voice as an integral part of the orchestra. As young as fifteen, he had looked down on the "tiresome monotony" of Italian opera's artificial divisions and championed Wagner as a tool with which to break the mould. Now it had been broken and composers, it was said, were free. But were they?

To the obligation to write arias, duets, ensembles has succeeded the ban on them. It is no longer permitted to sing in operas and, in this game, the beautiful art of song has been weakened and tends to disappear . . . Monotony, for having changed its type, is not for that less monotonous; it is even, perhaps, a little more boring . . .

Even worse than this attack on clear melodic lines were the theorists who approved of it. Saint-Saëns, increasingly devoted to lightness, simplicity and the sheer delight of vocal and instrumental sound, condemned those who "on the pretext that beauty is sometimes accessible only with difficulty, imagine that the inaccessible is necessarily beautiful". "A beautiful voice, singing a phrase of Gluck or Mozart, will always be enough to reduce vain and pretentious nonsense to nothing", he insisted. "Three notes from Mme Delna [a leading contralto at the Opéra] and the finest theories go up in smoke." But worst of all was the intolerance, fanaticism and mysticism, bred by this "taste for the mysterious and incomprehensible", which he had already condemned in *Problèmes et Mystères* and which he saw as out of place in a "scientific and utilitarian age". "Mysticism, source of ineffable delights, held in such great honour in the Middle Ages, has been judged. It is known where it leads, to weakness, nihilism, nothingness."[15]

As the harmonic system that had been the foundation of music for three centuries disintegrated around him – as he once foresaw that it would – Saint-Saëns became more than ever devoted to the classical tradition that had nurtured him. He told Malherbe:

I relish the fugues of Bach, the symphonies of Beethoven, the oratorios of Mendelssohn; as once Antaeus refound his strength on touching the earth, so I take new confidence in contact with these giants. I have studied them anew, and compared them, and sensing that the truth was in the line that runs through them, again I turned to them as before.[16]

And this consciousness of the sanctity of the classical past is woven into the fabric of his own music, whatever the new ground it breaks. After publication of the second piano trio Charles Lecocq wrote to him that "while everything in it has a modern ring, yet it turns its back on nothing of the art we learned at school".[17] Part of this sense of the worth of tradition is his devotion to Mozart, which had put him, he said, beyond "the fluctuations of fashion" in the form first of Italian opera and later of the Wagner cult. "All my life I have fought for him, first at the Conservatoire when I was a pupil . . . Preferring *Le Nozze di Figaro* to *Il Barbiere di Siviglia*, that was a crime."[18] In the same way, he explained, he defended Mozart against the Wagnerians' presentation of their hero as having eclipsed everything that had gone before. This claim was not only absurd, it was unforgivable. He told the *New York Times* in 1906 that they were

not satisfied with giving Wagner his deserved place but insisted on belittling the work of others. They said he was greater than Mozart and wished to thrust Mozart's work into a secondary place. It was then that I took up a position against them and was accused of taking a position against Wagner . . . Many who were belittling Mozart are turning to him again.[19]

Despite the perception of him in his younger days as a musical pioneer and innovator, Saint-Saëns was and remained a conservative in the sense that he believed in evolution rather than revolution, and distrusted the notion of progress for its own sake. To him, musical truth was, as he said, in the "line" that runs through the great works of the past. Romanticism had evolved naturally from previous eras as part of a "golden chain". But the process had now produced unacceptable excesses. "Harmonic heresy", made possible, he believed, largely by the development of the piano since the eighteenth century, had now become "so abundant that it must be permitted to deplore it".[20] Time-honoured laws were being broken by composers who, he was to complain,

> *mean to be laws unto themselves and reply to the most justifiable criticism with the one peremptory argument that they 'will do as they please'. Assuredly, art is the home of freedom, but freedom is not anarchy . . . The dissonance of yesterday, we are told, will be the consonance of tomorrow; one can grow accustomed to anything. Still, there are such things in life as bad habits, and those who grow accustomed to crime come to a bad end. It is impossible for me to regard scorn of all rules as being equivalent to progress, by which word we generally mean improvement. The true meaning of the word* progressus *is a going forward, but the end or object is not stated. There is such a thing as the progress of a disease, and this is anything but improvement.*[21]

Moving forward, which is what progress meant, involved leaving things behind as well as attaining new things, "and it happens often enough that what we have lost was worth more than what we have gained".[22]

True musical progress, he believed, involved "adding to the old rules principles which are the natural expression of time and experience",[23] instead of what he saw as the "casting aside of all rules and every restraint",[24] which were the safeguards against mediocrity and decadence. Rules were the backbone of art, of literature as well as music, forcing the artist to climb to the heights of creation. "Never forget", he told the poet Pierre Aguétant, quoting Théophile Gautier, "that beauty is a difficulty overcome."[25] At a time when rules were no longer recognised, he wrote in one of his essays, "the man with 'developed taste' is not the one who knows how to get new and unexpected results by passing from one key to another, like the great Richard did in *Die Meistersinger,* but rather the man who abandons all keys and piles up dissonances which he neither introduces nor concludes and who as a result, grunts his way through music as a pig through a flower garden".[26] He condemned the Impressionists for attaching too much importance to 'tonal colour' at the expense of linear clarity and harmonic logic. In his introduction to the collection of essays and reminiscences called *Ecole Buissonnière,* published in 1913, he says: "For me, music is an art that has its laws, its grammar, its syntax, things which are disregarded in a world where it is sought only to conjure up impressions, to create ambiences and 'atmospheres'." This music's many admirers "enjoy delights of which I have not the least idea, and which I shall never know."[27] The new attitudes, such as Debussy's denial that discords had to be resolved, were not only an artistic affront to the traditions and principles he prized, and which had been part of his make-up since infancy, but also seemed like a personal affront to the memory of the mother and great-aunt who had brought him up in those traditions.

Confronted with musical developments that seemed such an unacceptable break with the past, Saint-Saëns yet retained, for a while at least, a faith in the evolutionary process. He believed it would produce a reaction to the 'heresy' he so deplored, and which he saw as "destined to disappear one day, probably far distant, but inevitable, as a result of the same evolution that gave it birth . . . The fashion today is for endless complications, arabesques and ceaseless modulations; but it is a fashion, and nothing more."[28] Writing to the *Neue Freie Presse* in Vienna in 1906, he hoped that "a mighty genius may arise who, out of the present chaos, will evolve a state of order . . . where the tonalities, instead of dancing in a senseless and purposeless round, will assist each other."[29] He did not know at the time that in Vienna Schoenberg was about to ditch tonality completely.

In condemning the new music he inevitably made many enemies. The stance he came to adopt in relation to most of his contemporaries was derided, often virulently, as the sour grapes of an embittered old reactionary, as unhelpful as it was irrelevant. One of his more extreme critics, Jean-Aubry wrote that Saint-Saens had lost the right to respect because of his expressions of "sarcasm" and his "scowling and aggressive attitude towards young musicians".[30] If it had been left to him alone French music "would have become fossilised in imitations of the past", for he lacked "generosity of mind and heart".[31] The image of a veteran spitefully dismissive of younger composers needs some qualification. Certainly he professed to despise Debussy's landmark opera "*Pelléath et Méli-thande*", as he contemptuously pronounced it in his rasping lisp.[32] Yet he was friendly enough towards Debussy to introduce him to musical contacts in London in 1895 and to find him accommodation there (with a French professor in Belsize Park). And in 1914 he confessed to Hermann Klein that he saw great talent and originality in Debussy's works.[33] Perhaps he recognised in them that unique voice that he had so long dreamed would win for French music the independence from Italian and German models (Debussy had, after all, long since shaken off his early enthusiasm for Wagner). He was closer to Debussy's aesthetic than is generally appreciated, valuing the picturesque and the kind of tonal sensuousness that both men admired in Massenet's music. Both were interested in orchestral colour, clarity of declamation and modal variants in harmony. Although he recoiled from most of Ravel's works because of their intricacies and unconventional harmonies, he was one of the first to predict a distinguished career for Fauré's pupil when, as head of the Prix de Rome jury in 1901, he thought very highly of the cantata submitted by the twenty-six-year-old (it came third). Among Fauré's other pupils he was much taken with Jean Roger-Ducasse and by 1901 was "completely under Ducasse's spell, finding him remarkable in every way", Fauré told his wife.[34] Later still, he became friendly with Poulenc, of all twentieth-century composers perhaps the nearest heir to the Saint-Saëns aesthetic, and one of his last services was to help further the career of the Greek composer Dimitri Mitropoulos.

As a busy practising musician himself, he did not have the time to consider at length the compositions of apprentice composers, but that did not mean he would not have liked to do so. When Fauré's pupil Alfredo Casella called to show him some of his compositions, he explained that he was too busy, although "it would interest me very much" to see his work.[35] His apparent dismissiveness stemmed also from a conviction that a young composer of talent had no need of guidance in how to compose, as he "must know what he wants", and indeed was probably better off without it. "Nothing is more dangerous than to ask advice, except to give it", he once observed.[36] "Do you want some good advice?" he asked Casella. "Do as I have done; since I was seventeen years old I have never shown my work to anyone."[37] Asked by the *New York Times* about modern trends in French music he replied: "I do not wish to criticise the younger men. I am perfectly willing that they should do their work."[38]

In approaching Saint-Saëns, composers, like anyone else, were liable to come up against the abrupt, irritable manner for which he was well known. But, as always, once the gruff exterior was passed, those new to his acquaintance were surprised by his friendly charm, for as he told Pierre Aguétant, "I am not insensitive either to talent or amiability".[39] The young Arthur Rubinstein, who called on him on the eve of a performance of his second piano concerto, noted the difference between the composer at home, where "his manners certainly belied his bad reputation", and his aloofness in public. At home, when Rubinstein mentioned that he was Polish, Saint-Saëns "rushed to the piano shouting 'this is my favourite composition of Chopin' ". He then played the E major Scherzo – "a little too quick for my taste but technically perfect". At the rehearsal of the concerto, in contrast, he sat in stony silence, ignoring all friendly overtures, and left at the end after lisping the brief comment "th'était très bien". Later Rubinstein received a signed portrait of the composer, on which Saint-Saëns had written: "For AR, with admiration of his great talent."[40]

The organist Marcel Dupré also discovered this cordiality after an initial display of petulance, when the composer gave a casting vote in his favour in the Prix de Rome of 1914. Dupré called to thank him and was told: "I voted for you because you deserved it. You have nothing to thank me for." He then asked about Dupré's childhood as a musical prodigy, adding "I was one also" and from then on the meeting was entirely friendly. There was a similar result the following year, when Dupré called again. "Monsieur, tell me quickly what you want", Saint-Saëns snapped, then: "You came to see me and not to solicit a favour? That is rare!"[41]

But however willing he may have been to consider young musicians, he was simply unable to come to terms with the turn-of-the-century vanguard as a whole. As the *Glasgow Herald* neatly summed it up in its obituary, modern composers "seemed to him to make a cult of ugliness", to which he opposed "balanced form and transparent scoring, speaking of a fastidious sense of beauty".[42] Interestingly, he saw the breakdown of orthodox harmony and the apparent abandonment of 'beauty of form' as symptomatic of a general decline in artistic sense, in a civilisation that had reached a stage where art was no longer a necessity, but a luxury for the few. To the rest all that mattered was material progress and 'utility' – and he draws from this a conclusion that has striking relevance to today's environmental concerns. For as musical beauty is disregarded, so is natural beauty, and nature becomes simply raw material, so that animals are hunted to extinction, forests are destroyed for ever and waterfalls are "so much motor-power".[43]

His outspokenness invited scorn, yet it is of value because of the different perspective it puts on the musical developments of the time. His admirers, such as Fauré, Hahn, Taffanel, Malherbe and the Conservatoire Concerts Society secretary Dandelot, saw him as something of an oasis of sanity in a musical world that was going awry. His first English biographer Arthur Hervey typically expressed the grounds for this admiration in 1921:

A tendency among some of the younger composers of different nations appears to point to a thorough negation of the fundamental principles of music hitherto more or less generally accepted. The desire, praiseworthy in itself, of avoiding conventionality, has led to fearsome experiments in sound. Whereas in the past, respect for formalism was pushed too far and barred the way to the free development of music, the so-called modernists are now going to the other extreme and, throwing all precedent to the winds, are seemingly endeavouring to create an entirely new language of sound, the adoption of which would necessitate the scrapping of all the masterpieces of the past. This appears to be a retrograde movement rather than an advance, for it can only lead straight back to the chaotic conditions that prevailed before mankind was civilised and able to appreciate what is understood as music . . . Saint-Saëns, during his long and varied career, has always known how to steer clear of exaggeration, and has shown conclusively by the freedom with which he has treated different forms of music that imagination is not hampered by knowledge, that true progress does not consist necessarily in abandoning all the traditions of the past, but that these should not, on the other hand, prevent a composer from cultivating an entire independence in the expression of his thoughts.[44]

No appraisal of the radical changes then taking place would be complete without Saint-Saëns's conservative view of them. His contemporaries may have regarded him as outdated and irrelevant (Romain Rolland noted in the 1900s that it was possible to discuss the French musical scene without once mentioning his name), but a balanced retrospective of the period has to consider all sides of the debate. Too often Saint-Saëns is left out of it – a legacy of the hostility he aroused – and the relationship of his later works, and the aesthetic behind them, to the currents of early-twentieth-century music is largely unknown territory, as indeed are the later works themselves. For the compositions that date from the 1890s onwards tend more and more to a cool, dispassionate style and sparseness of texture usually associated with later composers. Sometimes, as in the second cello concerto, there is an attempt to return to the lyrical warmth and biting rhythms of the earlier, better known works, but generally these qualities decline in favour of greater refinement and transparency, the musical equivalent of the incognito traveller's invisible personal life. But the later works are no less personal for that, reflecting the spiritual calm and satisfaction expounded in *Problèmes et Mystères*, which sometimes produces an intensely esoteric quality.

The E minor string quartet of 1899 blends the two styles in a combination of passion and restraint. As with the Preludes and Fugues for organ, Saint-Saëns only then, in his sixties, and after several abortive attempts, felt able to overcome what he regarded as one of the severest tests of musical architecture and balance. This did not mean a rigid adherence to conventional form: he was still prepared to modify traditional structures in the search for a pleasing shape. Although the quartet is laid out in the usual four movements the two outer movements have unusual formal features. But these deviations are much less marked than in earlier, more radical works, and serve mainly to heighten the feeling of cool precision and a smooth flow of sound. The very opening, a single sustained note on the first violin joined by a high pianissimo chord from the rest of the ensemble, is an appropriate introduction to the rarefied atmosphere of so much of Saint-Saëns's later writing. The first violin breaks into a meandering cantilena as the first half of the first subject, the second half breaking in with an abrupt change of rhythm and tempo, characterised by tumbling groups of semiquavers and a persistent double-dotted figure which, in a lengthy development, accompanies a short fugue. The surprise comes with the recapitulation, announced by the second half of the main subject, much abbreviated, before the leisurely re-appearance of the flowing first half.

The rhythmically obsessive scherzo is perhaps the most successful movement, built on a simple theme and containing fugal episodes of various types, while the adagio, a free fantasia based on two contrasted ideas, is a brief concession to the old lyricism. A feature of the quartet is the occasional tonal uncertainty, and this is especially noticeable in the second subject of the finale, which seems to hover between two keys a major third apart. The first subject is characterised by that rhythmic monotony into which Saint-Saëns is so often inclined to slip, but the movement is unusual in that the two subjects are recapitulated almost without a break, and only then is there a development, including a reference back to the opening of the whole work as well as the customary fugal passage. A rapid coda then brings the music to an energetic conclusion. The quartet is dedicated to Ysaÿe, with whom Saint-Saëns appeared in several concerts in Brussels and London over the next two years.

Engagements took him further afield in June 1899 when he took the Italian steamer *The Duchess of Genoa* to Brazil. He landed at Rio de Janeiro on the 7th (not Buenos Aires, as some reports, ignorant of South American geography, had it) and stayed at Persepolis in the outskirts of the city. Over the next two months he gave two chamber concerts in the capital, which included the first performance of the string quartet, and two at São Paulo. The visit attracted considerable interest. Both cities had a flourishing musical life, especially in opera, which acknowledged its European inheritance. But it was also proud of its native elements, and Saint-Saëns caused some bad feeling by admitting that he did not know any South American composers or their music.

Returning to France, he went to Béziers, where he asked Fauré to conduct the two performances of *Déjanire* scheduled for the festival. In October Albert Carré, who had succeeded Carvalho at the Opéra-Comique after the latter's death in 1897, staged *Javotte* and a month later the revised version of *Proserpine* – after a three-year delay for which the theatre blamed a lack of suitable singers. The alterations did little to save the opera, but Béziers had revived Saint-Saëns's appetite for the theatre and during his next sojourn in the Canaries he accepted a libretto by Victorien Sardou, author of *Tosca*, and his colleague Pierre Gheusi. This was *Les Barbares*, planned for the open air theatre at Orange and set in that town in Roman times. Saint-Saëns, having studied the acoustics and layout of the theatre, thought the drama unsuited for production there and at first declined it, but was swayed by the persistence of the authors, their willingness to make alterations, and by the opportunity of recreating a period of French history. Before beginning the music he set to work with Sardou and Gheusi on adapting the libretto. This, and the request for a choral work to open the Paris Exhibition of 1900, forced him to cancel a second visit to South America.

The Paris Exhibition was set for the summer, and Saint-Saëns was asked to head the commission for the musical events. His own contribution was a fitting welcome to the twentieth century: *Le Feu Céleste* is a hymn, for soprano, chorus and orchestra, organ and narrator, in praise of electricity. Armand Sylvestre, co-librettist of *Henry VIII*, wrote the words, which matched the composer's own faith in scientific inquiry and the hopes for mankind that lay in it. The hymn builds up to a climax of trumpets and organ proclaiming a world lit brilliantly by the new electrical wonder. It was the first item in the first official concert of the exhibition, on 31st May, a programme of French music conducted by Taffanel at the Trocadero. Just a few days before, Saint-Saëns had the treat of witnessing an eclipse of the sun – a switching-off of natural light before the celebration of the man-made variety. *Le Feu Céleste*, together with his organisation of the musical events that were such a prominent feature of the exhibition, earned him promotion to Grand Officier of the Légion d'Honneur. Later in the year he was made honorary president of the International Music History

Congress, and his bust was carved by the sculptor Paul Dubois, creating a major talking point at the 1901 Paris Salon.

Before settling down to *Les Barbares* he produced two vocal works for soprano and orchestra, the set of five songs called *Lola*, and *La Nuit*, with chorus, which he dedicated to Colonne in gratitude for having done so much to promote his works over nearly thirty years. *Lola*, to poems by Stephan Bordèse, is a late manifestation of his Hispanic style, particularly in the evocative Tango. In the meantime he was helping Fauré towards the première of his *Prométhée* at Béziers. Fauré was still a little in awe of his old master and in June was apologising to him for not having the score ready "for your inspection", pleading a week later that "I am working as much as I can".[45] In mid-August Saint-Saëns arrived in Béziers for the performance on the 27th; on the 26th the town was hit by a severe storm which ripped the scenery and threw the whole production into chaos. During what Fauré described as "a terrifying two hours" a thunderbolt struck the stage, on the exact spot, he wryly noted, where Prometheus was due to steal the heavenly fire. Saint-Saëns, his health ever vulnerable to damp, was drenched; "fortunately he is not ill", Fauré wrote to his wife. The production staff worked overnight to repair the damage and the two performances went ahead, to much acclaim. Saint-Saëns told Fauré: "With your *Prométhée* you have astounded your colleagues, including me" and, perhaps thinking that his protégé may have felt awkward in his moment of glory about rivalling him in the theatre, added the assurance that "I do not feel the slightest resentment, rather the reverse". Fauré, ever the pupil, declared that this "satisfaction with my work has given me great pleasure,"[46] and in an evening concert after the performance joined his former teacher in the latter's Beethoven Variations.

Saint-Saëns was indeed far from resentful and in fact was extremely proud of Fauré's success. On returning to Paris he spread the news of it among his colleagues at the Academy of Fine Arts, of which he was now vice-president, and at the Institute as a whole, thinking this would be useful for Fauré's further advancement. But his own work now demanded his attention. After making a fresh survey of the theatre at Orange he moved to St Germain-en-Laye to begin the music for *Les Barbares*. As so often, composition was interrupted by commitments at the Institute, which demanded his presence in the capital, and in October he travelled to Brussels for a performance of *Samson et Dalila*. Once again, the strain of work and the onset of winter began to affect his health, and when he joined the theatre directors, Fauré and Durand for dinner at the Grand Hotel he could not eat. Nevertheless, despite more work at the Institute, he was able to give his publisher the first two acts of *Les Barbares* before leaving for Algiers in December. On the way he stopped at Marseilles to hear Fauré's Requiem conducted by Paul Viardot, and wrote to Marie Fauré that the performance was very fine and did her husband "great honour". After congratulating her on her contributions to astronomy and their recognition by the Astronomical Society, he apologised for the fact that work and his troubled state of health had prevented him from thinking about the New Year gifts he had promised for her two sons. "They will lose nothing by waiting", he assured her.[47]

In Algiers he worked on the third act of *Les Barbares* over the next two months, then headed north. He arrived in London for a festival of his works in which he played the *Africa* fantasy and the Mozart K.450 concerto, and Ysaÿe played the Rondo Capriccioso and the third violin concerto. He was delighted by Ysaÿe's performance and gave him a farewell hug at the station next morning, barely encompassing the violinist's burly frame. Ysaÿe declared afterwards that this gesture meant more to him than any amount of applause or acclaim, and he repaid it on another occasion in London when he was rehearsing the orchestra for the 'Egyptian' concerto. Calling the composer from the wings, he lifted him up off the ground and kissed him on both cheeks before leading him to the piano to join the rehearsal (which, astonishingly, had begun at 11.30 p.m., after a concert).[48]

Saint-Saëns completed *Les Barbares* in Paris during April 1901 – whereupon he collapsed from exhaustion and influenza, causing him to cancel a new ballet he had promised to write for the Béziers festival. Recovery was not helped by news that the theatre at Orange had been closed for safety reasons. The Opéra stepped in with the offer of a date in its next season, but it meant that the previous year's research at Orange was in vain, for the piece had now to be remodelled for the indoor stage. Although the offer was welcome there was an unfavourable precedent for the transfer to Paris of a work written for the open air of the provinces: soon after its Béziers debut *Déjanire* made a less happy appearance at the Odéon, its scenic effects missing in its modified form.

As well as retouching *Les Barbares*, Saint-Saëns also wrote a solo song, 'Elle', to a sonnet by Lecocq, who at first was reluctant to have his name attached to what he called "this opuscule", as he was not especially proud of it. Saint-Saëns insisted, arguing that his name allied to that of one of the most popular operetta composers of the day in the same composition would "titillate the public". He was less enthusiastic, however, when a theatre director suggested a collaboration in reverse; that Lecocq should set Saint-Saëns's comedy *La Crampe des Ecrivains* as an operetta, for production in September. Lecocq was tickled by the idea – "it is mad; and it is exactly that which appeals" – but Saint-Saëns refused, telling his colleague that *La Crampe* had been written for amateur actors at Algiers, that "it is the opposite of a masterpiece" and that "it is not musical". Nothing more was heard of the project.[49]

By this time he had recovered from his illness, and a visit to Béziers in August for a revival of *Prométhée*, and the company of Fauré and Ducasse in the southern sunshine, helped lift his spirits further. He was "affectionate and charming the whole time, with a childlike merriment", Fauré wrote to his wife. "I know he is entirely convinced of my affection for him, and this puts him in a good mood by confirming those feelings he may have been uncertain of."[50] In September came news that, following Verdi's death, he was to succeed to the German title of Foreign Knight of the Order of Merit, bestowed by the Kaiser, an award which, in view of the hornets nest he had stirred up in Germany, he must have viewed with a touch of irony.

Les Barbares, despite the fears about its adaptation, was well received at its Opéra première on 23rd October, and Saint-Saëns wrote a congratulatory letter to the conductor Taffanel and the performers. There is some significance in the fact that it was Pierre Gailhard, co-director of the Opéra, who had taken on the work. He had been largely responsible for bringing Wagner to the theatre during the 1890s, enlivening the neighbourhood with violent demonstrations in the process and *Les Barbares*, of all Saint-Saëns's operas, perhaps comes closest to the Wagnerian model. There is a more comprehensive use of representative themes, an air of doom, and a heaviness that is remarkably at odds with his usual style. It is as if he was hitting back at Wagner on his own ground rather than by contrast, as he had done in *Phryné*, and the subject seems to imply a response to the declaration of war on the Latin races which he saw in the finale of *Die Meistersinger*. Here the Germans are the enemy. In a long symphonic introduction a narrator sets the scene as Roman Gaul in 105 BC and the invasion of Orange (Arausio) by Teutonic hordes, "giants with red hair from the misty North". Their leader Marcomir falls in love with Floria, the local priestess of Vesta, who breaks her vow of chastity in return for his promise to spare the inhabitants. But Livia, widow of the Roman consul killed in battle, discovers that it was Marcomir who struck the fatal blow and she stabs him with a piece of the dagger she had taken from her husband's body. The change of musical direction towards a greater intensity failed to compensate for the fact that, yet again, Saint-Saëns's enthusiasm for historical subjects had led him to a dead end. Sardou, like Gallet, had a taste for poetic atmosphere rather than full-bloodied drama, and the libretto has a lifelessness which the music could not transform, the characters remaining as remote as the period in which they are set. The score, moreover, is of a patchy quality that suggests that the composer was ill at ease in the weightier style he had adopted, and could not maintain it. After a short run at the Opéra *Les Barbares* was never revived.

The winter brought on an attack of bronchitis, so Saint-Saëns left for Egypt at the end of November, spending two weeks at Cannes on the way, but not before belatedly keeping his promise of presents for Fauré's two teenage sons. Their arrival brought an "explosion of joy", wrote Fauré in his letter of thanks, adding that Saint-Saëns was wise to leave Paris. "The cold is intense! Take care of yourself and come back to us in the spring full of health. Music and all of us need you for a long, long time yet." Mme Fauré, in a separate thank you note, told him that "you are like a parent to us and your name is always spoken here", and said she intended to give her eighteen-year-old son Emmanuel *Problèmes et Mystères* to read. "I am sure he will love you the more for it, for he is well up in your ideas."[51] The family sent him some flowers at Cannes, from where he was able to tell them that his bronchitis and other ailments had cleared. Now he was set for the crossing to Egypt, taking with him a copy of *Parysatis*, a three-act drama by Jane Dieulafoy about the queen of ancient Persia at the time of the wars with the Greeks. He had been commissioned to write the incidental music for it by Castelbon at Béziers.

The winter was passed in idyllic surroundings: the Khedive's brother, the Pasha, allowed him the use of a pavilion on an island in the Nile near Cairo. There, in a palatial room with a gold-panelled ceiling topped by a cupola of Alhambra-style decoration, he worked both on *Parysatis* and a march to be played at the coronation of Edward VII. He paused only to conduct an Italian opera company in his *Hymne à Victor Hugo* at Alexandria on 26th February, in a festival to mark the poet's centenary. The pavilion at Cairo was to be his home again on later visits, and he told a musical journal: "I ask, when I am there, what I have done to deserve such paradise."[52]

In the summer he left "paradise" for London, to rehearse the *Coronation March* and take part in the London Musical Festival. Here he came to know the conductor Henry Wood. Early every morning he would be at the organ of the Queen's Hall for an hour's improvising before orchestral rehearsal began, and Wood, an organist himself, was often among the secret listeners. He recalled that Saint-Saëns seemed to have lost none of his social playfulness, but the wit of youth now looked more like the eccentricity of old age. On a visit to the Woods's home in company with Ysaÿe he kept singing at the top of his voice, declaring that he should have been a singer instead of a composer. When Mrs Olga Wood apologised for the lack of drawing room curtains, which were still at the cleaner's, "he dashed to the piano and proceeded to improvise a free fantasia to express the horror of his feelings at being asked into a drawing room without curtains. He laughed heartily . . ."[53] He shared the programme with Wood at the last concert of the London festival in May, conducting the introduction to *Les Barbares*, the entr'acte from *Phryné*, and the third violin concerto with Ysaÿe as soloist.

The performance of the *Coronation March* was unexpectedly delayed. Edward VII was due to be crowned on 26th June but was taken ill with peritonitis and the coronation was postponed. It finally took place on 9th August after a successful operation. Saint-Saëns's *March* was the second in a programme of seven festive pieces (four of them composed specially for the occasion) played in Westminster Abbey during the morning, before the entry of the king and queen. With its fanfares making full use of trumpet sonorities and the authentic theme from *Henry VIII* sung by the chorus, it was a fitting prelude to the proceedings. It was repeated in Paris later in the year under Colonne's baton, but did not survive as a concert piece, though it earned for its composer more titles to add to his collection – Commander of the Order of Victoria, Baronet and the special category knighthood for foreigners. His tribute to the king somehow symbolised the new friendly relations with England that were ending centuries of hostility and mistrust. The bearded figure of the composer was often mistaken for that of Edward: it was as if he was the king's French counterpart in the *entente cordiale* that was to be forged over the next two years.

Saint-Saëns's relations with the Edwardian monarchy were further strengthened when Queen Alexandra received him at Buckingham Palace along with the Dutch cellist Josef Hollmann. She was in mourning for her parents, Saint-Saëns's other royal patrons the king and queen of Denmark. She "was pale and looked feeble, but she welcomed us with the utmost cordiality", the composer recalled. Although she was deaf, she asked her guests to play, and rushed forward to help Saint-Saëns lift the piano lid "before the maids of honour could intervene". Afterwards she gave the two musicians a gold medal each, and "offered us a cup of tea which she poured herself with her royal and imperial hands".[54] He loved such displays of regal informality: on a visit to Portugal, he was delighted to be received by Queen Amelie entirely alone, without any of her attendants, "which allowed her to dispense with all etiquette and to seat me in a chair near her".[55]

From London he travelled to Béziers for the première of *Parysatis* on 17th August 1902, an event that was threatened by dull, wet weather and by the sudden indisposition of the main singer, who had suffered a miscarriage the previous night. Fortunately, another young soprano knew the part and was able to take over, "but", Fauré wrote to his wife, "you can imagine the uproar in the morning". As the performance time approached the weather cleared and *Parysatis* went ahead under a beautiful blue sky, among sets designed after bas-reliefs from Persepolis housed in the Louvre. As with *Déjanire*, harps played a prominent role, twenty of them surmounting a 450-strong orchestra with 250 choristers, conducted this time by Paul Viardot. The spectacle had the audience cheering wildly at the end, while Saint-Saëns and Mme Dieulafoy, in jacket and breeches, embraced on stage. Criticism, however, was mixed: it was not so much Olympian as Olympic, someone commented to Fauré, who confessed that "certainly there is sometimes a circus feel about it all".[56] Written for the special conditions of the Béziers arena, the production never travelled beyond its confines, and Saint-Saëns never tried to give it wider currency by transforming it into an opera, as he was to do with *Déjanire*. *Parysatis* was destined to remain a one-off, consigning the incidental music to virtual oblivion, which is a pity, because it is a substantial score, including a vigorous march, some lovely choruses, and a varied ballet featuring a wordless soprano imitating the nightingale. There are parts also for tenor and baritone solo, and the whole is redolent of that orientalism of which the composer was a past master, notably in the dark, brooding figure associated with the queen. After its first performance, the composer provided the festival audience with some light theatrical relief by directing his two comedies, *Botriocéphale* and *La Crampe des Ecrivains*.

If the orientalism, richness and colour of *Parysatis* represents a return to the earlier Saint-Saëns, so does the D minor cello concerto, written in the same year. He was moved to draw on his stylistic past by the demands of period setting for the former, and by the nature of the solo instrument in the latter. Ever since the childhood lessons with Franchomme he had had a special relationship with the cello, whose deep sonority had elicited from him some of his most memorable melodies. In this second concerto he indulges in the haunting lyricism, contrasted with strongly rhythmic passages, of his former years, although it never reaches the same heights as in the first concerto. He also adopts the condensed form of earlier concertante works – in this case, two movements each subdivided into two, the slow section ending the first movement. The andante, the heart of the concerto, seems to confirm that he was looking back with its mood of wistful nostalgia and even regret. The second movement opens with a vigorous perpetual motion for the cello, after which a thoughtful cadenza leads into the finale, based on material from the opening section. Here the orchestral passages become oddly old-fashioned, as if they had been written in the 1840s. Hollmann gave the first performance in Berlin in 1903, but since then the work has remained little more than a pleasant curiosity, never approaching its A minor predecessor in popularity.

The rest of 1902 was spent mainly on work for the Institute: Saint-Saëns was its representative at the unveiling of a monument to Liszt in Weimar, and he presented a paper to the Institute summing up his studies of ancient Greek instruments as he had seen them depicted in museums at Berlin, Alexandria and Naples, and on wall-paintings at Pompeii. Like his paper on ancient theatre decor, this essay on lyres and kitharas was a pioneering work of its time, bringing the practising musician's expertise to bear on theories as to how the instruments were played.

Classical literature too was very much on his mind at this time. Helen of Troy was one of the many subjects he had considered for operatic treatment as a young man, when he was still reaching towards the theatre. After Offenbach's famous send-up he realised that the story could no longer be taken seriously in the opera house and abandoned the idea, but now, nearly forty years after *La Belle Hélène*, he was coming round to it again. At the same time, a request for a new work came from Raoul Gunsbourg, director of the opera house at Monte

Carlo, which in 1892 had been one of the first to stage *Samson et Dalila* after its French première. Saint-Saëns, after so many operatic failures, was at first reluctant to oblige but, after reflecting on the success Massenet was having at Monte Carlo, decided to accept the opportunity to establish a foothold there. *Hélène* was to be the means of matching his rival in Monaco. He had very definite ideas on the character of Helen: she was "not simply a woman in love but the sport of destiny . . . a great figure whose sin excites no mockery but rather a kind of sacred terror" – rather like Proserpine, in fact. He therefore decided to write the libretto himself, basing it on the classical writers, rather than use a collaborator who "might ruin the simplicity of my conception".[57] His first choice for the title role was Nellie Melba, the Covent Garden prima donna who had so upstaged the London performances of *Henry VIII*.

But before beginning on the opera there was more theatre music on a classical theme to write. Sarah Bernhardt, who had been a formidable Andromache in Racine's tragedy, was planning to revive the play at her theatre in Paris, and asked Saint-Saëns to supply incidental music. He responded with a score consisting mainly of preludes to each of the four acts, and accompaniments for the entrance of key characters. Unlike the incidental music for *Antigone*, the *Andromache* music makes little attempt at integration with the drama itself, and no attempt to recreate the sound of ancient instruments, using instead the forces of a conventional symphony orchestra. Bernhardt played Hermione in the new production, which opened on 7th February 1903, with Colonne conducting. The first night audience responded with wild enthusiasm, so much so that someone who dared to hiss was nearly lynched and had to be escorted from the theatre. Critics, however, were divided. Charles Joly in *Le Figaro* praised in particular the preludes to the second and fourth acts, and the orchestration throughout as underlining the drama in subtle ways, as when "a simple note on the oboe, as for example in Andromache's explosion of grief, serves to indicate a feeling or emotion".[58] *Le Temps*, on the other hand, regarded the addition of music to Racine as little short of sacrilege, and its drama critic lamented the interference in characterisation. People, driven by strong passions, were instead forced by musical tempi "to enter pompously and exit with a dignified slowness". And Pierre Lalo, the paper's music critic, condemned the whole exercise of adding music to classical drama as "always useless, almost always injurious". Saint-Saëns, he noted, seemed to have agreed, because he had placed the music largely where the drama was not proceeding. Where the two did overlap, the result was unfortunate: the flutes' imitation of hissing serpents as Orestes is pursued by the Furies, said Lalo, reduced the scene to the level of operetta.[59]

Saint-Saëns was not present at the performance, having returned to Egypt to spend the winter of 1902–03 in the luxurious splendour of the Pasha's pavilion. There, after repaying His Highness for his hospitality by writing for him a piano piece, the *Valse Langoureuse*, he set to work on his libretto for *Hélène*. The pavilion provided ideal working conditions. "I enjoyed complete liberty and a calm undisturbed by visitors. These had probably been scared away by the guard of the palace gate, huge fellows in gorgeous costumes and formidably armed." But he had barely begun the poem when he was caught up in rehearsals for a concert of his works at the Khedive's theatre in aid of Breton sailors. This so disturbed his train of thought that he found it impossible to return to the subject of Helen, even after regaining the calm of the palace pavilion. So he moved into the desert at Ismailia – "a refuge of light and silence," as he called it – with a small colony of Suez Canal Company workers, so busy that "they people the solitude without disturbing it". There he finished the poem in twelve days, then left his winter quarters for Paris and a revival of *Henry VIII* at the Opéra. In June he took a short break at Biarritz and Cannes and at the beginning of July paid a courtesy call on Prince Albert of Monaco – a fellow member of the French Institute. The conversation doubtless centred on the new work for the prince's opera house. Saint-Saëns then set about working on the music in earnest, installing himself amid the flower-decked slopes of Mont Revard, above Aix-les-Bains. "It is thus that one should always work, in calm and silence, far from importunate visitors and all sorts of distractions, soothed by the wonderful sights of nature and the scent of flowers. When this is possible, work is more than a pleasure, it is a voluptuous delight." It was in this idyllic summer setting that *Hélène* was written, with only the orchestration left to be completed later in Paris.[60]

The opera is in one act divided into seven scenes, beginning at the court of Menelaus and ending as Helen leaves for Troy with her lover Paris after unsuccessfully resisting her fate and her passion. It is a curiously understated treatment of the story, a prime example of the composer's late style, with its classical reserve and even austerity. This is hardly calculated to bring to life the intense emotions the subject would seem to suggest, and the result is more like a tableau than an opera, decorative rather than dramatic. Saint-Saëns saw the central theme as in the tradition of *Samson et Dalila* – "temptation triumphant, the irresistible attraction of the forbidden fruit" – but by making the woman in love the central focus, whether or not she is also "the sport of destiny", he puts the spotlight on a subject with which he had little sympathy. Hence the qualities of elegance, grace and refinement deflect any obligation to emotional involvement. Even the sombre appearance of Pallas Athena and her warning of impending disaster, which was compared to that of Brunhilda in the second act of *Die Walküre*, hardly disturbs the serenity. There are moments of great charm, notably the chorus of Aphrodite's nymphs, and Saint-Saëns's enthusiasm for Gluck can be traced in the simplicity and clarity of the vocal writing. But the emotional detachment of the music made the characters seem cold and lifeless, and thus *Hélène*, of all the operas, is perhaps the clearest illustration of what came to be regarded as the fundamental weakness of Saint-Saëns's theatrical output. It is a style of opera that was in stark contrast to the hot-blooded contemporary works being written by Strauss and Puccini, but in the absence of live performances it is difficult to judge what impression it would make on audiences today, after nearly a century of anti-romanticism. As for Saint-Saëns himself, he regarded *Hélène* as the greatest and most perfect expression of his operatic ideals. When Pierre Aguétant complimented him on the poem he replied that it was "not bad, that's all . . . Your eulogies give me great pleasure, without enlarging the opinion I have of my poetic 'worth'. The music is worth more than the verse; there I know my craft and I strongly believe I have never exercised it better."[61]

In August he revisited Béziers, where both *Déjanire* and *Parysatis* were being revived, and brought with him a new contribution to the festival, a play called *Le Roi Apépis*. An adaptation of a novel by Victor Cherbuliez, it was a perfect vehicle for his natural wit, still as sharp as ever, and was an instant hit. As in all the best comedy, its humour is conveyed by the clarity, conciseness and precision of the dialogue, qualities that were as important to Saint-Saëns the author as to Saint-Saëns the composer. The organist Archibald Henderson wrote of him that his writing was always as finely tuned as his music: "there is never an unclear phrase or sentence".[62] Despite his display of modesty in reply to compliments on his writing, the care he took over prose and verse was as meticulous as it was over music, perhaps even more so. Fauré once encountered him in a fury because of a printing error in his words. "That affects him much more than mistakes in his music. Ever the violin of Ingres . . ."[63]

In October he travelled to Berlin to lay a wreath on a new statue of Wagner. His admiration for the composer's music was undiminished, but his well-publicised views on the Wagner legacy and philosophy, and his resentment at the number of Wagner performances in French theatres, left a taste of bitterness and mutual mistrust on his visits to Germany in the years to 1914. *A Capitulation* was still souring relations. In 1907 a German newspaper printed a letter arguing that Wagner's satire on the French nation was not an insult to France, to which Saint-Saëns countered that "in writing *A Capitulation*, and including it in his complete works, Wagner committed a blameworthy act which his patriotism will not excuse".[64] German cities had been the scene of some of his earliest triumphs as pianist and composer, and had given him recognition while he struggled to make his name at home, but the war of 1870 and subsequent controversies had cast a shadow over any feelings of friendliness and gratitude. As he once remarked to Hermann Klein, "I used to like the Germans, but not any more".[65]

A more poignant reminder of halcyon days of youthful comradeship, hopes and affections eclipsed by war was the death in 1903 of Augusta Holmes, aged fifty-six. She had continued to work in Paris, and had kept in touch with Saint-Saëns. He headed the committee to arrange for a monument to be placed on her tomb at the St Louis cemetery in Versailles, and at its unveiling, on 12th July 1904, he must have reflected on the present loneliness of his private and personal life, and on how different things might have been.

XIII • GRAND OLD MAN

WHILE SAINT-SAËNS CONTINUED TO COMPOSE AND PERFORM, TO WRITE, travel and discuss, in defiance of old age and recurring bouts of ill health, the image of the respected establishment figure grew as solid as the statue of him that was unveiled in Dieppe in 1907. Seventieth birthday greetings arrived from most of the European capitals, the one from Stockholm signed personally by King Gustav. Oxford University conferred an honorary doctorate to match that from Cambridge, and in 1913 came the highest award of the Légion d'Honneur, the Grand Croix. When, in 1909, the constitutional movement known as the Young Turks came to power in Turkey, its members, most of whom had been exiled in Paris, thought first of Saint-Saëns when the question arose as to who should write the new national anthem.[1] The suggestion was not taken up, but that it was made is an indication of his seniority in French musical life.

And while honours rained on him from on high, his fame seeped down to the humblest sections of society, where, it was said, his picture was revered by peasant families who had taken his name literally and adopted him as a saint with healing powers. Having survived most of his contemporaries he had become the grand old man of French music, part of the national fabric or, as he himself put it, "a little piece of the edifice". It was a position that presented him, to many, more as a curiosity than an elder statesman, a living relic of an age that had passed, and to those at the forefront of the musical developments he so strongly opposed he was an irritating – and in view of his long and frequent absences from Paris – ultimately a forgettable anachronism. The composer of symphonies and concertos was seen as representing those German influences which had prompted the revival of French music but which the national school was at last shaking off, leading Debussy to style himself, as if as an innovation, "*musicien français*".

The new hostility to the old forms was loudly expressed at two Colonne concerts in February and March 1904, when noisy demonstrations greeted performances of concertos by Saint-Saëns, Beethoven and Paderewski. For the demonstrators, such works were anathema to the process of musical rediscovery and the evolution of a distinctively national musical art, based on opera. The incidents were isolated but nevertheless symptomatic of a radicalism that was shaping a world of music in which Saint-Saëns could have no part. The first French performance of the D minor cello concerto, given by Hollmann at the Conservatoire on 5th February 1905, confirmed him as a man of the old school in the eyes of the vanguard. One writer, René Doire, writing in the *Courrier Musical* six years later, dismissed the concerto as "bad music well written",[2] a facile comment that was seized upon by Saint-Saëns's critics who then gleefully applied it virtually to the whole of his musical output. It has been repeated ever since, serving to stifle any fair and reasonable assessment of his works, and is still trotted out by commentators as a convenient blanket phrase with which to sum up eighty years of musical creation.

Those who, like Debussy, regarded him as "an unrepentant old symphonist" were not likely to be impressed by his continuing efforts to raise his standing in opera. But *Hélène* did keep his name alive in the theatre, for a time at least, as someone other than the composer of *Samson et Dalila*. After its Monte Carlo première in 1904 it went on to Covent Garden, with Nellie Melba in the title role at both theatres, and reached the Opéra-Comique in Paris in 1905, with Mary Garden (the first Mélisande). The work established his presence at Monte Carlo, as he had hoped, and his welcome there helped to make up for all the frustrations and disappointments he had experienced in the capital over the years. He grew to have a special fondness for the place, for its fresh, congenial climate and its botanic gardens, where he could often be seen making a close inspection of the plants. Before the première of *Hélène*, however, there was little time for relaxation. He arrived from Egypt in late January, in the company of Gabriel Geslin, a servant he had lately engaged, to help prepare the production. "I was so relaxed in the land of the pharoahs", he wrote to Marie Fauré. "Here it is quite the reverse, and from the time of my arrival I have had to apply myself to work – and what work! A mountain of orchestral parts to correct."[3]

As consolation he could look forward to a visit from Fauré and some relief from his work was provided by two performances of *Samson et Dalila* given in his honour, before the curtain finally went up on *Hélène* on 18th February for an annual charity gala. The new work was given in a double bill with Massenet's *La Navarraise*, an ironic coupling in view of the personal animosity between the two composers. Saint-Saëns had the satisfaction of receiving from Prince Albert the Grand Cross of the Order of St Charles, as Massenet had done two years before. However, if he entertained any idea that he might displace Massenet at Monte Carlo after rivalling him there he was to be disappointed, as the theatre retained connections with both men, who thereby were often to find themselves in awkward and uncomfortable proximity.

The pairing of *Hélène* with *La Navarraise*, repeated two days after the première and again in the two Covent Garden performances in June, also provided a curious contrast between the violent passion of the latter and the sedate treatment of the Homeric legend. The impression of lofty detachment in the new work was reinforced by Melba's dignified portrayal of the fated heroine, which was very much in line with her reputation for a certain coldness in interpretation as well as for vocal freshness and purity. This point was picked up by one of the few critics who did not find the opera dull. The *Musical Standard*'s reviewer wrote after the Covent Garden performances:

It seems to me that, dully played or not, it is wrong to sneer at operatic music as good as this. It may not be impressive in a creative sense, but there is individuality of method and phrase of a pronounced order. Nor is that all. We have a novel operatic treatment, musical and dramatic. I admired the stately and exquisitely refined tone of the whole creation. I also admired, even more deeply, the magnificent musicianship of the score . . . The chromatic chorus behind the scenes in the vision of Troy in flames, representing the suffering of the inhabitants, is an ear-haunting inspiration.

The work, he noted, drew on both Wagnerian and Italianate elements without being unduly influenced by either, so that Saint-Saëns "seems to have written set melody and yet avoided making that impression", and underlying it was "that harmonic refinement always associated with the work of the French composer".[4]

Melba's cold dignity was certainly in line with Saint-Saëns's perception of the role. Singer and composer became close companions during their stay in Monaco and often walked out together. Either through weariness or, more likely, inhibition in female company, he was for the most part uncharacteristically silent during these walks, Melba recalled, but the old talkativeness occasionally returned in "a volley of observations on music, opera and life in general". The vocal and intellectual boisterousness of the young man was still there, but Melba, like many of her contemporaries, saw only the elderly eccentric. She was particularly amused by an incident on the way to a party. Saint-Saëns left the seclusion of his hotel room reluctantly and joined her in the carriage in sullen mood. Suddenly he insisted on going back to the hotel for his toothbrush. On regaining the carriage he explained, in answer to her puzzled look, that he had no key but had found that his toothbrush opened the door, so he always carried it with him. And he patted the toothbrush "affectionately with his long, clever fingers". Once when he called on her, the servant forgot to tell her he was in the hall; he waited a short while then announced his presence himself by playing loud chords on the piano.[5]

From Monaco he travelled to Naples, but his stay there was troubled by his manservant's illness, an early indication of the cancer that was eventually to kill him. Concert life was about to resume with a vengeance. In April he was in Paris playing a Mozart concerto at the Conservatoire, in a programme otherwise consisting of his own works, including the C minor symphony and *Le Déluge*. In May he was in London to play his *Africa* fantasy with the Queen's Hall Orchestra under Henry Wood, and at the beginning of June he travelled to Edinburgh for a chamber concert of his works with the violinist Jacques Thibaud and the cellist Josef Hasselmans – both still in their twenties. (Thibaud was to die in an air crash in 1953.) His appearance was hailed as a momentous event in the artistic history of the city, comparable to previous visits by Chopin, Rubinstein and Grieg, for "since the death of Brahms, M. Saint-Saëns has generally been regarded as without rival in the excellence and variety of his musical compositions", commented the *Scotsman*. And there was a big audience, considering that it was out of the concert season. "The fair sex predominated, and the flush of summer costumes lent brilliance to the scene." The composer's age was in obvious contrast with the youth of his colleagues, which made his "hale and hearty appearance" all the more impressive.[6] The programme included the F major trio, the C minor cello sonata, the D minor violin sonata and the Havanaise. The composer was the soloist in his Caprice on *Alceste* and, as extras, Chopin's Etude Op. 10 No. 3 and an improvisation on the slow movement theme of Haydn's 'Surprise' symphony. The reviews of his playing confirm some of its essential features, the technical brilliance and the absence of expression, "a strange lack of sustained tone in cantabile passages", as the *Edinburgh Evening News* put it.[7] Archibald Henderson was in the audience and was struck by the "clear passage work and keen sense of rhythm".[8] "Years have not played havoc with the flexibility of his fingers and the firmness and certainty of his touch", said the *Scotsman*, aware that the concert was something special in the musical life of the city. "Everything was beautifully clear . . . The performance lifted the audience to a plane of art that is wholly above the level of the average concert. It was marked by a certain dignity and quietude that made an immediate appeal." The visit was felt to be quite a coup by Edinburgh's concert organisers: among the inducements was the provision of the composer's preferred make of piano, an Erard. After a rapturous ovation he was presented with a book on Edinburgh bound in vellum and gold and later completed his visit by an excursion to the Forth Bridge.[9]

From Edinburgh he returned to London to see *Hélène* at Covent Garden, which followed a concert of his chamber works at the new Aeolian Hall in Bond Street. There, he accompanied Wolff in the second violin sonata and the Australian contralto Ada Crossley sang two of his songs, 'La Cloche', and 'La Brise' from *Mélodies Persanes*. His Romance for violin, piano and organ, in which he took the organ part, was encored on demand. In between concerts he was writing music too, chiefly the *Caprice Andalou* for violin and orchestra.

Although he still travelled widely and frequently, Saint-Saëns gave up the homeless existence he had followed since the death of his mother and took a permanent address in Paris. On 21st June 1904, after the London première of *Hélène*, he moved into the ground floor at 17 Rue de Longchamp. Among his chief items of furniture were a piano surrounded by piles of scores and loose manuscripts, and a death mask of Beethoven. Arthur Rubinstein found when he visited "a small, fat man, baldish, with a short, rounded grey beard and two large warts asymmetrically positioned on either side of his nose". He looked like "a French bank official".[10] The disadvantage of a permanent address was, of course, that it made him more accessible to unwanted callers. Having settled in to his new home, he soon found the need again to escape the attention of favour-seekers. Over the next few years he acquired the habit of seeking refuge in the safe haven of rooms at a nearby hotel, letting it be known that he had "gone abroad". Thus he seemed to be more frequently absent from Paris than he really was. It became something of a standing joke to ask him, on a casual meeting, when he was leaving and, he confessed, "I don't always reply as politely as I should".[11]

As well as his faithful servant Geslin and his wife, the household consisted of two dogs, a griffon bitch called Lisette and her daughter Dalila. The dogs were Saint-Saëns's chief joy and he never ceased to be amused and fascinated by their ways, such as Dalila's habit of carrying a lump of sugar to her mother before taking one herself, or recognising the boom of the Eiffel Tower gun as the signal for lunch. He was especially intrigued by her reaction whenever he played the piano:

She uttered the most piercing cries. Whether she liked or detested it I do not know, for she came running up as soon as the music began instead of running away, though she raised such a series of howls that she had to be carried to the other end of the building as speedily as possible. Neither singing nor the playing of other instruments ever excited her to the same degree.

It reminded him of another dog he once had whose reaction to the piano was equally bizarre: it loved the sound and as soon as he began to play would get in the way by crouching by the pedals. To get rid of the animal, "all that was necessary was to play Chopin. Before eight bars had been played he had left the room, with dejected ears and his tail between his legs. However often the experiment was tried the result was invariably the same."[12]

Dogs seemed to bring out the child in him. Jacques Durand had a dog, and on entering his office one day, was astonished to find the composer, then over eighty, on all fours under the piano playing with it.[13] To Nellie Melba he was "one of the most amazingly youthful old men I have ever met".[14] It showed also in his boyish enthusiasm for new inventions, especially when they were allied to music. He was introduced to the gramophone as a by-product of his association with Melba in Monaco. The English Gramophone and Typewriting Company, keen to sign up the singer, sent its sales manager Sydney Dixon there to dazzle her with the wonders of the new machine. She was dining with Saint-Saëns when Dixon played them a record of Caruso, and they were both impressed by what was probably the first recorded music they had ever heard. The result was that Dixon secured the composer as well as the singer, for Melba went onto disc on her return to London, while in Paris Saint-Saëns became one of the first composers of any stature (the others being Brahms and Grieg) to be heard on record. The recordings, made in 1904, are of his own works, but piano rolls he made later for the Welte-Mignon piano-player also included Chopin's F sharp major Impromptu. They confirm his reputation for technical mastery, speed, and a pearly touch devoid of emotional intensity. The gramophone, by making music available to greater numbers of people, was in line with his belief in science as improving and elevating the life of man – as was the new medium of cinema. The film, like the gramophone, he saw as demonstrating the educational and practical value of the partnership of science and art, and in 1908 he became the first composer of rank to write film music.

L'Assassinat du Duc de Guise, about political events in 1563, was the first in a series of 'art films', sponsored by Charles Pathé, which sought to transfer onto the screen all the sophisticated techniques of the theatre, in acting, lighting, direction – and music. When filming was complete, Saint-Saëns was shown a preview and in due course supplied a score to accompany five scenes, for a small chamber group with piano or harmonium. The light, smooth-flowing style was admirably suited to the purpose, easy enough on the ear to insinuate itself into the action without distracting the viewer, yet distinctive enough to lend weight to atmosphere and mood. As with *Andromache*, there is no attempt at period recreation, but it is altogether a more satisfactory exercise than the Racine music. There was, of course, no spoken dialogue to consider, and as the play was already on film, pace and characterisation were in no danger of distortion. The music had to fit the drama, not the other way round. It was a project appropriate to a composer whose work for the theatre, from *Samson et Dalila* to the Béziers spectacles, has something of the cinematic about them. It is a pity, then, that despite his approval of the cinema in principle, Saint-Saëns made no further contribution to the medium. And he did not attend *L'Assassinat*'s public showing.

His chief scientific interest remained astronomy, in which Marie Fauré continued to share his enthusiasm. He arranged for her to use his telescope while it was with his cousin at Dieppe, and bought scientific instruments as gifts for her two sons. In November 1904, prior to a trip to Milan for an Italian version of *Hélène* at La Scala, he attended a conference on mirages at the Astronomical Society, contributing details of his experiences of the phenomenon during journeys on the Red Sea and in Suez. And in August 1905 he went to Burgos in Spain to observe a solar eclipse, "a sight even more marvellous than I expected", he enthused to Fauré, urging him to convey his excitement to Marie and the boys.[15] He was to witness another eclipse at St Germain-en-Laye six years later.

But music was still the tyrannical mistress. The *Caprice Andalou* was premièred by Wolff at a Lamoureux concert on 13th November 1904 and carries on the score a preface in praise of Cadiz, indicating that the piece was inspired by memories of the town. As *Parysatis* had provided an opportunity for a late indulgence in the orientalism of his earlier years, so the *Caprice* was a vehicle for another return to the Spanish idiom which had so delighted him over many years. The piece is built on melodies and rhythms noted during travels in Andalucia, chiefly around two contrasting themes; the first gently lilting, the second more boisterous. The violin part displays both lyrical and virtuoso writing of great finesse and brilliance, notably in the dazzling perpetual motion in the final section, which also introduces a habañera. Although some turns of phrase could now be described as clichéd, there are passages of great individuality, imagination and charm radiating from the clarity and delicacy of orchestration of which Saint-Saëns was a master. The music conveys a sense of well-being under the sunny skies that he loved, but, as in *Une Nuit à Lisbonne* and other musical pictures, there is also a melancholy haze of nostalgia for remembered delights.

He wrote the second cello sonata in February 1905 at Biskra, Algeria. It was an exceptionally bad winter there which made the health-sensitive composer ill at ease. Finding at least some sun farther south, he also took delight in the company of three gazelles he befriended during his stay there. The F major sonata, like its predecessor, contrasts with its near-contemporary concerto in its more regular form, with subtle deviations contained within four separate movements. There is very little, however, either of the C minor sonata's impassioned heaviness or its bleak austerity, the character here being one of sturdy optimism softened occasionally by an almost Slavic pathos and melancholy. Saint-Saëns told Servières that "music is a soft paste that can be shaped and moulded at will".[16] In this sonata, form as well as melodic content is moulded to the interests of an easy flow of sound, a marked feature of the composer's late works. There is a rippling interplay between cello and piano, between subject and counter-subject, rather than a working out of conflict and struggle. The adaptation of formal elements to this end is clearly demonstrated in the first movement, where the normal key relationships of sonata form are abandoned and the first subject consists of a group of contrasted melodic fragments, the chief of which are the bold opening flourish and a brief, more lyrical figure that returns in the recapitulation in the subdominant. The second subject, reminiscent of that of the slow movement of the D minor violin sonata, appears in the 'foreign' keys of D major and E flat.

The scherzo with eight variations is perhaps the sonata's finest movement, the theme recalling the macabre moods of the young Saint-Saëns and its delicate chromatic slides adding an extra touch of ghostly menace in fleeting shadows. The slow movement features an elegiac theme on the cello, introduced by soft chords floating upwards on the piano: twice the calm is interrupted by turbulent episodes in the minor key. The final allegro restores the mood of vigorous confidence stated at the outset, a sonata movement where the opening subject of answering phrases between cello and piano is a clear expression of Saint-Saëns's belief that "truth is in simplicity, purity and straightforwardness".[17] An extended development ends with the second half of this subject re-establishing the home key to bring the sonata to an energetic conclusion.

The sonata was first played by Hollmann at a Paris soirée later in 1905. By this time Saint-Saëns was working on a new opera for Monte Carlo, in response to a request from Prince Albert which reached him in Algiers in January. Still resentful of the apparent failure of most of his work for the theatre, he was not in a mood to make further efforts in that direction, but Monte Carlo seemed to offer new hope. *Hélène* was to be repeated there in March (with a new cast and coupled with Mascagni's *Amica*), and the composer was keen to maintain the friendly relations he had built up with the management. He liked the town, and it held the possibility of matching and perhaps outshining Massenet. A request from the French government for a new work for the Paris Opéra had less appeal: there, from long experience, he expected only trials and tribulations, with small reward. However, to deflect any ill-feeling there might have been from the Paris authorities he asked Gunsbourg to publish both Prince Albert's letter and his reply, to show that he already had a firm commitment. For the director, this was also good publicity for the forthcoming season, as Saint-Saëns's acceptance, posted from Algiers, suggested that the composer was coming out of retirement from the stage especially for the Monte Carlo opera house.

The theatre no longer attracts me and I very much thought that with Hélène, *I had said farewell to it for good. But how can I resist the request which Your Serene Highness deigns to express with an insistence so flattering to me? I shall strive to meet it to the best of my powers . . .*[18]

He took for his collaborator Augé de Lassus, the author of *Phryné*, who this time supplied a libretto of sombre, tragic character, a story of revenge in Corsica in Napoleonic times – fairly up to date by the standard of Saint-Saëns's operas. *L'Ancêtre* is a full-length work in three acts, which he worked on in the summer of 1905 while staying by Lake Maggiore and completed in Switzerland in August. He was dissatisfied with the finale and asked de Lassus to rewrite it. The revised version reached him on the eve of his departure for Paris, and he set it during a train halt at Pontarlier, on the French side of the Swiss border.

In the autumn his attention was diverted to events at the Conservatoire, where he was still a member of the governing body. Dubois resigned as director in a row over the barring of Ravel from the Prix de Rome after four failed attempts to win it. Ravel's teacher Fauré, who, though he had been professor of composition at the Conservatoire for nine years, had never been a pupil there, was the surprise choice to take over. The move represented a defeat for the conservatives, as Fauré began to instigate a number of far-reaching reforms.

Saint-Saëns was soon giving him stern advice, concerning a plan to institute a preparatory singing class, which he called "absurd". Never mind that his one-time pupil was now an established composer and director of the Conservatoire, he had to listen to his old master. Writing in his most peremptory manner, he tells Fauré: "I ignore your feelings on the matter, but I am determined to make mine known to you." He then explains, quite reasonably, that training the voice is not like training instrumentalists: there are so many different methods of voice training and it would be seriously damaging for a pupil to be taught one of them in a preparatory class only to have to switch to another, perhaps entirely contrary method, after moving to a higher class. As in his vocal writing, he was anxious to preserve and protect the purity and integrity of what he apparently regarded as the most treasured instrument of all. Fauré assured him that the idea of such a class was "a myth created by those who would like to have the job: there would be no question of it". He was used to the magisterial tone Saint-Saëns often adopted towards him and the two men were as cordial as ever. Fauré's first letter to him as Conservatoire boss recognised the debt he owed to his former teacher. "As it is you who raised me and to whom I am indebted for what I am, it is entirely just that the first words I should write on the directorial table should be addressed to you!" Whereas Saint-Saëns had for so long recommended Fauré for various posts, he now approached him with recommendations for other aspirants to musical positions. In addition, he was always ready to press his views on educational and editorial matters. When Dukas published an edition of Couperin, he wrote to Fauré complaining that Dukas was not competent enough to deal with questions of ornament in baroque music. He urged him to adopt at the Conservatoire a uniform system of ornamentation, recommending Leopold Mozart's violin method as the best source. This would help to deter "entirely erroneous" interpretations. Such a standard had never been drawn up before, and "it is up to you to make good the gap".[19]

He also understood that his own presence on the Conservatoire council might compromise the new chief's authority, so he resigned, thus also freeing himself from Conservatoire commitments. He was, in any case, increasingly out of step with the council membership, and later told Fauré that he left because he could no longer work with "people whom I detest", assuring him that there was "no other reason". At the same time Fauré received his resignation with dismay, fearing it would be used as ammunition by die-hard opponents of the reforms he had set in motion, and he begged him to keep it quiet.[20] But however much Saint-Saëns's departure may have been interpreted as conservative disapproval of the new regime, Fauré rode the storm and held the directorship for fifteen years, presiding over a flowering of musical talent. In December Saint-Saëns wrote to Marie Fauré from Cannes, on his way to Cairo ("I had to leave before the bad weather made me breathless"), that he was delighted to see her husband, "Monsieur le Directeur", in the position where he "had the right to be, by virtue of his good nature and high artistic conscience".[21]

While in Cairo he accepted the honorary presidency of a new musical society in Paris called the Salon Nouveau, and wrote to his old friend Paul Viardot, one of the organisers, that the society should be "as broad-minded as possible; reject neither the eccentric nor the conventional. Refuse only those works that have nothing in them; for the rest let the public be the judge."[22] The advice is another qualification of the image of a man implacably opposed to all young composers. Only six years before in *Portraits et Souvenirs*, he had lamented the fact that new works still had little chance of a hearing, that the situation that had prevailed when he was young, when new works had to struggle against hostility or indifference, seemed to be returning. "If we continue in this vein, French music will soon be nothing more than a museum . . ."[23]

His own latest work was soon to be presented to the public. As with *Hélène*, he had to leave his Cairo paradise for Monte Carlo in February 1906 to help prepare the première of *L'Ancêtre*. However, again as with *Hélène*, he could look forward to the company of Fauré, who was to review the opera for *Le Figaro*. Félia Litvinne took the title role, and there were four performances, from 24th February to 3rd March. During this period, Saint-Saëns had the uncomfortable honour of being invited to the palace with Massenet.

The story of *L'Ancêtre* concerns a vendetta between the Fabiani and the Nera, on the lines of *Romeo and Juliet*, the ill-fated lovers here being Tebaldo Nera and Margarita, foster-sister of Vanina Fabiani. A hermit, Raphael, is on the verge of sealing a peace between the warring factions when Vanina's brother Leandri is shot and Nunciata, the ancestress, demands war against the old enemy. Tebaldo tells the hermit he killed Leandri in self-defence, but Nunciata orders Vanina to shoot him to avenge the death. Vanina, who also loves Tebaldo, refuses, and when Nunciata takes up the gun, stands in the way, and is herself killed. As with *Hélène*, the chief feature of the music is its disembodied charm, which suffuses the whole work and is especially striking in the love scenes and in the hermit's address to the bees. But all the freshness and refined vigour of the composer's late period were not enough to compensate for what appeared to be a lack of personal involvement and the music's detachment from the action on stage, particularly in the more dramatic moments. Fauré's review was entirely favourable: ever loyal to his old mentor he was not the most impartial critic. It would, however, be uncharitable to suggest that his judgement was in any way affected by Saint-Saëns's declaration only a week before the première that he intended to buy the autograph of Chopin's F major Ballade to present to the Conservatoire library, a promise he kept. Despite Fauré's praise and the sumptuous dinner given by Prince Albert after the first night, *L'Ancêtre* was not given again in the principality after its four performances. It appeared instead at Toulouse the following year and at the Paris Opéra-Comique in 1911. It even crossed the Atlantic, being performed in Montreal in 1912, but after a further production in Antwerp it faded from view, to join the growing list of Saint-Saëns's forgotten operas.

After the last performance of *L'Ancêtre* at Monte Carlo in 1906, Saint-Saëns looked to Béziers again. For the festival he wrote a cantata, *La Gloire de Corneille*, to mark the tercentenary of Corneille's birth, with words by the Parnassian poet Sebastian-Charles Leconte. (He later dedicated it to Fauré.) He then embarked on a tour of Italy, conducting a programme of his works at the Academy of St Cecilia in Rome on 26th March. Two days later he was joined in Florence by the seventeen-year-old American-born violinist Albert Spalding in the third violin concerto. Spalding's wealthy family lived in one of the Florentine palaces. Saint-Saëns stayed overnight, occupying a bedroom of huge proportions, with an equally large bathroom adjoining in which the tub was situated in the very centre. At breakfast, he was asked if he had enjoyed his bath. "Bath?" he exclaimed, "I would as soon bath in Carnegie Hall than in a room that size!"[24] He was to help advance Spalding's career by introducing him to Hans Richter, with whom the young violinist made his London debut the following year.

May 1906 marked the sixtieth anniversary of Saint-Saëns's first public concert. As on the fiftieth, he took part in a concert of his works at the Salle Pleyel, demonstrating that at seventy he had lost none of his pianistic agility. Fauré wrote that "his sinewy, supple fingers, his clear playing, whether vigorous or charming, and his style, with that same nobility and moderation, are as deserving today as they have always been", and he called for a revival of the neglected third concerto.[25] The playing was still characterised also by a tendency to fast speeds, and Saint-Saëns still took a delight in accelerating the tempo to the consternation of fellow performers. Pierre Monteux, however, remembered one occasion when he went to the other extreme and set an unusually slow tempo. It was in a performance of the Schumann concerto at the Dieppe Casino one summer. Saint-Saëns asked for the concert not to be advertised, as it would attract too many holiday-makers and "it would be too crowded and hot". There was still a full house, and it *was* hot, Monteux recalled. And "with a sardonic smile" Saint-Saëns played the concerto finale *andante*, much to everyone's surprise and amusement. He afterwards told Monteux that he took the piece more slowly than usual because "it breathes of spring, love and Goëthe".[26]

In June 1906 he agreed to open the Berlin Philharmonic season, playing under Nikisch – his first concert engagement in the city since being hounded out twenty years before. In July he was in London, giving the English première of the second cello sonata at the Bechstein Hall with Hollmann. The scherzo variations were especially well-received, the *Musical Times* calling them "full of poetic grace and unbroken charm". In this and in other works, his playing, said the journal, "is not only remarkable for its unalloyed beauty, but furnished a welcome contrast to the noisy poundings of young and unrestrained virtuosi".[27] It was now over ten years since he had first seriously considered retiring from the concert platform; instead, the momentum of a long performing career had kept him going. Yet, he had still not visited the United States, having repeatedly turned down invitations for winter tours there, partly because of other commitments, but mainly because of his health, explaining that he was "subject to illness from cold" and couldn't bear the Paris winter let alone the North American winter.[28] Yet with every year that passed, he risked leaving it too late, and with his long-held desire to go to America no doubt rekindled by his contact with the Spalding family, he finally accepted an invitation from the Knabe Piano Company to give a series of concerts in the States. Towards the end of October 1906 he boarded the liner *La Provence* at Le Havre bound for New York, to follow in the footsteps of Tchaikovsky and Dvořák. The experience was to make him think that perhaps it really was time to give up.

Before leaving Paris he had caught a heavy cold; on the Atlantic crossing it developed into influenza and tonsillitis, and ultimately diphtheria, paralysing his hands and legs. At one stage it looked fatal. He recovered sufficiently to be able to walk down the gang plank on arrival, helped by the ship's purser and the tour manager, but he was shaken and began to doubt the wisdom of undertaking a punishing seven weeks of concerts and travel. A nurse was called to watch over him night and day – and here was his first lesson in how differently things were done in America.

I feared a slovenly old woman but instead saw an exquisite creature, bright as a rose and fresh as spring, perfectly educated, discreet and gracious without either coquetry or prudery, the very sight of whom was a comfort and a cure. She would get up at midnight dressed in a kimono to see if the fever had risen or if the doctor's directions had been observed. Sometimes, they say, these delightful nurses marry their patients when they are cured . . .[29]

He was too ill to keep his first date in Boston, but made his American debut with the New York Symphony Orchestra under Frank Damrosch at Carnegie Hall on 3rd November. It was an all-American reception; he stepped onto the platform to a blazing fanfare and at the end of the concert received a huge decoration of flowers and flags, to tumultuous applause. He had regained his "quick and rather precise movements", noted the *New York Times*, which praised his playing as "full of charm in his rippling passages and runs; he phrases and sings a melody with distinction and point, and all is done with perfect repose . . . [but] within restricted limits of dynamic contrast and tonal colour". The critic was less impressed by the programme. "Nothing that he played called for eloquence or for feeling that even scratched the surface; and he gave no sign of either." Certainly the works chosen were hardly calculated to make a strong first impression: they included the *Africa* fantasy, with a version of the 'Wedding Cake' caprice and an orchestrated version of the Allegro Appassionato. It is possible that Saint-Saëns did not yet feel strong enough to tackle longer works and that the programme had been a late substitution: the orchestra, reported the *New York Times*, sounded under-rehearsed and was not always in time with the composer. It was a programme of "trifles", and in *Africa* "the listener is dragged breathlessly on through one coruscation after another; everything is treated in the frankest manner . . . without thought of developing the musical interest." As for the purely orchestral works, the central section of *Le Rouet d'Omphale* was "dull" and *Danse Macabre* "has lost some of the point of its fantastic imagination".[30] It was hardly the most auspicious introduction to the New World. Indeed, there was a considerably smaller turnout for the second Carnegie Hall concert, in which Saint-Saëns played his second piano concerto and was at the organ in the C minor symphony. Ironically, the *New York Times* critic wrote rather more favourably of it. In the concerto Saint-Saëns "seemed at times to be carried away by the impetuosity of the music; the phrasing was now and again slighted, to the detriment of the rhythm, yet the grace of those captivating themes has not often been more persuasively presented". The writer, like so many other critics, thought the use of the piano in the symphony a "miscalculation" and was irritated by the "dryness and didactic repetition" of the last movement, but praised the work as a whole for its "fine and noble ideas".[31] At a third Carnegie Hall concert Damrosch conducted the A minor symphony, which, said the press, "has undeniable charm, for all its slight appeal to the deeper feelings of the listener", and other orchestral works, with the composer playing the fifth concerto (a late substitution for the fourth).[32]

The tour took Saint-Saëns, attended throughout by a doctor, to Philadelphia where he heard a concert performance of *Samson et Dalila*, to Washington where he played the second concerto before President Theodore Roosevelt, to Chicago and as far west as Minneapolis, where the city's orchestra had been founded only three years before. Following his return to New York he gave a piano recital at Carnegie Hall, creating a stir by wearing long white gloves which he carefully removed, finger by finger. He played what the *New York Times* called a "quaint list" of pieces by Rameau and Bach, Beethoven's Op. 26 sonata, Chopin's Barcarolle, a potpourri of themes from *Samson et Dalila*, the 'Surprise' symphony improvisation, four of his own waltzes and a transcription of the quartet from *Henry VIII*. It was, said the paper, a programme "no modern pianist would dream of putting forward". But the familiar qualities of clarity and brilliance were there, and the Barcarolle was "a sober Chopin, in a cool, dry light".[33] He cancelled an organ recital at Plymouth Church, Brooklyn, because he was by now too exhausted to tackle an unfamiliar instrument, but gave a piano recital there instead.

Considering the near-fatal illness at the start of the visit, and his constant battle against the symptoms, it was a remarkable feat of stamina and endurance by the seventy-one-year-old. He wrote later to Emile Renaud: "Don't ask me how I was able to do a brilliant concert tour while ill, I know nothing of it myself. I was getting up out of bed to play concertos! . . ."[34] But, spurred on by his natural curiosity, he did manage between concerts to take afternoon walks and long drives along Fifth Avenue, Broadway and over Brooklyn Bridge. In a very real sense it was a meeting of the old and new worlds. Saint-Saëns, steeped in a European tradition, was fascinated by skyscrapers, lifts, telephones, comfortable trains and all the modern conveniences of a new way of life, in a new century. Skyscrapers, he reported to *Le Figaro*,

are most agreeable to live in. One looks down from them as from the height of a balloon and grows intoxicated with space and light. One may mount them in a few seconds by means of the electric elevator, one of those useful mechanisms to lighten existence which render life so agreeable over there.

He liked the individuality of buildings, admiring the "great elegance" of neo-classical facades in Washington and the colourful and "not always unskilful" imitations of Greek, Roman and Renaissance architecture in New York, so different from the uniform grey stone of Paris. He praised audiences as the most "attentive, silent and enthusiastic" he had known, and was proud that Americans "have not forgotten the role that France played in their independence". But he was less happy about other aspects of American society: "bad taste" in the lighter forms of theatre, operetta and burlesque, for which he blamed the Italian influence, and religious fundamentalism existing side by side with material progress, so that "in a country where millions are spent on science, a sect prospers which has declared war on medicine and pretends to cure disease by prayer".

He was confident that the new American civilisation would develop its own music independent of European influences, excited "less by what America is today than by the idea of what she is able to become".[35] "The temperament is here and, I believe, the capability, and the time will come when America will cease to follow and will speak for itself", he told the *New York Times*. And he advocated, as part of that process, the study of Indian music, which "came from the soil", before it disappeared, and regretted that he had not had the opportunity to hear it for himself.[36]

But for all his enthusiasm for America, Saint-Saëns found the attentions lavished on him by strangers taxing his nerves, and he longed to withdraw from the socialising to the solitude of his hotel room. To the *New York Times* critic he appeared "sensitive as a child", who, it seemed, "avoids showing his feelings to a world that may not understand".[37] And for all his fascination with the wonders of the New World, his roots were firmly in the past. "Born in the first half of the nineteenth century, I belong to the past. In spite of all the comforts of the young Nation, I shall always prefer our old cities and the holy relics of the Old Continent."[38] There was to be no great musical tribute to his visit on the lines of Dvorˇ ák's *New World* symphony. Instead, a year later he wrote a modest setting of Psalm 150, which he sent and dedicated to the New York architect Whitney Warren. It is one of the few published works of his adult life he never heard played (a plan to conduct it in London in the summer of 1909 came to nothing).

After a farewell dinner in New York on 23rd December he set sail for home, now firmly resolved to give up concert work except for occasional appearances for charity. Again, it was a resolution he was not to keep: he was still, to use his own phrase, "like a fish in water" where music was concerned. In the first week of 1907, barely two weeks after his return, he was taking part in a Beethoven festival, conducting the ninth symphony at the Opéra – something of a curiosity, as he switched the usual order of the two inner movements, placing the adagio first.

There was more work in February in Monte Carlo, where the opera house, perhaps to compensate for not taking up *L'Ancêtre* again, was instead reviving *Le Timbre d'Argent*, his first opera, which had lately resurfaced in Germany. The cast included the eighteen-year-old English soprano Maggie Teyte, who had just made her Monte Carlo debut in Offenbach. There were three performances, between 26th February and 3rd March. "It made a big impact", he told Renaud, "and I took much pleasure in it."[39] A month later, after a week in Bordighera, he went to Berlin. There Prince Albert, a personal friend of the Kaiser, took his opera company to perform extracts from its repertory, including the first act of *Samson et Dalila*. As an attempt to improve Franco-German relations, it proved counter-productive: the prince was roundly condemned in the French press, and the Kaiser's lavish treatment of the visitors was criticised by his ministers as pandering to a potential enemy in an increasingly tense international climate. The visit was not entirely comfortable for Saint-Saëns either, as he encountered Massenet at official receptions (one of them attended also by Grieg), and stood with him to receive the applause after the final performance. As he already held the German Order of Merit, he did not share in the honours bestowed on the visiting artists, but received from the Kaiser a signed photograph instead.

A performance of *Salome* in Berlin confirmed Saint-Saëns's distaste for the work of Richard Strauss. He wrote later: "All tastes are in nature, and it is possible to love the music of *Salome* – as children love cod liver oil . . . [it is] music where you can hear, among other nice things, a voice singing in one key while the orchestra accompanies in another."[40] Reviewing the Paris première in *Le*

Temps, he described the opera as "a poem of hysterics" in which the orchestra alternately

quivers, sings, yelps, howls, goes mad, thunders, calms down, works itself into a passion, coughs, sneezes . . . At one moment it sounds like the slish-slash of silk being torn, at another like the smashing of a pane of glass . . . While one group of instruments is wandering about in one key, another, without hesitation, moves about in a neighbouring key, while the voices go off in another direction.[41]

But it was not only the technical liberties in the music that dismayed him: he was saddened too by what he regarded as the injurious treatment of the natural beauty of the human voice, an extension of the Wagnerian integration of voice and orchestra. In his article in the *Neue Freie Presse* in Vienna in 1906 he wrote that in contemporary opera

the human voice, formerly the undisputed mistress, has been reduced to a slave through the irritating abuse which is made of her power. The outcome of this state of things is the denying of all rules which have been evolved in the course of time, and the shaking of the very foundation on which the whole structure of music has been erected during the last four centuries.

He longed for a day when "the human voice, that living, god-inspired instrument, will regain the place which is its due, and line, shape and colour will unite in perfect equipoise."[42] But by 1921, the last year of his life, he had despaired of any such restoration, and declared that "the reign of the great singers has faded".[43] For this he blamed the influence of Wagner, who "would have liked to suppress the art of singing altogether" with his theories of vocal and orchestral integration. The popularity of the music dramas was due to the fact that Wagner "often forgot to apply this principle".[44] By 1913 Saint-Saëns's disillusion with Wagner was extending even to those aspects of the operas he had once admired. He still acknowledged "many beautiful things" in them, but

unhappily, apart from Tristan, *what tedious and useless longeurs there are in these works . . . Isolde and Brünnhilda at least are sublime, but we have heard so much of them! As for Parsifal, to whom the kisses of Kundry give stomach cramps, it really is too ridiculous.*[45]

The excesses of the post-Wagnerians left him, if not reconciled to, at least more respectful than formerly towards Italian opera. He disliked the trend towards realism in such works as *I Pagliacci* and *La Bohème*, which was directly opposed to his aspirations towards an historical and scenic beauty. He was especially scornful when the trend reached France in the form of Charpentier's *Louise*. He also remained critical of Italian comic opera, accusing it of "levity without point or moral".[46] But the Italians seemed to him closer to harmonic and melodic rectitude than the Germans, and he applauded serious Italian opera that was less obviously of the *verismo* kind. "Certainly all that glitters is not gold in the modern Italian school", he wrote in a letter of 1910. "But was this not always so in all that has come to us from Italy, even in the time when Italian works were sacred, and you were not allowed to find fault with them? . . . I take great delight in a production of *Tosca* or *Fedora*." The complaint here was more about the singers who still, as of old, embellished their roles without respect for the composer's intentions: he would have liked to hear new Italian operas "before singers added their abominable 'traditions' to them, for which it would be unfair to make the composers responsible".[47]

After being a guest of the Kaiser, it was Saint-Saëns's turn to play host when he returned to Paris in the spring of 1907, organising a reception at the Salle Pleyel for Rimsky-Korsakov, who had arrived for a series of concerts of Russian music. But he was soon on the move again, heading for his second and 'farewell' visit to Edinburgh, and stopping on the way in London to hear the Royal Choral Society sing *Samson et Dalila* at the Queen's Hall. Thibaud was again the violinist at Edinburgh but this time the cellist was Hollmann, and the programme included the second piano trio, the andante of which had to be repeated by popular demand, the F major cello sonata and the A major violin concerto (in piano reduction), which was as usual billed – to the composer's annoyance, no doubt – as a 'concert piece'. Again the reviews spotlighted some of the basic ingredients of his playing, including its formidable technique and its lack of tonal gradation: his "technical accomplishments", said the *Scotsman*, "do not carry him to those extremes of pianissimo and fortissimo in which the younger generation of virtuosi delight".[48]

In June he was in Oxford, to be presented with an honorary doctorate from the Chancellor, Lord Curzon, by Sir Hubert Parry. Glazunov was another recipient, as were such literary giants as Rudyard Kipling and Mark Twain. The ceremony took place at the Sheldonian Theatre, where Saint-Saëns played the prelude to *Le Déluge* and other pieces on the organ while the guests took their places. He had become France's unofficial musical ambassador, and if as he said, he was now part of the national fabric, he was indeed being carved in stone. In October he was at Dieppe to see a statue of himself unveiled, a rare experience for most people, let alone a composer. (The only previous example that springs to mind is that of Handel.) As he pointed out in reply to the mayor's tribute, statues were normally of dead people, who did not have to make a speech. As well as a concert of his music, an Ode to Saint-Saëns was read out, written by the director of the theatre in whose foyer the statue was placed, facing the sea. It showed the composer seated, writing a score perched on his knee. Complementing the Saint-Saëns museum and the Rue Saint-Saëns, it confirmed both his family links with the town and his status as a musician of eminence and long standing. It also cast him more than ever in the mould of an establishment figure, embodying an age that had passed, and to many in the musical world the man seemed like a museum piece himself. Few of the rising young composers of the period took him seriously. "It is the fashion just now – and not only in France – to regard him as lacking in modernity", as *The Times* delicately put it.[49] Elsewhere he was attacked for lacking emotional appeal, a point that carried some weight in the age of late romanticism but seems less relevant ninety years later. During his 1906 tour of the United States, the *New York Times* noted: "How often is the intelligence of the listener beguiled with a movement of impeccable skill and ingenuity to which the heart has completely refused to yield conviction."

More favourable critics countered that, in the words of Pierre Lalo,

it may be that other ways of feeling and expression seem more seductive and more touching than this limpid and concise manner, and that you require in the works you love a deeper soul. But you will not find in any of our contemporaries a more consummate knowledge, a more perfect technique, a style of writing at once more sober and more finished, or a more complete mastery of the art.[50]

To W. Wells-Harrison, writing in *The Strad* in 1915, this approach was indeed capable of drawing an emotional response, but of a special kind that showed that soul-searching profundity need not be the only means of achieving it.

It is, perhaps, in absolute greatness of utterance that he fails to attain that immortality which falls to the lot of the really great ones, but his music has the power to charm and occasionally lift us to emotional heights . . . Often his work reaches the heart where the ponderous efforts of the would-be profound composer fail miserably.[51]

Ravel, to the surprise of many, continued to hold Saint-Saëns up as a model for young composers. But perhaps the most loyal supporter was Fauré, who declared: "There is hardly a musician, in France or elsewhere, whose works are a source of beautiful and noble thoughts to the same degree as his."[52] Writing to his wife, Fauré lamented the fact that the

excessive polyphony, even though it is always quite justified, of Wagner, the chiaroscuro *effects of Debussy, the vulgar and passionate writhings of Massenet, these are the only things which move or attract the public today, while the clear, honest music of Saint-Saëns, which attracts me more than anything, leaves this same public indifferent. All this sends shivers up my spine!*[53]

Charles Malherbe defended Saint-Saëns against a public who "have trouble imagining that this man of simple style, an enemy of vulgar publicity, a stranger to artistic coteries, has his place marked out in the temple of memory, and carries on his brow the mark of the elect."[54]

As for Saint-Saëns himself, he was increasingly out of sympathy with the contemporary scene, and was coming to regard even Fauré as tainted by modernism. When in 1909 Fauré took the presidency of the new Independent Music Society (Société Musicale Indépendante), a breakaway from the National Society, he urged him to have nothing to do with "those hooligans". And in March 1913 he confessed to Lecocq that he was "making a superhuman effort to come to terms with *Pénélope*", Fauré's new opera.

I simply can't get used to never settling down in any key, to consecutive fifths and sevenths and to chords demanding a resolution that never comes . . . What an example for students to see their master constantly breaking the rules before they're taught . . . In travelling through all the keys without stopping, one experiences an overpowering fatigue . . . Prométhée, *now there was a masterpiece.*[55]

He had become a rare phenomenon, an established composer who had survived from the mid-nineteenth century into one of the most far-reaching periods of change in the history of music. One can only wonder what his near-contemporary Brahms would have made of it all if he had lived as long.

The most famous scene of battle between the conservatives and the progressives was, of course, the first performance of *Le Sacre du Printemps* at the Théâtre des Champs-Elysées on 29th May 1913, conducted by Monteux. Monteux's mother shared a box with Saint-Saëns and recalled that, as all hell broke loose in the theatre, he kept repeating "he's mad, he's mad" before walking out.[56] A year later he attended the first concert performance of the ballet, wrapped in furs and looking, according to Casella, "like a patient in a dentist's waiting room". At the first note of the opening solo he turned to Casella and asked: "What is that instrument?" On being told it was a bassoon he cried "It's a lie!" and stormed out, slamming the door.[57]

He had in fact slammed the door on most contemporary music and retreated to his own musical world, with its memories and ideals. He was not unduly troubled by the often bitter attacks made on him as a result of his outspoken views – "I am not absolutely frank with everyone, it's impossible, but with almost everyone, and that makes me many enemies!"[58] He remained, as always, impervious to criticism, attributing it largely to professional jealousy. He believed that his work was the best answer to it, and he would continue resolutely to compose and comment as he saw fit. Charges of chauvinism he readily and even proudly admitted: his family, he declared, boasted three army generals among their ancestors, so that by inheritance, "I was born a chauvinist and a chauvinist I shall remain until my last breath".[59] This sense of his own worth more than compensated for any hurt he may have felt from his critics. "I love to be loved, and do not understand that people hate me, who never did harm to anyone," he wrote to Pierre Aguétant. "I have written some considerable works, and that is enough. I realised it as soon as my brain began to outdo those of so many others, who have never forgiven me for it."[60] He did, though, begin to ponder the durability of his reputation as a composer after his death. He had suppressed *Le Carnaval des Animaux*, but he accepted that some of his published work might not survive him, that "certain works of mine will disappear", having been written in "a time of pausation, like the repose which comes after a day of toil".[61] Nevertheless, he remained defiantly confident that his name would live on. "Time alone will judge," he told the musicologist Jules Ecorcheville in 1909, "but on seeing the solid impression made by *Samson*, written thirty-seven years ago, and, the other day in Darmstadt, seeing the reception given to a quintet [the piano quintet] written by me fifty years ago, I cannot refrain from having some hope in my destiny." *Pelléas et Mélisande*, in contrast, he did not expect to last forty years.[62]

He was not always criticised on musical and artistic grounds. Some of the attacks were crudely personal, and even bizarre. Largely, it seems, because of his facial characteristics there was much speculation about his suspected Jewish ancestry, and that this was intended by some as a means of lowering his standing is perhaps not surprising in the France of the Dreyfus affair. To a Jewish writer, of course, such speculation would be of interest for opposite reasons. Gdal Salewski, for instance, writing after Saint-Saëns's death, argued that the composer's mother was of Jewish origin, and that *Samson et Dalila* was the only opera of his to endure because in it he had used the Hebrew scale, thereby remaining true to his "ancestral inspiration".[63] Equally far-fetched was the theory that he was Jewish on his father's side, and that his surname had been adopted to displace the patronymic of Kohn.[64]

In addition, the wildest rumours circulated about his private life, his frequent sojourns in North Africa leading to allegations of sexual activities with Arab boys. He had, it was reported in recognisably tabloid fashion, worn a "pink dress" when receiving a visit from the Archbishop of Carthage. Female impersonation was nothing new to Saint-Saëns – it had been his stock in trade at society charades over many years – but the likely explanation for the story is that the "dress" was a *galabeh*: the composer liked to go native in North Africa and often wore a fez. He was certainly fond of the company of talented and personable young men, many of whom were glad to be associated with his prestige and influence, and among those with whom he formed close relationships were his one-time pupil Reynaldo Hahn and Marcel Proust, both of whom were indeed homosexual. He sometimes used effusively endearing language in letters to male correspondents: "You are adorable, and I do not deserve to have friends such as you", says one.[65] Towards women, on the other hand, he could be as rude as ever, and professionally he scorned what he saw as their growing influence. One victim of his notorious rudeness was an importunate woman at a party who invited him to dinner and would not take no for an answer when he replied that he was too busy. "Couldn't you be very nice, just for me?" she cooed, to which he snapped "I don't want to be nice to you".[66] He expressed his professional mistrust of women while canvassing for Fauré's election to the Institute in 1909, urging him to cultivate the support of a countess he knew, with the sardonic comment that "it is above all through women" that people got in.[67] And he later told Fauré that he had resigned from the Conservatoire in 1905 partly because it had become "packed with journalists, theatre directors and women", who had laid it open to outside pressures.[68]

Yet one of the more distasteful stories about him demonstrates that his sexual preference was very definitely for women. Maggie Teyte came across him in Chicago during his second visit to the United States in 1915. She recalled that he caused a panic in the hotel by bursting in on the director of the Chicago Opera in a heated state, demanding a woman as a matter of urgency. A suitable professional was eventually found and taken to his room, where the seventy-nine-year-old was lying in a post-orgasmic languor, lamenting that she had arrived "too late".[69] John Philip Sousa, who met him in California on the same tour, noted that he "seemed always to have an eye" for the ladies, especially those of ample proportions. During their walks together "he would nudge me, calling my attention to 'yonder beaming beauty!' The broader the 'beam' the greater his delight!"[70] To Pierre Aguétant he argued that the male body was the more aesthetically pleasing because it was in line with classical proportions and not "exaggerated" but that "we prefer the body of a woman because we are men".[71] To the gossips, he remained indifferent. "If it is said that I have a bad character, I assure you that it is all the same to me. Take me as I am."[72]

The composer's fatherless upbringing and his strong devotion to his mother and her memory may be seen in post-Freudian days as strongly suggestive of a homosexual leaning. But there is no conclusive evidence to support such an idea. What is clear is that Saint-Saëns felt very deep affection for those close to him and would do everything in his power to help them. Fauré recognised the "discreet and loving machinations" of his mentor behind a request from the Prince of Monaco for a concert of his (Fauré's) music in the principality.[73] And he felt acute distress on hearing of illness and death, especially of young people. Finding Aguétant grown thin and pale, he took him in his arms and, with tears in his eyes, urged him to take up "physical culture" to build up his strength.[74] The advice recalls that which he gave to Godowsky thirty years earlier, when he is said to have wanted passionately to adopt him. This side of his character is most clearly evident in his deep attachment to his servant Geslin and his sometimes anxious concern for his health in the face of a spreading cancer. In 1914, when Geslin needed an operation, Saint-Saëns wrote to Renaud that "Gabriel is a part of me, I can well confess to you. I shall not be consoled at losing him."[75] From all this emerges a picture of a frustrated father rather than an aged homosexual, one who had shown a strong paternal instinct from at least the time when he taught at the Ecole Niedermeyer, and who had had those instincts cruelly thwarted by the deaths of his two infant children. In this light, his young friends, to whom he showed such strong emotion and even possessiveness, become a kind of substitute family, helping to soothe a deep sense of loneliness and isolation. This was made even sharper by seeing the sons of his favourite pupil, Fauré, grown up and distinguishing themselves. The tears and tender concern for young people, the sudden and dramatic abandoning of his wife, the seemingly inevitable personality clash with most women and the apparent inability to reconcile marriage with a demanding life in music, together suggest that the tragedy of Saint-Saëns's personal life was that he wanted to be a father without being a husband.

Fauré remarked to Jacques Durand that Saint-Saëns "keeps very quiet about his concerns for those he loves".[76] People who came to be on intimate terms with him still wondered what had become of the sour, ill-tempered ogre the public knew. Outbursts of angry impatience could alternate quite rapidly with genuine, friendly good humour. "I have said, re-said and written that it will not be possible for me to take part in the concert", he wrote in answer to a persistent request. "Will you have the grace at last to leave me in peace?" There followed almost immediately after a note to the same correspondent full of effusive expressions of affection.[77] In the autumn of 1910, while in London, he was invited by Sir Hubert Parry, director of the Royal College of Music, to take a student rehearsal of the C minor symphony. At one point he lost patience with the second violins and angrily ordered their leader, the young Eugene Goossens, to demonstrate how the passage should go. The terrified student fluffed it. After glaring at him "for what seemed ages", Goossens recalled, he removed his pince-nez and remarked in French to the whole orchestra: "Nice boy, but what a terrible violinist!" "I felt crushed and humiliated", says Goossens in his autobiography. "When he finished and started to leave the rostrum, we stood up. At that moment, the great man caught my eye – and winked!"[78]

Saint-Saëns spent the winter of 1907–08 in Egypt, where he wrote for the Khedive a march for military band, *Sur les bords du Nil,* one of very few works written at this time. In March 1908 he sailed for Monte Carlo, where *Henry VIII* was given two performances to close the season, the first a gala occasion in aid of the League of Hygiene's campaign against tar dust on the Nice-Menton road.

His domestic peace was disturbed in April 1908 by marital rows. Relations between Geslin and his wife had been deteriorating for a while, causing Saint-Saëns to take flight to a nearby hotel while the storm lasted. He recognised that a divorce was inevitable. As the couple lodged with him jointly he realised also that he had to dismiss them both, but he could not bear to be separated from his devoted servant, and wrote to a friend: "I *know* that I shall take Gabriel back when the crisis is over."[79] And he did take him back.

Fauré's interests too he continued to watch over. In the autumn of 1908 the Conservatoire director was working on his opera *Pénélope*, and Saint-Saëns was annoyed that Johann Wolff had written to him asking him to play at the Concerts Society. "I moaned at him [Wolff] for having disturbed your work", he told Fauré. "He does not know how odious the least correspondence is in such circumstances" and he added: "I absolutely forbid you to reply to me. When one has been working all day letter-writing is a torture which I well know and want to spare you from."[80] Aguétant records that Saint-Saëns's reaction to finding mail on his own desk was to fly into a rage then plunge his head into a basin of cold water.[81]

During the winter of 1908–09 he was busy canvassing support for Fauré's election to the Institute, writing from Las Palmas in February that "I have already written about forty letters and I shall write several more; and I shall do everything I can to be there at the critical moment".[82] True to his word, he broke away from rehearsals in Monte Carlo for incidental music he had written for Eugène Brieux's play *La Foi* to be in Paris for the vote on 13th March. Fauré was duly elected to the Institute, narrowly beating – after five counts – his rival Widor. Before leaving Monte Carlo he heard from a thankful Fauré that the Parisian weather had turned out "very mild. I was quite worried for you."[83] In fact, Saint-Saëns did catch cold but was well enough to take a rehearsal of *Phryné* at the Opéra-Comique.

The cold cleared on his return to Monte Carlo and he was able to devote his energies to *La Foi*, which was produced on 10th April. The play is set in Upper Egypt in the Middle Kingdom period. Besides its theme of the conflict between reason and blind faith, a favourite philosophical subject, as we have seen, it also appealed to Saint-Saëns because it allowed him to indulge his favourite exercise of period reconstruction, this time drawing on scales and folk melodies he had noted down during his many stays in Egypt and on his observations of instruments depicted in tomb paintings. The score includes music for guitar, cymbals and pipes, and notable pieces are two Hymns to Isis, in the first and fourth acts, a plaintive water-drawer's song, a funeral dirge and a march for the entrance of the high priest. *La Foi* opened in London on 14th September in a translation called *False Gods*, and ran at His Majesty's theatre for sixty-two performances over the next two months, with Herbert Beerbohm Tree as the high priest. The music was published the following year as 'three symphonic tableaux' and the whole production was revived at the Paris Odeon in May 1912, with Saint-Saëns conducting.

The London performances of *False Gods* were a kind of postscript to a major theatrical event earlier in the year: the English censor had finally passed *Samson et Dalila* for the stage – through the influence of a "highly placed person" widely believed to have been King Edward. It opened at Covent Garden on 24th April 1909. Louise Kirkby Lunn was Delilah, a role with which she was to become identified, in a lavish production that firmly established the opera in London. The composer joined the cast for the first night curtain call, but through the triumph *The Times* saw the irony of the opera's much delayed appearance. "We must regret that a work which belongs so very obviously to the last quarter of the nineteenth century should be presented as a novelty, since it cannot fail to strike all who are unfamiliar with its history as curiously old-fashioned."[84] It was still playing in June, when Charles Dalmorès took over the male lead from the unsatisfactory Maurice Fontaine, having already sung the role in Vienna and New York. The composer wanted to return to London to hear him but *L'Ancêtre* was to be given at Aix-les-Bains and he had to attend rehearsals there.

He had now achieved a lasting success on the London stage, but it was Monte Carlo that was to see the late and final flowering of his operatic endeavours. *Hélène* was given again there in 1909 and two seasons later the curtain went up on *Déjanire*. These last years in Monte Carlo also saw a mellowing of personal relations with Massenet, with whom Saint-Saëns had so often shared Prince Albert's hospitality. In March 1910 Massenet was ill in his room in the palace while his *Thérèse* was performed in a festival to mark the opening of the Oceanographic Museum in Monte Carlo. Saint-Saëns, a fellow guest, called on him with news of the opera's success and "lavished the most affectionate care on me constantly", Massenet recalled.[85]

Saint-Saëns's last opera, *Déjanire*, is a reworking of the incidental music to Gallet's play. The downfall of the hero through a woman, in this case Hercules at the hands of his jealous wife, was a theme that still appealed to him. Although the old intensity that produced *Samson et Dalila* is now replaced by a classical reserve that links the later opera with its immediate predecessors, there is a touch of sombre earnestness about it that suggests that the subject retained a strong meaning for the composer beyond mere atmospheric scene-painting. Pierre Lalo spoke of its "dignity, sobriety and grandeur", but also of its "sincerity"[86] which is perhaps most strikingly shown in the agonising discords that accompany the final death pangs of Hercules in the shirt of Nessus. In adapting the play Saint-Saëns modified Gallet's text as well as altering and extending the original music, in which material from the symphonic poem *La Jeunesse d'Hercule* makes a prominent appearance. The choruses in the new version, he explained,

are much more developed than in the first version. A dance chorus in the last act has disappeared and in its place is an epithalamion whose text imitates the Greek and whose music is in a Greek mode. Finally, all the spoken roles are sung now: these make up a new work for which the old is only the embryo.[87]

Déjanire was sung at Monte Carlo on 14th March 1911, travelling to the Paris

Opéra on 22nd November and to Brussels on 6th December. It stayed in the Opéra repertory for two years but thereafter went the way of most of his operas. Saint-Saëns saw it as the last of his major works, operatic or instrumental. "When you have the happiness to finish your career with *Déjanire*, it is best to keep to that", he declared. "I have written music for over sixty years; it's the end of huge enterprises and grand conceptions."[88] It was not quite – the oratorio *The Promised Land* was still to come.

His sense of having reached the end of a long road had been deepened by the deaths of more contemporaries. Sarasate died in 1908. In October of that year Saint-Saëns played, under Messager's baton, Mozart's C minor concerto at the Conservatoire in a memorial programme for the Concerts Society's conductor Georges Marty, who had died aged forty-eight. In 1909 the composer's long-time friend and publisher Auguste Durand died, leaving the firm in the hands of his son Jacques. The next year saw the deaths of Edouard Colonne, who had done much to promote his music, and of Pauline Viardot at the age of eighty-nine. At her funeral on 28th May at the Church of St Clotilde, Saint-Saëns, who at fourteen had been so dazzled by her artistry and erudition, and had been so stimulated by her company over so many years, paid tribute to the Delilah of his dreams. On the same day in London the funeral was taking place of King Edward VII.

But there were musicians living in whom he could still take pleasure. In the summer of 1908 he visited the composer-pianist Raoul Pugno at his country house at Gargenville, near Paris. There they rehearsed the *Africa* fantasy on a double-piano, the two keyboards arranged so that the players faced each other. Archibald Henderson turned the pages as Saint-Saëns played the orchestral part and, as Wagner had been years before, was astounded by his technical powers, his "readiness and resource in adapting orchestral texture to the piano". In the afternoon there was tea in the garden, where the guests also included the composer sisters Lili and Nadia Boulanger, the latter a pupil of Fauré who had just won the Second Order Prix de Rome. (Lili was to become the first woman to win the First Order five years later.)[89] Saint-Saëns was also a frequent guest at Paderewski's house at Morges in Switzerland, and played the Polonaise for two pianos with him at a concert in Geneva.

Among his many performing engagements at this time was a concert of his works in London on 7th June 1910 marking the twenty-fifth anniversary of Hollmann's first public appearance in England. He and the cellist were joined by Pugno, Ysaÿe and the singer Esta d'Argo in a programme that included the piano quartet, the second piano concerto, the F major piano trio, the Scherzo for two pianos, the septet and some songs. It also included a new work, *La Muse et le Poète* for violin, cello and orchestra. Written in Luxor the previous winter, it was suggested by a poem, 'Une Nuit d'Octobre'. This was one of four lyrics by Alfred de Musset in which the poet tells the Muse of his anguish at disappointed love, and seeks from her the consolation of poetic inspiration. Against the orchestral background the violin, as Muse, offers soothing answers to the complaints, sometimes melancholy, sometimes agitated, of the cello as Poet. In free fantasia form, it is a curious blend of early and late Saint-Saëns: the material represents a further advance of a stylistic trend hinted at in the second cello sonata, brief snatches of melody in a variety of moods worked out onto a broader lyrical canvas and here treated rhapsodically to an extent perhaps unprecedented in the composer's output. Yet it is expressed with all his accustomed luminescence and clarity, even to the light staccato orchestral chords. As in the second cello concerto, there is an orchestral episode, introducing the final section, that is straight out of the mid-nineteenth century.

A landmark in his performing career was the Mozart concerto series which began at the Bechstein Hall, London, on 8th June 1910, the day after the Hollmann anniversary evening, with a hand-picked orchestra. It showed remarkable evidence of the stamina of a seventy-four-year-old of fragile health. The concertos, mostly with his own cadenzas, were spread over three dates a week apart, and greatly boosted his prestige as a performer among the English public, though to some extent at the expense of his name as a composer. In the first concert were the concertos K.503, K.413, K.453 and K.488; in the second K.595, K.537 and K.491; and in the third K.271, K.467, K.450 (this, as he announced to the audience before playing, being the work he had played as a ten-year-old in 1846) and K.466. By laying the concertos side by side, as it were, the series highlighted the individual qualities of each, as well as helping to make them better known. *The Times* was warmly enthusiastic. In Saint-Saëns's playing a "manual dexterity that should be characteristic of a man in the prime of life is combined with a maturity of style and a wholehearted devotion to the musical ideals of the works presented that could only be attained in old age . . . To hear such an artist as the eminent composer give out some simple theme that in less sympathetic hands would be full of banality is a lesson in the higher and more restrained art." He "understands and appreciates the music from every point of view", so that "the force and variety of Mozart's melodic invention, the delicacy of his orchestration, the skill with which ornamental piano passages are combined with the orchestra were all perfectly shown". The only fault was noted in the final concert, when he "sometimes quickened the pace", leaving the orchestra to catch up.[90]

In September 1910 he conducted a concert of his works in Munich, and other engagements included an appearance at the (belated) Liszt centenary festival in Heidelberg in 1912, which he attended, reluctantly, at the invitation of the Association of German Musicians. He was still a member but had long ceased to take an active part in the association, ever since the row over Wagner in the 1880s. Apart from the long-standing rift with his association colleagues, he was worried also by the thought of having to share the festival platform with other, younger pianists like Busoni, but agreed to take part because, as he put it, "a refusal would have been misinterpreted".[91]

By now, all ideas of retirement, prompted by his illness on the 1906 American tour, had been laid aside. "There is simply no end to my interminable career," he remarked, a touch plaintively, to Henderson after his 1913 concert at the Salle Gaveau. The organist had complimented him on being able to give such a towering performance on the piano for a man of his age. "Not at all", he replied, "I am much too busy to get old."[92] He might have said of himself, as he said of Fauré, that "he has no age, and never will have".[93] Henderson noted that at the organ too Saint-Saëns's "feet as well as his hands had lost none of their cunning".[94]

If his concert life showed no sign of decline, neither did his writing and editing. He was as sharp as ever in his views on authenticity, particularly in pre-nineteenth century music, and continued to attack carelessness and misconceptions in both editing and performance. He urged the Opéra to use Pelletan's edition of Gluck, not, he insisted, because he had worked on it over many years, but because it was based on original sources. "There is a magnificent German edition which is completely erroneous, because it is not based on the same documents", he told the Opéra director Louis Broussan.[95] On another occasion he complained about the tedium inflicted on a performance of Gluck's *Iphigénie en Aulide* by unnecessarily slow speeds, explaining that "andante, in the eighteenth century, implied nothing of the idea of slowness we apply to it today. The term andante allegro is not uncommon in Handel; we should say today allegro giocoso."[96] Although the authority of Saint-Saëns's editions, which also include the Mozart sonatas and pieces by Liszt, no longer carries much weight in these days of Urtext, his contribution to the movement towards authenticity is nevertheless considerable, and proved to be a powerful corrective of many of the mistakes and excesses of nineteenth-century editors. In old age his mind retained its youthful alertness and vigour and when not conversing he was writing letters on matters of concern to newspapers and correspondents. From Cairo in January 1910, for instance, he wrote protesting about the proposed demolition of the old Conservatoire Concerts Society hall, "a little masterpiece" where, as a youth, he had first heard the orchestral works of Haydn, Mozart and Beethoven. While accepting that the hall was not suitable for the large orchestral forces required for more modern works he pleaded for it to be retained as a chamber music venue.[97] From 1911 he resumed regular journalism in a series of articles on music and other subjects for the *Echo de Paris* which were later incorporated in *Ecole Buissonnière*.

In the midst of this ceaseless round of work, his domestic life took a new direction – largely because of a dog. Lisette died and then in November 1909, Dalila followed. One day Geslin brought home a stray he had found near the Eiffel Tower, but the landlord at Rue de Longchamp took exception and refused to allow the premises to be turned into what he called a "zoological garden". Saint-Saëns therefore moved to an apartment on the third floor of 83 Rue de Courcelles with the new dog in June 1910, just after the London Mozart concerts. Berluron, as he called him, was to be his pet for the next six years, until he died a few months after his back paws were crushed by a passing vehicle. The Sorbonne librarian Jean Bonnerot was a regular visitor to the household as Saint-Saëns's secretary, and in June 1912 the composer engaged a cook after apologising to Fauré for the fare he was able to provide when inviting him to dinner. "Alas! There is nothing at my home of Vatel [a seventeenth-century steward to the aristocracy]. But there are, after all, stoves and saucepans; all sorts of things more or less edible will yet be made. The indulgence of the Society will be reclaimed."[98] He was still in the habit of taking rooms at the nearby Bedford Hotel to escape demands on his time, as in May 1911, after the exertions over *Déjanire*. "Here", he wrote to Fauré, "I am sheltered from unwelcome guests and wearisome matters."[99] In the winter, of course, he was genuinely absent, on his annual escape to warmer climes. In December 1911 he was at Blidah in Algeria, moving on to the resort of Hammam-r'Irha. He wrote to Renaud that it was "really hot in Blidah; here it is fresher but delightful all the same, and what is most delightful of all is the perfect, absolute silence".[100] Later that winter he left Algeria for Cairo, where he wrote the Six Studies for the left hand, at the request of the pianist Caroline de Serres, the dedicatee of the 'Wedding Cake' caprice and a frequent partner in piano duets.

After the next winter's sojourn in North Africa he travelled to Monte Carlo to see Fauré's new opera *Pénélope*. Although he could not come to terms with some of the more advanced aspects of the music, he was proud "and even a little moved" to learn that his old pupil had dedicated the opera to him. After the second performance on 11th March 1913 he sent Fauré a detailed criticism, mainly of certain points of production, confessing that the librettist René Fauchois had offended his classical and literary sensibilities by making "a travesty of the Odyssey". He could not see all of the Paris production in May because of an attack of colic, which he blamed on a milk diet, and which forced him to leave in a hurry during the second act. "I was only just in time", he told Fauré. But he was pleased to see in a later performance that some of the faults of staging he had pointed out had been corrected as he suggested.[101]

With Fauré and Dukas, he joined an unlikely combination with Debussy and d'Indy in the spring of 1913 in a promotion of French music at a concert to inaugurate the new Théâtre des Champs-Elysées. He conducted *Phaëton* and parts of *La Lyre et l'Harpe*. A fault occurred in the organ during the oratorio performance – Saint-Saëns cued the organist in but there was no sound, so he had to continue without it. It did not make him well-disposed towards the new theatre: he told Renaud that the event "was not a success, whatever the papers say; it was quite the contrary . . . The hall is not good, music is lost there".[102] At the same time, plans were afoot in London for a festival concert in his honour, which was to mark the summit of his prestige in England, as the award of the Grand Croix of the Légion d'Honneur in January had done in France.

The London concert was designed as a tribute to the composer on the lines of the Paris jubilee concerts of 1896 and 1906. This time the 'jubilee' was to mark the seventy-fifth anniversary of the beginning of his life in music, that is, of his first piano lesson at the age of two. The patronage of both Queen Alexandra and Queen Mary was an indication of the concert's high standing. Saint-Saëns arrived in London at the end of May, and took part in a selection of his works at a private soirée in Hyde Park Square as a curtain-raiser to the jubilee concert, which took place a few days later, on 2nd June, at the Queen's Hall. The programme, conducted by Thomas Beecham, covered a wide span of his life as a composer, from the 1854 *Ouverture d'un opéra-comique inachevé* (only just published) to the finale of the 'Egyptian' concerto, by way of the scherzo from the G minor concerto, the whole of the C minor symphony (an appropriate choice in view of the work's première in London) and the *Africa* fantasy. There was also the work now inevitably associated with any Saint-Saëns anniversary, the Mozart concerto K.450. Sir Alexander Mackenzie, head of the festival committee, presented the composer with an illuminated address and, while praising him as "the most gifted and most exalted representative" of French music, assured him that "his popularity is nowhere stronger than in England". Grace, wit and learning, he said, were the strengths of his art.[103] Beecham, who had not seen eye to eye with the composer over matters of tempo before the concert, tells the story that, at dinner that evening, he asked Saint-Saëns what he thought of his interpretations and was told: "My friend, there are only two types of conductor: one takes the music too fast, the other too slow."[104] The next evening Saint-Saëns attended a performance of *Samson et Dalila* at Covent Garden, and at the end of the second act was repeatedly called to the stage by prolonged applause and cheers.

This prestigious reminder of his long and eventful career put him in nostalgic mood. Among his personal effects was a box of notes and letters dating back to his earliest childhood and, looking over them, he was filled with a longing to recapture the peace and happiness he had known when, as a boy, he had gone to stay with his mother's relatives in the countryside at Wassy and Chaumont. Prompted by this yearning for the land of lost content, he travelled to the region in August, for the first time in seventy years, to picture little Camille in the village church and in his great-uncle's house, and driving his hoop along the avenue of trees. But it was a brief interlude: two weeks later he was back in England, to conduct his new oratorio, *The Promised Land*, at the Gloucester Three Choirs Festival.

The Promised Land was the long-delayed realisation of an idea that had been with Saint-Saëns ever since his youth, when he was first attracted to the subject of Moses in the Sinai desert. Several attempts to set the story had come to nothing over the years for one reason or another, but his travels in Egypt and more particularly work on *La Foi*, with its ancient Egyptian setting, prompted him to tackle the project afresh. Aware that oratorio was a form long out of favour in France, he aimed the work at the English market, and in the summer of 1912 asked Hermann Klein to revive the text he had provided for the abortive *Moses* oratorio of 1887. That winter he took the libretto, originally called *The Death of Moses* and adapted from the Bible, to Cairo and finished setting it after two months, on 15th February 1913. It was then chosen by the Gloucester Festival for performance that year, almost certainly through Klein's advocacy (and was not therefore a festival commission, as is sometimes stated). The choice marked a change of direction for the festival, which was including contemporary works by non-British composers for the first time in over fifty years: a choral work by Sibelius was also to be premièred in 1913. Saint-Saëns arrived in Gloucester in September; there he met Elgar, and on the evening of the 10th played Mozart's K.450 concerto at the Shire Hall. Next morning, in the cathedral, he conducted *The Promised Land*.

The work startled its audience with its starkly archaic format, solos, duets and choruses linked by recitatives and sprinkled with Handelian runs and Mendelssohnian devices which sounded like an over-enthusiastic and misguided appeal to an English choral tradition that had moved on. Lacking the strong Elgarian spiritual uplift that English audiences expected, it was never taken seriously by most people and soon joined *Le Déluge* and *La Lyre* among Saint-Saëns's forgotten choral works. Some of the musical media did, however, take it seriously, seeing in it a reaction to the over-ripe complexities of late romanticism: it is also a prime example of the composer's late style, with its emphasis on purposeful structure, simplicity of expression and purity of sound. The *Musical Times* said: "The simplicity of the vocal part here is remarkable, and the result is a great choral richness, because every singer can give attention to sonority."[105] Simplicity and sonority were words used also by *Le Figaro*, which saw *The Promised Land* as in the tradition of French seventeenth- and eighteenth-century motets, while dismissing suggestions that it was a mere Handelian pastiche. "In spite of some external and unimportant similarities, *The Promised Land* is quite original and written in the true manner of Saint-Saëns and of Saint-Saëns alone."[106] This individual voice is evident particularly in the music depicting the water bursting from the rock, the double-chorus which follows, which impressed the *Musical Times* with its "majestic effect", the duet of Moses and Aaron that opens part two, the song of Moses for bass and choir with pizzicato accompaniment and the death of Moses. But as with Saint-Saëns's operas, it was perceived as decorative rather than dramatic, and as such was not likely to win over hearts and minds among a public born in the nineteenth-century romantic age.

A month after the Gloucester Festival, Saint-Saëns was in Berlin for a Philharmonic concert in his honour, and to attend the 100th performance of *Samson et Dalila* at the Royal Opera. The events were the high-water mark of his rehabilitation with the German public – both were sold out well in advance – before war once again intervened. At the concert he played the *Africa* fantasy under Oskar Fried, and the 'Wedding Cake' caprice, and conducted his A minor symphony, which owed its première to Germany, and the *Danse Macabre*. The goodwill thus generated had been under threat from a row over the opera. Saint-Saëns's demands that it be given in its original form instead of "the mutilated and distorted form in which it has always been given in Berlin" had fallen on deaf ears, and he had therefore refused the invitation to conduct the 100th *Samson*.[107] But the row was resolved by the intervention of the Kaiser, who ordered the changes demanded by the composer, and Saint-Saëns conducted the 101st performance. Relations were further improved when *Proserpine* was included for the first time in plans for the German Opera.

The demanding concert schedule of 1913 left him, at the age of seventy-eight, longing more than ever for a quiet life, but, as he wrote to a friend, "fate doesn't wish it".[108] When he was persuaded to play at the Salle Gaveau on 6th November he billed the event, optimistically from his point of view, as his "last concert". The programme included the septet, piano and organ pieces, orchestral items and a Mozart concerto, conducted by Pierre Monteux. The proceeds went to a charity for French soldiers, a benefit prophetic of political events that were to reawaken that aggressively nationalistic side of the composer's character.

XIV • PATRIOT AGAIN

THE LAST MONTHS OF PEACE WERE RELATIVELY PEACEFUL IN A PERSONAL sense for Saint-Saëns after he withdrew, for the time being at least, from the concert circuit. He broke his retirement briefly in April 1914 to conduct the second act of *Les Barbares* in a gala evening at the Opéra, but the exertion made him aware of a growing feebleness which he could not help comparing with the seemingly boundless energy he had possessed as a young man. In a letter to Renaud he contrasted his present state with himself as a soldier during the Franco-Prussian war. "I no longer have the indomitable energy of forty years ago, that resilience that won the admiration of my comrades in the National Guard during the siege."[1]

His operas were still clinging to life, as the gala evening showed. In Brussels in early March he "walked on golden clouds", as he told Renaud,[2] after seeing *Le Timbre d'Argent* in a revised form, with recitatives he had supplied to replace the spoken dialogue. In June he went to Lisbon where *Proserpine* was being given. *Phryné*, meanwhile, scored such a success at the Gaieté theatre in Paris that the management decided to give (by way of contrast) *Proserpine* in October, which, Saint-Saëns explained to Renaud, "will prevent me from going to Vienna as I had promised".[3] He was not to know that Austria would soon be an enemy country, and that war, not opera, would prevent him going to Vienna.

His more relaxed lifestyle in the first months of 1914 was, however, overshadowed by his manservant's deteriorating health. This caused him to bring to his Paris home an Arab boy who had attended him in North Africa that winter. Then there were his own ailments, mainly a recurring congestion. He had rested from composition as he had done from performing, finding that, as he told a friend, "in the ordering of ideas the difficulties do not smooth themselves out with age".[4] The only significant work to date from 1914, apart from two unaccompanied church choruses, was the song cycle *La Cendre Rouge*, which he dedicated to Fauré in return for the dedication of *Pénélope*, "as I shall not do any more operas".[5] The ten settings of poems by Georges Docquois are a prime example of his later songwriting style, embodying a fastidious sense of declamation and verbal clarity which has all but eclipsed the rich, sensuous lyricism of the earlier period, such as in the *Mélodies Persanes*. "I do not dare call them melodies", he told Fauré, "because they are something else which I should not know how to define. There is something both of the amusing and the harsh in them, something for most tastes, not all."[6] The theme of the cycle is love and its aftermath ("Love, why have you left me? I can't do without you!"), and its moods vary from melancholy to joy. 'Jour de pluie' compares the gloom of the weather to the sorrow in the poet's heart, to a staccato accompaniment imitating raindrops, while in contrast 'Pâques', with its bare fourths suggesting tolling bells, joyfully celebrates the end of Lent and the coming of May. An important accompaniment figure is heard in 'Amoroso', four notes including a flattened seventh, reminiscent of a common jazz inflection. This appears again in the epilogue, which also includes an echo from the third song, 'Douceur', and transforms the flowing andante accompaniment of the opening prelude into a turbulent allegro appassionato, in a bitter, anguished recollection of lost love.

From seeing *Proserpine* in Lisbon, Saint-Saëns moved on to Madrid, returning to Paris by way of Bordeaux. During June he was engaged in rehearsals for a revival of *La Princesse Jaune*, and writing an article for the *Echo de Paris*. Just two weeks before the German declaration of war on 3rd August he decided to treat himself, by way of light relief, to a meal at the Magic City cabaret club. He was "not amused at all", he told Renaud. The sight of near-naked female dancers "disgusted me, with their fat legs and naked feet, which made me think of chiropodists rather than of love. And their faces were something else . . ."[7]

On the eve of war he was in Belgium preparing again to break his retirement from the concert platform by playing at a festival in his honour at Namur, which the king and queen had promised to attend. He stayed at Dinant, at the Hotel de la Citadelle, soon to be reduced to a pile of rubble. The festival never took place. Hermann Klein remembered a conversation with him in the hotel's palm garden, in which he denounced "that dog" the Kaiser as a charlatan, declared that he now hated the Germans, and made some irreverent impersonations of the domestic manners of the Wagners as he recalled them at Wahnfried. Neither he nor his companion could believe that the Germans would dare invade Belgium.[8]

As the Europe that Saint-Saëns had known since his youth began its campaign of self-destruction, and the earliest casualties of battle hardened the hearts of nations, the first weeks of war saw the aged composer nursing private wounds. The months of comparative musical inactivity initiated by exhaustion and the need to rest had left him frustrated, dissatisfied and even angry with himself. The gloom was deepened by daily visits to Gabriel Geslin at the clinic to which he had been readmitted following the apparent failure of his operation. Saint-Saëns wrote to Renaud complaining of "moral depression" and of lacking the courage to work, which was "distressing and humiliating". "Existence is bearable only thanks to the comfort which Bonnerot brings me; his devotion is boundless." At the end of August came an invitation from his old acquaintance Dr Félix Regnault to visit him at a hospital in his charge, set up in a casino at Houlgate on the Normandy coast. There, he promised, Geslin would have all the medical care he needed.

For Saint-Saëns, the visit provided an excuse to get away from Paris, where news of the German advance stirred grim memories of 1870–71. He had nightmares of occupation and of being taken hostage because of the German Order of Merit which he held, and which, he believed, "puts me in the spotlight just when it would be advantageous to be hidden in shade".[9] He need not have worried on those grounds: all honours bestowed by what were now enemy countries, chiefly Germany and Austria, were ordered to be given up. They included his membership of the Association of German Musicians, which he had held since 1869, and the German Order of Merit. In any case, he was to put himself in the firing line. After two months of war, his long-held anti-German sentiments boiled over in a furious attack on Wagner and the aggressive nationalism he represented. German troops had overrun Belgium and were on French soil, while a French offensive in the Ardennes had suffered heavy losses. Meanwhile, the *Echo de Paris* published a series of articles by Saint-Saëns, headed 'Germanophilie', calling for a complete ban on German music in France, and especially Wagner's, claiming – somewhat dubiously – that it had been imposed on a "reluctant people". The French, he argued, could no longer be expected to applaud works which the Germans regarded as embodying their national genius, and which were written by a man who hated France and had ridiculed French culture. "Would you applaud a famous singer who had insulted your mother?" he asked, using as extra ammunition the reports of German atrocities in Belgium which had so shocked the French public.

His criticism of Wagner on purely musical grounds, of his influence on melody, harmony and vocal style, and on philosophical grounds, of the idea of his operas as an absolute artistic truth, had been stated long before. Criticism on the cruder basis of race and national rivalry had now it seemed been unleashed under the impact of war. Saint-Saëns condemned Wagner as one of a race capable of war crimes, whose works had for years been pushing French music out of the theatres. In reality, of course, this nationalistic side of the argument also went back a long time, at least to 1871, when Saint-Saëns was smarting from Wagner's *Capitulation* satire and the defeat of France, and saw the process of national musical revival in strongly patriotic terms. The advent of the Wagner craze in France he saw as a threat to that revival, partly on the practical basis that performances of his operas meant fewer opportunities for French works to be heard, and partly because he saw it as somehow infecting and undermining French patriotism. Both considerations were spelled out in a letter to a member of the Conservatoire council in July 1896, when Wagner's operas were being given with greater frequency in French theatres.

How is it that no one sees the evil work that is done? It is not only the annihilation, the gradual emaciation of the French school, but even more: Wagnerism, under the flag of art, is a machine marvellously equipped to erode patriotism in France. It is the German soul infiltrating our public little by little.

Bayreuth was not raised,

> *as they say here, to the glory of Art, but to the glory of German Art, the Holy Art of Germany, as they sing at the end of* Die Meistersinger . . . *It is objected, with just cause, that there are no openings for our composers and that they are forced to go to Brussels to get a hearing. But, it will be said, Wagner's operas are played in Brussels. True, but their presence in Brussels is not as widespread as is believed; Gounod is played there more than Wagner . . . There is not at this time any other town, even in Germany – Bayreuth excepted – where the music of the author of* A Capitulation *is played so much [as in Paris].*[10]

As quoted earlier, in another letter of the same period he wrote: "Let us hope that the Wagnerian fever will pass, as everything passes in this world, and that a day will come when French music is played in France."[11] In the meantime he hoped that French music would make up for its apparent displacement at home by being played more often abroad, in a process of "reciprocal penetration".[12] For Saint-Saëns, music was not a matter of transcending national boundaries: if art has no country, he would argue, artists certainly do have one.

Publication of the 'Germanophilie' articles (republished in pamphlet form in 1916), far from matching a popular patriotic mood, unleashed a storm of controversy around their author. The implied criticism of French musicians and French opera house directors opened old wounds at a time when the nation was laying aside political, social, religious and philosophical divisions in the cause of defence. Saint-Saëns went on to stir the waters even further by attacking the formation of trade unions in Paris orchestras, with the militant syndicalism that had spread to many areas of public life in the last years of peace very much in mind. He regarded unions as the institutionalisation of ignorance and greed, and contrasted their aims with what he saw as the selfless dedication of the intellectual working to improve the lot of mankind. People

> *have no regard – in these days when they are constantly talking about their rights and urged to demand more wages for less work – for the young people who spend their best years leading a precarious existence, working day and night without hope of personal profit, with no end in view other than the discovery of new facts from which humanity might benefit.*[13]

Such views upset the 'sacred union' of a nation at war, and Saint-Saëns, far from securing a ban on Wagner's music, succeeded only in alienating French musicians to the extent that they turned their backs on him (on some occasions literally) and refused, for a time, to play his music. "How ridiculous our poor Camille is, with his need to be polemical and say such stupid things", Messager wrote to Fauré.[14]

What made him seem ridiculous was partly the tub-thumping on an issue – the influence of Wagner on French music – that had long ceased to concern most contemporary musicians and critics. "Saint-Saëns has lived so long at Cairo or in the Azores [*sic*] that he may well be unaware of what has taken place in France", wrote Jean-Aubry. "French music of today owes less to Wagner than Saint-Saëns does to Liszt and the German classics." The aim of young composers in wartime, he asserted, was not to insult the enemy, but to "oppose German art with French art".[15] Many suspected that Saint-Saëns's patriotism was a cloak to hide more selfish motives, and that he sought a Wagner ban to give his own operas more of a hearing. There is, no doubt, an element of truth in this. Yet he was not entirely alone in his stance against German music: Pierre Monteux, for instance, who had served in the trenches and fought at Verdun, refused to conduct a ballet based on *Till Eulenspiegel* while in America with the Ballets Russes in 1916. "I could not participate in a project that would send a considerable sum of money to Germany", he commented.[16] Less controversially, Saint-Saëns contributed, along with several prominent musicians, to the King Albert Book, a tribute to Belgian resistance.

Barred by war from his annual hibernation, he was troubled more by the prospect of winter than by the hostility he had aroused. "The summer over, I fear inclement weather", he wrote in November 1914.[17] And in January he was forced to overcome his scruples regarding animals and put on his furs, writing to Renaud of the "wickedness of thus taking possession of that which poor animals had on their backs for a shield against the rigours of the temperature. But this wickedness being generally allowed, I am as wicked as everyone else."[18] Escape had to wait until the spring, when he made his second visit to the United States, partly as musician, partly as lecturer and goodwill ambassador pleading for support for French war charities. He wrote a cantata, *Hail! California*, for performance at the Panama Pacific Exhibition in San Francisco, but was not really looking forward to the journey. "I shall certainly be bored", he told Renaud, "and I shall console myself with the taste of turtle soup." He also regretted not having had time to improve his English, so that "I shall be like an animal, not understanding a word that is said to me". He engaged an interpreter to go with him. He was cheered by a "splendid" performance of *L'Ancêtre* at Monte Carlo at the end of March, but left Bordeaux for New York on 24th April in sombre mood, having visited every day the Paris clinic where his manservant was still too weak to face a second operation.[19]

War made it inevitable that the 1915 visit to America was peppered with politics. To make it at all required some courage in view of the U-boat threat to shipping in the Atlantic, as was only too well demonstrated in the same week as his departure by the sinking of the *Lusitania*. The composer's official status was as delegate of the Franco-American Commission for the development of political, economic, literary and artistic relations, to give a series of talks arranged by the French government. He stepped into a row straight from the gang plank on arrival in New York harbour. The soprano Elsa Kutschera, whom he had often accompanied in recitals, was on the quayside and rushed forward to embrace him – only to be contemptuously brushed aside and told: "Go away, you are German!" Without another word, Saint-Saëns was driven away in a cab, leaving the singer distressed and humiliated. Born in Austria-Hungary and educated in Germany, she had lived for many years in Paris and was in America to raise funds for Belgian relief. That evening in her hotel she told reporters that she was Belgian, that her husband was in the Belgian army and that she had sons and nephews in the French army. Music knew no boundaries, she pleaded: Saint-Saëns had known many triumphs in Berlin, while she had sung his music at the Paris Opéra and he had "praised me to the skies". Asked about the incident after dining as a guest of the Franco-American Commission, Saint-Saëns replied only that "I will not see her. I have nothing to do with her now, that woman. I won't see her any more." She later wrote to him: "You will understand my astonishment at your ungallant manner. Your brutality has amused me. I know you are too obstinate to apologise." To this the composer replied by pointing out that Kutschera had been known in Paris before the war as a German Wagnerian singer, yet "since the war you declare yourself a Belgian. Why did you not say so before?" It would have irritated him to know that the singer regarded this reply as an apology.[20]

His snub to Mme Kutschera was thrown into sharper relief by his entirely different reaction at meeting Busoni, who, although Italian, had spent most of his musical life in Germany (Italy had not yet entered the war). News of their friendly conversation at a performance of *Carmen* at the Met was relayed back to Berlin, where it caused outrage, Busoni being seen as consorting with the enemy. Busoni, an admirer of the older composer, found the whole business annoying and stupid, writing, with a sense of the absurdity of it all: "Just think, this significant event was transmitted by cable!"[21]

Saint-Saëns reached San Francisco on 22nd May, after stops at Philadelphia and Chicago, "as chipper and spry as though he had not counted nearly eighty years," as the *San Francisco Chronicle* observed.[22] The next evening he went to hear the Boston Symphony Orchestra, in San Francisco for the exhibition, and two days later heard it play his C minor symphony, bowing to wild applause from his box at the end. In between concerts he enjoyed walks in the exhibition grounds with John Philip Sousa, whose band was also playing a prominent part in the programme of musical events. He declined to talk to reporters about what were for him the controversial issues of the war and contemporary music, and as in South America in 1899, made the undiplomatic admission that he had not heard anything by native composers. He expected, however, "as I shall probably write music for as long as I live", that his American experiences would provide the basis for a new work on his return home.[23] This was perhaps an attempt to appease local pride: there was to be no 'American' work, apart from the cantata he had brought with him. A secular hymn of praise on the lines of the *Hymne à Victor Hugo* and *Le Feu Celeste, Hail! California* was intended as a tribute to Franco-American relations, featuring in a free fantasia the *Marseillaise* and *The Star-Spangled Banner*, and adding a military band and an organ to the already large orchestral and choral forces in the triumphant finale. It was played in the first and last of three concerts of Saint-Saëns's works conducted by the composer, on 19th, 24th and 27th June, with Sousa's band providing the military back-up. It was a piece of bombast which did not impress the critics, still smarting perhaps from the composer's confessed ignorance of American music, and the score was not published. The last concert, before a four-thousand-strong audience, also featured *The Promised Land*, a not entirely satisfactory performance, it seems, for which lack of rehearsal time was blamed.

The American visit also featured the lectures Saint-Saëns gave, at each port of call, on the historical development of music, using a piano and a blackboard to illustrate various points. They helped to make the tour both a financial and a personal success. It raised not only 100,000 francs for the war charities but also the composer's sinking spirits. After a reception in San Francisco held for him by the Franco-American Commission on 1st July, he was quite reluctant to leave "delightful California" after his six weeks there.[24] He was pleasantly surprised to meet an old acquaintance in New York on the return journey, and boarded the ship in a "light-hearted and happy mood", according to the *New York Musical Courier*.[25] He was also impressed by how quickly he was able to cross an ocean and a whole continent, writing to Renaud on his return: "Yes indeed, it's me! You see, it's so simple, crossing the Atlantic and America; I come back in a better state than the one I went away in . . ." Geslin he found much better, but "still suffering".[26]

The boost to his own well-being did not last. He began to have a paralysis in his legs, and was recommended to take the waters at Bourbon-l'Archambault. Work followed him there in September, when he wrote to Renaud of having to deal with an "enormous correspondence," forwarded by Bonnerot, and with proofs to be corrected.

I don't know if the waters of Bourbon will do me good, but they had begun to give me terrible trouble; I had to stop the treatment and start it again on a lower level . . . The weather is admirable, the countryside ravishing, but I hardly enjoy it, not being able to go for walks; for I can go out only by car and I hate the car when I have to get in and out all the time. A rare thing, the food is excellent and varied, nothing like the monotonous, pretentious horrors of luxury hotels. If I had legs it would be delightful; but if I had legs I should not be here.

Apart from the food, he also took delight in the spa town's associations with Louis XIV and his mistresses.[27]

Life back in Paris was enlivened by the company of Fauré, increasingly deaf but still capable of lively conversation at fortissimo, as the two men dined at the Marguery restaurant, near the Conservatoire. They still corresponded too, about the Conservatoire, Fauré's new song cycle *Le Jardin Clos* and the prospect of Debussy's election to the Institute. Amid talk of reforms at the Conservatoire, Saint-Saëns suggested a literary course, "so composers can get to know, as you and I know, what the French language is all about". He was finding both the poetry (by van Lerberghe) and the music of *Le Jardin Clos* "inhospitable" but was delighted by Fauré's 12th Barcarolle, which had been played to him by its dedicatee Louis Diémer, a regular partner of Saint-Saëns in piano duets. As for Debussy, Saint-Saëns used all his influence to prevent his becoming a member of the Institute, especially after publication of the pieces for two pianos *En Blanc et Noir*. These, he said, were "quite unbelievable, and we must at all costs bar the door of the Institute against a man capable of such atrocities, fit to be placed beside Cubist paintings".[28] He need not have worried: Debussy had cancer and died less than three years later, before the next election took place. Loyal as Fauré was to his old teacher, this attitude must have saddened him, for his relations with Debussy were rather more cordial and respectful.

Although he was still weak in the legs, Saint-Saëns showed no sign of halting his musical activity, two years after his "last concert". His generosity with donations to and help for families of musicians killed or wounded in battle was matched by his readiness to take part in charity concerts. These included a performance of his Beethoven Variations with Alfred Cortot. In December 1915 he took part in a performance of the Polonaise for two pianos in a concert of his works, adding as an encore the *Valse Mignonne*, which "I played very well". "The hall was filled to overflowing, the enthusiasm indescribable", he reported to Renaud, although he wished for a better ensemble in the quartet from *Henry VIII*. He was also surprised (and no doubt irritated) to hear that everyone thought the Polonaise, which he had written nearly thirty years before, was a recent work.[29]

The composer's patriotism found fervent expression early in February 1916 when he conducted the *Marseillaise* – allowing himself, as *Le Figaro* noted, "a moment of rare emotion" – in a concert of French music organised by the Society of Authors, in which he also conducted his Op. 131 cantata *La Gloire*.[30] He was helping too with rehearsals for the first performance in France of *The Promised Land*, which the conductor Victor Charpentier had asked to include in his Grand Concerts series at the Théâtre des Champs-Elysées. This took place on 20th February (there was a second performance on 12th March), in a French translation made by Klein of his own text, with Saint-Saëns's co-operation. The composer was not fond of setting French prose, but, as he explained to *Le Figaro*, "I alter my view when dealing with a prose that is not the current prose of conversation but a prose moulded upon music itself, as is the case here, or a rhythmical, sonorous prose, lying halfway between prose and verse".[31] The concert was a sell-out, each number was applauded and the French critics were mostly enthusiastic. This was a success which far exceeded expectations, at a time when oratorio was not fashionable in France, and French choral forces were no match for those of the English, especially because of the war. The composer, though, was not there to see the triumph: when the performance ended and the audience was calling him to the platform, he had already left for Bordeaux to begin a concert tour of southern France, taking with him for company the Swiss interpreter who had been with him in America.

At Bordeaux, in a concert in aid of local war charities, he was honoured with extracts from *Samson et Dalila*, *Henry VIII* and *Les Barbares*. He also conducted the *Marche Héroïque*, played his *Menuet et Valse*, and accompanied Marcelle Demougeot, the first Dejaneira, in two of his songs, 'La Cloche' and, from *La Cendre Rouge*, 'Mai'. Then it was on to Tours, where he played Chopin and Liszt as well as his own pieces, in a recital with Hollmann and the soprano Martha de Villiers. There was another recital with Hollmann at the Casino in Nice, and at Monte Carlo he was called to the stage and loudly acclaimed after a performance of *Hélène*. But the strenuous itinerary proved too much, at the end of a winter when he had again been denied the warmth of North Africa and when there had been little rest. He had also begun writing music for a production at the Odéon in Paris of Alfred de Musset's comedy *On ne badine pas avec l'amour*. The strain soon began to tell: by the end of the tour he was in a fever and spitting blood, and was ordered to take a complete rest. He wrote to Renaud of his intention to retire to Menton, where he knew no one and where "I shall give myself up, in solitude, to literature and painting".[32]

Revived by the rest and the Mediterranean air, he was ready to work again after just a few days, and returned to Paris in time for a programme of his works given at the Sorbonne by the Conservatoire Concerts Society. He rescored his *Orient et Occident* for symphony orchestra, and conducted the new version at a Lamoureux-Colonne concert on 16th April, in a programme shared with other composer-conductors including Fauré, d'Indy and Dukas.

He was also supervising rehearsals for a new production of *Phryné* at the Opéra-Comique, an event he had been looking forward to ever since it was announced earlier in the year by Pierre Gheusi, the co-librettist of *Les Barbares*, who was now the Opéra-Comique's director. The singer for the title role was Mary Dorska (she liked her name billed as one word, Marydorska) who had lately made her operatic debut in *Manon*. When Saint-Saëns heard her in February he was full of enthusiasm. "She will be marvellous", he told Renaud. "She is very beautiful, gifted and with a ravishing voice . . . Everything is being done to make it a great success. I shall go home in triumph."[33] He conducted the first performance on 12th April, in a gala evening which also featured act one of *Manon*, act four of *Carmen* and a new ballet, with the *Marseillaise* ending the programme on a note of patriotic fervour. The event made 18,000 francs for the war effort in French Africa, and Saint-Saëns was delighted by the reception given to *Phryné*, for which he had always had a special fondness. His only regret was that he could not conduct the two further performances, on 27th April and 6th May, for on 23rd April he was due to set off on another long-distance voyage, this time to Argentina. Before leaving Paris he sent Gheusi some money for the stage hands – "what would we do without these humble but indispensable helpers?" – adding that he would have declined the invitation to South America if he had known earlier of the director's plans to revive *Phryné*. He was very grateful for the opera's "second birth": it would, he was sure, be more brilliant than the first. Work on the revival gave him "the greatest pleasure and in no way exhausted me, on the contrary! If I do not return from this voyage of adventure, I should have had the advantage of ending my existence with one of the greatest artistic joys of my interminable career . . ."[34]

The possibility of not returning from another journey across the ocean was a very real one. German submarines were again targeting passenger ships, having desisted for a while in response to American threats following the sinking of the *Lusitania*. The Spanish composer Granados and his wife were among the first victims when the *Sussex* was torpedoed in the Channel in March 1916. Granados had been one of several European composers invited to Argentina at the start of the year, along with Messager, Charpentier and Saint-Saëns. The last reached South America safely at the end of April, looking forward to "seeing again the Southern Cross, the Centaur, and Orion in reverse".[35] He took up residence at La Plata, east of Buenos Aires. His first major engagement was to conduct *Samson et Dalila* at the Colon Theatre in the capital, before an audience that included the Argentine president. He then appeared as pianist in a number of chamber concerts at the theatre and in the district of Cordoba, which were all of his own works except for a Chopin impromptu. Everywhere he attracted large audiences who were aware that his visit was an event of special interest. He was presented with a copy of Dante by a leader of the Italian colony but as the Grand Old Man of French music he aroused particularly strong enthusiasm among the French community in the city, a rallying point for national pride and patriotic feeling for the distant homeland in peril. He was taken on a tour of the port works and other French projects in the city, and at the end of June was joined in a packed hall by Messager and Xavier Leroux, newly arrived to conduct at the Colon Theatre, to hear an orchestral concert of his works organised by the Argentine Chamber of Music.

From Buenos Aires he crossed the Plate for a brief stay in Montevideo, where he played his fifth concerto, the *Rapsodie d'Auvergne* and Mozart's concerto K.488

at the Solis Theatre on 13th July. It seemed to him that he had never played better in his life. As on previous visits to the Americas, he astounded observers with the stamina that belied his age. The Montevideo newspaper *El Dia* noted his "extraordinary mental alertness, marvellous physical vigour and youthful spirit".[36] Interest here was if anything even greater than in Argentina. Uruguay, South America's most liberal and progressive democracy at the time, saw France as the model and beacon of liberty, and strongly supported the French cause in the war, so much so that the country had declared 14th July a national holiday the year before. Saint-Saëns's presence in the capital on that date boosted the celebrations, and led to a request from the Uruguayan government for a new national hymn. He responded with an orchestral *Hymne pour le 14 juillet*, but it created rather less impression even than the 1902 *Coronation March* and *Hail! California*, and the score was never published. There was in any case little chance of it being adopted as a national anthem because of subsequent political changes and because 25th August took precedence as Uruguay's official independence day. Nevertheless, the composer was paid 5,000 francs for it, which he donated to a charity for musicians on his return to France.

Towards the end of his stay in Montevideo, fatigue and the onset of a paralysis in his left hand caused him to cancel plans to go on to Brazil. He returned instead to La Plata, from where he took a train to the harbour and a ship bound for Lisbon on 27th July. His send-off was of the kind usually reserved for visiting heads of state. Crowds thronged the railway station to see him go, and as he took his seat in the compartment the municipal band played rousing marches, concluding with the *Marseillaise.*

Ahead lay the prospect of another autumn and winter in wartime Paris. At the beginning of November he was at a memorial ceremony at the Conservatoire for members killed or missing at the front, at which the prelude to *Le Déluge* was played along with extracts from Fauré's Requiem. "Your Pie Jesu is the *only* Pie Jesu, just as Mozart's Ave Verum is the only Ave Verum", he wrote to Fauré. "It was a beautiful ceremony. I should like to have said a few words at the end but I could not break through the crowd."[37] True to form, his health broke down again following the exertions of the spring and summer, and the onset of cold weather. In November, following a concert programme with Fauré at the Salle Gaveau in aid of refugee children from invaded territories, and a production of *Samson et Dalila* at the Opéra which he conducted, he succumbed to a severe attack of bronchitis. But when the illness had passed its worst, he used his enforced leisure to write the *Sept Improvisations* for organ, which he dedicated to his old pupil and friend Gigout. In terms of composition, the period 1916–17 was relatively fallow by Saint-Saëns's standards. Apart from the *Hyme pour le 14 juillet*, the most substantial score was that for *On ne badine pas avec l'amour* which opened at the Odéon on 8th February 1917. This was also a fairly lightweight composition, but it does show Saint-Saëns's supreme skill in the art of incidental music, setting the atmosphere and stressing the comic aspects with succinctness and subtlety. Henri Quittard in *Le Figaro*, one of a number of critics surprised that a composer of Saint-Saëns's seniority and stature should undertake so apparently trivial a task, was delighted by the music's "exquisite touch and delicate expression", in which abounded "youth and freshness of inspiration as much as variety, spirit and emotion", from the fountain scene prelude to the chapel scene finale with its "pure and serene beauty".[38]

The score, which was not published, was Saint-Saëns's last contribution to the theatre, though not the end of his association with it, as he continued to promote and occasionally conduct his operas. He remained intensely interested in the vocal art both in and outside the theatre. His other works dating from 1916–17 are all vocal: two unaccompanied church choruses, three part-songs and a solo song 'Honneur à l'Amérique', the last marking the entry of the United States into the war. He was to go on writing vocal pieces, solo and choral, until the last months of his life. And he praised Fauré for introducing at the Conservatoire a complete vocal training course – as opposed to the preparatory course he had denounced earlier – designed to teach both technique and performance accuracy:

Thanks to you there will no longer come from the school singers who know how to do neither a trill nor a scale . . . While you are in the process of making reforms in the singing department, how happy I should be to see you bring the axe to those abominable 'traditions', that habit of doing things which the composer never thought of . . . It is the duty of the Conservatoire to combat these horrors, and to forbid its professors to encourage and propagate them.[39]

He was also pleased that his second concerto had been chosen as the Conservatoire's test piece for cello students, believing that this would help bring the work from behind the shadow of the first concerto. He knew, however, with accurate foresight, that "it will never be as well-known as the first; it is too difficult". He offered to help judge the examination performances, and wanted to hear the opera and opéra-comique competitions as well. However, he realised that with concert and other commitments ahead, he would not have the time, as "one cannot be everywhere at once". In the summer of 1917, he was again taking the waters at Bourbon-l'Archambault to ease the paralysis that had returned to his legs and, more worryingly, was affecting his fingers too. The treatment seems to have been only partially successful: it "has restored my fingers", he wrote to Fauré. "As to my legs, they will no longer rival those of fleet-footed Achilles."[40]

The walking difficulties, and the bronchial and pulmonary illnesses that plagued him with greater frequency in the last years of his life served to heighten an awareness of age and isolation. Inviting Gigout to his birthday dinner in October 1917 he commented sardonically: "One is eighty-two only once in life; but it is not more fun for that. I need consolation."[41] The display of his sculpted bust at the Conservatoire only reinforced the feeling of belonging more to the dead than to the living; he suggested to Fauré that the bust should be placed in the library, "where I had my education".[42] It was perhaps this growing sense of isolation from the present that led to reconciliation with his old enemy Vincent d'Indy. D'Indy, now in his sixties, was clinging to a fast-fading post-Wagnerian glow, and was also, in his own way, coming to be regarded as a figure from the past. The reconciliation was marked by an agreement to differ over several aspects of the nature and purpose of music. D'Indy's views were outlined in his *Cours de Composition Musical.* Saint-Saëns replied in his booklet *Les Idées de Vincent d'Indy*, in which he takes issue with his old adversary on such matters as the origins of music, the expressive content of sixteenth-century music and the worth of César Franck. Saint-Saëns disputed the assertion that art originated out of a desire to express religious emotion, arguing that it came about rather to satisfy a need known as "aesthetic sense", which arose "when man, instead of being solely concerned with the utility of an object he had made, concerned himself with its form".[43] Contrary to d'Indy, he believed that sixteenth-century polyphony was designed to be sung as he had heard it as a young man in Rome, "without nuance or expressive intent", and that the view of it as expressive of high religious emotion was a modern romantic misconception. "The mentality of the sixteenth century was not ours . . . That at least is my hypothesis. I affirm nothing, I was not there. But I very much fear that this hypothesis is the truth", he told d'Indy in a letter. On Franck he remained adamant that his music was in general "graceless and charmless". But having stated their respective positions at some length, the two men felt the personal bond of past battles, in a world that was passing them by. Saint-Saëns wrote to d'Indy explaining his reasons for publishing his views:

If I were like you surrounded by pupils I should not have written this little book. But, not being in such favourable circumstances, I have no other means of pointing out, in the interests of musical education, those of your ideas which do not accord with mine . . . You will see that I have done you justice in not sparing you my approval when this was possible for me.[44]

Work, as always, was the means of escape from sombre moods. In November 1917 there were rehearsals to direct for a revival of *Henry VIII* at the Opéra, a talk to the Astronomical Society on ways of combating public ignorance of the sciences and a concert in Le Havre. When Fauré asked him to hear a promising pianist from the Conservatoire, Alfred Cortot's pupil Magdeleine Brard, he replied that he had no time, but would do his best to hear her recital at the Salle Gaveau on the morning of his departure for Le Havre. But while he was too busy to be despondent, personal sorrow was preparing to break in once more: on 20th November his beloved servant Geslin died in the clinic, after several operations. He heard the news from Jacques Durand. "I am much grieved", he told Fauré, "especially by the fact that I was not able to be there in his last moments."[45] Death, having robbed him of so many friends of his youth, had now taken a friend of his old age.

Again, the Opéra rehearsals helped to divert his mind. The revival of *Henry VIII* raised hopes for the work's future, especially as the great Italian singer Mattia Battistini was to take the title role. So keen was Saint-Saëns for him to succeed in it that he agreed to the part being transposed up a semitone to suit Battistini's high baritone. The revival opened the Opéra's season on 1st December. Battistini's Henry was, said *Le Figaro*, "a striking creation" in a strong cast that also included Marcelle Demougeot as Catherine,[46] but it was to prove one of the opera's last bursts of brilliance before it sank into obscurity.

The autumn's exertions, the death of Geslin and memories of the previous winter's assault on his health made the prospect of another winter in Paris unbearable. Saint-Saëns therefore headed south, passing through the Midi to Marseilles, where he stayed for a few weeks before moving on to Cannes. He was in the south for longer than he expected: the German offensive of spring 1918 and the bombardment of Paris made a return to the capital inadvisable. News of the deaths of civilians and the damage (including the mutilation of St Luke's statue on the outside of the Madeleine) intensified the bleakness of his mood, so that "at this time I think only of the war".[47] A consolation was his late-flowering friendship with the young poet Pierre Aguétant. Aguétant wrote to him at Cannes in April with samples of his work, partly because of Saint-Saëns's literary reputation and partly, no doubt, in the hope that he would bestow prestige on the verses by setting them. After the usual initial rebuff, Aguétant persisted in asking for comments and advice, sweetening his persistence with expressions of admiration. "Garlands are a matter of indifference to me", came the reply, "but I am not insensitive either to talent or amiability." Curiously, it was an outburst of indignant rage from the young man, in reply to a request to "leave your lyre in the hall", that won Saint-Saëns over. He replied that "my innocent pleasantries have unleashed a storm", but that the storm had cleared the air and "you are dearer to me after it . . . What more must you have? That I embrace your knees, as Priam did those of Achilles?" Increasingly beset by loneliness and despondency, he could not resist the chance of a new friendship with a proud and talented youth, who, after only a brief correspondence, had already become "*mon cher poète*". "Old age", he told him, "is such a little thing compared with youth and poetry." When he finally returned to Paris in the summer, after more treatment at Bourbon-l'Archambault, he invited Aguétant to dinner and welcomed him with great warmth and affection. "He opened his arms and closed them round me tenderly," recalled the poet. He thereafter became a close companion and confidant, accompanying the aged composer on walks in nearby Monceau Park, which was about as far as he could go on his weak legs. Saint-Saëns set two of Aguétant's poems, 'Où nous avons aimé' and 'Angelus'. "The crime is committed; the 'Angelus' is my victim – it is you who wished it", he declared. He was not sure at first that 'Angelus' was suitable for setting, but decided to go ahead "for the pleasure of seeing my name next to yours". Indeed, his fine ear for the musical potential of words sometimes put him in a delicate situation with the poet: when Aguétant wanted him to set his poem 'La Paix', he had to decline, but could not say why. "Your poem is ravishing but too literary to be set to music. That is not to say that your verse which I have set is not literary. It is so difficult to explain . . . "[48]

Composition in any case was made increasingly difficult by failing eyesight, which was particularly troublesome in 1918. Apart from the two Aguétant songs, the only other pieces written during the year were a song, 'Victoire', and the *Marche Interalliée* for military band. Depressed and disillusioned as he was by the continuing deadlock on the western front, he never lost his patriotic sentiments and beliefs in ultimate victory. "I am not a prophet, but I believe we are destined to see Germany defeated brusquely, like a balloon burst by a pin", he wrote in July 1918.[49] A large part of Belgian territory had been recovered by the Allies in September when he was invited by the Belgian queen, Elizabeth, to be her guest at a villa near the front line. He accompanied her on a walk in the forest, played to her on an old, worn piano, heard an orchestra of Belgian soldiers – "it has all the qualities of an experienced orchestra and, more than that, of youth, which nothing can replace" – and was woken at night by distant explosions and cannon fire. Early next morning the queen and her entire household saw him into the car taking him to Boulogne. The Belgian royal family, widely admired for their resistance to occupation, held a special place in his affections, and he saw them as a symbol of hope for civilisation. On 19th October he wrote: "I am happy to see my dear Belgian sovereigns re-enter their kingdom. One can never meet them enough; without them Europe is lost."[50]

His hatred of Germany was more intense than ever. As the Allies pushed back enemy lines he declared that "the force of German resistance would be admirable, if it was possible to admire criminals". Later he joined popular calls for Germany to be heavily punished after the war. "It's rich, when they say they will not accept a humiliating peace. What would they have imposed on us, if they had been the victors? One doesn't even care to think of it. We cannot make conditions too hard." Napoleon's attitude in victory, he believed, was entirely different from that to be expected from a victorious Kaiser. The French emperor, he insisted, forbade pillage and paid for the destruction his wars caused.[51]

It was in this mood of virtuous nationalism that he wrote his song 'Victoire', to words by Paul Fournier, writer of *Hail! California*, though he fully realised the artistic and technical limitations of this type of music. The vocal line had to be within the range of one octave, it had to be easy to sing and remember, and at the same time not sound too familiar, like the *Marseillaise*. There was wider scope, though not much, in the *Marche Interalliée*, inspired by meetings of the Inter-Allied Circle at a Paris hotel, where "you could hear English military music of the first order".[52]

Within a few weeks the war was over, but Saint-Saëns, beset by physical ailments and disability, and more than ever prone to dejection, could not share in the general rejoicing. "There is too much grief", he lamented. Haunted by images of death and destruction, and aware of the huge arms industry the war had created, he sensed that the Europe which had been his musical home all his life had gone for good, and felt only foreboding. On the day of the Armistice he wrote to Aguétant: "Europe begins a grave malady of which I cannot predict the outcome . . . among all the ruins that surround us."[53] The old belief in human advancement through artistic and scientific endeavour, which he had once so confidently espoused, had been confounded.

XV • WORLD WEARY

A MAJOR WAR HAD BROKEN IN UPON SAINT-SAËNS'S THOUGHT AND OUT-look for the second time in his life, adding a heightened political awareness to his personal and artistic philosophy. But whereas the defeat of 1871 had been the spur to greater achievements within the context of nationalism, the victory of 1918 brought only a mood of pessimism set against a background of international uncertainty. The chaos in central and eastern Europe disturbed his instinct for order; despite the victory of the Right in the French elections of 1919 he bemoaned the growing strength of socialist movements throughout the continent. His old love affair with England and the English was soured by distrust of British intentions in the peace talks. He believed it when a French marshal called Lloyd George "an evil man".[1] He watched the victory parade, from a window overlooking the Champs-Elysées, with a jaundiced eye, complaining that he could not hear the military music because of the cheering crowd. And while, at thirty-five, war had sharpened his faith in the destiny of his country as a great musical power, at eighty-three it left him only with cynicism. "What I believe we have now is the apathy after the war, the tendency of the French to forget everything too easily . . . There are too many people, alas, who see in the world their own personal interests."[2]

He had a growing feeling of having lived too long into an alien age. Most of his friends had died, more recently Clairin, Lecocq and Ecorcheville, the last of whom was killed in battle. He was given to lamenting the fact that he had been left behind to suffer ever more disabling bouts of illness, which now began to include heart trouble. Having lived with illness so often, he was calmly philosophical about the prospect of death. When stricken by bronchial congestion in August 1918 he told an anxious Aguétant not to "revolt against the inevitable; be used to the idea that no one lives forever and that at eighty years of age one will not have long . . . Is it so necessary to live a long time? The ancients thought otherwise and they are often right." Sometimes he was more hopeful of recovery. "The bad time cannot last forever", he wrote in January 1919, "and soon doubtless I shall be able to take my baths and my walks again." A year later he was more despondent. "Existence has become so disagreeable that I regret having lived so long. I should have died the day after the victory!"[3]

A consolation was being able to travel again to North Africa for the winter. From Algiers on 28th December 1918 he wrote: "I have seen the port, the sea, the distant mountains, a view I have known for a long time but which I see again." What was especially delightful was the sight of blue sky. He wrote from Cannes the following spring:

I never tire of it whereas I am soon wearied by a grey sky and the absence of sun and blue. True, beautiful, stormy clouds can be appreciated; they are even splendid, as long as they do not hide all the blue. The blue is very varied, according to the climate and the season. It is marvellous at Cannes, exquisite in Egypt, where it is clear and not at all dark . . .

But however marvellous the sky in southern France, it could not rival the climate of his beloved Algeria, as he wrote from Marseilles in April that year:

Oh, I would if I could stay in Algeria among the greenery and the flowers. Why must I return to the cold, which I detest? But one cannot escape fate. I used to dream at one time of ending my days in a small town on the outskirts of Algiers, with no other care than to put in plants and watch them grow. Instead of this, I shall be to my last day caught up in an unbearably giddy round.[4]

Despite the illnesses, the disability and the despondency, he was still able to dazzle audiences from the concert platform, his technique as brilliant as ever. Indeed, he was still working to improve it further. Just a month before his death, Jacques Durand heard him play Rameau with difficult trills executed to perfection, and was told that he had been working on them for a long time and that only then did he believe he had the technique for them.[5]

The post-war years also saw a final burst of composition. In a musical world he found increasingly incomprehensible, he turned more than ever inwards in these last works, to a private world of tradition and regularity. Yet these qualities are often coupled with quite startling harmonic experiments, which make the pieces something more than mere reproductions. The admirer of classical elegance sometimes wanders down unexplored paths to make his last statements of formal clarity combined with innovative content. The two elements are well-demonstrated in the string quartet no. 2 in G of 1919. Its opening could be taken for that of a classical quartet from the time of Haydn, and it continues in fairly regular sonata style, except that the second subject is not only in the unusual key of A major but makes its first appearance in the recapitulation also in that key. The sudden leap from F sharp major to G for the recapitulation is an example of some daringly abrupt key changes, but the movement is laced also with more subtle harmonic shifts, a feature which comes into its own in the molto adagio. This extraordinary piece, though based in C minor, seems of indeterminate key, the material changing shape like passing clouds. An andantino section in contrasted rhythm promises more stable contours but this too wanders off into distant tonalities, its final appearance in C major a short burst of sunshine before the gloom and uncertainty return briefly to end the movement.

The feeling of chromatic instability continues in the slow interlude that precedes the finale, a swirling mist out of which breaks at last the clear visibility of an allegretto rondo, announced by four pizzicato crotchets and a sustained dominant seventh chord which, together with a brief triplet figure, will later be integrated into the argument. The rondo theme, with its rising intervals of a fifth, restores us to the world of classical sobriety, and the subsidiary passages include an energetic fugue crowned by the reappearance of the pizzicato crotchets and dominant seventh. When he visited America in 1906 Saint-Saëns told the press that his ambition was to write "a really beautiful string quartet", implying that he had not succeeded in his first essay in the form.[6] If the second also fell short of his ideal, he could at least feel that he had made a creditable effort.

The harmonically less adventurous Morceau de Concert for harp and orchestra instead combines with classical elegance the virtuosity of the romantic concerto style. The stiff chordal opening, which also heralds the coda, gives way to three episodes. The first is based on a theme in folk style, the second is a tranquil fantasia and the third a march, with Mendelssohnian overtones, that breaks out – all too briefly – into a flowing lyricism. This is interrupted too soon and too easily by the return of the opening chords, an example of the old stylistic eagerness to regain emotionally safe ground, but this fault, though it slightly weakens the overall structure of the piece by foreshortening a potentially strong section of it, is more than made up for by fleeting passages of great beauty and brilliance.

Saint-Saëns's deepening sense of the value of tradition in a world seemingly more intent than ever on abandoning it found another expression in his insistence on the greatest possible accuracy and authenticity in the editing and performance of music. He was outraged over the insertion of a ballet into the last act of *Carmen*, already disfigured by Guiraud's recitatives. In October 1919 he wrote to Emile Straus, who had married Bizet's widow: "Such a procedure would be understandable if it concerned a work that needed support. But *Carmen*! Is there a more brilliant success?" The sacrilege might just have been tolerable if the music for the ballet had been taken from the previous acts: Saint-Saëns professed that he himself would have been willing to do this because the unity of the opera "would not then have been destroyed". But the music instead came from other works of Bizet "that are not at all Spanish in character". To the former Mme Bizet he wrote: "It is not only in Paris but in the whole world that this unfortunate ballet disfigures the last act of *Carmen*." He regarded the publisher Choudens as the chief culprit and suggested an appeal to the Society of Authors, but with little hope, as musicians were in a small minority in the group.[7] His lack of faith was justified: it was not until the 1970s that serious and sustained efforts were made to perform *Carmen* as Bizet wrote it, without the excrescences and distortions of a century.

For Saint-Saëns, of course, the issue was a personal as well as an artistic one. It touched the sanctity of the memory of a much-loved "friend and comrade", whom he contrasted with the rivals and enemies "under the guise of friendship" he had known. Bouts of nostalgia, brought on by thinking and writing about the musical greats who were part of his past, were frequent. When Henderson called at his home one day in 1920 he found him reading letters Gounod had written to him when he was a boy.[8] This retreat into the past is perhaps most strikingly expressed musically in the Six Fugues for piano, written in Algeria during the winter of 1919–20 for a friend and former pupil Isidor Philipp, professor of piano at the Conservatoire. In his letter asking him to accept the dedication, Saint-Saëns asserted whimsically that the fugues were inspired by "the climate, the couscous and perhaps some devil driving me on". They seem rather to represent an attempt to rediscover his roots, to recapture, from the vantage point of technical maturity and mastery, his childhood enthusiasm for Bach and his introduction by Boëly to a musical world which combined formal discipline with flights of harmonic fancy. The harmonies and modulations sometimes seem so wayward as to give the impression of an improvisation, but in fact each fugue is an ingenious treatment of its subject (two subjects in the last, a double fugue), the whole set using a number of technical tricks, especially inversion and augmentation. "You will find in them a distant reflection of the *Well-Tempered Clavier* despite my efforts to put aside the idea", he told Philipp, "but the demands of the genre inevitably lead to certain forms, as the demands of verse lead to similar forms in poetry." He demonstrated that they were far removed from the contemporary world with its supposed disregard for rules by making up an atonal theme of a type Schoenberg might have written. Such a theme, he said, would have prevented any comparison with the '48', "but what a response, what a counter-subject!"[9]

The fugues were written as Algiers was once more working its magic, restoring, to some extent, health and appetite. "I treat myself to enormous prawns which are found here, and fresh fish, my preferred diet. I no longer have bronchitis nor catarrh, and all would be for the better if my legs were more awake, but they are hardly that." But the weather could still turn cold, as he had found on previous visits. When it did so he moved, as before, further south to Hammam-r'Irha early in 1920 only to find snow even there. "The palm trees, all white, have a strange appearance . . . I have had to light a fire . . ."[10]

At the same time he was looking forward to his first visit to Greece, at the invitation of the Athens Conservatoire. A lifelong student of the classical world, he regretted having left it so late to see the great monuments of ancient Greek civilisation for himself, when his failing constitution made it more difficult to explore as much as he would have liked. For the bronchial pneumonia which the Algerian climate had helped to alleviate returned in the spring, and he had still not fully recovered when he arrived in Athens on 13th May. Straightaway he had to embark on a series of engagements as pianist and conductor, culminating in an open-air concert at the Odeon of Herodes Atticus at the foot of the Acropolis, in which he conducted *La Jeunesse d'Hercule*. Yet despite the demands, he found his two weeks in Greece wonderfully stimulating, being, as he said, "feted there as nowhere else". He met the charismatic prime minister Venizelos; the Conservatoire orchestra was "excellent, playing my works to perfection"; and everywhere he went he attracted large crowds shouting "Vive la France!" – a cry "that went to my heart".[11] After his last concert he was showered with flowers and students placed themselves in the harness to draw his carriage back to his rooms. Towards the end of his stay he was taken to see some of the principal archaeological sites of Attica, sufficiently invigorated to tackle also the arduous climb up to the Parthenon. There he was able to admire the grandeur and beauty of that famous ruin and the views across the city and the sea. Nevertheless, the effort seriously taxed his frail legs, and he could not help wishing he had made the journey to Greece as a younger man. "I made it too late. Still, as the proverb says, better late than never!"[12] One result of the visit was his promotion of the career of the young Greek composer Dimitri Mitropoulos, whose opera *Sister Beatrice* he heard while in Athens. He recommended Mitropoulos to Busoni in Berlin and praised him highly in the Paris press on his return.

The Greek experience did much to restore his zest for life. Yet even this pleasant memory had been soured by the end of the year, after the defeat of Venizelos in the October elections and the return of King Constantine, exiled during the war because of his pro-German views. Having been so delighted by the welcome he had received from the Greeks, by December he was denouncing them as "turncoats, who can be relied on for nothing".[13]

In the meantime there had been more public performances, an eighty-fifth birthday concert at the Paris Trocadero, a recital tour of Belgium and Switzerland later in October and conducting during the opera season in Algiers. It seemed as if he could go on forever. As Jacques Durand put it: "Despite the burden of years, he looked so full of life that the thought that one day he would be no more hardly entered my head."[14] Other projects included the working out of figured basses of seventeenth- and eighteenth-century viola sonatas by Tartini, Corelli and others, and the revision and orchestration of his 1862 cello suite. And he was still writing new music, albeit on a small scale. The three sonatas for wind instruments are small masterpieces each exploring a wide range of tonal expressiveness within a context of stylistic and formal simplicity.

The D major oboe sonata, dedicated to Louis Bas, principal oboist at the Conservatoire Concerts Society, is an echo of the second piano concerto in that its three movements are in order of increasing speed. A gentle andantino in sonata form is followed by a lilting allegretto in pastoral style, introduced and rounded off by a recitative, which gives way to the molto allegro of the finale. This is the most substantial portion of the work, and shakes off the rather dreamy serenity of the earlier movements with a vigorous working out of two main ideas, the first, in D minor, dominated by triplets, the second based on a falling chromatic sequence. As the music regains the tonic major, this second theme is given out by the oboe in broad, augmented form to usher in the triumphant coda.

The clarinet sonata in E flat begins and ends with a tender, flowing melody tinged with autumnal sadness, continuing in the first movement through a series of gentle harmonic twists until it dies away in a pianissimo fall down the tonic chord. A delicate allegro introduces a brighter mood but deep gloom follows in the lento, a solemn chorale that tests first the clarinet's lower register then its upper. This leads directly into the vigorous finale which, as in the oboe sonata, provides the main display of virtuosity. The material includes a curious six-note figure twice repeated, each time a semitone lower, and a modified recollection of the first movement theme. There is a brief pianissimo recalling a phrase from the second movement that gives way to a reprise of the sonata's opening melody, fully stated, bringing the work to a poignant close – a simple device yet effective in leaving a sense of thematic and formal unity.

In the G major sonata for bassoon the form is turned inside out, the central scherzo and adagio rather than the outer movements providing the main substance. It opens with a sonata movement of extreme conciseness, with a rippling piano accompaniment, that is little more than an introduction to the allegro scherzando, the main test of the instrument's technical possibilities, with its staccato leaps contrasted with a more lyrical subsidiary idea. The adagio features an extended song-like theme made up of a single rhythmic pattern whose constant repetition is a reminder of one of the composer's stylistic hallmarks from his earlier years, as is the promised build-up of emotional intensity that is instead reined in by a conventional return of the opening. A cadence in the unrelated key of B flat prepares the way for a finale so brief that it seems its sole function is to dispel, in a jovial romp back to the home key, any lingering melancholy. Saint-Saëns dedicated the sonata to Léon Letellier, principal bassoon at the Opéra and the Concerts Society.

The winter of 1920–21 in Algeria was again a cold one, but Saint-Saëns was not unduly troubled. "What is that beside the cold of Europe?" he asked.[15] He was saddened by not being able to walk as much as he wished, writing to Gigout on 10th January: "No, my dear friend, 1921 will not rejuvenate me. If it could only give me back my legs!"[16] But in February he had the pleasure of dining with Queen Victoria's daughter Princess Beatrice at the Algiers home of a rich Englishman. It was his first meeting with the princess since he accompanied her in front of her mother over forty years before. Also in February he was asked by students in Algiers for a march that could be played or sung, and duly obliged with a piece for chorus and/or military band. Two more choral pieces followed (though not the *Hymne à Jeanne d'Arc* he had contemplated the previous autumn), as well as several songs, including three settings of the sixteenth-century poet

Ronsard. His last published work, the *Feuillet d'Album* for piano, was written for a member of the Rothschild family.

In the spring he returned to his home in Rue de Courcelles for what was to be the last time. By now his rooms were crammed full of gifts and souvenirs from his many concerts around the world, enough for a second museum. He told Aguétant: "Above all, don't give me any presents. I no longer know where to put them!"[17] Still there were the inevitable engagements – and, like most celebrities, while he professed to find the "giddy round" unbearable, he did not like to be ignored either. He was hurt to find on returning to Paris that he had not been invited onto a government committee to organise three concerts at the Salle Gaveau as a tribute to French music. Worse, none of the concerts included any of his works. "To complain, to protest I cannot", he wrote to one of the organisers, "but I thought perhaps you could make some comment."[18]

An invitation to speak at the inauguration of a new American conservatory at Fontainebleau in June helped to make amends. While welcoming this new opportunity to strengthen the musical links between France and America, he used the occasion to make one last spirited defence of tradition and one last vigorous attack on the vanguard, warning against any further experimentation with "audacious dissonances". "The extreme limit has been reached", he declared.

To go beyond would mean a relapse into the cacophony from which we have emerged. Besides, there is no need for it. In the vast field of present-day music there is plenty of room for inventions which is practically, if not theoretically, endless. Innovation does not necessarily mean we must have recourse to dissonance . . .

He likened the readiness to tolerate ever more outlandish departures from traditional methods to his neighbour, who "makes painful efforts to play the piano". The piano is badly out of tune but she seems unaware that anything is wrong because she does nothing about it. The listener is in danger of falling into the same error in modern music. "One can become accustomed to uncleanliness, to vice, even to crime . . . Why cannot we understand that in art, as in everything else, there are some things to which we must not become accustomed?" And he advised students to avoid striving for originality for its own sake, which was likely to produce only "a blend of folly and weirdness". Music was best served by allowing "your personal contribution to it to express itself naturally" because – and here the conservative and traditionalist sums up his argument – "we do not keep a tree alive by hacking away at its roots".[19]

In August he gave a recital at the Casino in Dieppe, and announced at the end that he had played in public for the last time. He meant it this time. It was no matter for regret, he wrote to Aguétant, for it meant goodbye to all the pressures, "the obligation to work every day to keep the fingers in trim, not to have lunch if the concert is during the day, not to have dinner if it is in the evening;

and often one is ill at ease all the time beforehand". Then there was "the humiliation of feeling oneself to be the plaything of the public". With the Dieppe recital he felt he had bowed out in triumph, having played "brilliantly". "I shall not finish, as so many others do, on a pitiful decrescendo."[20] Yet even this "last recital" was not quite the last: he was still to give an organ recital at the Institute, and to play in his septet there. As he walked with difficulty to the platform for the septet performance, his beard (though not his hair) now completely white, a member of the Academy of Sciences remarked to him that "our old legs do not function so well any longer", to which he replied: "Our legs do not. But in a few moments you will see how my fingers function."[21] His fellow performers certainly did, for they had trouble in keeping pace with him as he indulged his cheeky habit of accelerating the tempo.

The technical powers that had once astounded Wagner were as alive as ever, as Durand was to discover when Saint-Saëns called at his office in the Place de la Madeleine and, after a conversation about Liszt's *Faust* symphony, proceeded to play the whole work on the piano from memory.[22] Neither did his lack of mobility prevent him from taking rehearsals for a revival of *Ascanio* which Hahn was to conduct at the Opéra in November as a belated eighty-sixth birthday tribute. Yet behind the image of the tireless veteran there arose a crushing sense of failure such as he had never felt before. The supreme self-confidence that had carried him through his long life and often difficult career seemed suddenly to evaporate. Durand met him during an interval at one of the *Ascanio* performances and found him "unusually despondent", convinced that the opera would never succeed. His publisher tried to argue him out of it but Saint-Saëns was "inconsolable". The next day he left for Algiers and Durand never saw him again.[23]

The more congenial climate of his favourite resort helped to restore him to his old business-like self. At Wolff's request he orchestrated his 1868 Romance for violin, piano and harmonium, and began to plan new projects – a sonata for cor anglais, orchestration of his *Valse Nonchalante* as a dance for the ballerina Napierkowska and the editing of some unpublished Mozart pianoforte manuscripts. He attended a performance of *Lakmé* at the Algiers Opéra, and the thought that his own *Samson et Dalila* would soon be receiving its five-hundredth performance at the Paris Opéra, an event to which he very much looked forward, lifted his spirits further. But as the weather again turned cold he caught a chill, and on 16th December decided to spend the day in his rooms at the Hotel Oasis, in the company of his servant Jean Laurendeau and Jean Bonnerot. According to Bonnerot, he was in good spirits, even singing some Verdi arias. He practised the piano, as usual, and wrote some letters, one of them including some reminiscences of Pauline Viardot and the difficulty she had, despite her linguistic facility, singing Polish in Chopin's songs. After playing dominoes with Laurendeau he felt unwell and went to bed early; before long he was struggling for breath as congestion of the lungs took hold. Bonnerot called a doctor, but it was too late. Shortly before eleven o'clock that night, after a brief period of ease, Saint-Saëns died. He never saw the five-hundredth *Samson*. Instead, death had come, as he had wished and as he had not dared to hope, amid the peace of Algiers and far from the hurly-burly of Paris. It was the same month that had seen the deaths of both his parents.

For an elder statesman, however, a return to the French capital after death was not to be avoided. There could be no simple funeral but instead all the pomp and ceremony due to a holder of the Grand Croix of the Légion d'Honneur. Nevertheless, he would have been proud and delighted by the message of sympathy to President Millerand from the Belgian king and queen, offering condolences on the loss of an "illustrious composer whose works and talent had so many admirers in Belgium".[24]

As a non-Christian, Saint-Saëns had stipulated that the religious part of the funeral service should be kept to a minimum, and as a last stand against the Italian influence in French music absolutely forbade the playing of Stradella's setting of the Pie Jesu. In fact, all the music played was to be his own. A service was held at the cathedral in Algiers attended by the governor-general and other colonial officials, with selections of Saint-Saëns's music played by the municipal orchestra. A large crowd watched as the cortege, attended with full military honours, moved to a chapel where the body awaited passage to France. It arrived in Marseilles the next day, where it was met by a relative and Saint-Saëns's old colleague from the Béziers days, Castelbon de Beauxhostes. A platoon of hussars escorted the funeral party to the railway station and a train bound for the capital, where a state funeral was held on 24th December at the Madeleine, scene of so many of the composer's finest hours. The church's facade was hung, like the coffin, with black drapes fringed with silver, and inside a huge silver cross was suspended above the high altar. Outside, crowds, troops and military bands thronged the route from the Place de la Concorde. Music played at the service, by a 250-strong orchestra drawn from the Conservatoire and the Opéra, included three extracts from the Requiem, the adagio from the C minor symphony and, as the coffin was carried from the church, the *Marche Héroïque*. Durand was among the bearers; as was Gigout, representing Saint-Saëns's old pupils from the Ecole Niedermeyer; the director of the Institute, Imbart de la Tour; the director of the Academy of Fine Arts, Paul Léon and Opéra director Jacques Rouché.

The funeral procession made its way through crowd-lined streets to the Montparnasse cemetery where, after speeches by representatives of government, the Institute and the arts, the body was interred in the family vault. Among the mourners, keeping a little apart from the relatives who ignored her, was the veiled figure of Mme Marie Saint-Saëns, the composer's widow.

XVI • THE LEGACY

THE YEARS HAD BROUGHT NO RECONCILIATION BETWEEN SAINT-SAËNS'S family and the wife he had spurned. She was still blamed for the deaths of the two children, and all contact with her was rigorously avoided. The state funeral was the only public event in his honour which the relatives were unable to prevent her attending. Saint-Saëns himself left her nothing in his will, so completely had he expunged her from his life. His extensive collection of books and manuscripts he bequeathed to the public library at Dieppe, the rest of his estate to his favourite cousin. But the family animosity towards Marie turned to outrage when she dared to contest the will, claiming an annual allowance from the cousin's daughter. When this was refused she went to court seeking outright ownership of half of Saint-Saëns's works published after their marriage, plus a stake in the proceeds from all his works. When this was rejected in July 1924 she appealed to a higher court, which, eighteen months later, also denied her outright ownership but granted rights to the proceeds, then estimated at 100,000 francs a year. On this she lived into a lonely old age until she died at her home near Bordeaux on 30th January 1950, at ninety-five. Her death, where it was reported at all, merited just a brief paragraph.

While Saint-Saëns's material legacy was being fought over, his musical legacy proved to be of more limited appeal. Just two years before his death the writer Jean Montargis, assessing the composer's place in French music, declared that "he is, with Rameau and Berlioz, our best claim to glory".[1] But after the death of "the last of the veterans", as the *Daily Telegraph* called him,[2] there followed a swift reaction to the praise and adulation he earned in life, a process of debunking not uncommon among composers' reputations. Saint-Saëns's fall from grace, however, was to be one of the most spectacular in musical history. For the debunkers were already well established in his lifetime, as we have seen, and it was their verdict that rang the loudest when his voice was silenced. There were some who praised him, notably Fauré in his obituary for the *Revue Musicale*, but even some of the praises carried undertones of fashionable disapproval. In his speech at the tomb, the composer and critic Alfred Bruneau spoke of an aspect of Saint-Saëns's work for which he was despised by some as much as he was admired by others. "Tradition captivated him more than innovation. In defence of it, when he felt it threatened, he fought with vivacity, courage and extraordinary violence."[3] The comment of Pierre Lalo in *Le Temps* was similarly double-edged. After hailing him as "the legitimate heir of the classical masters and at the same time one of the glories of French music . . . in the extraordinary precocity, facility and brilliance of his musical gift", he adds that "he is not their equal, and above all he is no Mozart".[4] Saint-Saëns himself would hardly have made such a claim (though there were those who did), and Lalo's argument carried less weight than that of Richard Aldrich in the *New York Times*. This was the view that was to remain and which has still not been dislodged: that Saint-Saëns's music had "invention, skill, ingenuity, a great feeling for form and rhythm, a mastery of resources", but rarely a "true creative force, passion, warmth, vivifying power or even spontaneity". Craftsmanship, Aldrich declared, was "not enough", and in his preoccupation with method rather than with matter, Saint-Saëns was content with themes that were "cold and grey".[5] This was echoed in London, where *The Times* obituary criticised him for not being always "fastidious" in his choice of themes, so that "the commonplace" jostled in the same composition, even in the same movement, with moments of "rare beauty and originality". The paper added that because Saint-Saëns was such a versatile composer time alone would put his reputation in perspective, and that "there is much that will probably be forgotten".[6]

One of the most uncompromising verdicts came from the thoroughly hostile Jean-Aubry, who wrote that Saint-Saëns lacked "generosity of mind and heart which, had he possessed it, might have imparted to his work the fullness and humanity we miss in it, in spite of its technical perfection". Jean-Aubry dismissed the works as "documents of musical history", rather than "living emanations of genius which will retain their vitality in spite of the passing of time and fashions".[7]

Time was indeed quick to consign the bulk of Saint-Saëns's works out of partial neglect to virtual oblivion. This was offset partly by publication in 1922 of the complete *Le Carnaval des Animaux*, on whose enormous popularity the fame of the composer largely came to rest, as he feared it would. The eclipse of his serious works was well advanced within three years of his death. When Fauré was breathing his last in November 1924 he told his sons:

When I am no longer here you will hear it said of my works 'After all, that was nothing much to write home about!' You must not let that hurt or depress you. It is the way of the world; it happened with Saint-Saëns and with others. There is always a moment of oblivion . . .[8]

For Saint-Saëns the moment was to last rather longer. In 1930, Dandelot complained about the "unjust and exaggerated disfavour into which Saint-Saëns's work has fallen", though he remained confident that, as with Mendelssohn, "posterity will do justice to a master who, if he had not the personality of a Gounod, a Fauré, a Debussy, had a superior talent and often attained strong and lasting beauty".[9] In 1935, the centenary of Saint-Saëns's birth, there was a brief rekindling of interest, when Hahn noted, with irony rather than pleasure, that "at last they play a bit of his music. His name is uttered. He is spoken about. It is all something new. For fifteen years he has been walled up in silence, as though we were ashamed of him."[10] But, with the exception of a handful of works, the silence soon closed in again, and the pedestal on which he had been placed at the height of his fame was cast down – literally, as well as figuratively. In 1944 his statue was destroyed, along with what was left of the sea-front buildings at Dieppe, as the German occupiers strengthened sea defences against Allied landings.

In the post-war years his music continued to lose ground, and critics continued to dismiss it as facile and heartless, in what was by now the received wisdom. The composer's old colleague Pierre Monteux attributed the neglect to a simple desire not to appear "old-fashioned". Much the same verdict has been passed by history on Mendelssohn, who, as noted by Dandelot, is in this respect a close parallel with Saint-Saëns. Both men have been dismissed as composers who had life too easy, being endowed with phenomenal gifts that made them brilliant technicians, but without soul and feeling. Mendelssohn's rehabilitation has been a slow process – his 150th anniversary has lately passed almost unnoticed. Similarly, Saint-Saëns's may yet be some way off, but that it is justified can be argued both from the point of view of his place in musical history and that of the music itself.

From the historical viewpoint, he is significant both in the French and in the wider European context, representing a sobering counter to romanticism in general and Wagner mania in particular. His contribution to the concert repertory is much greater than is generally recognised, notably in the concertos – especially the piano concertos – and the chamber works, while his songs would, if given the recognition they deserve, form a staple commodity in recital programmes. He also foreshadowed much of the twentieth-century style, its tendency to conciseness of utterance, its emotional restraint and its preference for lightness of texture. The concertos are particularly significant here, with their emphasis on balance between soloist and orchestra, while his stage and film scores are forerunners of an important aspect of the twentieth-century music industry.

By cultivating classical instrumental forms from an early age he acted as a kind of lightning conductor for the might of the European tradition to act on the French musical scene and help generate one of the great ages of French orchestral and chamber music, in the period to 1914. He represents, too, by virtue of his personality and his reaction to personal misfortune, a distinctive strand in the French style, one that was to be taken up by Ravel, Satie and others. This sees the composer less as a vehicle for personal expression and more as an impersonal observer, of the picturesque, the exotic, even the bizarre. The veteran Saint-Saëns, the incognito traveller seeking to lose his identity in ancient times and faraway places, embodies this particular aspect of the national aesthetic, and it is to be noted that none of his twelve operas treats of contemporary subjects.

But it is on the music itself that Saint-Saëns will ultimately be judged. The operas must remain something of a closed book in this respect in the face of a reluctance to test them on stage. The exception is *Samson et Dalila* which, though it has its critics, retains its popularity in the world's leading houses. Otherwise, we can see the ruthless orthodoxy of the modern world beginning to melt: a much wider range of Saint-Saëns's music is being recorded and broadcast, and more of his works are appearing in concert programmes. And as the music is more widely heard, the more it is appreciated, casting off the layers of prejudice that have smothered it for decades. Of course, much of the product of over eighty years of composition will stay forgotten, as Saint-Saëns himself realised, especially those works where his stylistic weaknesses are most apparent: the reluctance to follow through the emotional and dramatic implications of a theme, the over-use of a thematic or rhythmic pattern, the impression sometimes given of careless dismissal when a more expansive treatment might have been expected. But the music's positive qualities will provide a basis for the rediscovery of much of Saint-Saëns's considerable output, not just the technical flair but also the exuberance and vitality, the rhythmic drive, the contemplative moments, and the warmth and seductiveness of so many of the melodies, imbued with a sense of the greatness and dignity of the past, a poetic feeling for time and place. Time may yet do Saint-Saëns justice. In 1914 Jean Bonnerot wrote that it was too early to pass judgement on his works, and that he was a composer who "belongs to posterity".[11] The signs are that posterity will one day accept ownership.

APPENDICES

APPENDIX I • ESSAYS by SAINT-SAËNS

THE ESSAYS WHICH FOLLOW HAVE BEEN CHOSEN TO GIVE IN GREATER detail the arguments Saint-Saëns expounded on some key issues that concerned him in later life. They deal with the nature of artistic creation and form as its essence, and some of the absurdities of the Wagner craze, with a defence of Mendelssohn and Meyerbeer. They include one of his celebrated attacks on the modernists for disregarding centuries of musical evolution, and his account of the composition of *Hélène*, illustrating his approach to the medium of opera.

'Art for Art's Sake'

WHAT IS ART?

Art is a mystery – something which responds to a special sense, peculiar to the human race. This is ordinarily called the aesthetic sense, but that is an inexact term, for aesthetic sense signifies a sense of the beautiful and what is aesthetic is not necessarily beautiful. Sense of style would be better.

Some of the savage races have this sense of style, for their arms and utensils show a remarkable feeling for style, which they lose by contact with civilization.

By art let us understand, if you please, the fine arts alone, but including decorative art. Music ought to be included.

I shall astonish most of my readers, when I say that very few people understand music. For most people it is, as Victor Hugo said, an exhalation of art – something for the ear as perfume is for the olfactory sense, a source of vague sensations, necessarily unformed as all sensations are. But musical art is something entirely different. It has line, modelling, colour through instrumentation, all making up an ideal sphere where some, like the writer of these lines, live from childhood on, which others attain through education, while many others never know it at all. Furthermore, musical art has more movement than the other fine arts. It is the most mysterious of them all, although the others are mysterious as it is easy to see.

The first manifestation of art occurs through attempts to reproduce objects. Such attempts have been found which date back to prehistoric times. But what is primitive man's idea in such attempts? He wants to record by a line the contour of the object, the likeness of which he wishes to preserve. This contour and this line do not exist in nature. The whole philosophy of art is in that crude drawing. It bases itself on nature even while making something quite different in response to a special, inexplicable need of the human spirit. Accordingly nothing can be more chimerical or vain than the advice so often given to the artist to be truthful. Art can never be true, even though it should not be false. It should be true artistically, by giving an artistic translation which will satisfy the sense of style of which we have spoken. When art has satisfied this sense of style, the object of artistic expression has been attained; nothing more can be asked. But it is not the "vain effort of an unproductive cleverness," as our M. de Nun has said; it is an effort to satisfy a legitimate need, one of the loftiest and most honourable in human nature – the need of art.

If this is so, why should we demand that art be useful or moral? It is both in its own way, for it awakens noble and honest sentiments in the soul. That was the opinion of Théophile Gautier, but Victor Hugo disagreed. The sun is beautiful, he used to say, and it is useful. That is true, but the sun is not an object of art. Besides, many times Victor Hugo denied his own doctrine by writing verses which were merely brilliant descriptions or admirable bits of imagination.

We are, however, talking of art and not of literature. Literature becomes art in poetry but forsakes it in prose. Even if some of the great prose writers rendered their prose artistic through the beauty and harmony of their periods and the picturesqueness of their expressions, still prose is not art in its real nature. So, crude indecency aside, what would be immoral in prose ceases to be immoral in verse, for in poetry art follows its own code and form transcends the subject matter. That is why a great poet, Sully-Prudhomme, preferred prose to verse when he wanted to write philosophically, for he feared, on account of the superiority of form to substance in poetry, that his ideas would not be taken seriously. That explains as well why parents take young girls to hear an opera, when if the same piece was played without music they would be appalled at the idea. What Christian is ever shocked by *La Juive* or Catholic frightened away from *Les Huguenots*?

Because prose is far removed from art, it is unsuited to music, despite the fact that this ill-assorted union is fashionable today. In poetry there has been an effort to make it so artistic that form alone is considered and verse is written which is entirely without sense. But that is a fad which cannot last long.

Some time ago M. de Nun said:

Not to take sides is what the author is inhibited from doing. Art, to my way of thinking, is a setting forth of ideas. If it is not that – if it limits itself solely to considerations of form, to a worship of beauty for its own sake, without regard to the deeds and thoughts it brings to light, then it seems to me no better than the vain effort of an unproductive cleverness.

The eminent speaker is absolutely right as far as prose is concerned, but we cannot agree with him if poetry is considered.

Victor Hugo, in his marvellous ode *La Lyre et l'Harpe*, brings paganism and Christianity face to face. Each speaks in turn, and the poet in his last stanza seems to acknowledge that both are right, but that does not prevent the ode from being a masterpiece. That would not be possible in prose, but in the poem the poetry carries all before it.

Why is it that geniuses like Victor Hugo, distinguished minds, thinkers, and profound critics, refuse to see that art is a special entity which responds to a certain sense? If art accommodates itself marvellously, if it accords itself with the precepts of morality and passion, it is nevertheless sufficient unto itself – and in its self-sufficiency lies its heights of greatness. The first prelude of Sebastian Bach's *Well-Tempered Clavier* expresses nothing, and yet that is one of the marvels of music. The Venus de Milo expresses nothing, and it is one of the marvels of sculpture.

To tell the truth, it is proper to add that in order not to be immoral art must appeal to those who have a feeling for it. Where the artist sees only beautiful forms, the gross see only nudity. I have seen a good man scandalized at the sight of Ingres's *La Source.*

Just as morality has no function to be artistic, so art has nothing to do with morality. Both have their own functions, and each is useful in its own way. The final aim of morality is morality; of art, art, and nothing else.

FROM *Musical Memories*

'Anarchy in Music'

MUSIC IS AS OLD AS HUMAN NATURE. WE CAN GET SOME IDEA OF WHAT it was at first from the music of savage tribes. There were a few notes and rudimentary melodies with blows struck in cadence as an accompaniment; or, sometimes, the same primitive rhythms without any accompaniment – and nothing else! Then melody was perfected and the rhythms became more complicated. Later came Greek music, of which we know little, and the music of the East and Far East.

Music, as we now understand the term, began with the attempts at harmony in the Middle Ages. These attempts were laboured and difficult, and the uncertainty of their gropings, combined with the slowness of their development, excites our wonder. Centuries were necessary before the writing of music became exact, but slowly, laws were elaborated. Thanks to them the works of the sixteenth century came into being, in all their admirable purity and learned polyphony. Hard and inflexible laws engendered an art analogous to primitive painting. Melody was almost entirely absent and was relegated to dance tunes and popular songs. But the dance tunes of the time, on which, perhaps, erudition was not used sufficiently, were written in the same polyphonic style and with the same rigid correctness as the madrigals and the church music.

We simply do not know how they played anthems, masses and madrigals, in the absence of any indication of either the time or the emphasis. We find a few directions for expression, as in the first measures of Palestrina's Stabat Mater, but such directions are extremely rare. They are simply the first signs of the dawn of the far-off day of music with expression. Certain learned and well-intentioned persons endeavour to compare this music with ours, and we find in some of the modern editions instances of *molto espressivo* which seem to be good guesses. This exclusively consonant music, in which the intervals of fourths were considered dissonant, while the diminished fifth was the *diabolus in musica*, ought from its very nature to be antithetical to expression. Nothing in the Kyrie in *La Messe du Pape Marcel* gives the impression of a prayer, unless expressive accents, without any real justification, are introduced.

Expression came into existence with the chord of the dominant seventh from which all modern harmony developed. This invention is attributed to Monteverdi. No matter what has been said, however, it occurs in Palestrina's *Adoremus*. Floods of ink have been poured out in discussing this question, some affirming, while others – and not the least, by any manner of means – denying the existence of the famous chord. No equivocation is possible. It is a simultaneously played chord held by four voices for a whole measure. What is certain is that Palestrina, by putting aside the rules, made a discovery the significance of which he did not realise.

With the introduction of the seventh interval a new era began. It would be a grave error to believe that the rules were overturned, for, instead, new principles were added to old ones as new conditions demanded. They learned how to modulate, how to transpose from one key to the next key and finally to the keys farthest away. In his treatise on harmony Fétis studied this evolution in a masterly manner. Unfortunately his scholarship was not combined with deep musical feeling. For example, he saw faults in Mozart and Beethoven where there are only beauties, and beauties which even an ignorant listener – if he is naturally musical – will see without trouble. He did not understand the vast difference between the unlettered person who commits a solecism and Pascal, the inventor of a new syntax.

However that may be, Fétis gave us a comprehensive review in broad outlines of musical evolution down to what he justly called the 'omnitonic system', which Richard Wagner has achieved since. "Beyond that", he said, "I can see nothing more."

He did not foresee the atonic system, but that is what we have come to. There is no longer any question of adding to the old rules new principles which are the natural expression of time and experience, but simply of casting aside all rules and every restraint. "Everyone ought to make his own rules. Music is free and unlimited in its liberty of expression. There are no perfect chords, dissonant chords or false chords. All aggregations of notes are legitimate."

That is called, and they believe it, the *development of taste.*

He whose taste is developed by this system is not like the man who by tasting a wine can tell you its age and its vineyard, but he is rather like the fellow who with perfect indifference gulps down good or bad wine, brandy or whiskey, and prefers that which burns his gullet the most. The man who gets his work hung in the Salon is not the one who puts on his canvas delicate touches in harmonious tones, but he who juxtaposes vermilion and Veronese green. The man with a 'developed taste' is not the one who knows how to get new and unexpected results by passing from one key to another, as the great Richard did in *Die Meistersinger*, but rather the man who abandons all keys and piles up dissonances which he neither introduces nor concludes and who, as a result, grunts his way through music as a pig through a flower garden.

Possibly they may go farther still. There seems to be no reason why they should linger on the way to untrammelled freedom or restrict themselves within a scale. The boundless empire of sound is at their disposal and let them profit by it. That is what dogs do when they bay at the moon, cats when they mew, and the birds when they sing. A German has written a book to prove that the birds sing false. Of course he is wrong for they do not sing false. If they did, their song would not sound agreeable to us. They sing outside of scales and it is delightful, but that is not man-made art.

FROM *Musical Memories*

'Hélène'

LONG HAD I THE VISION OF HELEN FLEEING INTO THE NIGHT, ARRIVING crushed, all her strength gone, at the sea-side far from her palace, rejoined by Paris, the scene of passion, the resistance finally overcome, the last flight of the two lovers after a desperate struggle . . .

For never could I look upon Helen simply as a woman in love; she was the sport of Destiny, the victim of Aphrodite offered up by the goddess to her own glory, the prize of the Golden Apple, a great figure whose sin excites no mockery but rather a kind of sacred terror. See her on the walls of Ilion, the city upon which her very presence summons ruin and massacre. When she passes, the old men of Troy rise and greet her. Later on we find her in her husband's house, doing the honours of his palace with queenly dignity. No one dreams of reproaching her for the past, for leaving home, for the years spent in Troy and the many Greeks dead on her account! The daughter of Zeus meets with naught but universal regard and respect.

Consequently I had conceived the idea of depicting in music the hegira of the two lovers, had it not been so well-known how successfully this idea was parodied. To have these two epic characters, that had become comic, taken seriously, was for a long time not to be thought of; I had put off my plan, and, with the lapse of years, the very project itself had been forgotten.

A request made by M. Gunsbourg – which I at first rejected though afterwards he insisted upon my considering it carefully – sufficed to bring it all back again and to present Helen and Paris before me more living than ever.

My first intention – the intention of an idle man, I grant you – was to find someone who would collaborate with me. But who should this be? A collaborator might have wished to add his ideas on to my own and so ruin the simplicity of my conception, the result being that I made up my mind to work alone.

Alone? Not altogether. Following the example of our classical writers I had enlisted the services of Homer, Theocritus, Aeschylus, Vergil and even Ovid.

Without the help of Vergil should I have hazarded that description of Priam's palace, those gilded roofs and walls lined with shining polished brass, adorned with dazzling statues which in all probability were polychrome, that ensemble which gives almost a sense of verisimilitude to the strange architecture of Gustave Moreau? Should I have dared to utter the line: "Dans le sang de ses fils Priam est égorgé"?

Having made my notes and outlined my scenario, all I had to do was to set to work. At the time, I was in Cairo, the guest of His Highness Mohammed Ali, Pasha of Egypt, the Khedive's brother. I was in the enjoyment of complete liberty and of a calm undisturbed by visitors. These had probably been scared away by the guard of the palace gate, huge fellows in gorgeous costumes and formidably armed.

I cannot possibly say how I found the first musical phrase to which I subsequently adapted the line: "Des astres de la nuit tes yeux ont la clarté!".

I had reached this point when the director of the Khedive's theatre conceived the idea of giving a grand concert on behalf of the sailors of Brittany and of composing it entirely from my works.

Suddenly I found myself plunged into a round of rehearsals, compelled to take my own part in this solemnity. All this was incompatible with work that was in its initial critical stage. Regretfully I gave up *Hélène* and when, later on, I wished to take it up again, it was quite impossible. I was bewildered, out of tune so to speak. I had to quit my delightful abode in Cairo and proceed to the middle of the desert into the Thebaid of Ismailia – a refuge of light and silence – for what one is pleased to call 'inspiration'.

Ismailia, the favourite sojourn of the Prince of Arenberg, is a heavenly spot.

It is a *beata solitudo* inhabited by a number of highly civilised people of both sexes employed by the Suez Canal administration, a small though choice colony which included poets of no mean talent! And as these kindly folk are very busy, they people the solitude without disturbing it.

In twelve days I had written my poem. Then I set sail at Port Said for Paris, where preparations were in progress for a revival of *Henry VIII* at the Opéra. Once this was over, I was quite tired out; my 'composing machine' would not work any longer and I needed a week at Biarritz and another at Cannes to recover. Then I remembered that Aix-en-Savoie was close to a flowerdecked mountain, surrounded by a wonderful panorama and easy of access. Soon I found myself installed on Mount Revard where I sketched out almost the whole of the music of *Hélène* to be completed subsequently in Paris.

It is thus that one should always work, in calm and silence, far from importunate visitors and distractions of various kinds, soothed by the glorious sights of nature and the odours of flowers. When this is possible, work is more than a pleasure, it is voluptuous delight.

There has been noticed a certain analogy between the appearance of Pallas in *Hélène* and that of Brünnhilde in the second act of *Die Walküre.* Of this fact I was aware, though I found it impossible to avoid it.

Helen appeals for help to Zeus, her father. What can he do? Come himself? So formidable an appearance would not fit in with the framework of the opera. Send Mercury his messenger to her? The ancients might have permitted this, for Mercury conducted souls to the infernal regions; though in our opinion Hermes is not a god to be taken seriously, we cannot imagine him as threatening or terrible, predicting a catastrophe. On the contrary, such a role fell naturally to Pallas, the living antithesis of Cytherea who was also a daughter of Zeus; consequently hesitation was impossible.

In art, when logic commands, it must be obeyed and nothing else must be considered. Assuredly it is vexatious to find oneself in disaccord with one of the finest scenes on any stage; it would be even more vexatious to withdraw before an analogy which was necessarily inevitable.

Helen and Paris, Samson and Delilah, Adam and Eve, drama is always the same in its essence: the triumphant temptation, the irresistible attraction of the forbidden fruit.

Though protesting for form's sake, we have any amount of indulgence for and even sympathy with the vanquished.

Even the Church rejoices over Adam's lapse. *O felix culpa!* which had made necessary the Redemption, the very foundation of the Christian religion.

Suppose Helen and Paris, terrified by the predictions of Pallas, were to bid each other an eternal farewell, they would enlist our esteem but would interest us no more. Whoever took any interest in Menelaus?

This situation, which can be carried back to the Garden of Eden, is of a disquieting nature; it contains a problem which no one so far has succeeded in solving. It may be that the civilisation of which we are so proud, young enough in comparison with the age of humanity, is but transitory, a progress towards a higher state wherein that which now seems obscure will become clear, and certain things that appear to us essential will be nothing but words. Let us hope it will be so. As Carmen, that other incarnation of the same idea, says, it is always our privilege to hope.

FROM *Outspoken Essays on Music*

'Musical Digressions'

OPINIONS ON ART – ESPECIALLY ON MUSICAL ART – HAVE AT ALL TIMES been liable to strange aberrations. Art inspires a wealth of suggestion; along this line of thought, chalk can easily be passed off as cheese. The public willingly allows itself to be gulled. On perusing once again what Stendhal said of Cimarosa, what Balzac said of Rossini, one is amazed at the judgements they passed on their contemporaries. The latter listened with gaping mouths, imagining in their simplicity that the reason they did not find in this Italian music everything it was desired to make them see was that they were incapable of understanding it.

Fifty years ago, one dared not express a doubt as to the value of famous operas which nowadays it is the fashion to regard as devoid of melody, of harmony, of instrumentation, of everything. At that time, Beethoven, the divine Beethoven, was the unknown quantity in music. Do not think that I am making up all this; one does not invent such things.

Without, therefore, making useless personal allusions, let us not exhibit amazement at certain judgements; here, as elsewhere, there is nothing new under the sun. May we not, however, warn sincere readers and put them on their guard against the assertions of certain persons, doubtless of the utmost good faith, though excessively liable to suggestion? It may be divined that I am alluding to those, well known to be a numerous band, who flock to the banner of the mighty Richard, and beneath its shade engage in a fight that has long been inconclusive.

They are not content that their god should triumph; there must even be victims sacrificed on his altars. Mendelssohn first of all. Certainly there is lack of uniformity in his work. But what of *Elijah*, the *Midsummer Night's Dream*, the sonatas for the organ, the preludes and fugues for the pianoforte, the *Scottish* symphony, the *Reformation* symphony? . . . Try to accomplish a like task!

They would have us believe that when he first appeared he was accepted without a struggle, his 'mediocrity' having at the outset placed him on a level with the masses.

Do not believe anything of the kind.

I was present at the very first performance of the *Midsummer Night's Dream* and of the symphonies given before a Parisian public, and I still remember that I broke more than one lance in his defence. At the first performances of the *Midsummer Night's Dream* I saw old *habitués* of the Conservatoire holding their heads in their hands as they asked in tones of anguish why the Concerts Society inflicted such horrors on its subscribers . . . Only by degrees did this public discover the Berceuse, then the Scherzo, then the March, then the Agitato, and finally the Overture. It was a tedious process!

Another victim: Meyerbeer. It was mainly against his *Huguenots* that an outcry was raised, by reason of its popular and long unchallenged success. Robert Schumann lent powerful aid in this direction through an article he wrote which declared that *Les Huguenots* was not 'music'.

Unfortunately, when Schumann applied his marvellous talent to opera, he created *Geneviève*. Now, *Geneviève* is assuredly charming music, though of a kind ill adapted to the theatre. Henceforth, so far as *Les Huguenots* is concerned, Schumann's judgement is lacking in authority. On the other hand, we have the opinion of Berlioz – who is known to be anything but indulgent in criticism – and he in his famous *Traité d'Instrumentation* quotes fragments of the great duo, "cette scène immortelle". This, in my opinion, is praise of no negligible kind.

Immolated victims! We must act in such fashion that the god be right in everything (otherwise he would no longer be a god); we must recognise not only the many dazzling qualities he possesses but also those he lacks.

For instance, his clarity will be extolled, as also his wealth of melody. Certainly, he is clear whenever he wishes to be, just as certain women are virtuous when it pleases them; though they are not the ones whose virtue one is in the habit of praising. It is not in Helen but in Penelope that virtue is extolled; it is in Mozart that clarity is personified, not in Wagner.

Apologists have gone so far as to claim that there is no difficulty which the orchestra cannot overcome in the Bayreuth repertory, and that the latter does not even contain any gaucheries; though certain passages are not only difficult or gauche, but quite impossible of execution.

I have before me a very interesting and well-written article on 'The Future of the Lyrical Drama'. In it the author has criticised kings, heroes, gods, rich costumes, everything legendary or mysterious, the almost universal disposition to place the action in faraway lands and far-distant times. As I read, I was afraid I might be proceeding in the direction of a negation of Wagner's work, for it had always appeared to me that this dealt with gods and heroes, legends and mysteries, and that whenever the author decided to venture into real life, he had had recourse to the costumes and the customs of antiquity.

Such was not the case. Siegfried's forge, the shoes of Hans Sachs suffice to make the Tetralogy and *Die Meistersinger* realistic works. Do not, however, imagine that Wagner is capable of coarse realism! Like Beethoven, he repudiates the direct imitation of nature; he does not imitate the sound of the iron, he substitutes the man for the thing, the smith for his tool, expressive art for pure imitation. The author dwells on this at considerable length.

This is all very fine, but it is not true. An anvil – a real anvil – exists in the orchestra, written in the score. The effects obtained by Wagner are very picturesque, and if he has not substituted "expressive art for pure imitation, the smith for his tool", I humbly confess I will not take exception to it. In *Das Rheingold*, too, he has introduced an entire orchestra of anvils, large, middle-sized, and small, which clang away for some considerable time. They strike *crescendo* whilst the orchestra is gradually dying away, and continuing *decrescendo* whilst the orchestra gradually resumes its proper role; their appearance and their disappearance blend in the ensemble. The effect is original and striking in the extreme. I heard it for the first time in Munich, at the performance organised by command of Ludwig the Third [*sic*], against the wish of the author himself, who refused to put in an appearance. The anvil solo passage caused a sense of giddiness in the listener, and no doubt this was displeasing to Wagner, when he heard it at Bayreuth, for he suppressed it during the rehearsals. I regretted this, as I have always missed the castanets that were originally played to a trimetrical rhythm on resuming the Bacchanale motive in *Tannhäuser*. They too have been discontinued.

Gods and heroes, far-off lands and bygone times: all this is unquestionably very useful in lyrical drama, but not indispensable, as M. Charpentier has triumphantly demonstrated in *Louise*. But M. Charpentier, like the true man of the theatre he is, has diverted the difficulty in all sorts of ingenious ways; he has even transported us right into fairyland in his vision of an illuminated Paris as seen from the heights of Montmartre.

To return to what we were saying, can we not see things as they really are? What aberration is it that makes us delight in erroneous reasoning when we can reason correctly, as is possible in the case of those I have mentioned? One of them may well say: "In its essence, art does not change; men only change their minds as to its methods and its limitations. Once they become certain that these latter are purely arbitrary and that everything in the realm of the beautiful has a right to live, they will the more easily conceive of the inexhaustible fecundity of art."

Let us think over these noble words, and desire – though without expecting it – that they may be rightly read and valued, and may serve as a guide for future judgements.

FROM *Outspoken Essays on Music*

APPENDIX II • POEMS by SAINT-SAËNS

THE FOLLOWING SELECTION, AS WELL AS ILLUSTRATING SAINT-SAËNS'S poetic style – didactic, ironic, pessimistic – touches on some of the subjects that prompted him to verse: foreign travel, the impulse to respond creatively to nature and the inevitability of death.

La Mer

La mer tente ma lyre avec ses épouvantes,
Ses caresses de femme et ses goëmons verts.
O mer trois fois perfide! alors que tu me hantes
Sur mon indignité j'ai les yeux grands ouverts.

Je pourrais comme un autre en alignant des rimes
Dire ton glauque azur aux vastes horizons;
Je pourrais par des mots semés sur tes abîmes
Faire comme les flots s'entrechoquer des sons.

Mais non, je suis trop peu pour cette rude tâche;
Tu m'as découragé par ton immensité.
L'effort est superhumain et je me sens trop lâche
Pour peindre dans mes vers ta terrible beauté.

Que d'autres plus hardis t'adressent la parole,
Comparent ton murmure à celui du sapin;
Je n'ose pas. Et puis ce serait chose folle
De te chanter encore après Jean Richepin.

FROM *Rimes Familières* (1902 ed.)

The Sea

The sea tempts my lyre with its terrors, its feminine caresses and its green weed. O, thrice treacherous sea! Now that you haunt me in my unworthiness, my eyes are wide open.

Like anyone else lining up rhymes, I should have the power to speak of your blue-green to the wide horizons, by scattering words over your depths make sounds interplay like the waves.

But no, I am too unworthy for such a mighty task; you have discouraged me by your immensity. Such exertion is superhuman and I feel too cowardly to depict your terrible beauty in my verse.

Let others more daring address you in words, compare your murmur to that of the fir trees. After Jean Richepin*, it would be madness to sing of you.

*Jean Richepin (1849–1926), poet and dramatist.

Les Heures

Toutes nous blessent, la dernière
Nous tue, ayant enfin pitié
Quand elle achève sans colère
L'oeuvre faite plus d'à moitié.

Les autres, même la plus douce,
Hélas! nous usent lentement,
Et chacune d'elles nous pousse
Vers le funèbre monument.

Funèbre? non. Quelle caresse
Vaut le sommeil sans lendemain?
Vienne l'heure, pâle maîtresse
Qu'on espère jamais en vain!

Elle viendra, consolatrice,
Tarir la source des remords:
Nulle passion tentatrice
Ne trouble le repos des morts.

* * *

Ces heures, pleines d'espérance,
De terreur ou de volupté,
Ne sont pourtant qu'une apparence,
Un rêve sans réalité.

Le temps, l'espace: vain mirage,
Mots creux auxquels rien ne répond;
Bruit de la vague sur la plage,
Du caillou dans le puits profond!

The Hours

All wound us, the last kills us, having pity at last when it finishes without anger the work more than half done.

The rest, even the sweetest, alas! slowly wear us out, and each one pushes us towards the dismal gravestone.

Dismal? No. What caress is worth the sleep without a tomorrow? Let the hour come, pale mistress who is never hoped for in vain! She will come, the comforter, to dry up the well of remorse: no tempting passion troubles the sleep of the dead.

* * *

These hours, full of hope, dread or delight, are but an illusion, a dream without reality. Time, space: empty mirage, hollow words to which nothing replies; sound of the wave on the shore, of the pebble in the deep pit!

Avec le mètre et l'heure, infime,
L'homme prétend jauger les mers
Dont l'infini creuse l'abîme,
Qui pour flots ont des univers!

Sonnez, sonnez, Heures futiles,
Mensonge par l'homme inventé!
Résonnez! vos sons, inutiles
Se perdent dans l'éternité.

FROM *Rimes Familières* (1902 ed.)

Mors

Pourquoi craindre la mort? pourquoi s'effrayer d'elle?
La mort est chose naturelle.
Naître, vivre et mourir, c'est tout l'homme en trois mots,
Comme aux flots succèdent les flots,
Comme un clou chasse l'autre, un homme prend la place

De celui qui vivait hier, et qui n'est plus;
    On s'en va sans laisser de trace.
    C'est la loi. Les derniers venus

Reprennent le fardeau qui tombe de l'épaule
Des anciens fatigués par le rude chemin
    Qui va de l'un à l'autre pôle.
Ils ont marché longtemps; le repos vient enfin.
On devrait le bénir, et comme une caresse
Accueillir le baiser de l'obscure déesse.

With his humble measurements of time and space, man aspires to gauge the seas, whose depths are infinite, and whose waves are whole universes!

Ring out, futile hours, illusion invented by man! Again, ring out! Your sounds are lost, useless, in eternity.

Death

Why fear death? Why be daunted by it? Death is a natural thing. To be born, to live, to die, this is the whole of man in three words; as waves follow waves, as one nail drives out the other, so a man takes the place of him who lived yesterday and is no more. He goes leaving no trace. It is the law.

Those who come after take up the burden that falls from the shoulder of the old who are worn out by the hard road that leads from one pole to the other. They walked a long time; rest came at last. One comes to bless it, and like a caress to welcome the kiss of the dark goddess.

Ah! dit l'homme, autrefois, quand on avait l'espoir
D'un bonheur éternel, en s'endormant au soir
De la vie, on croyait que sous la froide pierre
S'ouvrait un gouffre de lumière;
La mort était alors un bien.
Mais quoi! songer, en mon destin morose,
Qu'après avoir vécu je ne serai plus rien . . .

Crois-tu donc être quelque chose?

FROM *Rimes Familières* (1902 ed.)

Le Nil

Fleuve auguste: ton flot intarissable et fort
Reflète l'azur clair de l'Egypte! Sans effort
Et sans bruit, à travers les siècles innombrables
(Depuis qu'aux vastes mers ont succédé les sables
Et la mort à la vie en ces pâles déserts),
Tu ramènes la vie, éclose aux pays verts
Et lointains, où la pluie éternelle et féconde
Prodigue fleurs et fruits aux terres qu'elle inonde.
Large et lourd, le beau Nil s'épand dans la clarté;
Sa puissance est égale à sa tranquillité.

Written after visiting Luxor and Aswan, January 1910.
FROM Dandelot, *La vie et l'oeuvre de Saint-Saëns.*

Ah! says man, once, when we had hope of eternal bliss, in going to sleep in the evening of life, we believed that under the cold stone there opened up a gulf of light; death was then a blessing.

But really! To think, that it is my gloomy destiny that I shall be no more after having lived… do you then believe in being something?

The Nile

Majestic river, your strong, inexhaustible flow reflects the clear blue sky of Egypt! Without effort or fuss, across the unnumbered centuries (since the sands replaced wide seas and death life in these deserts), you restore life, open out on green, far-flung lands, where the prolific, unending wet lavishes flowers and fruits on the earth it floods. Wide and sultry, the beautiful Nile spreads out in its brightness; her power is as great as her tranquillity.

APPENDIX III • WORKS by SAINT-SAËNS

ORCHESTRAL

	OPUS	DATE
Symphony in A	posth.	1850
Symphony in E flat (no. 1)	2	1853
Ouverture d'un opéra-comique inachevé	140	1854
Symphony in F (*Urbs Roma*)	posth.	1856
Symphony in A minor (no. 2)	55	1859
Symphony in D	—	1859
Overture: *Spartacus*	—	1863
Suite	49	1863
Rapsodie Bretonne	76	1866
Marche Héroïque	34	1871
Le Rouet d'Omphale	31	1871
Phaëton	39	1873
Danse Macabre	40	1874
La Jeunesse d'Hercule	50	1877
Suite Algérienne	60	1880
Une nuit à Lisbonne	63	1880
Jota Aragonese	64	1880
Symphony in C minor (no. 3), 'Organ'	78	1886
Sarabande et Rigaudon	93	1892
Coronation March for Edward VII	117	1902
Ouverture de fête	133	1909
Hymne pour le 14ième juillet	—	1916

PIANO and ORCHESTRA

	OPUS	DATE
Concerto no. 1 in D	17	1858
Concerto no. 2 in G minor	22	1868
Concerto no. 3 in E flat	29	1869
Concerto no. 4 in C minor	44	1875
Allegro appassionato	70	1884
Rapsodie d'Auvergne	73	1884
Africa	89	1891
Concerto no. 5 in F, 'Egyptian'	103	1896

VIOLIN and ORCHESTRA

	OPUS	DATE
Concerto no. 2 in C	58	1858
Concerto no. 1 in A	20	1859
Introduction and Rondo Capriccioso	28	1863
Romance in C	48	1874
Concerto no. 3 in B minor	61	1880

	OPUS	DATE
Morceau de Concert	62	1880
Havanaise	83	1887
Caprice Andalou	122	1904

CELLO and ORCHESTRA

	OPUS	DATE
Concerto no. 1 in A minor	33	1872
Concerto no. 2 in D minor	119	1902

OTHER CONCERTANTE WORKS

	OPUS	DATE
Tarantella, for flute and clarinet	6	1857
Romance in D flat, for flute	37	1871
Romance in F, for horn or cello	36	1874
La Muse et le Poète, for violin and cello	132	1909
Morceau de Concert, for harp	154	1919
Cyprès et Lauriers, for organ	156	1919
Odelette, for flute	162	1920

MILITARY BAND

	OPUS	DATE
Orient et Occident	25	1869
Hymne Franco-Espanol	—	1900
Sur les bords du Nil	125	1908
Vers la victoire	152	1918
Marche Interalliée	155	1918
Marche dediée aux étudiants d'Alger (with optional chorus)	163	1921

CHAMBER MUSIC

	OPUS	DATE
Piano Quintet in A minor	14	1855
Six Duos for harmonium and piano	8	1858
Suite for cello and piano	16	1862
Piano Trio no. 1 in F	18	1863
Serenade for piano, organ, violin and viola	15	1866
Romance for piano, organ and violin	27	1868
Berceuse in B flat, violin and piano	38	1871
Cello Sonata no. 1 in C minor	32	1872
Romance in C, for violin and piano	48	1874
Piano Quartet in B flat	41	1875
Allegro Appassionato, for cello and piano	43	1875
Romance in D, for cello and piano	51	1877
Septet for trumpet, strings and piano	65	1881

	OPUS	DATE
Romance for horn and piano (from suite, op. 16)	67	1885
Violin Sonata no. 1 in D minor	75	1885
Valse Caprice, for piano and strings ('Wedding Cake')	76	1886
Le Carnaval des Animaux, for two pianos and chamber (or full) orchestra	posth.	1886
Caprice sur des airs Danois et Russes, for flute, oboe, clarinet and piano	79	1887
Morceau de Concert, for horn and piano	94	1887
Chant Saphique, for cello and piano	91	1892
Piano Trio no. 2 in E minor	92	1892
Violin Sonata no. 2 in E flat	102	1896
Barcarolle, for violin, cello, harmonium and piano	108	1898
String Quartet no. 1 in E minor	112	1899
Cello Sonata no. 2 in F	123	1905
Fantaisie, for violin and harp	124	1907
Triptyque, for violin and piano	136	1912
Elégie, for violin and piano	143	1915
Cavatina, for tenor trombone and piano	144	1915
String Quartet no. 2 in G	153	1919
Prière, for cello and organ	158	1919
Deuxième Elégie, for violin and piano	160	1920
Oboe Sonata	166	1921
Clarinet Sonata	167	1921
Bassoon Sonata	168	1921

PIANO SOLO

	OPUS	DATE
Six Bagatelles	3	1855
Mazurka no. 1 in G minor	21	1862
Gavotte in C minor	23	1871
Mazurka no. 2 in G minor	24	1871
Romance sans paroles	—	1871
Six Studies, Book 1	52	1877
Menuet et Valse	56	1878
Mazurka no. 3 in B minor	66	1882
Allegro Appassionato (solo version)	70	1884
Album	72	1884
Souvenir d'Italie	80	1887
Les cloches du soir	85	1889
Valse Canariote	88	1890
Suite	90	1891
Thème varié	97	1894
Souvenir d'Ismalaïa	100	1895
Valse Mignonne	104	1896
Valse Nonchalante	110	1898
Six Studies, Book 2	111	1899

	OPUS	DATE
Valse Langoureuse	120	1903
Six Studies for the left hand	135	1912
Valse Gaie	139	1913
Six Fugues	161	1920
Feuillet d'album	169	1921

PIANO DUET

	OPUS	DATE
Duettino	11	1855
King Harald Harfagar	59	1880
Feuillet d'album	81	1887
Pas redoublé	86	1887
Berceuse	105	1896

TWO PIANOS

	OPUS	DATE
Variations on a theme of Beethoven	35	1874
Polonaise	77	1886
Scherzo	87	1889
Caprice arabe	96	1894
Caprice héroïque	106	1898

ORGAN

	OPUS	DATE
Fantaisie no. 1	—	1856
Bénédiction Nuptiale	9	1859
Trois Rapsodies sur des cantiques Bretons	7	1866
Three Preludes and Fugues, Book 1	99	1894
Fantaisie no. 2	101	1895
Marche religieuse	107	1897
Three Preludes and Fugues, Book 2	109	1898
Seven Improvisations	150	1917
Fantaisie no. 3	157	1919

HARMONIUM

	OPUS	DATE
Three Pieces	1	1852
Elévation ou Communion	13	1865

HARP

	OPUS	DATE
Fantaisie	95	1893

INCIDENTAL MUSIC

	AUTHOR(S)	FIRST PRODUCED
Antigone	Vacquerie/Meurice (after Sophocles)	1893, Comédie Française, Paris
Déjanire	Gallet	1898, Béziers
Parysatis	Dieulafoy	1902, Béziers
Andromaque	Racine	1903, Sarah Bernhardt Theatre, Paris
La Foi	Brieux	1909, Monte Carlo
La Fille du tourneur d'ivoire	Mme Ferrare, from Mme Bertheroy's novel	1909, Paris (private performance)
On ne badine pas avec l'amour	de Musset	1917, Paris Odeon

FILM MUSIC

	DIRECTOR	PREMIÈRE
L'assassinat du Duc de Guise	Lavedan	1908, Paris

BALLET

	SCENARIO/CHOREOGRAPHY	COMPLETED	1ST PRODUCED
Javotte	J. L. Croze/Mariquita	1896	1896, Lyons

OPERAS

	LIBRETTIST(S)	COMPLETED	FIRST PRODUCED
Le Château de Roche Cardon, ou Les Cruautés du Sort	Saint-Saëns	1861	(unpublished)
Le Timbre d'Argent	Barbier/Carré	1865	1877, Théâtre Lyrique, Paris
La Princesse Jaune (Op. 30)	Gallet	1871	1872, Opéra-Comique, Paris
Samson et Dalila (Op. 47)	Lemaire	1873	1877, Weimar
Etienne Marcel	Gallet	1878	1879, Lyons
Henry VIII	Détroyat/Sylvestre	1882	1883, Paris Opéra
Proserpine	Gallet	1886	1887, Opéra-Comique, Paris
Ascanio	Gallet	1888	1890, Paris Opéra
Phryné	de Lassus	1893	1893, Opéra-Comique, Paris
Frédégonde, Acts 3 & 4*	Gallet	1895	1895, Paris Opéra
Les Barbares	Sardou/ Gheusi	1901	1901, Paris Opéra
Hélène	Saint-Saëns	1903	1904, Monte Carlo
L'Ancêtre	de Lassus	1905	1906, Monte Carlo
Déjanire	Gallet/Saint-Saëns	1910	1911, Monte Carlo

[*Guiraud's opera completed by Saint-Saëns]

VOICE and ORCHESTRA

	OPUS	POET	DATE
Le Retour de Virginie	—	A. Barbier	1852
Ode à Sainte Cécile	—	Nibelle	1852
Scène d'Horace (soprano & baritone)	10	Corneille	1860

	OPUS	POET	DATE
Ivanhoé (mezzo-soprano)	—	Roussy	1864
Hoche Cantata	—	anon.	1868
La fiancée du timbalier (mezzo-soprano)	82	Hugo	1887
Pallas Athène (soprano)	98	Croze	1894
Lever du soleil sur le Nil (contralto)	—	Saint-Saëns	1898
Lola (soprano)	116	Bordèse	1900

SOLO SONGS

	POET	DATE
'Le Soir'	Desbordes-Valmore	1842
'La maman'	Mme Tastu	1842
'Ariel'	?	1842
'Tandis que sur vos ans'	?	1844
'Reçois mes hommages'	?	1844
'Nous qu'en ces lieux'	?	1844
'La golfe de Baya'	Lamartine	c. 1847
'Le lac'	Lamartine	1850
'Le poète mourant'	Lamartine	1850
'Ruhethal'	Uhland	c. 1850
'Antwort'	Uhland	c. 1850
'A quoi bon entendre'	Hugo	c. 1850
'La cigale et la fourmi'	La Fontaine	c. 1850
'Guitare'	Hugo	1851
'Rêverie'	Hugo	1851
'Le pas d'armes du roi Jean'	Hugo	1852
'La feuille du peuplier'	Mme Tastu	1853
'La chasse du Burgrave'	Hugo	1855
'Le sommeil des fleurs'	Penmarch	1855
'Lever de la lune'	after Ossian	1855
'La cloche'	Hugo	c. 1855
'L'attente'	Hugo	c. 1855
'Plainte'	Mme Tastu	c. 1855
'La madonna col bambino'	Lignori	c. 1855
'La mort d'Ophélie'	Legouvé	c. 1857
'Souvenances'	Lemaire	c. 1858
'Alla riva del Tebro'	(Italian)	1860
'Extase'	Hugo	c. 1860
'Etoile du matin'	Distel	c. 1860
'Soirée en mer'	Hugo	1862
'Canzonetta Toscana'	(Italian)	c. 1863
'Le matin'	Hugo	c. 1864
'L'enlèvement'	Hugo	1865
'Clair de lune'	Mendès	c. 1865
'Sérénade' (Op. 15)	Mengeot	1866
'La cocinelle'	Hugo	1868
'Maria Lucrezia'	Legouvé	1868

	POET	DATE
'Chant de ceux qui s'en vont sur mer'	Hugo	1868
'Tristesse'	Lemaire	c. 1868
'Marquise, vous souvenez-vous?'	Coppée	c. 1869
Mélodies persanes (cycle of six songs, Op. 26)	Renaud	1870
'S'il est un charmon gazon'	Hugo	1870
'Si vous n'avez rien à me dire'	Hugo	1870
'Désir de l'Orient'	Saint-Saëns	1871
'A Voice by the Cedar Tree'	Tennyson	1871
'Dans ton coeur'	Cazalis	1872
'Danse Macabre'	Cazalis	1873
'Chanson triste'	Cazalis	c. 1873
'Vogue, vogue la galère' (with harmonium)	Aicard	c. 1877
'Night Song to Preciosa'	Ginner	1879
'Dans les coins bleus'	Sainte-Beuve	1880
'Chanson à boire du vieux temps'	Boileau	1885
'Une flûte invisible' (with flute and piano)	Hugo	1885
'Suzette et Suzon'	Hugo	1888
'Présage de la Croix'	Bordèse	1890
'Guitares et Mandolines'	Saint-Saëns	1890
'Aimons nous'	de Banville	1891
'Amour viril'	Boyer	1891
'Les Fées'	de Banville	1892
'Là-bas'	Croze	1892
'Madeleine'	Tranchant	1892
'Le Rossignol'	de Banville	1892
'Primavera'	Stuart	1893
'Fière Beauté'	Mahot	1893
'La Sérénité'	Barbier	1893
'Vive Paris, vive la France!'	Tranchant	1893
'La Libellule'	Saint-Saëns	1894
'Peut-être'	Croze	1894
'Pourquoi rester seulette?'	Croze	1894
'Alla riva del Tebro' (arrangement of a madrigal by Palestrina)	anon.	1898
'Les vendanges'	Sicard	1898
'Si je l'osais'	Tranchant	1898
'Sonnet'	Saint-Saëns	1898
'Les cloches de la mer'	Saint-Saëns	1900
'Nocturne'	Quinault	1900
'Thème varié'	Saint-Saëns	1900
'Desir d'amour'	Perpina	1901
'Elle'	Lecocq	1901
'Soeur Anne'	Pressat	1903
'L'arbre	Moréas	1903
'Le fleuve'	Audigier	1906
'Violons dans le soir' (with violin and piano)	Ctesse de Noailles	1907
'L'amour oyseau'	Ronsard	1907

	POET	DATE
'Soir romantique'	Ctesse de Noailles	1907
'L'étoile'	Prince Haidar Pasha	1907
'Le vent dans la plaine'	Verlaine	1913
'Les sapins'	Martin	1914
'Ne l'oubliez pas'	Mme Félix Regnault	1915
'La Française'	Zamaçois	1915
'God Save the King' (adaptation)	traditional	1915
La Cendre Rouge (cycle of ten songs, Op. 146)	Docquois	1915
'Vive la France!'	Fournier	1915
'Honneur à l'Amérique'	Fournier	1917
'Angelus'	Aguétant	1918
'Papillons'	de Léché	1918
'Victoire'	Fournier	1918
'Où nous avons aimé'	Aguétant	1918
'Grasselette et maigrelette'	Ronsard	1921
Vieilles chansons:		1921
i. 'Temps nouveau'	Charles d'Orleáns	
ii. 'Avril'	Belleau	
iii. 'Villanelle'	Fresnaye	
'A Saint Blaise'	Ronsard	1921
'L'amant malheureux'	Ronsard	1921
'Amour blessé'	Ronsard	1921

UNDATED: 'Demand à l'oiseau', 'Méditation', 'La nature souriante', 'Le papillon et l'étoile', 'Le bonheur est chose légère', 'Puisque ici bas toute âme' (Hugo), 'Si tu veux faisons un rêve' (Hugo).

VOCAL DUETS

	POET	DATE
'Pastorale'	Destouches	1855
'Viens!'	Hugo	c. 1855
'Le soir descend sur la colline'	Saint-Saëns	1857
'El Desdichado'	Jules Barbier	1871
'Les cygnes' (Op. 26b)	Armand Renaud	1891
'Vénus'	Saint-Saëns	1896

VOCAL MUSIC for the CHURCH

	OPUS	DATE
Mass	4	1856
Tantum ergo	5	1856
Oratorio de Noël	12	1858
Psalm 18 (19)	42	1865
Requiem	54	1878
Panis Angelicus (tenor and strings or organ)	—	1898
Offertoire pour la Toussaint (4 voices and organ)	—	1898
Psalm 150	127	1908

	OPUS	DATE
Ave Maria (mezzo-soprano and unaccompanied chorus)	145	1914
Tu es Petrus (unaccompanied chorus)	147	1914
Quam dilecta (unaccompanied chorus)	148	1916
Laudate Dominum (unaccompanied chorus)	149	1916

ALSO: 4 canticles, 36 motets

SECULAR CHORAL WORKS

	OPUS	LIBRETTIST/POET	DATE
Les Noces de Prométhée	19	Cornut	1867
Super flumina	—	anon.	1874
Le Déluge	45	Gallet	1875
Les Soldats de Gédéon (unaccompanied double male chorus)	46	Gallet	1876
Chanson de grand-père & *Chanson d'ancêtre*	53	Hugo	1878
La Lyre et l'Harpe	57	Hugo	1879
Hymne à Victor Hugo	69	Saint-Saëns	1881
Calme des nuits & Les fleurs et les arbres	68	anon	1882
Les Marins de Kermor & *Les Titans* (unaccompanied male chorus)	71	St-Félix	1884
Saltarelle (unaccompanied male chorus)	74	Deschamps	1885
Les Guerriers (unaccompanied male chorus)	84	Audigier	1888
Nuit Persane	—	Renaud	1891
Chants d'automne (unaccompanied male chorus)	113	Sicard	1899
La Nuit	114	Audigier	1900
Le Feu Céleste	115	Sylvestre	1900
Romance du soir (unaccompanied)	118	Croze	1902
A la France (unaccompanied)	121	Combarieu	1903
La Gloire de Corneille (cantata)	126	Leconte	1906
La Gloire (cantata for male voices)	131	de Lassus	1909
Aux aviateurs (unaccompanied male chorus)	134	Bonnerot	1912
Aux mineurs (unaccompanied male chorus)	137	Bonnerot	1913
Hymne au printemps (unaccompanied male chorus)	138	Bonnerot	1913
Des pas dans l'allée & *Trinquons*	141	Béranger	1913
Hymne au travail (male voices)	142	Bonnerot	1913
The Promised Land	—	Klein, fr. the Bible	1913
Hail! California	—	trad.	1915
Chanson des aiguilles (female voices)	151	Bonnerot	1917
Salut au Chevalier Printemps (female voices)	151	Fournier	1917
Le Sourire (female voices)	151	Mirval	1917
Hymne à la Paix	159	Jean Louis Fauré	1919
Aux conquérants de l'air	164	anon.	1921
Le Printemps	165	anon.	1921

ALSO: Madrigal for tenor and male chorus from Molière's *Psyché*, and various part-songs.

TRANSCRIPTIONS and ARRANGEMENTS

COMPOSER	ORIGINAL WORK	INSTRUMENT	DATE
Bach	Six transcriptions, 1st set	piano	c. 1861
	Six transcriptions, 2nd set	piano	c. 1872
	Prelude to sixth violin sonata	violin, piano	1884
	Sarabande	violin, piano	1889
Beethoven	Dervishes Chorus (*The Ruins of Athens*)	piano	1869
	Three transcriptions from string quartets	piano	c. 1869
Berlioz	Hymne de la Fête de Pâques (*La Damnation de Faust*)	piano	c. 1855
	Lélio	vocal score	1855
Bizet	Scherzo (*Les Pêcheurs de Perles*)	piano	1886
Chopin	Sonata in B flat minor	two pianos	1908
	Nocturne in E	violin, piano	1913
Duparc	*Lénore*, symphonic poem	two pianos	1875
Durand, Jacques	*Chanson des Maucroix*	piano	1884
Duvernoy	Nocturne (*Helle*)	piano	1897
Gluck	Caprice sur les airs de ballet d'*Alceste*	piano	c. 1867
	Menuet (*Orphée*)	piano	1873
Gounod	Kermesse et Valse (*Faust*)	piano	1862
	Paraphrase sur *Gallia*	piano	1871
	Kermesse et Valse (*Faust*)	piano	1887
	Suite Concertante	two pianos	1888
Haydn	Andante (Symphony no. 94)	piano	c. 1868
Liszt	Improvisation sur la Beethoven Cantate	piano	1870
	Orpheus	violin, cello & piano	1885
	'St Francis of Assisi preaching to the birds'	organ	?
Lvov	Fantaisie sur l'Hymne National Russe	piano	1896
Massenet	*La Mort de Thaïs*, concert paraphrase	piano	1895
Mendelssohn	Scherzo (*A Midsummer Night's Dream*)	piano	c. 1858
Milan de Valence	Two Fantasies (lute)	piano	1898
Mozart	Andante (piano concerto K.467)	violin, piano	?
Paladilhe	*La Mandolinata*, paraphrase	piano	1869
	La Islena, paraphrase	piano	?
Reber	Four symphonies	piano duet	1858–9
Schumann	*Abendlied*	piano	1878
Wagner	Religious March (*Lohengrin*)	piano, violin & organ	1868

ALSO: cadenzas for Beethoven's fourth piano concerto (1878) and violin concerto (1900) and for Mozart's piano concertos K.482 and K.491, and concerto for two pianos K.365.

PARODIES

	DATE
Gabriella di Vergy	1885
Les Odeurs de Paris	undated

MAIN LITERARY WORKS

	DATE OF FIRST PUBLICATION	/ PUBLISHER
La Matérialisme et la musique	1882	?
Harmonie et Mélodie	1885	Calmann Lévy
Note sur les décors de théâtre dans l'antiquité Romaine	1886	Baschet
Rimes Familières	1891	Calmann Lévy
La Crampe des Ecrivains	1892	Calmann Lévy
Charles Gounod et le Don Juan de Mozart	1893	Ollendorff
Preface to L. A. Niedermeyer, *Vie d'un compositeur moderne*	1893	Librairie Fischbacher
Problèmes et Mystères	1894	Flammarion
Portraits et Souvenirs (2nd. ed., 1909)	1899	Société d'édition artistique
'Essai sur les lyres et cithares'	1902	Didot
Botriocéphale (in 1902 ed. of *Rimes Familières*)	1902	Calmann Lévy
Le Roi Apépi	1903	Calmann Lévy
La parenté des plantes et des animaux	1906	Flammarion
Ecole Buissonnière	1913	Pierre Lafitte
Au courant de la vie	1914	Dorbon-Ainé
Germanophilie	1916	Dorbon-Ainé
Les Idées de M. Vincent d'Indy	1917	Pierre Lafitte

APPENDIX IV • SELECT DISCOGRAPHY

CURRENTLY OR RECENTLY AVAILABLE RECORDINGS

Among the latest releases to be especially welcomed are the Medici Quartet playing the two string quartets and the song recital by François le Roux with Graham Johnson, which includes the *Mélodies Persanes*. Of much interest also is the reissue of a historic 1919 recording of Saint-Saëns playing his own transcription of the *Suite Algérienne*.

ORCHESTRAL

The early symphonies in A and F (*Urbs Roma*), and symphonies 1–3: Jean Martinon, Orchestre National de la RTF. EMI CZS5 69683-2.

Symphonies nos. 2 and 3: Yan Pascal Tortelier, Ulster Orchestra. Chandos 8822.

Symphony no. 3: Barenboim, Chicago Symphony Orchestra. DG 415 847-2.

Danse Macabre, Phaëton: Lorin Maazel, Pittsburgh Symphony Orchestra. Sony SK 53979.

La Jeunesse d'Hercule, Symphony no. 3: Georges Prêtre, Vienna Symphony Orchestra. Erato 0630-15620-2.

La Foi, incidental music: Michel Plasson, Toulouse Capitole Orchestra. EMI CDC5 55584-2.

Le Carnaval des Animaux: Itzhak Perlman, Atlanta Symphony Orchestra. Telac CD80443.

CONCERTANTE

Cello Concerto no. 1: Piatigorsky, Chicago Symphony Orchestra, Frederick Stock (1940). Sony MHK62876; Yo Yo Ma, Orchestre National de France, Lorin Maazel (with the Lalo concerto). CBS MK 35848.

Cello Concerto no. 2, Allegro Appassionato: M. Kliegel, Bournemouth Sinfonietta, J. F. Monnard. Naxos 8 553039.

Piano Concertos nos. 1–5: Pascal Rogé, Philharmonia Orchestra, Charles Dutoit. Decca 417 351-2.

Piano Concerto no. 5: Philippe Entremont, Toulouse Capitole Orchestra, Michel Plasson (1970). Sony SBK63211.

Violin Concerto no. 1: Kyung Wha Chung, Montreal Symphony Orchestra, Charles Dutoit (with Lalo's *Symphonie espagnole*). Decca 411952-2.

Violin Concerto no. 1, Havanaise, Introduction and Rondo Capriccioso, Morceau de Concert, Romance in C, Sarabande et Rigaudon: Kantorow, Tapiola Sinfonietta. BIS CD860.

Violin Concerto no. 3: Chee-Yun, London Philharmonic Orchestra, J. Lopez-Cobos. Denon CO-180 17; Itzhak Perlman, Orchestre de Paris, Barenboim (with Lalo's *Symphonie espagnole*). DG 429 977-2.

Cello Suite: M. Kliegel, Bournemouth Sinfonietta, J-F. Monnard. Naxos 8 553039.

Havanaise, Introduction and Rondo Capriccioso: Ruggiero Ricci, London Symphony Orchestra, Pierino Gamba. Bela 461 369-2.

CHAMBER

Caprice on Danish and Russian airs: Rotholz, Dine, Kay, Winn. BIS CD9079.

Le Carnaval des Animaux, Piano Trio no. 1 in F, Septet: Nash Ensemble. Virgin VC 790751-2.

Clarinet Sonata: M. Edwards, T. Bach. Crystal CD735.

Septet: Darré, Delmotte, Logerot, Pascal Quartet. EMI CZS569470-2.

String Quartets nos. 1 and 2: Medici Quartet. Schwann 364842.

Violin Sonata no. 1: Heifetz, B. Smith (1967). RCA 09026 61776-2.

VOCAL

Parysatis: G. Catley, orch., H. Ringold (1948). Dutt CDLX7022.
Samson et Dalila: Elena Obraztsova, Placido Domingo, Robert Lloyd, Paris Orchestra and Chorus, Barenboim. Polygram DG CD413 297-21; Jon Vickers, Rita Gorr, Paris Opéra Orchestra, Georges Prêtre. EMI CDS 47895-8; Renata Tebaldi, New Philharmonia, A. Guadagno (1969). Decca 452 456-ZDM2.
Songs (including *Mélodies Persanes*): François le Roux, Graham Johnson. Hyperion CDA66856.

KEYBOARD

Etudes, op. 52, op. 111; Etudes for the Left Hand, op. 135; Thème Varié, op. 97: Piers Lane. Hyperion CDA67037.
Beethoven Variations: Philippe Entremont and Georges Casadesus (1970s). Sony SBK63211.
Suite Algérienne (transcription): Saint-Saëns (1919). EMI CMS5 66182-2.
Organ works: S. J. Bleicher. Artn. 74321 35088-2.

HISTORICAL RECORDINGS

It goes without saying that any of Saint-Saëns's own recordings are rare collectors' items. At the opposite end of the scale, the number of recordings on 78 and LP of the *Danse Macabre*, *Le Carnaval des Animaux* and the third symphony are legion. Among recordings to look out for specially in old record shops is *Le Carnaval* with Ogden Nash's verses read by Noël Coward, any Rubinstein recordings of the second piano concerto and Ansermet's third symphony.

Le Carnaval des Animaux: André Kostelanetz and his orchestra, with pianists Leonid Hambro and Jascha Zeyde, and Ogden Nash's verses spoken by Noël Coward. Philips NBR 6001; John Ogdon and Brenda Lucas, City of Birmingham Symphony Orchestra, Louis Frémaux. Klavier 527 (no verses); Leonard Bernstein, conductor and narrator, New York Philharmonic Orchestra. Columbia D3S-785.
Suite Algérienne: Frankenland State Symphony Orchestra, Barati. Lyrichord 7103E.
Septet: Groupe Instrumentale de Paris, Lafarge (piano), Lagorce (trumpet). Seraphim S-6081.
Symphony no. 3: Ernest Ansermet, Suisse Romande Orchestra, with Pierre Segon. Decca VIV51.
Danse Macabre, Phaëton, Le Rouet d'Omphale, La Jeunesse d'Hercule, Marche Héroïque: Philharmonia Orchestra, Charles Dutoit. Decca SXL 6975.
Cello Concertos nos. 1 and 2, Cello Suite, Allegro Appassionato: Christine Walewska, Monte Carlo Opera Orchestra, Eliahu Inbal. Philips Sequenza 416 980-1.
Piano Concerto no. 2: Arthur Rubinstein, Philadelphia Orchestra, Eugene Ormandy (with de Falla's *Nights in the Gardens of Spain*). RCA SB 6841.
Piano Concerto no. 4: Grant Johannesen, Philharmonia Orchestra, Georges Tzipine (with Milhaud's *Carnaval d'Aix*). HMV CLP 1149.
Piano Concertos nos. 1–3: Aldo Ciccolini, Orchestre de Paris, Serge Baudo. HMV 29 05711.
Etude en forme de valse, Toccata (recital): Cécile Ousset. Decca Ace of Diamonds SDD R-435.
Violin Concerto no. 3: Alfredo Campoli, London Philharmonic Orchestra, Pierino Gamba (1956). Decca Eclipse ECS 663.
Danse Macabre: Stokowski, Philadelphia Orchestra. HMV D.B.3077 (78).

NOTES

INTRODUCTION

1. Romain Rolland, trans. by Mary Blaiklock, *Musicians of Today* (London: Kegan Paul, Trench, Trubner, 1917), p. 267.

CHAPTER I. CHILD PRODIGY

1. Jean Bonnerot, *Saint-Saëns, sa vie et sa oeuvre*, 2nd ed. (Paris: Durand, 1922), p. 9.
2. Georges Servières, *Saint-Saëns* (Paris: Librairie Félix Alcan, 1923), p. 5.
3. Ibid., p. 4.
4. Arthur Dandelot, *La vie et l'oeuvre de Saint-Saëns* (Paris: Editions Dandelot, 1930), p. 15n.
5. Camille Saint-Saëns, trans. by Edwin Gile Rich, *Musical Memories* (London: John Murray, 1921), p. 3.
6. Ibid., pp. 3–4.
7. Bonnerot, *Saint-Saëns*, p. 11.
8. Harold Schonberg, *Lives of the Great Composers* (London: Davis-Poynter, 1971), p. 328.
9. Saint-Saëns, *Musical Memories*, p. 13.
10. Ibid., p. 4.
11. *L'Illustration*, May 1846.
12. Saint-Saëns, *Musical Memories*, p. 5.
13. Ibid., p. 3.
14. Ibid., p. 175.
15. Ibid., p. 5.
16. Ibid., pp. 1–2.
17. Ibid., p. 5.
18. James Harding, *Saint-Saëns and his Circle* (London: Chapman and Hall, 1965), p. 15.
19. Saint-Saëns, *Musical Memories*, pp. 7–8.
20. Saint-Saëns, trans. by Fred Rothwell, *Outspoken Essays on Music* (London: Kegan Paul, Trench, Trubner, 1922), pp. 54–55.
21. Saint-Saëns, *Musical Memories*, pp. 5–6.
22. Ibid., p. 7.
23. *L'Illustration*, May 1846.
24. *Moniteur Universel*, 1st August 1840.
25. Saint-Saëns, *Musical Memories*, p. 6.
26. Harding, *Saint-Saëns*, pp. 19–20.
27. Saint-Saëns, *Outspoken Essays*, pp. 158–59.
28. Saint-Saëns, *Musical Memories*, pp. 273–74.
29. Ibid., p. 276.
30. Bonnerot, *Saint-Saëns*, pp. 18–19.
31. Saint-Saëns, *Musical Memories*, p. 10.
32. Vernon Loggins, *Where the Word Ends* (Baltimore: Louisiana State University Press, 1958), pp. 54–55.
33. Saint-Saëns, *Musical Memories*, pp. 11–13.
34. Servières, *Saint-Saëns*, pp. 11–12.
35. Ibid., pp. 19–20, 26.
36. D. G. Mason, *From Grieg to Brahms* (New York: Outlook, 1903), p. 101.
37. *L'Illustration*, May 1846.
38. Saint-Saëns, *Musical Memories*, p. 10.
39. Letter to Pierre Aguétant, 13th May 1918, in Aguétant, *Saint-Saëns par lui-même* (Paris: Editions Alsatia, 1938), p. 61.
40. Letter to M. Levin, 9th September 1901. Quoted in Dandelot, *La vie*, p. 181.
41. Bonnerot, *Saint-Saëns*, p. 23.
42. Saint-Saëns, *Musical Memories*, p. 11.

CHAPTER II: STUDENT

1. Harry Haskell, *The Early Music Revival, A History* (London: Thames and Hudson, 1988), pp. 13–16.
2. Saint-Saëns, *Ecole Buissonnière* (Paris: Pierre Lafitte, 1913), p. 249.
3. Haskell, *The Early Music Revival*, p. 19.
4. Saint-Saëns, trans. by Edwin Gile Rich, *Musical Memories* (London: John Murray, 1921), p. 15.
5. Ibid., p. 16.
6. Jacques Durand, *Quelques Souvenirs d'un éditeur de musique* (Paris: Durand, 1924), p. 2.
7. J. Cooper, *The Rise of Instrumental Music and Concert Series in Paris 1828–1871* (Michigan: UMI Research Press, 1983), passim.
8. Saint-Saëns, *Musical Memories*, pp. 208–09.
9. B. Schwarz, *French Instrumental Music between the Revolutions 1789–1830* (New York: Da Capo, 1987), p. xi.
10. Hector Berlioz, trans. by Rachel and Eleanor Holmes, *Memoirs* (New York: Dover Publications, 1966), p. 364.
11. Ibid., pp. 245–46.
12. Ibid., pp. 358–59.
13. Quoted in James Harding, *Saint-Saëns and*

his Circle (London: Chapman and Hall, 1965), p. 40.
14. Saint-Saëns, *Musical Memories,* p. 20.
15. Quoted in Edward Burlingame Hill, *Modern French Music* (London: George Allen & Unwin, 1924), p. 26.
16. Saint-Saëns, *Harmonie et Mélodie* (Paris: Calmann Lévy, 1885), p. 283.
17. Saint-Saëns, *Musical Memories,* pp. 189–90.
18. Ibid., p. 19.
19. Jean Bonnerot, *Saint-Saëns, sa vie et sa oeuvre,* 2nd ed. (Paris: Durand, 1922), p. 25.
20. Saint-Saëns, *Musical Memories,* p. 19.
21. Marguérite Long, trans. by Olive Senior Ellis, *At the Piano with Fauré* (London: Kahn & Averil, 1980), p. 20.
22. Saint-Saëns, *Harmonie et Mélodie,* p. xxii.
23. Quoted in Arthur Hervey, *Saint-Saëns* (London: The Bodley Head, 1921), pp. 28 and 42.
24. Charles Gounod, trans. by W. Hely Hutchinson, *Autobiographical Reminiscences* (London: Heinemann, 1896), pp. 211–12.
25. Romain Rolland, trans. by Mary Blaiklock, *Musicians of Today* (London: Kegan Paul, Trench, Trubner, 1917), p. 111.
26. Saint-Saëns, *Musical Memories,* p. 275.
27. Ibid., p. 182.
28. Saint-Saëns, *Portraits et Souvenirs* (Paris: Société d'édition artistique, 1899), p. 98.
29. Saint-Saëns, *Musical Memories,* pp. 180–81.
30. Ibid., pp. 183, 186–87.
31. Ibid., p. 14.
32. Ibid., p. 26.
33. Ibid., pp. 26–28.
34. Ibid., p. 28.
35. Frits Noske, *French Song from Berlioz to Duparc* (New York: Dover Publications, 1970), pp. 221–29.
36. Saint-Saëns, *Musical Memories,* pp. 145–46, 151–52.
37. Saint-Saëns, *Portraits et Souvenirs,* pp. 48–50.
38. Ibid., p. 51.
39. Ibid., p. 87.
40. Quoted in Arbie Orenstein, *Ravel, Man and Musician* (New York: Dover Publications, 1991), p. 124.
41. Saint-Saëns, *Portraits et Souvenirs,* p. 15; *Musical Memories,* pp. 191–92.
42. Saint-Saëns, *Portraits et Souvenirs,* pp. 32–33.
43. Letter from Las Palmas, May 1899, quoted in Arthur Dandelot, *La vie et l'oeuvre de Saint-Saëns* (Paris: Editions Dandelot, 1930), p. 29.
44. Quoted in Harding, *Saint-Saëns,* p. 47.

CHAPTER III: ORGANIST

1. Saint-Saëns, trans. by Edwin Gile Rich, *Musical Memories* (London: John Murray, 1921), pp. 195–96.
2. Quoted in Arthur Dandelot, *La vie et l'oeuvre de Saint-Saëns* (Paris: Editions Dandelot, 1930), pp. 30–31.
3. Saint-Saëns, *Musical Memories,* p. 101.
4. Letter of Berlioz to Saint-Saëns, April 1855, in the Saint-Saëns Museum, Dieppe, mentioned in *Berlioz and the Romantic Imagination,* the catalogue to an exhibition held at the Victoria & Albert Museum, London, to mark the centenary of the death of Berlioz (London: The Arts Council, 1969), p. 79.
5. James Harding, *Saint-Saëns and his Circle* (London: Chapman and Hall, 1965), pp. 56–57.
6. Harry Haskell, *The Early Music Revival, A History* (London: Thames and Hudson, 1988), pp. 18–19.
7. Ibid., p. 18.
8. Quoted in Dandelot, *La vie,* p. 56.
9. Letter to Vincent d'Indy, in *Revue Musicale,* February 1947.
10. Letter dated 9th December 1877, in Edward N. Waters, ed., trans. by William R. Tyler, *The Letters of Franz Liszt to Olga von Meyendorff 1871–1886* (Washington: Dumbarton Oaks, 1979), pp. 300–01.
11. Saint-Saëns, *Musical Memories,* pp. 104, 105–06.
12. *Musical Quarterly,* January 1916.
13. Saint-Saëns, *Musical Memories,* pp. 105–07.
14. Saint-Saëns, *Ecole Buissonnière* (Paris: Pierre Lafitte, 1913), p. 332.
15. Quoted in Harding, *Saint-Saëns,* p. 57.
16. Ibid., p. 58–59.
17. Saint-Saëns, *Ecole Buissonnière,* p. 330.
18. Saint-Saëns, *Portraits et Souvenirs* (Paris: Société d'édition artistique, 1899), p. 103.
19. Michael Stegemann, trans. by Ann Sherwin, *Camille Saint-Saëns and the French Solo Concerto 1850–1920* (Aldershot: Scolar, 1991), p. 23.

20. Saint-Saëns, trans. by Fred Rothwell, *Outspoken Essays on Music* (London: Kegan Paul, Trench, Trubner, 1922), p. 113.
21. Stegemann, *Camille Saint-Saëns*, pp. 25–26.
22. Saint-Saëns, *Outspoken Essays*, p. 113.
23. Ibid., p. 113–14.
24. Ibid., p. 39.
25. Quoted in Saint-Saëns, *Musical Memories*, p. 36.
26. J. Cooper, *The Rise of Instrumental Music and Concert Series in Paris 1828–1871* (Michigan: UMI Research Press, 1983), pp. 101, 155.
27. Ibid., p. 130.
28. Saint-Saëns, *Harmonie et Mélodie* (Paris: Calmann Lévy, 1885), p. 207.
29. Saint-Saëns, *Portraits et Souvenirs*, pp. 124, 193–94.
30. Cooper, *Instrumental Music*, p. 128.
31. Saint-Saëns, *Portraits et Souvenirs*, pp. 10–11.
32. Quoted in Harding, *Saint-Saëns*, p. 53.
33. Letter to M. Levin, dated 9th September 1901, quoted in Dandelot, *La vie*, p. 181.
34. Quoted in Jean-Michel Nectoux, trans. by Roger Nichols, *Gabriel Fauré: A Musical Life* (Cambridge: Cambridge University Press, 1991), p. 35.
35. Saint-Saëns, *Musical Memories*, pp. 107–08.
36. Ibid., pp. 201, 203–05, 206–07.
37. Quoted in Gerald Norris, *Stanford, The Cambridge Jubilee and Tchaikovsky* (Newton Abbot: David and Charles, 1980), p. 225.
38. Georges Servières, *Saint-Saëns* (Paris: Librairie Félix Alcan, 1923), p. 18.
39. Harold Schonberg, *The Great Pianists* (London: Gollancz, 1964), p. 265.
40. Martin Gregor-Dellin and Mack Dietrich, eds., trans. by Geoffrey Skelton, *Cosima Wagner's Diaries, vol. 1, 1869–77* (London: Collins, 1978), p. 1142n.

CHAPTER IV: TEACHER

1. Quoted in Arthur Dandelot, *La vie et l'oeuvre de Saint-Saëns* (Paris: Editions Dandelot, 1930), pp. 44–45.
2. Preface by Saint-Saëns to *Vie d'un compositeur moderne* (Paris: Librairie Fischbacher, 1893), p. x.
3. Jean-Michel Nectoux, trans. by Roger Nichols, *Gabriel Fauré: A Musical Life* (Cambridge: Cambridge University Press, 1991), p. 29.
4. Quoted in James Harding, *Saint-Saëns and his Circle* (London: Chapman and Hall, 1965), p. 86.
5. Saint-Saëns, trans. by Edwin Gile Rich, *Musical Memories* (London: John Murray, 1921), p. 177.
6. Jean-Michel Nectoux, ed., *Saint-Saëns et Fauré Correspondance, 60 ans d'amitié* (Paris: Heugel, 1973), pp. 36, 38–39.
7. Robert Orledge, *Gabriel Fauré* (London: Eulenburg, 1979), p. 7.
8. Quoted in J. Barrie Jones, ed. and trans., *Gabriel Fauré: A Life in Letters* (London: Kahn & Averill, 1980), p. 19.
9. Letter of Fauré to Marie Fauré, dated 14th July 1922, in ibid., p. 200.
10. Marguérite Long, trans. by Olive Senior-Ellis, *At the Piano with Fauré* (London: Kahn & Averill, 1980), p. 19.
11. Quoted in Jean-Michel Nectoux, trans. by J. A. Underwood, *Gabriel Fauré: His Life through his Letters* (London: Marion Boyars, 1984), p. 13.
12. *Revue Musicale*, 1st February 1922.
13. Marguérite Long, *At the Piano with Fauré*, p. 20.
14. Unpublished letter, undated, in the Bibliothèque nationale de France, Paris.
15. J. Barrie Jones, *Gabriel Fauré*, p. 18 and n. 5.
16. In a letter dated 17th September 1920, Saint-Saëns tells Fauré: "I have turned my old suite for cello and piano into one for cello and orchestra, with some new pieces." In Jean-Michel Nectoux, ed., *Saint-Saëns et Fauré Correspondance*, p. 125.
17. Dandelot, *La vie*, pp. 49–50.
18. Quoted in Mina Curtiss, *Bizet and his World* (London: Secker and Warburg, 1959), p. 128.
19. Winton Dean, *Bizet* (London: Dent, 1965), p. 49.
20. Saint-Saëns, *Portraits et Souvenirs* (Paris: Société d'édition artistique, 1899), p. 126.
21. Quoted in Curtiss, *Bizet*, p. 128.
22. Edmond Galabert. Introduction to Georges Bizet, *Lettres à un ami, 1865–1872* (Paris: Calmann-Levy, 1909), p. 8.
23. Saint-Saëns, *Portraits et Souvenirs*, p. 67.
24. Ibid., p. 152. Saint-Saëns gives a detailed account of the reconstruction of *Orphée* in

his *Ecole Buissonnière*, translated in *Musical Memories*.
25. Saint-Saëns, *Musical Memories*, p. 38.
26. Ibid., p. 38.
27. Ibid., pp. 37–38.
28. Unpublished letter, undated, in the Bibliothèque nationale de France, Paris.
29. Saint-Saëns recalled that he was as young as eighteen when he was "accused so prettily by Gounod of lacking inexperience". Camille Bellaigue, *Souvenirs de Musique et des Musiciens* (Paris: Nouvelle Librairie Nationale, 1921), p. 59. The remark has mistakenly been attributed to Berlioz.
30. Saint-Saëns, *Musical Memories*, p. 39.

CHAPTER V: PIANIST

1. Saint-Saëns, trans. by Edwin Gile Rich, *Musical Memories* (London: John Murray, 1921), p. 10.
2. *Musical Times*, August 1906.
3. Quoted in James Harding, *Saint-Saëns and his Circle* (London: Chapman and Hall, 1965), p. 200.
4. Quoted by M. D. Calvocoressi in the *Musical Times*, June 1912.
5. Joseph Horowitz, *Conversations with Arrau* (London: Collins, 1982), pp. 93–94.
6. Quoted in Arthur Dandelot, *La vie et l'oeuvre de Saint-Saëns* (Paris: Editions Dandelot, 1930), pp. 44–45.
7. Quoted in Harold Schonberg, *The Great Pianists* (London: Gollancz, 1964), p. 267.
8. Quoted in Michael Stegemann, trans. by Ann Sherwin, *Camille Saint-Saëns and the French Solo Concerto 1850–1920* (Aldershot: Scolar, 1991), p. 109.
9. *Musical Times*, June 1912.
10. Romain Rolland, trans. by Mary Blaiklock, *Musicians of Today* (London: Kegan Paul, Trench, Trubner, 1917), p. 105.
11. Dandelot, *La vie*, p. 26.
12. *New York Times*, 4th November 1906.
13. Quoted in Stegemann, *Camille Saint-Saëns and the French Solo Concerto*, p. 108.
14. *New York Times*, 16th November 1906.
15. Quoted in Bertita de Harding, *Concerto: The Story of Clara Schumann* (London: Harrap, 1962), p. 218.
16. Quoted in Sacheverell Sitwell, *Liszt* (New York: Dover Publications, 1967), p. 240.
17. Quoted in the *New York Times*, 17th December 1921.
18. Saint-Saëns, *Portraits et Souvenirs* (Paris: Société d'édition artistique, 1899), p. 21.
19. Saint-Saëns, *Musical Memories*, p. 271.
20. J. Cooper, *The Rise of Instrumental Music and Concert Series in Paris 1828–1871* (Michigan: UMI Research Press, 1983), pp. 77–78.
21. *The Times*, 19th December 1921.
22. *The Times*, 3rd June 1913.
23. Cooper, *The Rise of Instrumental Music*, pp. 125–26, 256.
24. Saint-Saëns, *Portraits et Souvenirs*, p. 117–18.
25. J. Barrie Jones, ed. and trans., *Gabriel Fauré: A Life in Letters* (London: Batsford, 1989), p. 20–21.
26. Andrew Thomson, *The Life and Times of Charles Marie Widor* (Oxford: Oxford University Press, 1987), p. 10.
27. Saint-Saëns, *Musical Memories*, p. 38.
28. Letter to Humbert Ferrand, dated 17th January 1866, in Humphrey Searle, ed. and trans., *Hector Berlioz, a Selection from His Letters* (London: Gollancz, 1966), p. 200.
29. Saint-Saëns, *Portraits et Souvenirs*, p. 12.
30. Letter to Humbert Ferrand, dated 17th January 1866, in Humphrey Searle, ed. and trans., *Hector Berlioz*, p. 200.
31. Saint-Saëns, *Portraits et Souvenirs*, pp. 7–8, p. 12.
32. Saint-Saëns, *Musical Memories*, pp. 39–41.
33. Quoted in Stegemann, *Camille Saint-Saëns and the French Solo Concerto*, p. 27.
34. *The Times*, 6th May 1867.
35. Letter to Humbert Ferrand, dated 11th June 1867, in Humphrey Searle, ed. and trans., *Hector Berlioz*, p. 206.
36. Georges Bizet, *Lettres à un ami 1865–1872* (Paris: Calmann Lévy, 1909), p. 119.
37. Quoted in Mina Curtiss, *Bizet and his World* (London: Secker and Warburg, 1959), pp. 197–98.
38. Quoted by D.C. Parker in *Musical Quarterly* (October 1919), p. 562.
39. Quoted in Harding, *Saint-Saëns*, p. 97.
40. Jean Bonnerot, *Saint-Saëns, sa vie et sa oeuvre*, 2nd ed. (Paris: Durand, 1922), p. 50.
41. Quoted in Curtiss, *Bizet*, p. 206.
42. Saint-Saëns, trans. by Fred Rothwell,

Outspoken Essays on Music (London: Kegan Paul, Trench, Trubner, 1922), p. 172.
43. Saint-Saëns, *Portraits et Souvenirs*, pp. 103–04.
44. Quoted in Dandelot, *La vie*, pp. 55–56.
45. Stegemann, *Camille Saint-Saëns and the French Solo Concerto*, pp. 164–65. See also the *Mercure de France*, 1st January 1922.
46. Attributed to the pianist Zygmund Stojowski.
47. Quoted in Stegemann, *Camille Saint-Saëns and the French Solo Concerto*, p. 28.
48. Saint-Saëns, *Portraits et Souvenirs*, p. 63.
49. Quoted in René Pichard du Page, *Augusta Holmès, Une Musicienne Versaillaise* (Versailles: Librairie M. Dubois; Paris: Librairie Fischbacher, 1921), p. 10.
50. Ibid., pp. 17–19.
51. Arthur Duparc, ed., *Correspondance de Henri Regnault* (Paris: Charpentier, 1872), p. 38.
52. Quoted in du Page, *Augusta Holmès*, p. 16.
53. Saint-Saëns, *Harmonie et Mélodie* (Paris: Calmann Lévy, 1885), pp. 225, 228–29.
54. Letter to Pierre Aguétant, 1918, in Pierre Aguétant, *Saint-Saëns par lui-même* (Paris: Editions Alsatia, 1938), p. 37.
55. Saint-Saëns, *Portraits et Souvenirs*, pp. 12–13.
56. Quoted in Stegemann, *Camille Saint-Saëns and the French Solo Concerto*, p. 29.
57. Ibid., p. 30.
58. Saint-Saëns, *Outspoken Essays*, p. 75.
59. Letter dated 2nd September 1874, quoted in Jean-Michel Nectoux, trans. by Roger Nichols, *Gabriel Fauré: A Musical Life* (Cambridge: Cambridge University Press, 1991), p. 44.
60. Saint-Saëns, *Outspoken Essays*, p. 77.
61. Quoted in Stegemann, *Camille Saint-Saëns and the French Solo Concerto*, p. 30.
62. Quoted in Dandelot, *La vie*, p. 60.
63. Saint-Saëns, *Outspoken Essays*, p. 173.

CHAPTER VI: PATRIOT

1. Martin Gregor-Dellin and Mack Dietrich, eds., trans. by Geoffrey Skelton, *Cosima Wagner's Diaries, vol. 1, 1869–1877* (London: Collins, 1978), pp. 245, 247.
2. Ernest Newman, *Life of Richard Wagner*, vol. 4 (New York: Knopf, 1960), p. 268n.
3. Quoted in J. Barrie Jones, ed. and trans., *Gabriel Fauré: A Life in Letters* (London: Batsford, 1989), p. 269.
4. Saint-Saëns, trans. by Edwin Gile Rich, *Musical Memories* (London: John Murray, 1921), p. 281.
5. *New York Times*, 6th June 1922.
6. Quoted in Harold Schonberg, *The Great Pianists* (London: Gollancz, 1964), p. 265.
7. Romain Rolland, trans. by Mary Blaiklock, *Musicians of Today* (London: Kegan Paul, Trench, Trubner, 1917), p. 268.
8. *Musical Standard*, 10th June 1871.
9. C. E. Hallé, *Notes from a Painter's Life* (London: John Murray, 1909), pp. 79–80.
10. Jean Bonnerot, *Saint-Saëns, sa vie et sa oeuvre*, 2nd ed. (Paris: Durand, 1922), p. 62.
11. *Musical Times*, September 1871.
12. *Musical Standard*, 1st July 1871.
13. Saint-Saëns, *Portraits et Souvenirs* (Paris: Société d'édition artistique, 1899), pp. 194–95.
14. *The Orchestra*, 25th August 1871.
15. Bonnerot, *Saint-Saëns*, p. 12.
16. Letter, dated 10th October 1871, in the Bibliothèque nationale de France, Paris.
17. Saint-Saëns, *Musical Memories*, pp. 50–51, 59; *Portraits et Souvenirs*, pp. 128–30.
18. Winton Dean, *Bizet* (London: J. M. Dent, 1965), p. 95.
19. Saint-Saëns, *Harmonie et Mélodie* (Paris: Calmann Lévy, 1885), p. 211.
20. Saint-Saëns, *Au courant de la vie* (Paris: Dorbon-Ainé, 1914), p. 42.

CHAPTER VII: SYMPHONIC POET

1. Quoted in Arthur Hervey, *Saint-Saëns* (London: The Bodley Head, 1921), p. 86.
2. Ibid., pp. 86–87.
3. Ibid., pp. 85–86.
4. *New York Times*, 9th December 1934.
5. Jacques Durand, *Quelques Souvenirs d'un éditeur de musique* (Paris: Durand, 1924), pp. 17–18.
6. Saint-Saëns, trans. by Edwin Gile Rich, *Musical Memories* (London: John Murray, 1921), p. 193.
7. Saint-Saëns, *Harmonie et Mélodie* (Paris: Calmann Lévy, 1885), pp. 211–12.
8. Saint-Saëns, *Portraits et Souvenirs* (Paris: Société d'édition artistique, 1899), pp. 195–96.
9. Elaine Brody, *Paris: The Musical Kaleidoscope*

1870–1925 (London: Robson Books, 1988), p. 46.
10. Quoted in Mina Curtiss, *Bizet and his World* (London: Secker and Warburg, 1959), p. 349.
11. Quoted in D. G. Mason, *From Grieg to Brahms* (New York: The Outlook Company, 1903), pp. 103–04.
12. Winton Dean, *Bizet* (London: Dent, 1965), p. 100.
13. Saint-Saëns, *Musical Memories*, p. 43.
14. Quoted in Arthur Dandelot, *La vie et l'oeuvre de Saint-Saëns* (Paris: Editions Dandelot, 1930), pp. 66–67.
15. *The Orchestra*, 25th August 1871.
16. Quoted by M. D. Calvocoressi in the *Musical Times*, June 1912.
17. Ibid.
18. Saint-Saëns, *Portraits et Souvenirs*, pp. 125–26.
19. Saint-Saëns, *Musical Memories*, p. 49.
20. Saint-Saëns, *Ecole Buissonnière* (Paris: Pierre Lafitte, 1913), pp. 91–92.
21. Quoted in Jean Bonnerot, *Saint-Saëns, sa vie et sa oeuvre*, 2nd ed. (Paris: Durand, 1922), p. 70.
22. General Yusuf. See Saint-Saëns, *Musical Memories*, p. 270.
23. James Harding, *Saint-Saëns and his Circle* (London: Chapman and Hall, 1965), p. 122.
24. J. Barrie Jones, ed. and trans., *Gabriel Fauré: A Life in Letters* (London: Batsford, 1989), p. 30.
25. Ibid., pp. 27–28.
26. Hervey, *Saint-Saëns*, p. 11.
27. Sacheverell Sitwell, *Liszt* (New York: Dover Publications, 1967), p. 277.
28. Saint-Saëns, *Musical Memories*, p. 277.
29. Ibid., pp. 29–30.
30. Ibid., pp. 148–150.
31. Quoted in Mason, *From Grieg to Brahms*, pp. 103–04.
32. Ibid., p. 104.
33. Undated letter in the Bibliothèque nationale de France, Paris.
34. Bonnerot, *Saint-Saëns*, p. 72.
35. Ibid., p. 73.
36. Undated note in the Bibliothèque Gustav Mahler, Paris.
37. Georges Servières, *Saint-Saëns* (Paris: Librairie Félix Alcan, 1923), pp. 196–97.
38. *Musical Times*, January 1922.
39. Arthur Foote, *An Autobiography* (New York: Da Capo, 1979), p. 44.
40. Saint-Saëns, *Portraits et Souvenirs*, p. 26.
41. Quoted in Mason, *From Grieg to Brahms*, p. 113.
42. Quoted in Dandelot, *La vie*, pp. 63–64.
43. Ibid., p. 86. According to Dandelot, it was Truffot who suggested his sister as a wife for Saint-Saëns.

CHAPTER VIII: HUSBAND and FATHER

1. Quoted in James Harding, *Saint-Saëns and his Circle* (London: Chapman and Hall, 1965), p. 134.
2. Mina Curtiss, *Bizet and his World* (London: Secker and Warburg, 1959), p. 134.
3. Quoted by J. G. Proudhomme in the *Musical Quarterly*, October 1922.
4. Michael Stegemann, trans. by Ann Sherwin, *Camille Saint-Saëns and the French Solo Concerto 1850–1920* (Aldershot: Scolar, 1991), p. 34.
5. Ibid., p. 35.
6. *Le Figaro*, 26th February 1889, quoted in Arthur Dandelot, *La vie et l'oeuvre de Saint-Saëns* (Paris: Editions Dandelot, 1930), p. 77.
7. Quoted in Rosa Newmarch, *Tchaikovsky* (London: Grant Richards, 1900), pp. 148–49.
8. Saint-Saëns, trans. by Edwin Gile Rich, *Musical Memories* (London: John Murray, 1921), pp. 129, 140–41.
9. Quoted in David Brown, *Tchaikovsky: A Biographical and Critical Study*, vol. ii (London: Gollancz, 1982), p. 55.
10. Modest Tchaikovsky, trans. by Rosa Newmarch, *The Life and Letters of P. I. Tchaikovsky* (London: The Bodley Head, 1906), p. 176.
11. Letter to Vladimir Stasov, dated 23rd November 1875, in Jay Leyda and Sergei Bertensson, eds. and trans., *The Mussorgsky Reader* (New York: Da Capo, 1970), pp. 318–319.
12. Jean Bonnerot, *Saint-Saëns, sa vie et sa oeuvre*, 2nd ed. (Paris: Durand, 1922), pp. 78–79.
13. Brown, *Tchaikovsky*, p. 56.
14. Letter to Durand, dated 24th March 1876. Correspondence to Durand referred to

here and below, as well as in the text, are from the Collection of Jean-Manuel Mobillion de Scarano, kept in the Bibliothèque Gustav Mahler, Paris.

15. Saint-Saëns, *Harmonie et Mélodie* (Paris: Calmann Lévy, 1885), pp. 37–98. This contains Saint-Saëns's lengthy report of the Bayreuth Festival.
16. Ibid., pp. 41–42.
17. Ibid., pp. 38, 98.
18. Richard and Cosima Wagner, ed. L. Guichard, *Lettres à Judith Gautier* (Paris: Gallimard, 1964), p. 317.
19. Saint-Saëns, *Musical Memories*, pp. 45–47.
20. Quoted in Bonnerot, *Saint-Saëns*, p. 82.
21. Quoted in Arthur Hervey, *Saint-Saëns* (London: The Bodley Head, 1921), p. 47.
22. Georges Servières, *Saint-Saëns* (Paris: Librairie Félix Alcan, 1923), p. 38.
23. Quoted in Hervey, *Saint-Saëns*, p. 46.
24. Saint-Saëns, *Musical Memories*, p. 47.
25. Quoted in Dandelot, *La vie et l'oeuvre de Saint-Saëns*, p. 82.
26. Ibid., p. 245.
27. Bonnerot, *Saint-Saëns*, p. 86.
28. Letter dated 18th April 1877.
29. Saint-Saëns, *Musical Memories*, p. 53.
30. Letters to Durand, dated 6th and 13th November 1877.
31. Letter dated 23rd November 1877.
32. Quoted in Bonnerot, *Saint-Saëns*, p. 89.
33. Saint-Saëns, *Musical Memories*, p. 23.
34. Jean-Michel Nectoux, trans. by J. A. Underwood, *Gabriel Fauré: His Life through His Letters* (London: Marion Boyars, 1984), pp. 65–66. Fauré was mistaken in recalling that Liszt was present at this supper.
35. Edward N. Waters, ed., trans. by William R Tyler, *The Letters of Franz Liszt to Olga von Meyendorff 1871–1886* (Washington: Dumbarton Oaks, 1979), p. 300.
36. Letter dated 9th December 1877.
37. Waters, ed. *The Letters of Franz Liszt*, p. 309.
38. Saint-Saëns, *Musical Memories*, p. 124.
39. Richard and Cosima Wagner, *Lettres à Judith Gautier*, p. 201.
40. Review contained in a letter from Saint-Saëns to Durand, from Strasbourg, dated 2nd April 1878.
41. Letter dated 9th April 1878.
42. The account given by the pianist Leopold Godowsky, who came to know Saint-Saëns nearly ten years later, is that the composer, returning from an unsuccessful hunting trip, saw blood on the pavement and quipped: "It looks as though I had been hunting here." The concierge could not face telling him the news, which he learned only on reaching his rooms. See Jeremy Nicholas, *Godowsky, the Pianist's Pianist* (Hexham: Appian, 1989), p. 22. The picture of Saint-Saëns as a hunter sits oddly with his much-publicised love of animals and hatred of cruelty to them.
43. J. G. Proudhomme in the *Musical Quarterly*, October 1922.
44. *The Times*, 17th June 1878.
45. Quoted in Harding, *Saint-Saëns*, p. 55.
46. Letter to Marie Clerc, dated 3rd October 1878 in Nectoux, *Gabriel Fauré: His Life through His Letters*, p. 81.
47. Letter dated 12th November 1880.
48. Saint-Saëns, *Musical Memories*, p. 218. Massenet, never one to air his grudges in public, insisted in old age that "I was and always have been" Saint-Saëns's friend as well as "great admirer". Saint-Saëns wrote to his contacts in Weimar on Massenet's behalf as early as 1867, after the younger composer was narrowly beaten in the Universal Exhibition opera competition, telling him he had done so because "there are so many good and beautiful things in your score". This approach, however, was unsuccessful. See Jules Massenet, trans. by H. Villiers Barnett, *My Recollections* (Boston: Small, Maynard & Co., 1919), pp. 118 and 71.
49. Saint-Saëns, *Musical Memories*, pp. 214, 216–17.
50. Felix Weingartner, trans. by Marguerite Wolff, *Buffets and Rewards* (London: Hutchinson, 1937), p. 312.
51. Quoted in Bonnerot, *Saint-Saëns*, pp. 94–95.
52. *New York Times*, 17th November 1879.
53. Reprinted in *Harmonie et Mélodie*, p. 2.
54. Saint-Saëns, trans. by Fred Rothwell, *Outspoken Essays on Music* (London: Kegan Paul, Trench, Trubner, 1922), pp. 16–19.
55. Letter dated 16th February 1879.
56. Letter dated 17th March 1879.
57. Hermann Klein, *Thirty Years of Musical Life*

in *London 1870–1900* (London: Heinemann, 1903), pp. 173–74.
58. *The Times*, 29th August 1879.
59. Ibid.
60. Saint-Saëns's account of his experiences at and thoughts on the 1879 Birmingham Festival is given in full in his *Harmonie et Mélodie*, pp. 141–54.
61. Saint-Saëns, *Portraits et Souvenirs* (Paris: Société d'édition artistique, 1899), p. 84.
62. Ibid., p. 137.
63. Letter to Durand, 9th December 1879.
64. Letter to Durand, 16th February 1880.
65. Letter to Durand, 29th June 1880.
66. Saint-Saëns, *Musical Memories*, pp. 262–63.
67. Quoted in Harding, *Saint-Saëns*, p. 162.
68. Ibid., p. 162.
69. Letter to Durand, July 1879.
70. D. C. Parker in *The Strad*, 1918.
71. Letter to Durand, 12th November 1880.
72. Quoted in Bonnerot, *Saint-Saëns*, p. 106.
73. Letter dated 24th March 1881.
74. Letter dated 25th July 1881.
75. Quoted in Harding, *Saint-Saëns*, p. 156.
76. Pierre Aguétant, *Saint-Saëns par lui-même* (Paris: Editions Alsatia, 1938), p. 101.

CHAPTER IX: THE IMMORTAL

1. Saint-Saëns, trans. by Edwin Gile Rich, *Musical Memories* (London: John Murray, 1921), pp. 32–33.
2. Saint-Saëns, *Notice sur Henri Reber* (Paris: Firman Didot, 1881), p. 10.
3. Jean Bonnerot, *Saint-Saëns, sa vie et sa oeuvre*, 2nd ed. (Paris: Durand, 1922), p. 109.
4. Quoted in Gerald D. Turbow, 'Art and Politics: Wagnerism in France', in *Wagnerism in European Culture and Politics*, edited by David C. Large and William Weber (Ithaca and London: Cornell University Press, 1984), p. 155.
5. Georges Servières, quoted in Gill Chesney, 'Some Wagnerian Repercussions in France after 1880', in *Wagner 1876: A Celebration of the Bayreuth Festival* (London: The Wagner Society, 1976), p. 238.
6. Saint-Saëns, *Harmonie et Mélodie* (Paris: Calmann Lévy, 1885), p. xxii.
7. Letter dated 6th March 1881.
8. Saint-Saëns, *Harmonie et Mélodie*, p. 297; Saint-Saëns, trans. by Fred Rothwell, *Outspoken Essays on Music* (London: Kegan Paul, Trench, Trubner, 1922), p. 40.
9. Letter to Emile Lemoine dated 23rd May 1898, quoted in Arthur Dandelot, *La vie et l'oeuvre de Saint-Saëns* (Paris: Editions Dandelot, 1930), p. 163.
10. Quoted in Bonnerot, *Saint-Saëns*, pp. 100–01.
11. Quoted in Dandelot, *La vie*, p. 96.
12. Letter dated 27th January 1882.
13. Letter dated 17th March 1882.
14. Quoted in Henri Collet, *Samson et Dalila de Saint-Saëns* (Paris: Librairie Delaplane, 1922), p. 42.
15. Letter to Durand, dated 27th January 1882.
16. Quoted in Elaine Brody, *Paris: The Musical Kaleidoscope 1870–1925* (London: Robson Books, 1988), p. 56.
17. Saint-Saëns, *Harmonie et Mélodie*, p. 97.
18. James Harding, *Saint-Saëns and his Circle* (London: Chapman and Hall, 1965), pp. 144–45.
19. Jacques Durand, *Quelques Souvenirs d'un éditeur de musique* (Paris: Durand, 1924), pp. 20–23.
20. Quoted in Dandelot, *La vie*, pp. 101–02.
21. Charles Gounod, trans. by W. Hely Hutchinson, *Autobiographical Reminiscences* (London: Heinemann, 1896), pp. 211–12, p. 221.
22. Felix Weingartner, trans. by Marguerite Wolff, *Buffets and Rewards* (London: Hutchinson, 1937), p. 208.
23. Reprinted in *Harmonic et Mélodie*, p. 281.
24. Saint-Saëns, *Musical Memories*, p. 34.
25. *Yorkshire Post*, 19th November 1885.
26. Letter to Durand, 18th November 1885.
27. *The Times*, 21st November 1885.
28. Saint-Saëns, *Harmonie et Mélodie*, p. 98.
29. Ibid., pp. 307–08.
30. Ibid., p. 313. Saint-Saëns was not the first to draw attention to the 'war on the Latins' exhortation in *Die Meistersinger*. It was noted by the critic Charles Bannelier after the first performance in 1868.
31. Ibid., pp. 314–15.
32. Letter dated 21st January 1886.
33. Letter dated 24th January 1886.
34. Letters to Durand, dated 26th and 31st January, 19th February 1886.

35. But see Chapter 8, note 42.
36. Saint-Saëns, *Outspoken Essays on Music*, pp. 127–30, 135–36.
37. Francesco Berger, *Reminiscences, Impressions and Anecdotes* (London: Sampson and Low, 1913), pp. 115–16.
38. J. Barrie Jones, ed. and trans., *Gabriel Fauré: A Life in Letters* (London: Batsford, 1989), pp. 58–59.
39. Letter dated 19th February 1886.
40. Quoted in Harding, *Saint-Saëns*, p. 172.
41. Letter dated 18th May 1886.
42. *Daily Telegraph*, 21st May 1886.
43. Bonnerot, *Saint-Saëns*, pp. 125–26.
44. *Daily Telegraph*, 20th and 21st May 1886.
45. Quoted in Harding, *Saint-Saëns*, p. 173.
46. Ibid., p. 173.
47. G. Jean-Aubry, trans. by Edwin Evans, *French Music of Today* (London: Kegan Paul, Trench, Trubner, 1919), p. 69.
48. G. Jean-Aubry in the *Musical Times*, January 1917.
49. Quoted in Léon Vallas, trans. by Hubert Foss, *César Franck* (London: Harrap, 1951), p. 193.
50. Ibid., p. 193.
51. Romain Rolland, trans. by Mary Blaiklock, *Musicians of Today* (London: Kegan Paul, Trench, Trubner, 1917), p. 271.
52. Léon Vallas, *César Franck*, pp. 137–38.
53. Francis Poulenc, trans. by Cynthia Jolly, *Emmanuel Chabrier* (London: Dobson, 1981), p. 62.
54. Letter of Saint-Saëns to Vincent d'Indy in the *Revue Musicale*, February 1947.
55. Quoted in Dandelot, *La vie*, p. 169.
56. Saint-Saëns, *Outspoken Essays*, pp. 46, pp. 48–49.
57. Quoted in Vallas, *César Franck*, p. 193.

CHAPTER X: MAN of the THEATRE

1. Letter to Durand, 14th February 1886.
2. Saint-Saëns, trans. by Fred Rothwell, *Outspoken Essays on Music* (London: Kegan Paul, Trench, Trubner, 1922), pp. 22–23.
3. Saint-Saëns, *Portraits et Souvenirs* (Paris: Société d'édition artistique, 1899), p. 91.
4. Saint-Saëns, *Outspoken Essays*, p. 181.
5. Saint-Saëns, *Portraits et Souvenirs*, p. 89.
6. Ibid., p. 231.
7. Ibid., p. 183.
8. Georges Servières, *Saint-Saëns* (Paris: Librairie Félix Alcan, 1923), p. 181.
9. Saint-Saëns, trans. by Edwin Gile Rich, *Musical Memories* (London: John Murray, 1921), p. 55.
10. Saint-Saëns, *Outspoken Essays*, pp. 130–31.
11. Quoted in Servières, *Saint-Saëns*, p. 185.
12. Letter dated 29th March 1887 in the Bibliothèque nationale de France, Paris.
13. *The Stage*, 25th March 1887.
14. Saint-Saëns, *Musical Memories*, p. 55.
15. Wilhelm Ganz, *Memories of a Musician* (London: John Murray, 1913), p. 264. The pianist Jeanne-Marie Darré (1905–99) once played all five concertos in one concert.
16. *The Times*, 21st June 1887.
17. Wilhelm Ganz, *Memories*, pp. 264–66.
18. Letter dated 10th May 1880.
19. Wilhelm Ganz, *Memories*, p. 265.
20. *Musical Times*, January 1922.
21. Watson Lyle, *Camille Saint-Saëns, His Life and Art* (London: Kegan Paul, Trench, Trubner, 1923), pp. 69–70.
22. Rollo Myers, *Emmanuel Chabrier and His Circle* (London: Dent, 1969), p. 131.
23. *Musical Times*, January 1922.
24. Quoted in Harold Schönberg, *Lives of the Great Composers* (London: Davis-Poynter, 1971), p. 329.
25. Quoted in the *New York Times*, 9th December 1934.
26. *Musical Times*, January 1922.
27. Jacques Durand, *Quelques Souvenirs d'un éditeur de musique* (Paris: Durand, 1924), p. 9.
28. *Musical Quarterly*, October 1922.
29. Quoted in Watson Lyle, *Camille Saint-Saëns*, p. 71.
30. Henri Fevrier, *André Messager* (Paris: Amiot-Dumont, 1948), p. 33.
31. Jan Paderewski and Mary Lawton, *The Paderewski Memoirs* (New York: Da Capo, 1980), pp. 136–37.
32. Quoted by J. G. Proudhomme in *Musical Quarterly*, October 1922.
33. Jeremy Nicholas, *Godowsky, the Pianist's Pianist* (Hexham: Appian, 1989), pp. 22–25.
34. Robert Orledge, *Gabriel Fauré* (London: Eulenburg, 1979), pp. 13–14.

35. Letter dated 23rd January 1887, in J. Barrie Jones, ed. and trans., *Gabriel Fauré: A Life in Letters* (London: Batsford, 1989), p. 61.
36. Letters dated 13th May 1918 and 10th May 1918 in Pierre Aguétant, *Saint-Saëns par lui-même* (Paris: Editions Alsatia, 1938), pp. 59, 61–62.
37. Saint-Saëns, *Musical Memories*, pp. 54–55.
38. Hermann Klein, *Thirty Years of Musical Life in London 1870–1900* (London: Heinemann, 1903), pp. 175–76.
39. Quoted in Arthur Dandelot, *La vie et l'oeuvre de Saint-Saëns* (Paris: Editions Dandelot, 1930), p. 116.
40. Jean Bonnerot, *Saint-Saëns, sa vie et sa oeuvre*, 2nd ed. (Paris: Durand, 1922), pp. 134–35.
41. Saint-Saëns, *Musical Memories*, p. 55.
42. Letter in the Bibliothèque nationale de France, Paris.
43. Quoted in Dandelot, *La vie*, p. 116.
44. J. Barrie Jones, ed. and trans., *Gabriel Fauré*, p. 63.
45. Quoted in Dandelot, *La vie*, p. 116.
46. Letters dated 11th, 16th and 21st January 1889.
47. Letters dated 2nd and 3rd February, 1889.
48. Letter dated 6th February 1889, in the Bibliothèque nationale de France, Paris.
49. Quoted in Dandelot, *La vie*, p. 116.
50. Quoted in Bonnerot, *Saint-Saëns*, p. 139.
51. The poem is contained in Saint-Saëns, *Rimes Familières* (Paris: Calmann Lévy, 1891), and reprinted in Appendix II.
52. Quoted in Dandelot, *La vie*, p. 117.
53. Quoted in *Le Figaro*, 1st March 1890.
54. Letter dated 30th November 1889, in the Bibliothèque Gustav Mahler, Paris.
55. Letter dated 30th November 1889.
56. *New York Times*, 17th November 1906.
57. 'Adam and Eve', in *Rimes Familières*.
58. Letter dated 28th May 1918, in Pierre Aguétant, *Saint-Saëns par lui-même*, p. 34.
59. *Le Figaro*, 22nd April 1890.
60. *Musical Times*, June 1890.
61. *The Times*, 28th March 1890.
62. *The Stage*, 23rd March 1890.
63. Ibid.
64. *Le Figaro*, 23rd March 1890.
65. *The Times*, 24th March 1890.
66. *Le Temps*, 23rd March 1890.
67. *Musical Times*, April 1890.
68. *New York Times*, 13th April 1890.
69. Emma Eames, *Some Memories and Reflections* (New York: Appleton, 1927), pp. 102–03.
70. *Musical Times*, April 1890.
71. *The Times*, 24th March 1890.
72. Hermann Klein, *Thirty Years*, p. 287.
73. Letter dated 28th May 1890, in the *Revue Musicale*, February 1924.
74. Quoted in the *New York Times*, 17th November 1935.
75. *Le Figaro*, 22nd April 1890.
76. Henry Wood, *My Life of Music* (London: Gollancz, 1938), p. 81.
77. *Le Figaro*, 22nd April 1890.
78. Jacques Durand, *Quelques Souvenirs*, pp. 71–72.
79. Quoted in Arthur Hervey, *Saint-Saëns* (London: The Bodley Head, 1921), pp. 66–67.
80. Quoted in Dandelot, *La vie*, pp. 282–83.
81. *New York Times*, 17th November 1935.
82. Servières, *Saint-Saëns*, p. 57.

CHAPTER XI: THE TRAVELLING PHILOSOPHER

1. Charles Gounod, trans. by W. Hely Hutchinson, *Autobiographical Reminiscences* (London: Heinemann, 1896), pp. 257–58.
2. Letter from Las Palmas dated 2nd February 1894, quoted in Arthur Dandelot, *La vie et l'oeuvre de Saint-Saëns* (Paris: Editions Dandelot, 1930), p. 138.
3. Letter from St Germain-en-Laye dated 13th May 1889, in the Bibliothèque nationale de France, Paris.
4. *Musical Times*, January 1922.
5. Georges Servières, *Saint-Saëns* (Paris: Librairie Félix Alcan, 1923), p. 195.
6. Saint-Saëns, *Ecole Buissonnière* (Paris: Pierre Lafitte, 1913), p. 320.
7. Ibid., p. 322.
8. Letter in the Bibliothèque nationale de France, Paris.
9. Letter dated 11th March 1892, in the Bibliothèque nationale de France, Paris.
10. Letter from Marseilles, dated 11th May 1892, quoted in Dandelot, *La vie*, p. 137.
11. Ibid., p. 138.

12. Letter from Paris, dated 17th August 1892, in the Bibliothèque nationale de France, Paris.
13. Jacques Durand, *Quelques Souvenirs d'un éditeur de musique* (Paris: Durand, 1924), pp. 91–92.
14. Letters dated 1st January 1892 and 19th September 1892, in Jean-Michel Nectoux, ed., *Saint-Saëns et Fauré Correspondance, 60 ans d'amitié* (Paris: Heugel, 1973), p. 50, pp. 51–52.
15. Quoted in Henri Février, *André Messager* (Paris: Amiot-Dumont, 1948), p. 70.
16. Ibid., pp. 71–72.
17. Jean Bonnerot, *Saint-Saëns, sa vie et sa oeuvre*, 2nd ed. (Paris: Durand, 1922), pp. 155–56.
18. Ibid., p. 155.
19. Quoted in Gerald Norris, *Stanford, the Cambridge Jubilee and Tchaikovsky* (Newton Abbot: David and Charles, 1980), p. 353.
20. Ibid., p. 353.
21. Letter dated 3rd June 1893, in Modest Tchaikovsky, trans. by Rosa Newmarch, *The Life and Letters of P. I. Tchaikovsky* (London: The Bodley Head, 1906), p. 707.
22. Francesco Berger, *Reminiscences, Impressions and Anecdotes* (London: Sampson and Low, 1913), p. 117.
23. Norris, *Stanford*, p. 360.
24. Saint-Saëns's account of his experiences at the Cambridge jubilee is given in full in his *Portraits et Souvenirs* (Paris: Société d'édition artistique, 1899), pp. 133–47.
25. Quoted in Norris, *Stanford*, p. 393.
26. Saint-Saëns, *Portraits et Souvenirs*, pp. 142–43.
27. Saint-Saëns, *Harmonie et Mélodie* (Paris: Calmann Lévy, 1885), p. 142.
28. Wilhelm Ganz, *Memories of a Musician* (London: John Murray, 1913), p. 265.
29. Sir Frederick Cowen, *My Art and My Friends* (London: Edward Arnold, 1913), pp. 231–32.
30. Quoted in Harold Rosenthal, *Two Centuries of Opera at Covent Garden* (London: Putnam, 1958), pp. 257–58.
31. *The Times*, 27th September 1893.
32. *The Stage*, 29th September 1893.
33. Cowen, *My Art*, p. 232.
34. Ibid.
35. Quoted in Bonnerot, *Saint-Saëns*, p. 155.
36. Letter dated 21st October 1893, in Nectoux, *Saint-Saëns et Fauré Correspondance*, p. 54.
37. *Revue musicale*, February 1924.
38. Saint-Saëns, *Portraits et Souvenirs*, pp. 206–11, 214–17, 155, 186–87.
39. Quoted in Arthur Hervey, *Saint-Saëns* (London: The Bodley Head, 1921), p. 34.
40. Saint-Saëns, trans. by Fred Rothwell, *Outspoken Essays on Music* (London: Kegan Paul, Trench, Trubner, 1922), pp. 4–5.
41. Saint-Saëns, trans. by Edwin Gile Rich, *Musical Memories* (London: John Murray, 1921), p. 81.
42. Letter from Cairo dated 4th February 1907, quoted in the *Revue des Deux Mondes*, April 1926.
43. Saint-Saëns, *Musical Memories*, p. 81.
44. Letter from Dieppe dated 21st September 1894, quoted in Dandelot, *La vie*, p. 139.
45. Letter dated 2nd February 1894, ibid., p. 138.
46. Letter dated 18th June 1894, in the *Revue Musicale*, February 1924.
47. Quoted in Marc Bredel, *Erik Satie* (Paris: Musique Mazarine, 1982), pp. 48–49.
48. Quoted in Dandelot, *La vie*, p. 133.
49. Ibid., p. 134.
50. Saint-Saëns, *Ecole Buissonnière*, p. 324.
51. Letters quoted in Dandelot, *La vie*, pp. 134–35.
52. Arthur Dandelot, *La Société des Concerts du Conservatoire*, 3rd ed. (Paris: G. Havard, 1894), p. 142.
53. Durand, *Quelques Souvenirs*, pp. 107–8.
54. Quoted in Dandelot, *La vie*, pp. 142–43.
55. Ibid., pp. 145–47.
56. Bonnerot, *Saint-Saëns*, p. 163.

CHAPTER XII: REACTIONARY and ROYAL FAVOURITE

1. Quoted in Arthur Dandelot, *La vie et l'oeuvre de Saint-Saëns* (Paris: Editions Dandelot, 1930), p. 230.
2. Letter to M. L. Boëmann, 1894, in the Bibliothèque nationale de France, Paris.
3. Pierre Aguétant, *Saint-Saëns par lui-même* (Paris: Editions Alsatia, 1938), p. 154.
4. Quoted in the *New York Times*, 8th January 1922.
5. Aguétant, *Saint-Saëns*, p. 97.

6. Saint-Saëns, trans. by Edwin Gile Rich, *Musical Memories* (London: John Murray, 1921), p. 268.
7. Ibid., pp. 269–70.
8. Doris Monteux, *It's All in the Music* (New York: Farrar, Straus and Giroux, 1965), pp. 36–37.
9. *The Times*, 15th July 1898.
10. *The Stage*, 21st July 1898.
11. Saint-Saëns, *Musical Memories*, pp. 264–65, p. 266.
12. Ibid., p. 271.
13. Letter dated 14th September 1898, in *Saint-Saëns: Correspondance inédite* (Paris: *Revue Musicale*, 1983), p. 24.
14. Quoted in J. Barrie Jones, ed. and trans. *Gabriel Fauré: A Life in Letters* (London: Batsford, 1989), p. 79.
15. Saint-Saëns, *Portraits et Souvenirs* (Paris: Société d'édition artistique, 1899), pp. 21, 219, 26–27, 219, 22, vii–viii, 38, 240, 185, 155, 187, 189.
16. Quoted in Dandelot, *La vie*, p. 171.
17. Letter dated 9th January 1893, in the *Revue Musicale*, February 1924.
18. Letter to Malherbe, quoted in Dandelot, *La vie*, pp. 182–83.
19. *New York Times*, 25th November 1906.
20. Saint-Saëns, *Portraits et Souvenirs*, p. 21.
21. Saint-Saëns, trans. by Fred Rothwell, *Outspoken Essays on Music* (London: Kegan Paul, Trench, Trubner, 1922), pp. 6, 8.
22. Quoted in Arthur Hervey, *Saint-Saëns* (London: The Bodley Head, 1921), p. 136.
23. Saint-Saëns, *Musical Memories*, p. 95.
24. Ibid.
25. Letter dated 26th August 1918, in Aguétant, *Saint-Saëns*, p. 33.
26. Saint-Saëns, *Musical Memories*, p. 96.
27. Saint-Saëns, *Ecole Buissonnière* (Paris: Pierre Lafitte, 1913), p. viii.
28. Saint-Saëns, *Portraits et Souvenirs*, p. 21, pp. 109–10.
29. Quoted in the *Musical Times*, August 1906.
30. G. Jean-Aubry, trans. by Edwin Evans, *French Music of Today* (London: Kegan Paul, Trench, Trubner, 1919), pp. 4, 69.
31. G. Jean-Aubry in *The Chesterian*, January 1922.
32. James Harding, *Saint-Saëns and his Circle* (London: Chapman and Hall, 1965), p. 215.
33. Hermann Klein in the *Musical Times*, January 1922.
34. Letter dated 30th August 1901, in J. Barrie Jones, ed. and trans., *Gabriel Fauré: A Life in Letters* (London: Batsford, 1989), p. 107.
35. Alfredo Casella, ed. and trans. by Spencer Norton, *Music in My Time* (Norman: University of Oklahoma Press, 1955), pp. 81–82.
36. Letter dated 29th August 1918, in Aguétant, *Saint-Saëns*, p. 35.
37. Casella, *Music in My Time*, pp. 81–82.
38. *New York Times*, 25th November 1906.
39. Letter dated 14th April 1918, in Aguétant, *Saint-Saëns*, p. 13.
40. Arthur Rubinstein, *My Young Years* (London: Cape, 1973), pp. 131, 132–33, p. 136.
41. Marcel Dupré , ed. by R. Kneeream, *Recollections* (New York: Belwin Mills, 1972), pp. 61–62.
42. *Glasgow Herald*, 19th December 1921.
43. Saint-Saëns, *Outspoken Essays*, p. 9.
44. Arthur Hervey, *Saint-Saëns* (London: The Bodley Head, 1921), pp. ix–x.
45. Letters dated 20th and 28th June 1900, in Jean-Michel Nectoux, ed., *Saint-Saëns et Fauré Correspondance, 60 ans d'amitié* (Paris: Heugel, 1973), pp. 63–64.
46. Letters dated 27th and 28th August 1900, in J. Barrie Jones, *Gabriel Fauré*, pp. 100–01.
47. Letter dated 24th December 1900, in Nectoux, *Saint-Saëns et Fauré*, p. 66.
48. Lev Ginsburg, ed. by H. R. Axelrod, trans. by X. M. Danko, *Ysaÿe* (New Jersey: Paganiniana, 1980), pp. 107, 484.
49. *Revue Musicale*, February 1924.
50. Letter dated 31st August 1901, in Barrie Jones, *Gabriel Fauré*, p. 108.
51. Letters dated 30th November 1901, in Nectoux, *Saint-Saëns et Fauré*, p. 67.
52. Quoted in Dandelot, *La vie*, p. 160.
53. Henry Wood, *My Life of Music* (London: Gollancz, 1938), p. 159.
54. Saint-Saëns, *Musical Memories*, pp. 267–69.
55. Ibid., p. 270.
56. Letter dated 18th August 1902, in Barrie Jones, *Gabriel Fauré*, p. 109.
57. Saint-Saëns, *Outspoken Essays*, pp. 106, 107.
58. *Le Figaro*, 8th February 1903.
59. *Le Temps*, 8th February 1903.
60. Saint-Saëns, *Outspoken Essays*, pp. 108–10.

61. Letter dated 22nd October 1918, in Aguétant, *Saint-Saëns*, p. 30.
62. A. M. Henderson, 'Memories of some distinguished French organists', *Musical Times*, June 1937.
63. Letter to Marie Fauré dated 10th August 1900, in Barrie Jones, *Gabriel Fauré*, p. 96.
64. Quoted in Dandelot, *La vie*, pp. 210–11.
65. Hermann Klein, 'Saint-Saëns as I knew him', *Musical Times*, January 1922.

CHAPTER XIII: GRAND OLD MAN

1. *New York Times*, 20th June 1909.
2. *Courrier Musical*, 15th February 1911, quoted in Arthur Dandelot, *La vie et l'oeuvre de Saint-Saëns* (Paris: Editions Dandelot, 1930), p. 204.
3. Letter dated 18th February 1904, in Jean-Michel Nectoux, ed., *Saint-Saëns et Fauré Correspondance, 60 ans d'amitié* (Paris: Heugel, 1973), p. 71.
4. *Musical Standard*, 25th June 1904.
5. Nellie Melba, *Melodies and Memories* (London: Hamish Hamilton, 1980), pp. 135–36, 185–86.
6. *Scotsman*, 6th June 1904.
7. *Edinburgh Evening News*, 6th June 1904.
8. A. M. Henderson, 'Memories of some distinguished French organists', *Musical Times*, June 1937. Henderson mistakenly gives the date of this concert as 1906.
9. *Scotsman*, 6th June 1904.
10. Arthur Rubinstein, *My Young Years* (London: Jonathan Cape, 1973), pp. 130–31.
11. Letter from Algeria dated 27th February 1920, in Pierre Aguétant, *Saint-Saëns par lui-même* (Paris: Editions Alsatia, 1938), p. 81.
12. Saint-Saëns, trans. by Fred Rothwell, *Outspoken Essays on Music* (London: Kegan Paul, Trench, Trubner, 1922), p. 133, pp. 134–35.
13. Jacques Durand, *Quelques Souvenirs d'un éditeur de musique* (Paris: Durand, 1924), p. 129.
14. Nellie Melba, *Melodies and Memories*, p. 135.
15. Letter dated 29th September 1905, in Nectoux, *Saint-Saëns et Fauré*, p. 75.
16. Georges Servières, *Saint-Saëns* (Paris: Librairie Félix Alcan, 1923), p. 198.
17. Quoted in Aguétant, *Saint-Saëns*, p. 14.
18. Letter dated 1st February 1906, quoted in Dandelot, *La vie*, p. 203.
19. Letters dated 23rd and 29th September 1905, and 22nd May 1908, in Nectoux, *Saint-Saëns et Fauré*, pp. 74, 76, 80–81.
20. Letters dated 12th October 1905 and 31st July 1920, ibid., pp. 76–77, 123.
21. Letter dated 3rd December 1905, ibid., pp. 77–78.
22. Quoted in the *Musical Standard*, 24th February 1906.
23. Saint-Saëns, *Portraits et Souvenirs* (Paris: Société d'édition artistique, 1899), pp. 40–41.
24. J. A. Maltese, ed., *The Accompanist: the Autobiography of André Benoist* (New Jersey: Paganiniana, 1978), p. 255.
25. Quoted in Nectoux, *Saint-Saëns et Fauré*, p. 79, n. 2.
26. Doris Monteux, *It's All in the Music* (New York: Farrar, Straus and Giroux, 1965), pp. 37–38.
27. *Musical Times*, August 1906.
28. *New York Times*, 17th November 1906.
29. Ibid., 17th March 1907.
30. Ibid., 4th November 1906.
31. Ibid., 16th November 1906.
32. Ibid., 19th November 1906.
33. Ibid., 28th November 1906.
34. Letter from Monaco, dated 5th March 1907, in *Saint-Saëns: Correspondance Inédite* (Paris: *Revue Musicale*, 1983), p. 26.
35. Quoted in the *New York Times*, 17th March 1907.
36. Ibid., 25th November 1906.
37. Ibid.
38. Ibid., 17th March 1907.
39. Letter from Monaco, dated 5th March 1907, in *Saint-Saëns: Correspondance Inédite*, p. 25.
40. Quoted in Dandelot, *La vie*, pp. 248–49.
41. Quoted in the *Musical News*, 11th May 1907.
42. Quoted in the *Musical Times*, August 1906.
43. Letter to Camille Bellaigue, dated 23rd April 1921, in the Bibliothèque nationale de France, Paris.
44. Saint-Saëns, *Outspoken Essays*, p. 181.
45. Letter dated 20th January 1913, in the Bibliothèque nationale de France, Paris.

46. Quoted in the *New York Times*, 17th March 1907.
47. Letter from Cairo, dated 8th February 1910, in the Bibliothèque nationale de France, Paris.
48. *Scotsman*, 19th May 1907.
49. *The Times*, 8th June 1910.
50. *New York Times*, 4th November 1906, 8th January 1922.
51. *The Strad*, July 1915.
52. From Fauré's review of *Déjanire*, 1911, quoted in Robert Orledge, *Gabriel Fauré* (London: Eulenburg, 1979), p. 232.
53. Letter dated 1st October 1909, in J. Barrie Jones, ed. and trans., *Gabriel Fauré: A Life in Letters* (London: Batsford, 1989), p. 136.
54. Quoted in Dandelot, *La vie*, p. 171.
55. Quoted in Jean-Michel Nectoux, trans. by Roger Nichols, *Gabriel Fauré: A Musical Life* (Cambridge: Cambridge University Press, 1991), p. 238, and Orledge, *Gabriel Fauré*, p. 35.
56. Doris Monteux, *It's All in the Music*, p. 91.
57. Alfredo Casella, ed. and trans. by Spencer Norton, *Music in My Time* (Norman: University of Oklahoma Press, 1955), pp. 120–21.
58. Aguétant, *Saint-Saëns*, p. 56.
59. Quoted in Dandelot, *La vie*, p. 181.
60. Letter from Bourbon-l'Archambault, dated 17th July 1918, in Aguétant, *Saint-Saëns*, p. 18.
61. Quoted by J. G. Proudhomme, in the *Musical Quarterly*, October 1922.
62. Letter dated 16th June 1909, quoted in Arbie Orenstein, ed., *A Ravel Reader* (New York: Columbia University Press, 1990), p. 4.
63. Gdal Salewski, *Famous Musicians of a Wandering Race* (New York: Bloch, 1927), pp. 70–71.
64. J. G. Proudhomme, in the *Musical Quarterly*, October 1922.
65. Letter to unidentified recipient, dated 17th August 1907, in *Saint-Saëns: Correspondance Inédite*, p. 97.
66. Nellie Melba, *Melodies and Memories*, p. 136.
67. Letter from Las Palmas, dated 24th February 1909, in Nectoux, *Saint-Saëns et Fauré*, p. 84.
68. Letter dated 31st July 1920, ibid., p. 123.
69. Garry O'Connor, *The Pursuit of Perfection: A Life of Maggie Teyte* (London: Gollancz, 1979), p. 125.
70. John Philip Sousa, *Marching Along* (Boston: Hale, Cushman and Flint, 1928), p. 304.
71. Aguétant, *Saint-Saëns*, p. 38.
72. Ibid., p. 11.
73. Letter to Jacques Durand, dated 3rd September 1918, in Jean-Michel Nectoux, trans. by J.A. Underwood, *Gabriel Fauré, his Life through his Letters* (London: Marion Boyars, 1984), p. 301.
74. Aguétant, *Saint-Saëns*, p. 22.
75. Letter dated 14th June 1914, in *Saint-Saëns: Correspondance Inédite*, p. 54.
76. Letter dated 3rd September 1918, in Nectoux, *Gabriel Fauré, His Life through His Letters*, p. 301.
77. Letter dated 21st April 1913, in the Bibliothèque nationale de France, Paris.
78. Eugene Goossens, *Overture and Beginners* (London: Methuen, 1951), p. 79.
79. Letter dated 21st April 1908, in *Saint-Saëns: Correspondance Inédite*, pp. 98–99.
80. Letter dated 1st September 1908, in Nectoux, *Saint-Saëns et Fauré*, p. 82.
81. Aguétant, *Saint-Saëns*, p. 19.
82. Letter dated 24th February 1909, in Nectoux, *Saint-Saëns et Fauré*, p. 83.
83. Letter dated 9th March 1909, ibid., p. 85.
84. *The Times*, 25th April 1909.
85. Jules Massenet, trans. by H. Villiers Barnett, *My Recollections* (Boston: Small, Maynard & Co., 1919), p. 265.
86. Quoted in Jean Bonnerot, *Saint-Saëns, sa vie et sa oeuvre*, 2nd ed., (Paris: Durand, 1922), p. 192.
87. Quoted in Dandelot, *La vie*, pp. 241–42.
88. Ibid., p. 237.
89. *Musical Times*, June 1937.
90. *The Times*, 9th, 16th and 23rd June 1910.
91. Saint-Saëns, trans. by Edwin Gile Rich, *Musical Memories* (London: John Murray, 1921), p. 122.
92. *Musical Times*, June 1937.
93. Marguérite Long, trans. by Olive Senior-Ellis, *At the Piano with Fauré* (London: Kahn Averill, 1980), p. 9.
94. *Musical Times*, June 1937.
95. Letter dated 9th August 1910, in the Bibliothèque nationale de France, Paris.

96. Quoted in Dandelot, *La vie*, p. 217.
97. Ibid., p. 234.
98. Letter dated 17th May 1912, in Nectoux, *Saint-Saëns et Fauré,* p. 93.
99. Letter dated 1st May 1911, ibid., p. 91.
100. Letter dated 16th December 1911, in *Saint-Saëns: Correspondance Inédite*, p. 28.
101. Letters dated 7th and 12th March, 10th May and 12th June 1913, in J. Barrie Jones, *Gabriel Fauré,* pp. 151–53.
102. Letter dated 1st April 1913, in *Saint-Saëns: Correspondance Inédite*, p. 36–37.
103. *The Times*, 3rd June 1913.
104. Quoted in James Harding, *Saint-Saëns and his Circle* (London: Chapman and Hall, 1965), p. 209.
105. *Musical Times*, October 1913.
106. *Le Figaro*, 15th September 1913.
107. *New York Times*, 28th September 1913.
108. Quoted in Bonnerot, *Saint-Saëns*, p. 206.

CHAPTER XIV: PATRIOT AGAIN

1. Letter dated 29th April 1914, in *Saint-Saëns: Correspondance Inédite* (Paris: *Revue Musicale*, 1983), p. 52.
2. Letter dated 7th March 1914, ibid., p. 45.
3. Letter dated 14th June 1914, ibid., p. 54.
4. Quoted in Robert Orledge, *Gabriel Fauré* (London: Eulenburg, 1979), p. 182.
5. Letter from Lisbon, dated 3rd June 1914, in Jean-Michel Nectoux, ed., *Saint-Saëns et Fauré Correspondance, 60 ans d'amitié* (Paris: Heugel, 1973), p. 102.
6. Ibid.
7. Letter dated 20th July 1914, in *Saint-Saëns: Correspondance Inédite*, p. 57.
8. *Musical Times*, January 1922.
9. Letters dated 26th August and 1st September 1914, in *Saint-Saëns: Correspondance Inédite*, pp. 59–61.
10. Quoted in Arthur Dandelot, *La Société des Concerts du Conservatoire*, 3rd ed. (Paris: G. Havard, 1897), pp. 62–63.
11. Undated letter to M. L. Boëmann in the Bibliothèque nationale de France, Paris.
12. Arthur Dandelot, *La vie et l'oeuvre de Saint-Saëns* (Paris: Editions Dandelot, 1930), p. 230.
13. Saint-Saëns, trans. by Edwin Gile Rich, *Musical Memories* (London: John Murray, 1921), pp. 86–87.
14. Letter from Nice, dated 28th November 1914, in J. Barrie Jones, ed. and trans., *Gabriel Fauré: A Life in Letters* (London: Batsford, 1989), p. 162.
15. *Musical Times*, January 1917.
16. Doris Monteux, *It's All in the Music* (New York: Farrar, Straus and Giroux, 1965), p. 97.
17. *Saint-Saëns: Correspondance Inédite,* pp. 124–25.
18. Ibid., p. 66.
19. Letter dated 3rd April 1915, ibid., pp. 69–70.
20. *New York Times,* 13th and 16th May 1915.
21. Letter dated 18th July 1915, in Ferruccio Busoni, trans. by A. Beaumont, *Selected Letters* (London: Faber, 1987), p. 205.
22. *San Francisco Chronicle*, 22nd May 1915.
23. Ibid., 22nd and 23rd May 1915.
24. Letter to Renaud, dated 2nd August 1915, in *Saint-Saëns: Correspondance Inédite,* pp. 72–73.
25. Quoted in the *San Francisco Chronicle,* 2nd July 1915.
26. Letter dated 2nd August 1915, in *Saint-Saëns: Correspondance Inédite,* pp. 72–73.
27. Letter dated 17th September 1915, in ibid., pp. 75–76.
28. Letters dated 16th October and 27th December 1915, in J. Barrie Jones, *Gabriel Fauré,* pp. 165–66.
29. Letter dated 20th December 1915, in *Saint-Saëns: Correspondance Inédite,* pp. 77–78.
30. *Le Figaro,* 10th February 1916.
31. Ibid., 19th February 1916.
32. Letter dated 18th March 1916, in *Saint-Saëns: Correspondance Inédite,* p. 84.
33. Letter dated 19th February 1916, ibid., p. 82.
34. *Le Figaro,* 23rd April 1916.
35. Quoted in Jean Bonnerot, *Saint-Saëns, sa vie et sa oeuvre,* 2nd ed. (Paris: Durand, 1922), p. 207.
36. *El Dia,* 13th July 1916.
37. Letter dated 2nd November 1916, in Nectoux, *Saint-Saëns et Fauré,* p. 110.
38. *Le Figaro,* 13th February 1917.
39. Letter from Bourbon-l'Archambault, dated 1st July 1917, in Nectoux, *Saint-Saëns et Fauré,* p. 116.

40. Ibid.
41. Letter dated 7th October 1917, in the Bibliothèque nationale de France, Paris.
42. Letter dated 13th November 1917, in Nectoux, *Saint-Saëns et Fauré*, p. 118.
43. Saint-Saëns, trans. by Fred Rothwell, *Outspoken Essays on Music* (London: Kegan Paul, Trench, Trubner, 1922), p. 3.
44. Letters published in the *Revue Musicale*, February 1947.
45. Letter dated 21st November 1917, in Nectoux, *Saint-Saëns et Fauré*, p. 119.
46. *Le Figaro*, 4th December 1917.
47. Pierre Aguétant, *Saint-Saëns par lui-même* (Paris: Editions Alsatia, 1938), p. 130.
48. Ibid., pp. 11–16, 42.
49. Ibid., p. 133.
50. Ibid., pp. 97–99.
51. Ibid., pp. 133–35, 146.
52. Ibid., pp. 42–43.
53. Ibid., p. 142.

CHAPTER XV: WORLD WEARY

1. Pierre Aguétant, *Saint-Saëns par lui-même* (Paris: Editions Alsatia, 1938), p. 140.
2. Letter dated 18th October 1918, ibid., p. 145.
3. Ibid., pp. 149, 26, 78–79, 143.
4. Ibid., pp. 84, 83, 76.
5. Jacques Durand, *Quelques Souvenirs d'un éditeur de musique* (Paris: Durand, 1924), p. 76.
6. *New York Times*, 4th November 1906.
7. Letters dated 22nd and 26th October 1919, in Mina Curtiss, *Bizet and his World* (London: Secker and Warburg, 1959), p. 462.
8. *Musical Times*, June 1937.
9. Letter dated 17th February 1920, quoted in Georges Servières, *Saint-Saëns* (Paris: Librairie Félix Alcan, 1923), pp. 95–97.
10. Letters dated 3rd January and 10th March 1920, in Aguétant, *Saint-Saëns*, pp. 85, 87.
11. Letter from Marseilles, dated 16th June 1920, and letter from Paris, dated 30th June 1920, in ibid., pp. 89, 90–91.
12. Letter dated 30th June 1920, in ibid., pp. 90–91.
13. Letter dated 21st December 1920, in ibid., p. 91.
14. Durand, *Quelques Souvenirs*, p. 131.
15. Letter dated 21st December 1920, in Aguétant, *Saint-Saëns*, p. 86.
16. Letter in the Bibliothèque nationale de France, Paris.
17. Aguétant, *Saint-Saëns*, p. 94.
18. Letter dated 26th April 1921, in the Bibliothèque nationale de France, Paris.
19. Saint-Saëns, trans. by Fred Rothwell, *Outspoken Essays on Music* (London: Kegan Paul, Trench, Trubner, 1922), pp. 177–80.
20. Letter dated 21st August 1921, in Aguétant, *Saint-Saëns*, pp. 130–31.
21. Marcel Dupré, ed. by R. Kneeream, *Recollections* (New York: Belwin Mills, 1972), p. 64.
22. Durand, *Quelques Souvenirs*, p. 128.
23. Ibid., pp. 130–31.
24. *Daily Telegraph*, 23rd December 1921.

CHAPTER XVI: THE LEGACY

1. Jean Montargis, *Camille Saint-Saëns, l'oeuvre, l'artiste* (Paris: La Renaissance du Livre, 1919), p. 126.
2. *Daily Telegraph*, 19th December 1921.
3. Quoted by Hermann Klein in the *Musical Times*, January 1922.
4. Quoted in the *New York Times*, 8th January 1922.
5. Ibid., 25th December 1921.
6. *The Times*, 19th December 1921.
7. *The Chesterian*, January 1922.
8. Quoted in Robert Orledge, *Gabriel Fauré* (London: Eulenburg, 1979), p. 30.
9. Foreword to Arthur Dandelot, *La vie et l'oeuvre de Saint-Saëns* (Paris: Editions Dandelot, 1930).
10. *New York Times*, 17th November 1935.
11. Preface to Jean Bonnerot, *Camille Saint-Saëns, sa vie et sa oeuvre* (Paris: Durand, 1914).

BIBLIOGRAPHY

1A. UNPUBLISHED SOURCES

Miscellaneous letters in the Bibliothèque nationale, Paris, and the British Library, London. Letters to Auguste Durand (Saint-Saëns's publisher) in the Gustav Mahler Library, Paris. The Saint-Saëns museum in Dieppe, which houses a collection of the composer's correspondence, was closed during the period of the author's research. There is also a large, uncatalogued collection of letters at Northwestern University, Evanston, USA, and a smaller collection in the New York Public Library for the Performing Arts.

1B. PUBLISHED PRIMARY SOURCES

Aguétant, Pierre. *Saint-Saëns par lui-même.* Paris: Editions Alsatia, 1938.

Nectoux, Jean-Michel, ed. *Saint-Saëns et Fauré Correspondance, 60 ans d'amitié.* Paris: Heugel, 1973.

Saint-Saëns: Correspondance inédite. Paris: Revue Musicale, 1983.

1C. ESSAYS, REMINISCENCES ETC. BY SAINT-SAËNS

Ecole Buissonnière. Paris: Pierre Lafitte, 1913.

Harmonie et Mélodie. Paris: Calmann Lévy, 1885.

Musical Memories. Translated by Edwin Gile Rich. London: John Murray, 1921 (a translation of selections from *Ecole Buissonnière).*

Outspoken Essays on Music. Translated by Fred Rothwell. London: Kegan Paul, Trench, Trubner, 1922.

Portraits et Souvenirs. Paris: Société d'édition artistique, 1899.

Preface to Louis Alfred Niedermeyer, *Vie d'un Compositeur Moderne.* Paris: Librairie Fischbacher, 1893.

Problèmes et Mystères. Paris: Flammarion, 1894.

Rimes Familières. Paris: C. Levy, 1891.

2. BIOGRAPHIES OF SAINT-SAËNS

Bonnerot, Jean. *Saint-Saëns, sa vie et sa oeuvre.* Paris: Durand, 1914; 2nd ed. 1922.

Dandelot, Arthur. *La vie et l'oeuvre de Saint-Saëns.* Paris: Editions Dandelot, 1930.

Harding, James. *Saint-Saëns and his Circle.* London: Chapman and Hall, 1965.

Hervey, Arthur. *Saint-Saëns.* London: The Bodley Head, 1921.

Lyle, Watson. *Camille Saint-Saëns: His Life and Art.* London: Kegan Paul, Trench, Trubner, 1923.

Montargis, Jean. *Camille Saint-Saëns: l'oeuvre, l'artiste.* Paris: La Renaissance du Livre, 1919.

Servières, Georges. *Saint-Saëns.* Paris: Librairie Félix Alcan, 1923.

3. SAINT-SAËNS STUDIES

Collet, Henri. *Samson et Dalila de Saint-Saëns.* Paris: Librairie Delaplane, 1922.

Cooper, Martin. 'Camille Saint-Saëns'. In *The Concerto,* edited by Ralph Hill. London: Penguin, 1952.

Mason, D. G. *From Grieg to Brahms.* New York: The Outlook Company, 1903.

Rolland, Romain. *Musicians of Today.* Translated by Mary Blaiklock. London: Kegan Paul, Trench, Trubner, 1917.

Salewski, Gdal. *Famous Musicians of a Wandering Race*. New York: Bloch, 1927.
Schonberg, Harold. *The Great Pianists*. London: Gollancz, 1964.
———. *Lives of the Great Composers*. London: Davis-Poynter, 1971.
Stegemann, Michael. *Camille Saint-Saëns and the French Solo Concerto 1850-1920*. Translated by Ann Sherwin. Aldershot: Scolar, 1991.

4. AUTOBIOGRAPHY, REMINISCENCES, LETTERS, ETC.

Barrie Jones, J., ed. and trans. *Gabriel Fauré: A Life in Letters*. London: Batsford, 1989.
Bellaigue, Camille. *Souvenirs de musique et des musiciens*. Paris: Nouvelle Librairie Nationale, 1921.
Berger, Francesco. *Reminiscences, Impressions and Anecdotes*. London: Samson and Low, 1913.
Berlioz, Louis Hector. *Memoirs*. Translated by Rachel and Eleanor Holmes. New York: Knopf, 1932; New York: Dover Publications, 1966.
Busoni, Ferruccio. *Selected Letters*. Translated by A. Beaumont. London: Faber, 1987.
Casella, Alfredo. *Music in my Time*. Edited and translated by Spencer Norton. Norman: University of Oklahoma Press, 1955.
Cowen, Sir Frederick. *My Art and My Friends*. London: Edward Arnold, 1913.
Duparc, Arthur, ed. *Correspondance de Henri Regnault*. Paris: Charpentier, 1872.
Dupré, Marcel. *Recollections*. Edited by R. Kneeream. New York: Belwin-Mills, 1972.
Durand, Jacques. *Quelques Souvenirs d'un éditeur de musique*. Paris: Durand, 1924.
Eames, Emma. *Some Memories and Reflections*. New York: Appleton, 1927.
Foote, Arthur. *An Autobiography*. New York: Da Capo, 1979.
Galabert, Edmond. Introduction to Georges Bizet. *Lettres a un ami 1865–1872*. Paris: Calmann Lévy, 1909.
Ganz, Wilhelm. *Memories of a Musician*. London: John Murray, 1913.
Goossens, Eugene. *Overture and Beginners*. London: Methuen, 1951.
Gounod, Charles. *Autobiographical Reminiscences*. Translated by W. Hely Hutchinson. London: Heinemann, 1896.
Gregor-Dellin, Martin and Mack Dietrich, eds. *Cosima Wagner's Diaries, vol. i, 1869–1877*. Translated by Geoffrey Skelton. London: Collins, 1982.
Hugo, H.E., ed. and trans. *Letters of Franz Liszt*. Cambridge, Massachusetts: Harvard University Press, 1953.
Klein, Hermann. *Thirty Years of Musical Life in London 1870–1900*. London: Heinemann, 1903.
Long, Marguérite. *At the Piano with Fauré*. Translated by Olive Senior-Ellis. London: Kahn and Averill, 1980.
Maltèse, J. A., ed. *The Accompanist: the autobiography of André Benoist*. New Jersey: Paganiniana, 1978.
Massenet, Jules. *My Recollections*. Translated by H. Villiers Barnett. Boston: Small, Maynard & Co., 1919.
Melba, Nellie. *Melodies and Memories*. London: Hamish Hamilton, 1980.
Nectoux, Jean-Michel. *Gabriel Fauré, His Life through His Letters*. Translated by J. A. Underwood. London: Marion Boyars, 1984.
Nichols, Roger. *Ravel Remembered*. London: Faber, 1987.
Paderewski, Jan and Mary Lawton. *The Paderewski Memoirs*. New York: Da Capo, 1980.
Rubinstein, Arthur. *My Young Years*. London: Jonathan Cape, 1973.
Searle, H., ed. and trans. *Hector Berlioz, a Selection from His Letters*. London: Gollancz, 1966.
Sousa, John Philip. *Marching Along*. Boston: Hale, Cushman and Flint, 1928.
Wagner, Richard and Cosima. *Lettres à Judith Gautier*. Edited by L. Guichard. Paris: Gallimard, 1964.

Waters, Edward N., ed. *The Letters of Franz Liszt to Olga von Meyendorff 1871-1886*. Translated by William R. Tyler. Washington: Dumbarton Oaks, 1979.

Weingartner, Felix. *Buffets and Rewards*. Translated by Marguerite Wolff. London: Hutchinson, 1937.

Wood, Henry. *My Life of Music*. London: Gollancz, 1938.

5. GENERAL BIOGRAPHY

Barzun, Jacques. *Berlioz and the Romantic Century*. 3rd ed. New York and London: University of Columbia Press, 1969.

Berlioz and the Romantic Imagination. Catalogue to an exhibition held at the Victoria & Albert Museum, London. London: Arts Council, 1969.

Bredel, Marc. *Erik Satie*. Paris: Musique Mazarine, 1982.

Brown, David. *Tchaikovsky: A Biographical and Critical Study, vol. ii, The Crisis Years 1874–1878*. London: Gollancz, 1982.

Curtiss, Mina. *Bizet and his World*. London: Secker and Warburg, 1959.

Dean, Winton. *Bizet*. London: Dent, 1965.

Dent, Edward. *Ferruccio Busoni*. Oxford: Oxford University Press, 1933.

Février, Henri. *André Messager*. Paris: Amiot-Dumont, 1948.

Fifield, Christopher. *Max Bruch, His Life and Works*. London: Gollancz, 1988.

———. *True Artist, True Friend*. Oxford: Clarendon Press, 1993.

Fitzlyon, April. *The Price of Genius: A Life of Pauline Viardot*. London: John Calder, 1964.

Gavoty, Bernard. *Reynaldo Hahn*. Paris: Buchet Chastel, 1976.

Ginsburg, Lev, and H. Axelrod, eds. *Ysaÿe*. Translated by X. M. Danko. New Jersey: Paganiniana, 1980.

Gregor-Dellin, Martin. *Richard Wagner, His Life, His Work, His Century*. Translated by J. Maxwell Brownjohn. London: Collins, 1983.

Grover, R. S. *Ernest Chausson*. London: Athlone, 1980.

Harding, Bertita de. *Concerto: the Story of Clara Schumann*. London: Harrap, 1962.

Holmes, Paul. *Debussy*. London: Omnibus, 1989.

Holoman, D. Kern. *Berlioz*. London: Faber, 1989.

Horwood, W. *Adolphe Sax, His Life and Legacy*. Baldock: Egon, 1983.

Loggins, Vernon. *Where the Word Ends*. Baltimore: Louisiana State University Press, 1958.

Monteux, Doris. *It's All in the Music*. New York: Farrar, Straus and Giroux, 1965.

Myers, Rollo. *Emmanuel Chabrier and his Circle*. London: Dent, 1969.

Nectoux, Jean-Michel. *Gabriel Fauré: A Musical Life*. Translated by Roger Nichols. Cambridge: Cambridge University Press, 1991.

Newman, Ernest. *Life of Richard Wagner, vol. iv*. New York: Knopf, 1960.

Newmarch, Rosa. *Tchaikovsky*. London: Grant Richards, 1900.

Nicholas, Jeremy. *Godowsky, the Pianist's Pianist*. Hexham: Appian, 1989.

O'Connor, Gary. *The Pursuit of Perfection: A Life of Maggie Teyte*. London: Gollancz, 1979.

Orledge, Robert. *Gabriel Fauré*. London: Eulenberg, 1979.

Orenstein, Arbie. *Ravel, Man and Musician*. New York: Columbia University Press, 1975; New York: Dover Publications, 1991.

———. *A Ravel Reader*. New York: Columbia University Press, 1990.

Page, Réné Pichard du. *Augusta Holmès, Une Musicienne Versaillaise*. Versailles: Librairie M. Dubois; Paris: Librairie Fischbacher, 1921.

Poulenc, Francis. *Emmanuel Chabrier*. Translated by Cynthia Jolly. London: Dobson, 1981.

Schneider, Louis. 'Charles Lecocq'. In *Les Maîtres de l'operette française*. Paris: Librairie Académique, 1924.

Sitwell, Sacheverell. *Liszt*. London: Cassell, 1955; New York: Dover Publications, 1967.
Thomson, Andrew. *The Life and Times of Charles Marie Widor*. Oxford: Oxford University Press, 1987.
Vallas, Léon. *César Franck*. Translated by Hubert Foss. London: Harrap, 1951.
Vuillermoz, Emile. *Gabriel Fauré*. Translated by Kenneth Schapin. Philadelphia: Chilton, 1960.

6. MUSICAL STUDIES

Dandelot, Arthur. *La Société des Concerts du Conservatoire*, 3rd ed. Paris: G. Havard, 1897.
Haskell, Harry. *The Early Music Revival, A History*. London: Thames and Hudson, 1988.
Huebner, Steven. *The Operas of Charles Gounod*. Oxford: Clarendon Press, 1992.
Moore, J. F. *A Voice in Time: The Gramophone of Fred. Gaisberg*. London: Hamish Hamilton, 1976.
Norris, Gerald. *Stanford, the Cambridge Jubilee and Tchaikovsky*. Newton Abbot: David and Charles, 1980.
Noske, Frits. *French Song from Berlioz to Duparc*. New York: Dover Publications, 1970.
Rosenthal, Harold. *Two Centuries of Opera at Covent Garden*. London: Putnam, 1958.
Scudo, Pierre. *La musique en l'année 1862*. Paris: Collection Hetzel, 1863.
Spark, Frederick, and Joseph Bennett. *History of the Leeds Musical Festivals*. Leeds: Spark and Jackson, 1892.
Walsh, T. J. *Monte Carlo Opera 1879–1909*. Dublin: Gill and Macmillan, 1975.

7. BACKGROUND

Brody, Elaine. *Paris, The Musical Kaleidoscope 1870–1925*. New York: George Braziller, 1967; London: Robson Books, 1988.
Chesney, Gill. 'Some Wagnerian Repercussions in France after 1880'. In *Wagner 1876: A Celebration of the Bayreuth Festival*. London: The Wagner Society, 1976.
Cooper, J. *The Rise of Instrumental Music and Concert Series in Paris 1828–1871*. Michigan: UMI Research Press, 1983.
Hill, Edward Burlingame. *Modern French Music*. London: George Allen and Unwin, 1924.
Jean-Aubry, Georges. *French Music of Today*. Translated by Edwin Evans. London: Kegan Paul, 1919.
Lang, Paul Henry. *Music in Western Civilisation*. London: Dent, 1942.
Locke, A. W. *Music and the Romantic Movement in France*. London: Kegan Paul, 1920.
Lockspeiser, Edward. 'French Chamber Music'. In *Chamber Music*, edited by Alec Robertson. Harmondsworth: Penguin, 1957.
Schrade, L. *Beethoven in France*. New Haven: Yale University Press, 1942.
Schwarz, B. *French Instrumental Music Between the Revolutions 1789–1830*. New York: Da Capo, 1987.
Turbow, Gerald D. 'Art and Politics: Wagnerism in France'. In *Wagnerism in European Culture and Politics*, edited by David C. Large and William Weber. Ithaca and London: Cornell University Press, 1984.

8. REFERENCE

Baker's Biographical Dictionary of Musicians. 7th ed. Oxford: Oxford University Press, 1984.
Beaumont, Cyril. *The Complete Book of Ballets*. London: Putnam, 1951.
Grout, Donald Jay. *A Short History of Opera*, 3rd ed. New York and London: University of Columbia Press, 1988.
Grove's Dictionary of Music and Musicians, 4th ed. London: Macmillan, 1940.

Murray, Peter and Linda. *The Penguin Dictionary of Art and Artists*. 6th ed. London: Penguin, 1989.
The New Grove Dictionary of Music and Musicians. London: Macmillan, 1980.
The New Grove Dictionary of Opera. London: Macmillan, 1992.
Reid, Joyce M. H., ed. *The Concise Oxford Dictionary of French Literature*. Oxford: Oxford University Press, 1976.
Rosenthal, Harold and John Warrack. *The Concise Oxford Dictionary of Opera*. 2nd ed. Oxford: Oxford University Press, 1979.

9. NEWSPAPERS, PERIODICALS

Buenos Aires Herald, 1899, 1916
The Chesterian, 1922
El Dia, 1916
Daily Telegraph, 1886, 1921
Edinburgh Evening News, 1904
Le Figaro, 1890, 1903, 1907, 1913, 1916, 1917, 1921, 1922
Glasgow Herald, 1921
L'Illustration, 1846
Mercure de France, 1920, 1922
Moniteur Universel, 1840
Monthly Musical Record, 1946
Musical News, 1902, 1907
Musical Quarterly, 1916, 1919, 1922
Musical Standard, 1871, 1902, 1904, 1906, 1907, 1915, 1916
Musical Times, 1871, 1890, 1902, 1906, 1907, 1912, 1913, 1917, 1922, 1937
New York Times, 1879, 1890, 1901, 1906, 1909, 1921, 1922, 1926, 1934, 1935, 1936
Revue des Deux Mondes, 1926
Revue Musicale, 1922, 1924, 1947
San Francisco Chronicle, 1915
Scotsman, 1904, 1907
South American Journal, 1899
The Stage, 1887, 1890, 1893, 1898, 1909
The Strad, 1915
Le Temps 1890, 1903, 1921
The Times, 1878, 1879, 1880, 1885, 1886, 1887, 1890, 1893, 1898, 1909, 1910, 1913, 1921, 1922
Yorkshire Post, 1885

INDEX